BOSTON: VOICES AND VISIONS

BOSTON: VOICES AND VISIONS

Shaun O'Connell

Edited by

SHAUN O'CONNELL

October, 2012

For Joan and Patrick Pahlquist, who nourished new friendships with Jae and Ellen in their 40th Anniversary Journey through Ireland, September, 2012

UNIVERSITY OF MASSACHUSETTS PRESS

Amherst and Boston

LC 2010019059
ISBN 978-1-55849-820-4 (paper); 819-8 (library cloth)

Designed by Sally Nichols
Set in Goudy Oldstyle
Printed and bound by Thomson-Shore, Inc.

Library of Congress Cataloging-in-Publication Data

Boston : voices and visions / edited by Shaun O'Connell.
p. cm.
Includes bibliographical references.
ISBN 978-1-55849-820-4 (pbk. : alk. paper) — ISBN 978-1-55849-819-8 (library
cloth : alk. paper)
1. Boston (Mass.)—Literary collections. 2. American literature—21st century.
I. O'Connell, Shaun. PS509.B665B67 2010
810.8'0974461—dc22
2010019059

British Library Cataloguing in Publication data are available.

The editor and publisher gratefully acknowledge the permission granted to reproduce
the copyrighted material in this volume. Every effort has been made to trace copyright
holders and to obtain their permission for the use of copyrighted material. The publisher apologizes for any errors or omissions and would be grateful if notified of any
corrections that should be incorporated in future reprints or editions of this book.
Since this page cannot accommodate all copyright notices, the acknowledgments
constitute an extension of the copyright page.

Boston: Voices and Visions is dedicated to all in my family who have made Greater Boston such a memorable and meaningful place for me. To Dorothy, my wife of more than half a century. To Michael, our son, and his family: Patricia, his wife, Angela and Niall, their children. To Liam, our son, and his family: Feng, his wife, and Sophie, their daughter. To Kathleen, our daughter, and her family: Jay, her husband, and Seamus, their son. So we make way for the ducklings.

CONTENTS

VI. "THERE IT WAS": BOSTON, CITY OF SELF AND SPIRIT 263

ACKNOWLEDGMENTS

Boston: Voices and Visions had its origins in many essays and reviews on Greater Boston writers I have published in various journals, but particularly in an essay I wrote for *New England Journal of Public Policy,* "Imagining Boston" (Summer/Fall 1986), for which I thank *NEJPP* editor Padraig O'Malley. I am grateful to Dan Wakefield for encouraging me to expand this essay into a book and for bringing the project to the attention of Beacon Press. The result was *Imagining Boston: A Literary Landscape* (Beacon Press, 1990), for which I thank Beacon Press editor Wendy Strothman. Students and colleagues at the University of Massachusetts Boston have enriched my sense of Greater Boston. UMB administrations—chancellors, provosts, Arts and Sciences deans, and English Department chairs—have supported and encouraged this effort for the last decade. I am particularly grateful to Katherine D. Scheuer for her scrupulous reading of this manuscript and to Duncan Nelson, my UMB colleague and friend, for the keen and sensitive editorial attention he has given the sections I have written for this anthology. At University of Massachusetts Press, I am deeply indebted to Bruce Wilcox and Paul Wright for their sustained support of this large and long-delayed project. Finally, I must again salute the three great teachers who taught me to see the city upon a hill and the New England mind anew: Professors Sidney Kaplan, Jules Chametzky, and Perry Miller.

I thank the following publishers and individuals for permission to reprint material included in this collection:

Excerpts from Letters (1935) of Fred Allen. From *Fred Allen: His Life and Wit* by Robert Taylor. Copyright © 1989 by Robert Taylor. By permission of Little, Brown and Company.

"The Hub," from *The Proper Bostonians* by Cleveland Amory. Copyright 1947, renewed © 1975 by Cleveland Amory. Used by permission of Dutton, a division of Penguin Group (USA) Inc.

"Quiet Has a Hidden Sound." From *Selected Poems.* Copyright 1948 by William Stanley Braithwaite, copyright renewed © 1975 by Katherine K. Arnold and Arnold D. Braithwaite. Used by permission of Coward-McCann, Inc., a division of Penguin Group (USA) Inc.

PREFACE

"New England was founded consciously, and in no fit of absence of mind," observed historian Samuel Eliot Morison of the establishment of the Bay Colony on the exposed, narrow, mountainous Shawmut peninsula of Eastern Massachusetts in 1630. That self-conscious presence of mind has endured for nearly four centuries. Boston has been shaped and sustained by observation, imagination, and interpretation. As a result, a compelling literary record constitutes the book of Boston. This anthology presents many of the writers—preachers, politicians, poets, novelists, essayists, diarists—representative men and women who have recorded, revised, and redefined evolving visions of Boston.

John Winthrop initiated the discussion in "A Model of Christian Charity," a sermon delivered aboard the *Arbella,* before his followers landed in the place they would call Boston. ("The land was ours before we were the land's," wrote Robert Frost in "The Gift Outright," a poem he recited at John F. Kennedy's presidential inauguration in 1961.) Winthrop's "city upon a hill" sermon made Boston the focal point of the Puritan "errand into the wilderness," a mission that eventually was enlarged into what Samuel Sewall called "the promise of American life," as Boston led the nation to separation from Great Britain during the years of the Revolution, then through its disputations and reunification during the era marked by abolitionism, immigration, and the Civil War. Boston became the nation's vital literary center during the mid-nineteenth century; after which its authority gradually diminished and New York City rose in importance during "the American Century." Boston was often divided against itself while it was transformed by the arrival of waves of immigrants who added fresh voices and a more inclusive vision to the city's discourse. Despite sustained debate over the city's identity and mission, Boston writers continued to invoke the high purposes for which the city was founded, sometimes in praise of the city, but often in works which called attention to the city's failures to fulfill its promises, as in Robert Lowell's "For the Union Dead" (1960), a poem that both honors the city's noble past and illustrates its ignoble present. In the twenty-first century some writers continue both to celebrate and to castigate the city, while others look back to Boston's origins to reassess its founders and renew the city's covenant of high purpose.

Boston: Voices and Visions is an interpretive anthology; that is, it includes commentary as well as anthology selections. At the beginning of each of the six sections, an introduction provides historical and biographical context, offers analysis which stresses the thematic relevance of each selection, and explores the pattern of their relations. Rather than present a random array of writers who happen to have been Greater Bostonians, this anthology focuses upon those authors who possessed a commitment to the sense of place, those who addressed Boston not only as a geographical, social, and political entity, but as an image, idea, and site of symbolic values. This anthology draws upon my previous work, *Imagining Boston: A Literary Landscape* (Beacon Press, 1990) and other essays on Greater Boston writers, for some sources and commentary.

BOSTON, FROM WINTHROP TO HAWTHORNE

In "The Minister's Vigil," chapter XII of Nathaniel Hawthorne's *The Scarlet Letter* (1850), Rev. Arthur Dimmesdale climbs the scaffold at the center of Puritan Boston on a dark May night. There, seven years before, he had stood, a silent witness, while Hester Prynne was punished for adultery, though he had been her lover and was the father of their child, Pearl. Conflicted, he now sought expiation, but, shrouded by night, he also knew that he was safe from discovery. Suddenly a lantern appeared as Rev. John Wilson approached, coming from the death bed of John Winthrop, Massachusetts Bay Colony founder in 1630 and its long-term governor. Dimmesdale, the sinner lurking in the dark on the scaffold, saw the saintly Wilson pass by in "a radiant halo, . . . as if the departed Governor had left him an inheritance of his glory, or as if he had caught upon himself the distant shine of the celestial city."[1] So does Hawthorne mark the death of Winthrop, the man who first envisioned Boston as a city upon a hill, here seen from the perspective of Rev. Dimmesdale, a beloved minister who secretly betrayed his calling and hid his sinfulness. John Winthrop died in March (not May) 1649, so, in Hawthorne's revisionist reading of Boston's history, the effort to establish a Christian utopia in the new world lasted less than two decades.

Hawthorne, like Winthrop before him, saw Boston as a place of mind over matter, spirit over flesh, image over actuality, but Hawthorne, a man of imagination, portrayed the city's depth and darkness, while Winthrop, a man of faith, envisioned its height and light. Two hundred years after Winthrop's death, Hawthorne composed a romance which called into question all that Winthrop had believed Boston should embody. As historian Samuel Eliot Morison wryly put it, Hawthorne reinvented and reinterpreted Boston's Puritan history. "Hawthorne, more than any other man, was responsible for the somber picture of early New England dear to popular illustrators, and already embalmed in tradition."[2] Despite Morison's implied complaint, Hawthorne's view of Boston's Puritan history has prevailed: a "righteous

Colony of the Massachusetts, where iniquity is dragged out in the sunshine!" as the Beadle put it before Hester Prynne, wearing her scarlet A, was led from the prison to stand before the scaffold and be judged by the self-righteous, wrathful citizens of Boston.[3]

John Winthrop, a lawyer and manor lord from Suffolk who rejected England as a sinful nation, drew his exalted vision of Boston, a place that then existed only in his great expectations of what it might become, from the Sermon on the Mount: "Ye are the light of the world. A city that is set upon a hill cannot be hid" (Matthew 5:14). This mission to found an actual city and then transform it into a city of God was thereafter fixed in Boston's sense of itself.[4] Winthrop's grand trope has long both inspired and haunted Boston as an ideal of polity and purpose. "A Model of Christian Charity," Winthrop's 1630 sermon, delivered aboard the *Arbella* before his followers arrived in America, articulated the mixture of idealism and anxiety which has characterized conceptions of Boston over the centuries. Winthrop's assertion of the need to sustain a Christian community spoke both to his hope for brotherhood and to his fear of the tensions, class and personal, which threatened to divide the colony. They "must delight in each other," he insisted, and fulfill their covenant, or God would surely punish them.[5] Winthrop's *Arbella* speech, it has been argued, may have been designed as part of "a larger restoration campaign associated with the idealized English past" as much as it was a mission statement for their errand into the wilderness.[6] That granted, Winthrop's vision of Boston came to be seen by succeeding generations as his expression of faith, his creation of mind, his invocation of the promise of American life.

Puritan colonists came to New England and founded Boston "to rebuild the most glorious Edifice of Mount Sion in a Wilderness," as Edward Johnson arrestingly put it in his *Wonder-Working Providence of Sions Savior* (1653).[7] "The forme of the Towne is like a heart, naturally situated for Fortifications, having two Hills, on the frontice part thereof next to the Sea." Johnson—in a style that ranged from contorted to poetic, but was always dogmatic and assured—set out to show that God's chosen people had successfully built a new Jerusalem, at once a heart and a fort, in the howling wilderness of the new world, centered in Boston, supported by Winthrop, its "pillar."[8]

In *Magnalia Christi Americana* (1702), Cotton Mather, New England's most influential minister in the early eighteenth century, superimposing Old Testament models onto Winthrop, described him not only as "the father of New England," but also as "our New English Nehemiah, the part of a ruler in managing the public affairs of our American Jerusalem." Thus Winthrop, who had an exalted vision of the city upon a hill before he saw it, was, in turn, retrospectively memorialized and mythologized as another "Moses."[9] Mather's work, a mixture of celebratory history and honorific biography, was also another example of the jeremiad, a vivid warning to his generation of Bostonians that they would surely be doomed unless they adhered to the old faith and emulated the purposeful lives of Boston's founders, offering Winthrop and others as exemplary models. Mather insisted that New England was exceptional in its mission: "My New England has one thing that will weigh down more than forty of the best things that other countries can brag of; that is, religion, religion, religion!"[10] However, after Winthrop articulated his great expectations for Boston, even greater anxieties seized its settlers and descendants.

Not long after settling on the small harbor peninsula that would become Boston—an exposed, narrow, hilly, and unpromising landscape—Winthrop expressed his fears over the future of the colony. Within two months of their arrival, he saw "Satan's forces bending against us" and doubted the dedication of some colonists to commit themselves to Boston's saintly ways: "some persons who never shewed so much wickednesse in England as they have done here."[11] Then, in a 1632 journal entry, he recounted "a great combat between a mouse and a snake," seeing in it a parable in which good and evil contended. He accepted Rev. John Wilson's interpretation of the struggle that the snake represented Satan and the mouse was the "poor contemptible people." The mouse prevailed over the snake, but Winthrop's account showed his need for Rev. Wilson's reassurance that "a marvelous goodly church" would "arise out of the earth" of the new world, just as they dreamed it would before they fled the corruptions of England.[12]

Looking back on his Puritan ancestors from the mid-nineteenth century, Hawthorne saw Winthrop's visionary dreams as delusions. As Hawthorne ironically puts it in the first chapter of *The Scarlet Letter*, the settlers of a "new colony, whatever Utopia of human virtue and happiness they might originally project," find "it among their earliest practical necessities to allot a portion of the virgin soil as a cemetery, and another portion as the site of a prison."[13] That is, he implied, the committed founders will surely die and some colonists will inevitably stray from proper and pious paths as time and experience compromise the original settlers' noble intentions. Winthrop's assertions of faith and hope for the Puritan community, set against Hawthorne's account of their failure to fulfill their original covenant, illustrate the dialectical debate over the vision of the city that has persisted among Boston writers for nearly four centuries.

In "The Custom-House," his extended preface to *The Scarlet Letter*, Hawthorne was particularly bitter about his own Puritan ancestors. William Hathorne—as the family name was spelled before Nathaniel changed it to distance himself from the family legacy—arrived in Boston among the original settlers in 1630, becoming a member of the House of Delegates and a major in the Salem Militia. This figure haunted his great-great-great grandson, for "he had all the Puritan traits, both good and evil. He was likewise a bitter persecutor," particularly of Quakers. John Hathorne, son of William, "inherited the persecuting spirit," continuing the family tradition of righteous wrath against sinners by serving as a judge at the Salem witchcraft trials of 1692 and thereafter, unlike his fellow judge Samuel Sewall, refusing to repent his actions. Nathaniel Hawthorne said of these stern ancestors, "I, the present writer, as their representative, hereby take shame upon myself for their sakes"; and he prayed "that any curse incurred by them . . . may be now and henceforth removed."[14] Thus did Hawthorne disown his ancestors before he set out to radically revise our sense of the Puritan past.

His Puritan forefathers, of course, saw themselves and their mission in a virtuous light. The zeal of the founders and their descendants is codified in Samuel Danforth's *A Brief Recognition of New England's Errand into the Wilderness* (1670), which identified the colonists with the children of Israel who went forth into the wilderness to build the city of God in a new homeland, contributing, as Joseph A. Conforti puts it in *Imagining New England*, to "a grand *American* narrative of New England's origins that mythologized the first generation of settlers."[15] Garry Wills points out that "wilderness was a theologically charged term" for these Puritan settlers. "It did not mean an uninhabited place." It meant 'the devil's lair' for them, just as it had when Jesus was tempted by the devil in the wilderness.[16] However, writing a generation after their arrival, with evidence of their collective failure to fulfill their utopian goals, Danforth, a Harvard-educated minister, wondered "why hath the Lord smitten us with blasting and mildew now seven years together, super-adding sometimes severe drought, sometimes great tempests, floods, and sweeping rains that leave no food behind them?" Why else but to test their faith and commitment is his answer, following the pattern of the jeremiad, the characteristic Puritan sermon genre that first lays blame, then invokes prospects of damnation, and finally issues pleas for repentance. The people of Boston must "cleave to the Lord, to his prophets, and his ordinances" to be saved.[17]

Other Puritan founders turned to more personal forms to articulate their sense of strangeness in a strange land. Anne Bradstreet was the first woman to land from the *Arbella* in 1630. Daughter of Thomas Dudley, who would succeed Winthrop as governor, Anne grew up in an atmosphere of aristocratic ease in Northampton, England. She was eighteen, two years married to Simon Bradstreet, who would also become the colony's governor, when she arrived. Accustomed to an untroubled, pious life on the estate of the Earl of Lincoln, she was stunned by her initial encounter with the new world, first in Charlestown, then in Newtowne, which came to be called Cambridge. She "found a new world, and new manners, at which [her] heart rose," as she reflected near the end of her life. Though she wished to return to the culture and comforts of England, Anne remained and made the best of it, persuading herself that she was fulfilling God's design. "But after I was convinced it was the way of God, I submitted to it and joined to the church at Boston."[18]

In writing "To My Dear Children" (1656) Bradstreet abandoned "the gestures of public poetry in favor of a quieter voice," note two historians of Puritan New England in a joint essay, thus establishing in America the importance of what would come to be seen as the spiritual autobiography, a form that would be favored by self-reflective and doubt-tortured Boston Puritans.[19] She offered herself as a model "pilgrim," exemplifying the triumph of faith over fears. In the process, perhaps without fully realizing it, she became an American, overcoming her occasions of doubt, drawing evidence of God's presence from the flourishing world of nature around her, particularly the thick forests of North Andover, where her family settled, and the swift waters of the nearby Merrimack River, in which she saw God's purpose illustrated.

> "O happy flood," quoth I, "that hold thy race
>   Till thou arrive at thy beloved place, . . .
>   So may we press to that vast mansion ever blest."[20]

Bradstreet's poems were first published, without her agreement, by her brother-in-law in London under the title *The Tenth Muse, Lately Sprung Up in America*, in 1650, thus establishing poetry as a legitimate form of Puritan self-expression. In public poetry and private prose, she gave voice to lyrical feelings that swell beneath Puritan rigor, particularly in "Before the Birth of One of Her Children," a love poem addressed to her husband, though even here she pointed up the lesson of proper subservience to God's will, just as she had after her arrival in America. The city she sought was located in a higher realm than Boston or Andover. As she puts it in one of her "Meditations Divine and Moral," "we must, therefore, be here as strangers and pilgrims, that we may plainly declare that we seek a city above and wait all the days of our appointed time till our change shall come."[21] Sensing death, "she decided to write a spiritual autobiography for the benefit of her children," writes Charlotte Gordon in *Mistress Bradstreet*. The poet dedicated her writing to the betterment of "after-comers," urging them "to devote themselves to the true god as well as to Massachusetts, God's chosen land."[22] Bradstreet, like her fellow Puritans, could never fully accept the world as she found it and saw herself passing though this world to the next. However, more than most Puritans, she yielded to its bountiful presence and turned to forms of personal expression in poetry and prose that would persist, with telling variations, for centuries: testimonies which weigh personal preferences against community commitment, writings which explore the tensions between self-expression and the quest to ascend from the city upon a hill to the "city above."

Born in Boston in 1706, a generation after Bradstreet's death, Benjamin Franklin abandoned the hypothetical city upon a hill for the purported city of brotherly love, Philadelphia. For Franklin, Boston meant coercion; Philadelphia promised liberty. One of fifteen children, Franklin had to leave school and work for his father, a tallow chandler and soap boiler. At age twelve he was forced into apprenticeship, employed by his harsh brother James, a printer. Benjamin not only learned the printing trade, but he also began to write and publish satirical works under an assumed name, Silence Dogood, an opinionated country clergyman, in *The New England Courant*. This garrulous persona gave young Franklin a new identity, a voice free from self-censure and community judgment. His essays, written in imitation of those he read in London's *Spectator*, were offensive to Puritan elders, particularly to Cotton Mather, the city's moral exemplar. Mather's *Bonifacius, Or Essays to Do Good* (1710) called for a life of service which Franklin's Silence Dogood letters seemed to mock, though Franklin's life would be dedicated to just such public service. After Franklin wrote "Dogood Papers, No. 4" in 1722, an essay that mocked self-important Harvard as "that famous Seminary of Learning," *The New England Courant* was banned and his brother arrested.[23] Though Benjamin carried on its publication for a while, he soon grew weary of Boston's censorial ways and incessant talk of the city above. He made his way to Philadelphia—an actual, attainable, alternative city, three hundred miles away—where his inventive character and experimental mind had latitude to develop. Franklin delighted in telling this tale of escape and self-transformation in his *Autobiography* (1791). He would not be the last Bostonian to find a better, less self-exalted world elsewhere.

That said, Franklin never wholly freed himself from the lessons he had learned in Boston, as his *Autobiography* demonstrates. However, he added a fresh, American, go-getter element to the genre. More than a century after Anne Bradstreet turned to poetic autobiography to recount her quest, to show how she struggled to submit her will to divine purpose in order to attain heavenly reward, Franklin employed the form, in prose, to affirm the more immediate rewards in the practice, even in the pretense, of virtue. Both, however, saw Boston as a moral and symbolic landscape.

As a boy, Benjamin had read Cotton Mather's *Essays to Do Good* with more care than Mather might have imagined, for Franklin incorporated its focus on self-examination and moral purpose into his own life and writings. Indeed, when, after establishing himself in Philadelphia, Franklin returned to Boston for a visit, he called upon Mather to pay his respects. Mather, though he had been attacked frequently by the Franklin brothers in the *Courant,* was cordial to this curious lamb who had strayed from the Boston flock. After their meeting concluded, as Franklin was leaving, Mather shouted, "Stoop, stoop!" But Franklin, not understanding Mather's warning, bumped his head on a low doorjamb. Like any true son of Puritan Bostonian, Franklin was able to make a parable from this painful incident and draw a moral lesson, but he was also able to turn it into a joke at his own expense. "I often think of [Mather's words] when I see pride mortified, and misfortunes brought upon people by their carrying their heads too high."[24] Benjamin Franklin came to assume many personae—satirist, polemicist, inventor, revolutionary, statesman—and while he moved with ease and authority through France and the nation he helped to found, he carried with him the voices and visions he first heard in Boston.

Nearly a century after Bradstreet's death, Phillis Wheatley, her spiritual and poetic descendant, arrived in Boston in 1761, a nine-year-old slave from Senegal, aboard the *Phillis*, and was bought by John Wheatley, a respected tailor. Thus was her new name and identity assigned. She too must have found in Boston a new world and new manners at which her heart rose. Phillis Wheatley, like Anne Bradstreet, would learn to submit to Boston ways, though, also like Bradstreet, Wheatley would retain an assertive voice of her own. She received an education from her mistress that far surpassed that offered to most white children in the colony, and she became a devout Christian. By age fourteen she was publishing poetic tributes and elegies in praise of Boston's values and worthies. By 1773 her *Poems on Various Subjects, Religious and Moral* was published to amazement and acclaim in London, where Wheatley was celebrated as a colonial oddity, then eventually accepted as another unlikely muse lately sprung up in America. Wheatley's poetic persona was a creation of Boston's missionary zeal: named for the slave ship on which she arrived, trained in Boston's Calvinistic faith, and identified in her book as the "Negro Servant to Mr. John Wheatley, of Boston, in New England."

Like Bradstreet before her, Wheatley focused on the shock of her arrival and the consolations of Christianity. In "On Being Brought from Africa to America" she rationalized her capture, enslavement, and abduction into a parable of salvation. However, as Boston had much to teach Wheatley about the Christian way to heaven, she had a moral lesson to impart to pious, patriarchal, prejudiced Boston: that *all* men and women have equal opportunity for salvation. She learned from Boston's ceaseless sermonizing to weave such a lesson into her poetry.

In 1774, replying to a minister who invited her to join his "Evangicals" in his mission to Christianize Africans, Wheatley declined, saying she could not speak their language. With pointed irony she would, she said, look like a "Barbarian" to the "Natives." "I can promise that my tongue shall be quiet/ for a strong reason indeed/ being an utter stranger to the language of the Anamaboe."[25] That is, having appropriated Boston's dress and language, she could no longer pass as a true African. Boston may have shaped Phillis Wheatley's language, religion, and identity, but she used her powerful poetic voice to remind Bostonians of its unfulfilled promise, as she so eloquently instructed privileged Harvard students in "To The University of Cambridge, in New-England."

John Adams was one of those later deemed "Eminent Bostonians" who carried forward the mission to build a city upon a hill for other, lesser sites to emulate, but Adams, unlike Winthrop, was more interested in creating a place of polity and purpose in *this* world than in the next.[26] Adams's passionate dedication to equal representation and balanced government made Boston a center of influence during and after the Revolution, when he was elected the new nation's second president. Born in 1735, the son of a farmer, Adams grew up just south of Boston in what is now Quincy, a city identified with the Adams family and the site of three Adams residences that illustrate his rise from yeomanry to eminence, a status sustained by his distinguished descendants. Adams went to Harvard College, class of 1755, but, like his Revolutionary-era friend and colleague Benjamin Franklin, Adams turned away from the "frigid" Calvinism there offered. He took up the study of law and, in 1764, married Abigail Smith, daughter of a Congregational minister. Their long, loving, and fruitful marriage of equals has become legendary, particularly since it is recorded in so many eloquent and witty letters, written during their many separations when his duties called him away from home. They moved to Boston in 1768, to Brattle Square, where Adams demonstrated his complexity of mind by successfully defending British soldiers accused of murdering civilian demonstrators during the Boston Massacre of 1770 and by campaigning against the Stamp Act. Elected as a delegate to the First Continental Congress, Adams left for Philadelphia to help instigate a revolution, write a constitution, and shape a nation.

Though John Adams spent some ten of the next twenty-six years away from home, occasioning the wonderful exchange of letters between him and his wife, and turned his attention away from local to national and international matters, he retained a rich sense of his place of origin. This is clear in a 1775 letter to Abigail in which he argues his "Overweening Prejudice in Favor of New England." Adams, ever the lawyer, listed the points in support of his case that "New England has in many Respects the Advantage of every other Colony in America." Adams focused upon the region, while Winthrop had focused upon the city. New England's "Support of Religion, Morals and Decency," its "public institutions," its territorial divisions, and its laws made the region exemplary for Adams, though he qualified his endorsement with mention of "Disadvantages," particularly "the exorbitant Prerogatives of our Governors &c.," which he and his fellow rebels were setting about to correct.[27]

Abigail Adams too had a large vision of nationhood, but she stayed at home, bearing five children (two died), tending the Adams household and fields, worrying about smallpox, provisions, and money while her husband conferred and conspired in Philadelphia. Thus Abigail's sense of place is far more local. "I hope to give you joy of Boston," wrote Abigail to John on March 3, 1775, "even if it is in ruins, before I send this away. I am too much agitated to write as I ought, and languid for want of rest." So she wrote in response to the Siege of Boston by General William Howe's British forces and the ensuing Battle of Bunker Hill that spring. The Adams family's humble farmhouse shook from cannon shots while she and her children watched rebel forces march by toward battle. They could see Bunker Hill aflame across Boston Harbor. Abigail was there, in the midst of the nation's defining moment, and wrote to tell John how terrible yet exhilarating it was.

In another, now famous letter, she told him that the nation that he and his fellow representatives to the colonial Congress were envisioning should be one in which all men and *women* are created equal. "Remember the Ladies, and be more generous and favourable to them than your ancestors," she enjoined, in a playful but firm tone.[28] John Adams and the Congress did not take her advice, though he never neglected to consult and rely upon his wife and "dearest friend" throughout their long marriage. When she told him that the new nation would need "learned women," he knew that he and the nation already had one in Abigail Adams.[29]

Nathaniel Hawthorne possessed an intense sense of local place and its cosmic implications, though he never looked kindly upon Boston. He remained a citizen of elsewhere in other American and European places, and he retained a detached, critical perspective on the city where ancestor William Hathorne distinguished himself by persecuting Quakers two centuries earlier. Boston, for Nathaniel Hawthorne, was a site of moral trials, where innocent, idealistic newcomers encountered disillusionment, released passion, evidenced hypocrisy, and demonstrated other human failings. Above all, the city was a challenge to his brooding imagination and served as a fitting emblem for his greatest romance.

When Hawthorne was thirty he saw Cotton Hill, the central peak of Trimountain, reduced to supply landfill for property development at the base of Beacon Hill. He mourned the destruction of the spacious estates that had graced the heights of Cotton Hill and the loss of "an admirable view of the city, being almost as high as the steeples and the dome of the State House, and overlooking the whole mass of brick buildings and slated roofs, with glimpses of streets far below. It was really a pity to take it down."[30] Many of his tales of the 1830s–'40s portray Boston as a diminished, even a fallen city. In "My Kinsman, Major Molineux" Hawthorne showed how a young man was corrupted by the city's drama, mystery, and sinfulness in the pre-revolutionary era. In "The New Adam and Eve" Hawthorne portrayed these two mythic innocents touring a Boston mysteriously without citizens. The pure couple recoil from the city's "squareness and ugliness," from its "unrenewed decay" and its signs of prejudice. In "Sights from a Steeple" a voyeur looks down, literally and figuratively, upon a Boston that has failed to fulfill its self-appointed mission.[31]

In 1839 Hawthorne worked unhappily as a weigher and gauger in the Boston Custom House, then left that position to become a charter member of Brook Farm, the short-lived utopian commune along the Charles River in West Roxbury. After he failed to adapt to communal ways, he married Sophia Peabody and they moved to Concord, living in impoverished happiness in the Emerson-Ripley Old Manse. Then the Hawthorne family moved back to his native Salem; then to Lenox, in western Massachusetts; then to Liverpool and Rome before returning to Concord for his final years. Though Boston reappeared in his fiction, in *The House of the Seven Gables* (1851) and *The Blithedale Romance* (1852), he never chose to live in the city again.

In *The Scarlet Letter*, Hawthorne makes a somewhat strained link between Boston and Salem, two seventeenth-century centers of New England Puritanism, the two cities in which his persecuting ancestors inflicted their righteous wrath upon those who deviated from their Calvinist faith. In "The Custom-House" preface he claims to have discovered evidence of Hester Prynne's story in the upper room of the Salem Custom House, where he worked in the late 1840s. He purports to have come upon the actual scarlet letter, wrapped in "a small roll of dingy paper" which bore an account of the tale written by one Jonathan Pue, former Surveyor of Boston. Here Hawthorne not only attempts to authenticate his romance but also to provide its rationale, for the ghostly voice of Pue seems to enjoin him to "give

your predecessor's memory the credit which will rightly be its due!"—
to which Hawthorne replies, "I will!," though his "credit" is critical.[32]
Hawthorne's claimed discovery of the letter and Pue's account provided the
novelist with license and purpose to portray the secret history of Boston
Puritanism as a system of heartless persecution and its victim, Hester
Prynne, as the city's unlikely heroine. Hawthorne thus linked Boston and
Salem into the same exemplary romance.

For Hawthorne, two places, as we have seen, defined Puritan Boston's concerns with death and judgment, secular and divine: the prison and the burial
ground. The opening chapter of *The Scarlet Letter* qualifies these stern images
with a rose-bush which, in Hawthorne's symbolic landscape, grows beside the
prison door. Hawthorne sets up a dialectic of contrasting Boston images, speculating that the rose-bush might be interpreted either as the product of
"Nature" or as a magical growth "that had sprung up under the footsteps of
the sainted Ann [sic] Hutchinson," who had been banished from the colony
for expressions of heresy in 1638. Either way, the rose-bush represents natural
passion and moral compassion, both outlawed in Puritan Boston, and pre-
pares the reader to sympathize with Hester Prynne, who is about to emerge
from the prison to receive the harsh judgment of the Boston community,
including her hypocritical lover, Rev. Arthur Dimmesdale. Hawthorne under-
scores his point by suggesting that the rose-bush "may serve, let us hope, to
symbolize some sweet moral blossom, that may be found along the track, or
relieve the darkening close of a tale of human frailty and sorrow."[33]

John Winthrop led the state prosecution's successful case against Anne
Hutchinson during her 1637 heresy trial. Winthrop announced the verdict:
"Mrs. Hutchinson, the sentence of the court you hear is that you are banished from out of our jurisdiction as being a woman not fit for our society,
and are to be imprisoned till the court shall send you away."[34] Hawthorne, it
might be said, readmits into Boston society his fictional variation on
Hutchinson in the figure of Hester, deemed an adulteress by Puritan elders,
whose *A* is eventually reimagined to represent "Angel" in the minds of the
belatedly compassionate Boston citizenry. After the truth—about her lover
Dimmesdale's hidden sin and her husband Chillingworth's manipulative
evil—finally emerged, Hester was seen as not only fit to join the Boston
community but as the city's "prophetess" who assured them that "a new
truth would be revealed, in order to establish the whole relation between
man and woman on surer ground of mutual happiness."[35]

Anne Hutchinson's heresy was to challenge the congregational theocracy of the colony by pursing salvation through personal revelation, so she was banished.[36] Hester Prynne's transgression was an act of love. Both Hutchinson and Hester were women whose actions went against the grain of Boston's strict, communal beliefs and, as a result, were punished for it, but Hawthorne rewrote the Hutchinson parable of defiance and banishment into a tale of victimization and salvation for the city.[37] In *The Scarlet Letter* Nathaniel Hawthorne removed "any curse incurred by" his Puritan ancestors and redefined Boston's mission to incorporate passion and grant compassion.

Though *The Scarlet Letter* was generally well received, some found Hawthorne's choice of subject "revolting," and Orestes Brownson, transcendentalist reformer turned Catholic intellectual, thought the romance would contribute to "an unsound state of public morals."[38] Hawthorne, however, remained unapologetic, and his work immediately entered the literary canon. If Samuel Eliot Morison is right in suggesting that Hawthorne transformed our sense of Boston Puritanism, he did not do so alone. Only a few years later, Oliver Wendell Holmes, the esteemed "Autocrat of the Breakfast Table," published in *Atlantic Monthly*, the house-organ for the Boston literary community, a satiric poem that has come to be seen as a biting satire on Puritanism, "The Deacon's Masterpiece; or The Wonderful 'One-Hoss Shay'" (1858). The Deacon's shay was built with such care and logic that it could never break down until, all of a sudden, it did just that! Similarly, New England Puritanism "came to smash," as Barrett Wendell, Harvard professor and celebrator of Brahmin Boston, put it.[39] Holmes, trained as a doctor in the rational humanism of Paris, came to see the Calvinism of New England Puritanism, the views of Jonathan Edwards in particular, which emphasized predestination and punishment, as intolerable, the theological counterpart of medical quackery.[40] Thus, the exalted goal of John Winthrop, stated in 1630, to build a city upon a hill, had become by the 1850s a subject of anguished reappraisal by Nathaniel Hawthorne and a topic of poetic sport for Oliver Wendell Holmes. Boston was not only a harbor community at the juncture of two rivers; it was an image and ideal open to interpretation.

SELECTIONS

John Winthrop, from "A Model of Christian Charity" (1630)

John Winthrop (1588–1649) led a group of English Puritans to settle the Massachusetts Bay Colony in 1630 and was elected their governor. "A Model of Christian Charity" was delivered aboard the *Arbella* before their arrival. Winthrop set the idealistic goal for Boston, to "be as a city upon a hill," but he soon expressed anxieties over the city's failure to fulfill its promise.

God Almighty in His most holy and wise providence hath so disposed of the condition of mankind as in all times some must be rich, some poor; some high and eminent in power and dignity, others mean in subjection.

The reason hereof: First, to hold conformity with the rest of His works, being delighted to show forth the glory of His wisdom in the variety and difference of the creatures and the glory of His power, in ordering all these differences for the preservation and good of the whole, and the glory of His greatness: that as it is the glory of princes to have many officers, so this great King will have many stewards, counting Himself more honored in dispensing his gifts to man by man than if He did it by His own immediate hand.

Secondly, that He might have the more occasion to manifest the work of His Spirit: first, upon the wicked in moderating and restraining them, so that the rich and mighty should not eat up the poor, nor the poor and despised rise up against their superiors and shake off their yoke; secondly, in the regenerate, in exercising His graces in them—as in the great ones, their love, mercy, gentleness, temperance etc., in the poor and inferior sort, their faith, patience, obedience, etc.

Thirdly, that every man might have need of other, and from hence they might be all knit more nearly together in the bond of brotherly affection. From hence it appears plainly that no man is made more honorable than another, or more wealthy, etc., out of any particular and singular respect to himself, but for the glory of his creator and the common good of the creature, man. Therefore God still reserves the property of these gifts to Himself (Ezek. 16, 17). He there calls wealth His gold and His silver, etc. (Prov. 3, 9). He claims their service as His due: "Honor the Lord with thy riches." All men being thus (by divine providence) ranked into two sorts, rich and poor, under the first are comprehended all such as are able to live comfortably by their own means duly improved, and all others are poor, according to the former distribution.

There are two rules whereby we are to walk, one towards another: justice and mercy. These are always distinguished in their act and in their object, yet may they both concur in the same subject in each respect: as sometimes there may be an occasion showing mercy to a rich man in some sudden danger of distress, and also doing of mere justice to a poor man in regard of some particular contract.

There is likewise a double law by which we are regulated in our conversation one towards another: in both the former respects, the law of nature and the law of grace, or the moral law or the law of the Gospel—to omit the rule of justice as not properly belonging to this purpose, otherwise than it may fall into consideration in some particular cases. By the first of these laws, man, as he was enabled so, withal [is] commanded to love his neighbor as himself; upon this ground stand all the precepts of the moral law, which concerns our dealings with men. To apply this to the works of mercy, this law requires two things: first, that every man afford his help to another in every want or distress; secondly, that he perform this out of the same affection which makes him careful of his own good according to that of our savior (Matt. 7, 12): "Whatsoever ye would that men should do to you." . . .

Thus stands the cause between God and us: we are entered into covenant with Him for this work; we have taken out a commission, the Lord hath given us leave to draw our own articles. We have professed to enterprise these actions, upon these and these ends; we have hereupon besought Him of favor and blessing. Now if the Lord shall please to hear us, and bring us in peace to the place we desire, then hath He ratified this covenant and sealed our Commission, [and] will expect a strict performance of the articles contained in it. But if we shall neglect the observation of these articles, which are the ends we have propounded, and, dissembling with our God, shall fall to embrace this present world and prosecute our carnal intentions, seeking great things for ourselves and our posterity, the Lord will surely break out in wrath against us, be revenged of such a perjured people, and make us know the price of the breach of such a covenant.

Now the only way to avoid this shipwreck, and to provide for our posterity, is to follow the counsel of Micah: to do justly, to love mercy, to walk humbly with our God. For this end, we must be knit together in this work as one man. We must entertain each other in brotherly affection; we must be willing to abridge ourselves of our superfluities, for the supply of others' necessities; we must uphold a familiar commerce together in all meekness, gentleness, patience and liberality. We must delight in each other, make others' conditions our own, rejoice together, mourn together, labor and suffer together, always having before our eyes our commission and community in the work, our community as members of the same body. So shall we keep the unity of the spirit in the bond of peace, the Lord will be our God, and delight to dwell among us, as His own people, and will command a blessing upon us in all our ways, so that we shall see much more of His wisdom, power, goodness and truth than formerly we have been acquainted with. We shall find that the God of Israel is among us, when ten of us shall be able to resist a thousand of our enemies, when He shall make us a praise and glory, that men shall say of succeeding plantations: "the Lord make it like that of New England." For we must consider that we shall be as a city upon a hill, the eyes of all people are upon us. So that if we shall deal falsely with our God in this work we have undertaken, and so cause Him to withdraw His present help from us, we shall be made a story and a by-word through the world: we shall open the mouths of enemies to speak evil of the ways of God and all professors for God's sake; we shall shame the faces of many of God's worthy servants, and cause their prayers to be turned into curses upon us, till we be consumed out of the good land whither we are going.

Anne Bradstreet, "Before the Birth of One of Her Children" (1678), and from "Meditations Divine and Moral" # 53

Anne Bradstreet (1612–1672) was America's first poet. An original settler in Boston in 1630, she was both the daughter and the wife of a governor of Massachusetts. Her poetry established the importance of the spiritual autobiography as a primary form of self-expression in Boston. Her *Meditations*, composed as a diary and left to her children, were not published until 1867. "Before the Birth of One of Her Children" and this passage from her diary show her translation of her actual journey to Boston as a spiritual quest for "the city above."

Before the Birth of One of Her Children

All things within this fading world hath end,
Adversity doth still our joys attend;
No ties so strong, no friends so dear and sweet,
But with death's parting blow is sure to meet.
The sentence past is most irrevocable.
A common thing, yet oh, inevitable.
How soon, my Dear, death may my steps attend,
How soon't may be thy lot to lose thy friend,
We both are ignorant, yet love bids me
These farewell lines to recommend to thee,
That when the knot's untied that made us one,
I may seem thine, who in effect am none.
And if I see not half my days that's due,
What nature would, God grant to yours and you.
The many faults that well you know I have
Let be interred in my oblivious grave;
If any worth or virtue were in me,
Let that live freshly in thy memory
And when thou feel'st no grief, as I no harms,
Yet love thy dead, who long lay in thine arms.
And when thy loss shall be repaid with gains
Look to my little babes, my dear remains.
And if thou love thyself, or loved'st me,
These O protect from step-dame's injury.
And if chance to thine eyes shall bring this verse,
With some sad sighs honor my absent hearse;
And kiss this paper for thy love's dear sake,
Who with salt tears this last farewell did take.

Meditation # 53

He that is to sail into a far country, although the ship, cabin, and provision be all convenient and comfortable for him, yet he hath no desire to make that his place of residence, but longs to put in at that port where his business lies. A Christian is sailing through this world unto his heavenly country, and here he hath many conveniences and comforts; but he must beware of desiring to make this the place of his abode, lest he meet with such tossing that may cause him to long for shore before he sees land. We must, therefore, be here as strangers and pilgrims, that we may plainly declare that we seek a city above, and wait all the days of our appointed time till our change shall come.

Benjamin Franklin, from *The Autobiography of Benjamin Franklin* (1771)

Benjamin Franklin (1706–1790), a founding father of the nation, was a man of many talents: writer, publisher, inventor, diplomat, scientist, and philosopher. A year after his death, his autobiography, written for his son William, then the governor of New Jersey, was published in Paris, entitled *Mémoires de la Vie Privée de Benjamin Franklin.*The first English translation, *The Private Life of the Late Benjamin Franklin, LL.D. Originally Written By Himself, And Now Translated From The French*, was published in London in 1793. Franklin's Boston was a Puritan prison from which he escaped, though he carried many Bostonian values with him as he joined others in inventing America during and after the Revolution.

My brother had, in 1720 or 1721, begun to print a newspaper. It was the second that appeared in America, and was called the *New England Courant*. The only one before it was the *Boston News-Letter*. I remember his being dissuaded by some of his friends from the undertaking, as not likely to succeed, one newspaper being, in their judgment, enough for America. At this time (1771) there are not less than five-and-twenty. He went on, however, with the undertaking, and after having worked in composing the types and printing off the sheets, I was employed to carry the papers through the streets to the customers.

He had some ingenious men among his friends, who amused themselves by writing little pieces for this paper, which gained it credit and made it more in demand, and these gentlemen often visited us. Hearing their conversations, and their accounts of the approbation their papers were received with, I was excited to try my hand among them; but, being still a boy, and suspecting that my brother would object to printing anything of mine in his paper if he knew it to be mine, I contrived to disguise my hand, and, writing an anonymous paper, I put it in at night under the door of the printing-house. It was found in the morning, and communicated to his writing friends when they called in as usual. They read it, commented on it in my hearing, and I had the exquisite pleasure of finding it met with their approbation, and that, in their different guesses at the author, none were named but men of some character among us for learning and ingenuity. I suppose now that I was rather lucky in my judges, and that perhaps they were not really so very good ones as I then esteemed them.

Encouraged, however, by this, I wrote and conveyed in the same way to the press several more papers which were equally approved; and I kept my secret until my small fund of sense for such performances was pretty well exhausted and then I discovered it, when I began to be considered a little more by my brother's acquaintance, and in a manner that did not quite please him, as he thought, probably with reason, that it tended to make me too vain. And, perhaps, this might be one occasion of the differences that we began to have about this time. Though a brother, he considered himself as my master, and me as his apprentice, and accordingly, expected the same services from me as he would from another, while I thought he demeaned me too much in some he required of me, who from a brother expected more indulgence. Our disputes were often brought before our father, and I fancy I was either generally in the right, or else a better pleader, because the judgment was generally in my favor. But my brother was passionate, and had often beaten me, which I took extremely amiss; and, thinking my apprenticeship very tedious, I was continually wishing for some opportunity of shortening it, which at length offered in a manner unexpected. I fancy his harsh and tyrannical treatment of me might be a means of impressing me with that aversion to arbitrary power that has stuck to me through my whole life.

One of the pieces in our newspaper on some political point, which I have now forgotten, gave offence to the Assembly. He was taken up, censured, and imprisoned for a month, by the speaker's warrant, I suppose, because he would not discover his author. I too was taken up and examined before the council; but, though I did not give them any satisfaction, they contented themselves with admonishing me, and dismissed me, considering me, perhaps, as an apprentice, who was bound to keep his master's secrets.

During my brother's confinement, which I resented a good deal, notwithstanding our private differences, I had the management of the paper; and I made bold to give our rulers some rubs in it, which my brother took very kindly, while others began to consider me in an unfavorable light, as a young genius that had a turn for libeling and satire. My brother's discharge was accompanied with an Order of the House (a very odd one), that "James Franklin should no longer print the paper called the New England Courant."

There was a consultation held in our printing-house among his friends, what he should do in this case. Some proposed to evade the order by changing the name of the paper; but my brother, seeing inconveniences in that, it was finally concluded on as a better way, to let it be printed for the future under the name of *Benjamin Franklin.* And to avoid the censure of the Assembly that might fall on him as still printing it by his apprentice, the contrivance was that my old indenture should be returned to me, with a full discharge on the back of it, to be shown on occasion, but to secure to him the benefit of my service, I was to sign new indentures for the remainder of the term, which were to be kept private. A very flimsy scheme it was, but however, it was immediately executed, and the paper went on accordingly, under my name for several months.

At length, a fresh difference arising between my brother and me, I took upon me to assert my freedom, presuming that he would not venture to produce the new indentures. It was not fair in me to take this advantage, and this I therefore reckon one of the first errata of my life. But the unfairness of it weighed little with me, when under the impressions of resentment for the blows his passion too often urged him to bestow upon me, though he was otherwise not an ill-natured man: perhaps I was too saucy and provoking.

When he found I would leave him, he took care to prevent my getting employment in any other printing-house of the town, by going round and speaking to every master, who accordingly refused to give me work. I then thought of going to New York, as the nearest place where there was a printer; and I was rather inclined to leave Boston when I reflected that I had already made myself a little obnoxious to the governing party, and, from the arbitrary proceedings of the Assembly in my brother's case, it was likely I might, if I stayed, soon bring myself into scrapes; and farther, that my indiscrete disputations about religion began to make me pointed at with horror by good people as an infidel or atheist. I determined on the point, but my father now siding with my brother, I was sensible that, if I attempted to go openly, means would be used to prevent me. My friend Collins, therefore, under-took to manage a little for me.

He agreed with the captain of a New York sloop for my passage, under the notion of my being a young acquaintance of his, that had got a naughty girl with child, whose friends would compel me to marry her, and therefore I could not appear or come away publicly. So I sold some of my books to raise a little money, was taken on board privately, and as we had a fair wind, in three days I found myself in New York, near 300 miles from home, a boy of but 17, without the least recommendation to, or knowledge of any person in the place, and with very little money in my pocket.

My inclinations for the sea were by this time worn out, or I might now have gratified them. But, having a trade, and supposing myself a pretty good workman, I offered my service to the printer in the place, old Mr. William Bradford, who had been the first printer in Pennsylvania, but removed from thence upon the quarrel of George Keith. He could give me no employ-ment, having little to do, and help enough already; but says he, "My son at Philadelphia has lately lost his principal hand, Aquila Rose, by death; if you go thither, I believe he may employ you." Philadelphia was a hundred miles further; I set out, however, in a boat for Amboy, leaving my chest and things to follow me round by sea. . . .

[In Philadelphia] I walked up the street, gazing about till near the market-house I met a boy with bread. I had made many a meal on bread, and, in-quiring where he got it, I went immediately to the baker's he directed me to, in Second Street, and asked for biscuit, intending such as we had in Boston; but they, it seems, were not made in Philadelphia. Then I asked for a three-penny loaf, and was told they had none such. So not considering or knowing the difference of money, and the greater cheapness nor the names of his bread, I made him give me three-penny worth of any sort. He gave me, ac-cordingly, three great puffy rolls. I was surprised at the quantity, but took it, and, having no room in my pockets, walked off with a roll under each arm, and eating the other. Thus I went up Market Street as far as Fourth Street, passing by the door of Mr. Read, my future wife's father; when she, standing at the door, saw me, and thought I made, as I certainly did, a most awkward, ridiculous appearance. Then I turned and went down Chestnut Street and part of Walnut Street, eating my roll all the way, and, coming round, found myself again at Market Street wharf, near the boat I came in, to which I went for a draught of the river water; and, being filled with one of my rolls, gave the other two to a woman and her child that came down the river in the boat with us, and were waiting to go farther.

Thus refreshed, I walked again up the street, which by this time had many clean-dressed people in it, who were all walking the same way. I joined them, and thereby was led into the great meeting-house of the Quakers near the market. I sat down among them, and, after looking round awhile and hearing nothing said, being very drowsy through labor and want of rest the preceding night, I fell fast asleep, and continued so till the meeting broke up, when one was kind enough to rouse me. This was, therefore, the first house I was in, or slept in, in Philadelphia.

Walking down again toward the river, and, looking in the faces of people, I met a young Quaker man, whose countenance I liked, and, accosting him, requested he would tell me where a stranger could get lodging. We were then near the sign of the Three Mariners. "Here," says he, "is one place that entertains strangers, but it is not a reputable house; if thee wilt walk with me, I'll show thee a better." He brought me to the Crooked Billet in Water Street. Here I got a dinner; and, while I was eating it, several sly questions were asked me, as it seemed to be suspected from my youth and appearance, that I might be some runaway.

After dinner, my sleepiness returned, and being shown to a bed, I lay down without undressing, and slept till six in the evening, was called to supper, went to bed again very early, and slept soundly till next morning. Then I made myself as tidy as I could, and went to Andrew Bradford the printer's. I found in the shop the old man his father, whom I had seen at New York, and who, traveling on horseback, had got to Philadelphia before me. He introduced me to his son, who received me civilly, gave me a breakfast, but told me he did not at present want a hand, being lately supplied with one; but there was another printer in town, lately set up, one Keimer, who, perhaps, might employ me; if not, I should be welcome to lodge at his house, and he would give me a little work to do now and then till fuller business should offer.

Phillis Wheatley, from *Poems on Various Subjects, Religious and Moral* (1773)

Born in Gambia (now Senegal), Phillis Wheatley (1753–1784) became a slave at age seven. Taken to America in 1761 aboard a slave ship called *Phillis*, she was purchased and named in Boston by John Wheatley and his family. The Wheatley family educated her and she was baptized at Old South Meeting House. In 1773 Wheatley published her only book, *Poems on Various Subjects, Religious and Moral.* She not only learned to master English verse forms, but incorporated Puritan moral and religious values into her experience as a slave in Boston.

On Being Brought from Africa to America

'Twas mercy brought me from my pagan land,
Taught my benighted soul to understand
That there's a God, that there's a Savior too:
Once I redemption neither fought nor knew,
Some view our sable race with scornful eye,
"Their color is a diabolic die."
Remember, Christians, Negroes, black as Cain,
May be refined, and join the angelic train.

To The University of Cambridge, in New England

While an intrinsic ardor prompts to write,
The muses promise to assist my pen;
'Twas not long since I left my native shore
The land of errors, and Egyptian gloom:
Father of mercy, 'twas Thy gracious hand
Brought me in safety from those dark abodes.

Students, to you 'tis given to scan the heights
Above, to traverse the ethereal space,
And mark the systems of revolving worlds.
Still more, ye sons of science ye receive
The blissful news by messengers from Heav'n,

How Jesus' blood for your redemption flows.
See Him with hands out-stretched upon the cross;
Immense compassion in His bosom glows;
He hears revilers, nor resents their scorn:
What matchless mercy in the Son of God!
When the whole human race by sin had fall'n,
He deigned to die that they might rise again,
And share with Him in the sublimest skies,
Life without death, and glory without end.

Improve your privileges while they stay,
Ye pupils, and each hour redeem, that bears
Or good or bad report of you to Heav'n.
Let sin, that baneful evil to the soul,
By you be shunned, nor once remit your guard;
Suppress the deadly serpent in its egg.
Ye blooming plants of human race divine,
An Ethiop tells you 'tis your greatest foe;
Its transient sweetness turns to endless pain,
And in immense perdition sinks the soul.

Letters from Abigail Adams to John Adams

John Adams (1735–1826), a founding father, was the second President of the United States (1797–1801). In 1764, Adams married Abigail Smith (1744–1818), the daughter of a Congregational minister, in Weymouth, Massachusetts. Abigail Adams wrote these memorable letters to her husband while he was in Philadelphia, attending the Continental Congresses.

Braintree 16 July, 1775: The appointment of the generals Washington and Lee, gives universal satisfaction. The people have the highest opinion of Lee's abilities, but you know the continuation of the popular breath depends much upon favorable events. I had the pleasure of seeing both the generals and their aid de camps soon after their arrival, and of being personally made known to them. They very politely express their regard for you. . . .

As to intelligence from Boston, 'tis but very seldom we are able to collect any thing that may be relied upon, and to report the vague, flying rumors, would be endless. I heard yesterday, by one Mr. Rolestone, a goldsmith, who got out in a fishing schooner, that their distress increased upon them fast. Their beef is all spent, their malt and cider all gone, all the fresh provisions they can procure they are obliged to give to the sick and wounded. 19 of our men who were in jail, and were wounded at the Battle of Charlestown, were dead. No man dared now to be seen talking to his friend in the street, they were obliged to be within, every evening, at ten o'clock according to martial law, nor could any inhabitant walk any street in town after that time, without a pass from Gage. He has ordered all the molasses to be stilled up into rum for the soldiers, taken away all licenses, and given out others, obliging to a forfeiture of ten pounds I.M. if any rum is sold without written orders from the General. . . .

As to the situation of the camps, our men are in general healthy, much more so at Roxbury than Cambridge, and the camp is in vastly better order. General Thomas has the character of an excellent officer. His merit has certainly been overlooked, as modest merit generally is. I hear General Washington is much pleased with his conduct.

Every article here in the West India way is very scarce and dear. In six weeks we shall not be able to purchase any article of the kind. I wish you would let Bass get me one pound of pepper, and 2 yards of black caliminco for shoes. I cannot wear leather, if I go barefoot for the reason I need not mention. Bass may make a fine profit if he lays in a stock for himself. You can hardly imagine how much we want many common small articles, which are not manufactured amongst ourselves, but we will have them in time. Not one pin to be purchased for love nor money. I wish you could convey me a thousand by any friend traveling this way. 'Tis very provoking to have such a plenty so near us, but tantalus like, not be able to touch. I should have been glad to have laid in a small stock of the West India articles, but I cannot get one copper. No person thinks of paying any thing, and I do not choose to run in debt. I endeavor to live in the most frugal manner possible, but I am many times distressed. . . .

Braintree March 31, 1776: . . . Do you not want to see Boston; I am fearful of the small pox, or I should have been in before this time. . . . The town in general is left in a better state than we expected, more owing to the precipitate flight than any regard to the inhabitants, though some individuals discovered a sense of honor and justice and have left the rent of the houses in which they were, for the owners, and the furniture unhurt, or if damaged sufficient to make it good.

Others have committed abominable ravages. The Mansion House of your President is safe and the furniture unhurt whilst both the house and furniture of the Solicitor General have fallen a prey to their own merciless party. Surely the very fiends feel a reverential awe for virtue and patriotism, whilst they detest the parricide and traitor.

I feel very differently at the approach of spring to what I did a month ago. We knew not then whether when we had toiled we could plant or sow with safety, whether when we had toiled we could reap the fruits of our own industry, whether we could rest in our own cottages, or whether we should not be driven from the sea coasts to seek shelter in the wilderness, but now we feel as if we might sit under our own vine and eat the good of the land.

I feel a gaieti de Coar [sic] to which I before was a stranger. I think the sun looks brighter, the birds sing more melodiously, and Nature puts on a more cheerful countenance. We feel a temporary peace, and the poor fugitives are returning to their deserted habitations.

Though we felicitate ourselves, we sympathize with those who are trembling lest the lot of Boston should be theirs. But they cannot be in similar circumstances unless pusillanimity and cowardice should take possession of them. They have time and warning given them to see evil and shun it.—I long to hear that you have declared an independency—and by the way in the new code of laws which I suppose it will be necessary for you to make I desire you would remember the ladies, and be more generous and favorable to them than your ancestors. Do not put unlimited power into the hands of the husbands. Remember all men would be tyrants if they could. If particular care and attention is not paid to the ladies we are determined to foment a rebellion, and will not hold ourselves bound by any laws in which we have no voice or representation. That your sex are naturally tyrannical is a truth so thoroughly established as to admit of no dispute, but such of you as wish to be happy willingly give up the harsh title of master for the more tender and endearing one of friend. Why then, not put it out of the power of the vicious and the lawless to use us with cruelty and indignity with impunity. Men of sense in all ages abhor those customs which treat us only as the vassals of your sex. Regard us then as beings placed by providence under your protection and in imitation of the Supreme Being make use of that power only for our happiness.

Nathaniel Hawthorne, "The Prison Door," from *The Scarlet Letter* (1850)

Nathaniel Hawthorne (1804–1864), novelist and tale-teller, was a central presence in the American literary renaissance. Along with the works of John Winthrop in the seventeenth century and Robert Lowell in the twentieth, Hawthorne's mid-nineteenth-century romance, *The Scarlet Letter*, was most influential in shaping the idea of Boston. His dark vision of the city is evident in the first chapter on *The Scarlet Letter*.

A throng of bearded men, in sad-colored garments and grey steeple-crowned hats, intermixed with women, some wearing hoods, and others bareheaded, was assembled in front of a wooden edifice, the door of which was heavily timbered with oak, and studded with iron spikes.

The founders of a new colony, whatever Utopia of human virtue and happiness they might originally project, have invariably recognized it among their earliest practical necessities to allot a portion of the virgin soil as a cemetery, and another portion as the site of a prison. In accordance with this rule it may safely be assumed that the forefathers of Boston had built the first prison-house somewhere in the vicinity of Cornhill, almost as seasonably as they marked out the first burial-ground, on Isaac Johnson's lot, and round about his grave, which subsequently became the nucleus of all the congregated sepulchres in the old church-yard of King's Chapel. Certain it is, that, some fifteen or twenty years after the settlement of the town, the wooden jail was already marked with weather-stains and other indications of age, which gave a yet darker aspect to its beetle-browed and gloomy front. The rust on the ponderous iron-work of its oaken door looked more antique than anything else in the new world. Like all that pertains to crime, it seemed never to have known a youthful era. Before this ugly edifice, and between it and the wheel-track of the street, was a grass-plot, much overgrown with burdock, pig-weed, apple-peru, and such unsightly vegetation, which evidently found something congenial in the soil that had so early borne the black flower of civilized society, a prison. But, on one side of the portal, and rooted almost at the threshold, was a wild rose-bush, covered, in this month of June, with its delicate gems, which might be imagined to offer their fragrance and fragile beauty to the prisoner as he went in, and to the condemned criminal as he came forth to his doom, in token that the deep heart of Nature could pity and be kind to him.

This rose-bush, by a strange chance, has been kept alive in history; but whether it had merely survived out of the stern old wilderness, so long after the fall of the gigantic pines and oaks that originally overshadowed it,—or whether, as there is fair authority for believing, it had sprung up under the footsteps of the sainted Ann Hutchinson, as she entered the prison-door,— we shall not take upon us to determine. Finding it so directly on the threshold of our narrative, which is now about to issue from that inauspicious portal, we could hardly do otherwise than pluck one of its flowers, and present it to the reader. It may serve, let us hope, to symbolize some sweet moral blossom that may be found along the track, or relieve the darkening close of a tale of human frailty and sorrow.

Oliver Wendell Holmes, "The Deacon's Masterpiece or, the Wonderful 'One-Hoss Shay' A Logical Story" (1858)

Oliver Wendell Holmes (1809–1894)—physician, essayist, Fireside Poet, and "Autocrat of the Breakfast Table"—was the poet laureate of Brahmin Boston.

> Have you heard of the wonderful one-hoss-shay,
> That was built in such a logical way
> It ran a hundred years to a day,
> And then, of a sudden, it—ah, but stay,
> I'll tell you what happened without delay,
> Scaring the parson into fits,
> Frightening people out of their wits,—
> Have you ever heard of that, I say?
>
> Seventeen hundred and fifty-five.
> *Georgius Secundus* was then alive,—
> Snuffy old drone from the German hive!
> That was the year when Lisbon-town
> Saw the earth open and gulp her down,

And Braddock's army was done so brown,
Left without a scalp to its crown.
It was on the terrible Earthquake-day
That the Deacon finished the one-hoss-shay.

Now in building of chaises, I tell you what,
There is always *somewhere* a weakest spot,—
In hub, tire, felloe, in spring or thill,
In panel, or crossbar, or floor, or sill,
In screw, bolt, thoroughbrace,—lurking still,
Find it somewhere you must and will,—
Above or below, or within or without,—
And that's the reason, beyond a doubt,
That a chaise *breaks down*, but doesn't *wear out.*

But the Deacon swore (as Deacons do,
With an "I dew vum," or an "I tell *yeou*,")
He would build one shay to beat the taown
'n' the keounty 'n' all the kentry raoun';
It should be so built that it *couldn'* break daown:
—"Fur," said the Deacon, "'t's mighty plain
Thut the weakes' place mus' stan the strain;
'n' the way t' fix it, uz I maintain,
Is only jest
T' make that place uz strong uz the rest."

So the Deacon inquired of the village folk
Where he could find the strongest oak,
That couldn't be split nor bent nor broke,—
That was for spokes and floor and sills;
He sent for lancewood to make the thills;
The crossbars were ash, from the straightest trees;
The panels of white-wood, that cuts like cheese,
But lasts like iron for things like these;
The hubs of logs from the "Settler's ellum,"—
Last of its timber,—they couldn't sell 'em,
Never an axe had seen their chips,
And the wedges flew from between their lips,
Their blunt ends frizzled like celery-tips;

Step and prop-iron, bolt and screw,
Spring, tire, axle, and linchpin too,
Steel of the finest, bright and blue;
Thoroughbrace bison-skin, thick and wide;
Boot, top, dasher, from tough old hide
Found in the pit when the tanner died.
That was the way he "put her through."—
"There!" said the Deacon, "naow she'll dew!"

Do! I tell you, I rather guess
She was a wonder, and nothing less!
Colts grew horses, beards turned gray,
Deacon and deaconess dropped away,
Children and grandchildren—where were they?
But there stood the stout old one-hoss-shay
As fresh as on Lisbon-earthquake-day!

EIGHTEEN HUNDRED;—it came and found
The Deacon's Masterpiece strong and sound.
Eighteen hundred increased by ten;—
"Hahnsum kerridge" they called it then.
Eighteen hundred and twenty came;—
Running as usual; much the same.
Thirty and forty at last arrive,
And then come fifty, and FIFTY-FIVE.

Little of all we value here
Wakes on the morn of its hundredth year
Without both feeling and looking queer.
In fact, there's nothing that keeps its youth,
So far as I know, but a tree and truth.
(This is a moral that runs at large;
Take it.—You're welcome.—No extra charge.)

FIRST OF NOVEMBER,—the Earthquake-day,—
There are traces of age in the one-hoss-shay,
A general flavor of mild decay,
But nothing local, as one may say.
There couldn't be,—for the Deacon's art

Had made it so like in every part
That there wasn't a chance for one to start.
For the wheels were just as strong as the thills,
And the floor was just as strong as the sills,
And the panels just as strong as the floor,
And the whippletree neither less nor more,
And the back-crossbar as strong as the fore,
And spring and axle and hub *encore*.
And yet, *as a whole*, it is past a doubt
In another hour it will be *worn out!*

First of November, 'Fifty-five!
This morning the parson takes a drive.
Now, small boys, get out of the way!
Here comes the wonderful one-hoss shay,
Drawn by a rat-tailed, ewe-necked bay.
"Huddup!" said the parson.—Off went they.

The parson was working his Sunday's text,—
Had got to *fifthly*, and stopped perplexed
At what the—Moses—was coming next.
All at once the horse stood still,
Close by the meet'n'-house on the hill.
—First a shiver, and then a thrill,
Then something decidedly like a spill,—
And the parson was sitting upon a rock,
At half past nine by the meet'n'-house clock,—
Just the hour of the Earthquake shock!
—What do you think the parson found,
When he got up and stared around?
The poor old chaise in a heap or mound,
As if it had been to the mill and ground!
You see, of course, if you're not a dunce,
How it went to pieces all at once,—
All at once, and nothing first,—
Just as bubbles do when they burst.

End of the wonderful one-hoss-shay.
Logic is logic. That's all I say.

II

BOSTON AND THE AMERICAN RENAISSANCE

James T. Fields traveled to Salem from Boston to visit Nathaniel Hawthorne in late 1848, hoping to draw a manuscript from the secretive author for Ticknor & Fields, then "the publishing centre of Boston," as Van Wyck Brooks put it in *The Flowering of New England*.[1] Advanced by this publisher, Hawthorne, author of tales and romances on human frailty and sorrow, would become the sweet moral blossom of the flowering of New England letters. Ticknor & Fields achieved respect in part because William D. Ticknor, though not required by copyright law to do so, paid English authors for publishing their works. Their offices in The Old Corner Bookstore, at the intersection of Washington Street and School Street, in the heart of the city, became not only the publishing but the literary center of Boston and, by extension, America before and after the Civil War. On this site Anne Hutchinson once lived and near this site Nathaniel Hawthorne would imagine a scaffold, the symbol of Puritan judgment in *The Scarlet Letter*. As Paul M. Wright puts it, Ticknor & Fields "offered in one small building a cultural center and one focal point for a rapidly expanding and still undefined American nation."[2] There, authors came and went—Henry Wadsworth Longfellow, Harriet Beecher Stowe, Ralph Waldo Emerson, Oliver Wendell Holmes, and many more—drawn into a loose literary association. Fields served as host, friend, promoter, and publisher, solidifying Boston's claims of cultural eminence. Emerson, the region's most esteemed literary figure, deemed Fields "the guardian and maintainer of us all."[3]

Fields's visit to Hawthorne in Salem showed that however disbursed New England's authors might be, however seldom they met, whatever opinions they privately held about each other, they found their vital center in Boston and constituted America's first true literary community. Fields's influence extended well beyond Boston, in one famous instance to the Berkshires of western Massachusetts, as illustrated in his account of the August 1850 climb and picnic on Great Barrington's Monument Mountain, an outing which included Nathaniel Hawthorne, then living in the tiny Red House in nearby Lenox; Oliver Wendell Holmes, whose 2,600-acre estate, Holmsdale, was set in Pittsfield; Edward Duyckink, visiting New York publisher; and Herman Melville, who lived on a farm, Arrowhead, a few miles up the road, also in Pittsfield. Melville—a native New Yorker and seafarer who had taken up farming in a remote, rural region of Massachusetts, a writer thus cut off from nurturing literary contacts—was so moved by the event that he immediately composed a rapturous tribute to Hawthorne, "Hawthorne and His Mosses," published quickly by Duyckink in his New York journal, *Literary World*, in which Melville spoke of the thrill he felt at encountering a fellow writer of genius. Thus the literary community that centered in Boston extended its presence and influence to include this isolated New Yorker who was then writing *Moby-Dick*, which he would dedicate to his new friend, Hawthorne, whose fame Melville spread to New York City. As Melville put it, "genius, all over the world, stands hand in hand, and one shock of recognition runs the whole circle round."[4]

Fields had come to Boston from a New Hampshire farm, an ambitious young man drawn to the city's cultural heights. Through pluck, luck, perseverance, and charm he worked his way up from bookseller to publisher by demonstrating determination and insight, as he showed in his visit to Hawthorne. Fields shrewdly guessed that the romancer, while employed as a Surveyor in the Salem Custom House (1846–1849), must have been writing something that Ticknor & Fields could publish. Hawthorne said no, there was no manuscript stored in the cabinet that had caught the publisher's eye, but, as Fields was leaving to board his train back to Boston, Hawthorne, impressed by Fields's instinct that he was holding something back, impulsively pulled papers from the cabinet and pressed upon Fields a sheaf of papers that would become *The Scarlet Letter*.

Though Hawthorne's romance satirized Puritan Boston and he kept his distance from the city, where he had worked unhappily as a writer-editor of the *American Magazine of Useful and Entertaining Knowledge* (1836) and as a Custom House Weigher and Gauger (1839–1841), Fields drew him back into the city's cultural center. Hawthorne came to love his visits to Ticknor & Fields, where he exchanged literary gossip with the convivial Fields in his green-curtained, book-strewn office overlooking the Old South Meeting House.[5]

Ticknor & Fields became the publishing and promotional center of what

Van Wyck Brooks called "a renaissance in Boston" by issuing souvenir volumes of "Boston Authors," which contained plates of Longfellow's Craigie House, James Russell Lowell's Elmwood, and other local literary manses, suggesting that Greater Boston was literally the home of authors. The firm published and made famous American authors whereas rival publishers were pirating English writers before copyright laws prevented them. "Few were our native authors," wrote Henry James in "Mr. and Mrs. James T. Fields," a nostalgic 1915 tribute, and "the friendly Boston house had gathered them all in."[6] Ticknor & Fields published, then distributed nationally and internationally "little brown editions" of Emerson, Hawthorne, Holmes, Longfellow, and Stowe. Famous English authors—Browning, Tennyson, De Quincey—were persuaded by Fields, who went to Europe to court them, to offer him their works, thus enhancing through association the prestige of his New England authors and building Boston's cultural claims abroad.[7]

Ticknor & Fields also published Oliver Wendell Holmes, professor of anatomy and physiology at Harvard Medical School, a poet and essayist who embodied and expressed the enlightened rationalism that had replaced Boston's narrow, long-standing Puritanism. Holmes's father had been the liberal-leaning minister of the First Congregational Church in Cambridge who was forced out of his pulpit after being caught up in the conflict between orthodox Calvinists like Lyman Beecher and revisionist Unitarians like William Ellery Channing. (King's Chapel, the first Anglican church in this country, adopted the tenets of Unitarianism and rejected belief in the Trinity.) Oliver, as a Harvard student, recoiled from Puritanism and turned to science through his study of medicine.[8] Characteristically positive and rational, Holmes, as we have seen in his "One-Hoss Shay," was scathing about the city's history of dark, deterministic Puritanism and imagined a brighter, freer, more rational Boston.

Holmes's popular and influential essays for *Atlantic Monthly*—later published in anthologies under the titles *The Autocrat of the Breakfast Table*, *The Professor at the Breakfast Table*, and *The Poet at the Breakfast Table*, collected as *The Breakfast-Table Series* (1882)—were designed to refute the image of America as the vulgar Jacksonian democracy which was portrayed in Frances Trollope's *Domestic Manners of the Americans* (1832). Mrs. Trollope used the boarding-house table as a setting to present a cross-section of Americans who eat like animals in silence, while Holmes used the boarding-house table as a setting where Americans ate with delicacy and talked ceaselessly in an "idealized Boston," as William C. Dowling puts it in *Oliver Wendell Holmes in Paris*. "Holmes's imaginary breakfast table gradually becomes a magical space in which opinions never before publicly heard in Boston are not only fearlessly uttered, but meant to be overheard by a large audience of *Atlantic Monthly* readers throughout the English-speaking world."[9]

Holmes saw Fields, his Beacon Hill neighbor, as his "literary counselor and friend."[10] For Holmes the city upon a hill and the eminent Bostonians who populated it literally set the measure of value for all things. "We all carry the Common in our heads as the unit of space, the State House as the standard of architecture, and measure off men in Edward Everetts as with a yard stick."[11] Everett, an esteemed Whig politician, served as congressman, senator, president of Harvard, governor of Massachusetts, and secretary of state. It was Holmes who defined what it meant to be a member of the "Brahmin caste" in his 1861 novel, *Elsie Venner*. This "harmless, inoffensive, untitled aristocracy" possessed an "aptitude for learning" which is "congenital and hereditary." Though Holmes did not quite say so, he implied that the exclusive Brahmin caste which resulted from the determinism of "Nature's republicanism" made outcasts of the Irish immigrants who were suddenly crowding Boston.[12] It was Holmes who, with playful and loving irony, dubbed Boston "the Hub of the solar system" and "the thinking centre of the continent, and therefore of the planet."[13] Holmes did his best to make the city just that by maintaining friendly and intellectually stimulating relations with a range of writers, including Emerson, Hawthorne, Lowell, Longfellow, and others who appeared at the Saturday Club meetings. Those meetings, starting in 1855, were held in the Parker House, on the corner of Tremont and School Streets, across from King's Chapel, just up School Street from the offices of Ticknor & Fields. Emerson was Boston's grey eminence, Hawthorne its celebrated romancer, Lowell its intellectual guide, and Longfellow its revered poet who, in turn, honored Boston's history, particularly in "Paul Revere's Ride," a poem written at the outbreak of the Civil War, designed to remind Greater Bostonians of their dedication to the ideal of a united nation.

In 1884 Holmes, looking back on Boston's fading glories with characteristic whimsy and nostalgia, paid tribute to the memory of those luminaries who dined at Parker House gatherings in "At the Saturday Club."

Such guests! What famous names its record boasts,
Whose owners wander in the mob of ghosts!
Such stories! Every beam and plank is filled
With juicy wit the joyous talkers spilled,
Ready to ooze, as once the mountain pine
The floors are laid with oozed its turpentine![14]

There Fields had introduced Charles Dickens to twenty-two eminent Bostonians in November 1867; Dickens drank what Holmes called "a jug anglice,"
or gin punch, and Longfellow called the gathering "a delightful dinner."[15]
Holmes here codified Boston's literary standing in jingling, commemorative
verse, just as he had celebrated the city's military glory in "Old Ironsides" in
praise of USS *Constitution*, which was saved from destruction by his poem.
In honoring the emblems of the Revolutionary period, Holmes cast reflected
glory on the Boston of his day and struck the tone of nostalgia, wistful
remembrances of things past that characterizes many of the writings on
Boston. In "The Last Leaf," he celebrated a fading figure of the Revolution,
Major Thomas Melvill (grandfather of Herman Melville), "the last of the
cocked hats," who had been one of the "Indians" at the Boston Tea Party.
Characteristically, Holmes mixes in humor, but without mockery, in his
verse celebrating a man and an era all but gone but still exemplary for contemporary Boston.

Holmes and Fields were among the founders of *Atlantic Monthly* in 1857,
a journal which gave voice to Greater Boston's "Yankee cultural elite," as
Ellery Sedgwick puts it in his history of the journal. "They were largely Anglo-
Saxon, middle-class liberal Protestant, and, in politics, Conscience Whigs,
Free Soil, and Radical Republican."[16] This group of high-minded, principled
men—after the Civil War the *Atlantic Monthly* family would include women
writers—illustrated how much the Boston elite had shifted their goals from
the founding of a communal theocracy in Winthrop's era to the establishment of an entrepreneurial, high-culture Athens of America in their own
time, while sustaining but also transforming their commitment to the long-
standing vision of Boston as a city upon a hill. For Brooks, the founding of
Atlantic Monthly "marked [the] high tide of the Boston mind."[17] This Boston-
based Yankee elite would stir the conscience and shape the culture of the
nation through war and peace for decades, after which the city's faded glories would be frequently memorialized in story and poem. Indeed, Boston

may resonate best in literary expressions of great expectations and in remembrances of things past.

When, on the eve of World War II, Harvard professor F. O. Matthiessen looked back on the major works of the half-decade 1850–1855 produced by Greater Bostonians (Emerson, Hawthorne, Thoreau) and New Yorkers (Melville, Whitman), a time that culminated in the publication of *Atlantic Monthly*, he deemed it "America's way of producing a renaissance, by coming to its first maturity and affirming its rightful heritage in the whole expanse of art and culture."[18] Yet this intense expression of American letters occurred in an era divided by debate and marked by violence, particularly in Boston, then the hub of the contentions over issues surrounding immigration and slavery.

During and after the devastating famine in Ireland of 1845–1850, the influx of poor Irish Catholic immigrants into Boston transformed the city and tested the ideals of its long-standing ruling elite. "As the Irish flooded into the city during the mid-1850s they confronted the solid ranks of a Brahmin class that dominated virtually the whole range of the city's cultural and educational institutions," notes historian Thomas H. O'Connor.[19] Alarmed at the threatening prospect of an enfranchised Irish voting bloc, the "American Party," also called the "Know-Nothing Party" for its secretiveness, was formed to protect long-established American citizens from the "insidious wiles of foreigners."[20] In the 1854 elections these nativists seized political power in Massachusetts, setting forth an agenda of "Temperance, Liberty, and Protestantism" to counter "Rome, Rum and Robbery," their caricature of Irish immigrants' values.[21]

The year 1854 also saw passage of the Kansas-Nebraska Act, which created two territories, opened new lands, and allowed settlers to determine if they would grant slavery within their boundaries, thus extending the reach of slavery into the American West and intensifying bitter debate throughout the nation. Boston abolitionists, many of whom held the same views as members of the "American Party," became even more incensed in their opposition to slavery and immigration. Fierce abolitionist Reverend Theodore Parker, for example, bemoaned the fact that Boston had become "the Dublin of America."[22]

Unsurprisingly, the city's immigrant Irish were generally hostile to these single-minded Yankee reformers. Indeed when, in June 1854, escaped slave Anthony Burns, who briefly found freedom in Boston, was arrested, many

Irish troops made up the Columbian Artillery which marched him from prison, down State Street, past lines of angry abolitionists, to the waiting ship which returned him to slavery in Virginia. Abolitionists accused Boston's Irish Catholics of complicity with slavery, but most Boston immigrant Irish saw the ruling that returned Burns as "a perfect triumph of law and order," as the Catholic newspaper, *The Pilot*, put it.[23]

Boston's Yankee-Brahmin rulers were also divided in these years leading up to the Civil War. The city's business community, particularly the textile manufacturers who depended upon Southern cotton to run the mills in Lawrence and Lowell that supported their standing and culture, resented the abolitionist pamphleteering of William Lloyd Garrison and supported Senator Daniel Webster, who was willing to tolerate slavery for the sake of preserving the union. His "compromise" of 1850 instituted the Fugitive Slave Law that required federal officials to recapture and return runaway slaves, including Anthony Burns.

Wendell Phillips, called "Beacon Hill's premier renegade," used his social standing and his Harvard education to chastise his fellow Boston Brahmins for their moral compromise and profit motives. Phillips became known as "the golden trumpet" of Garrison's abolitionist movement, denouncing Webster and stirring Bostonians to remember what their city should stand for: "The community which dares not protect the humblest and most hated member in the free utterance of his opinions . . . is only a gang of slaves."[24] When Phillips died in 1884, by then reconciled Bostonians honored him with a near-state funeral viewing in Faneuil Hall.[25]

Thomas Wentworth Higginson—noted minister, author, abolitionist, and decorated soldier—had tried but failed to free Anthony Burns in 1854, leading a group to break down the court house door while Phillips and Parker stirred an outraged abolitionist crowd in Faneuil Hall. Higginson was a lifelong political activist, agitating, in Henry James's ironic view, "on behalf of everything, almost, but especially of the negroes and the ladies."[26] During the Civil War, Higginson served as colonel of the 1st South Carolina Volunteers, the first federally authorized African American regiment, from 1862 to 1864. However, despite his demanding political activism and war service, he wrote poetry and published many essays in *Atlantic Monthly*. One of these essays, "Letter to a Young Contributor," written early in the war when Higginson was busy raising troops for his first regiment, subsequently became famous because Emily Dickinson, the reclusive Amherst poet, replied, asking Higginson if he was "too deeply occupied to say if my Verse is alive?"[27] Clearly Higginson was not too deeply preoccupied by military and political matters to recognize that her verse was, indeed, alive, if also at times beyond his comprehension. He replied, contributing to a rich, mostly epistolary relationship with "the belle of Amherst," showing that he believed, as he put it in his "Letter," that in the presence of living poetry "all these present fascinating trivialities of war and diplomacy ebbed away, like Greece and Rome before them, and there seemed nothing real in the universe." Thus did Higginson embody the ideals of *Atlantic Monthly* in his commitment both to political freedom and to poetic expression.

The conflicted year of 1857 was the right moment for the Yankee ascendancy to publish *Atlantic Monthly*, for the national debate was increasingly bitter and intense. Just the year before, pro-slavery Congressman Preston Brooks of South Carolina attacked the anti-slavery Massachusetts Senator Charles Sumner at his Senate desk, beating Sumner senseless with a cane for calling the Kansas-Nebraska Act a crime. In 1857, Chief Justice Roger B. Taney handed down the Dred Scott Decision, which declared African Americans to be "beings of an inferior order, and altogether unfit to associate with the white race."[28] Kansas was "bleeding" that year, in turmoil over the extension of slavery after a bloody attack upon slaveholders at Pottawatomie Creek, led by John Brown, a righteous figure strongly supported by Boston abolitionists and Concord transcendentalists. The new Boston publication would provide a forum for anti-slavery views, mainstreaming the once-radical opinions expressed since 1831 in William Lloyd Garrison's *Liberator*. However, *Atlantic Monthly* aspired to more than political purposes; the journal would help to shape an American culture by calling attention to the nation's literary achievements, most of them centered in Greater Boston, thus mainstreaming the claims initiated in the *Dial*, the journal of Concord's transcendentalists, published between 1840 and 1844. Though *North American Review*, founded in Boston in 1815, was the nation's oldest literary magazine, *Atlantic Monthly* quickly passed it in circulation and influence. This upstart journal declared itself "Devoted to Literature, Art, and Politics" and, by implication, to the eminence of the Boston literary and intellectual community.[29]

Atlantic Monthly's founders included James Russell Lowell, the poet and Harvard professor who became its first editor, and Ralph Waldo Emerson, its inspiring philosopher who had called for just such a publication devoted to a vigorous and original American literature in his "American Scholar" essay of 1837. "We have listened too long to the courtly muses of Europe. . . . We will walk on our own feet; we will work with our own hands; we will speak our own minds. The study of letters shall be no longer a name for pity, for doubt, and for sensual indulgence."[30] The first issue showed the journal's range of styles and concerns by including an abstract essay by Emerson, "Illusions," and a humorous essay by Holmes, "Autocrat of the Breakfast Table," which defined his avuncular, whimsical persona of Yankee rationalism. Emerson, Longfellow, and Whittier contributed poetry. James T. Fields oversaw the publication of *Atlantic Monthly* in a proper, plain brown buff cover.[31]

Fields served as *Atlantic Monthly*'s second editor, creating a synergy between journal and book publication that would be crucial to establishing, sustaining, and promoting Boston as a literary-cultural center. The journal was conceived as a monthly "book" designed to reflect and preserve the state of the culture, so it was a natural step to republish *Atlantic Monthly* authors in actual book form. By 1880, the former Ticknor & Fields, after three reformulations of the firm, merged their operations with Riverside Press, founded by Henry Oscar Houghton in 1852, forming a new partnership named Houghton, Mifflin & Company.[32] There Fields promoted and published his *Atlantic Monthly* authors: Lowell, Emerson, Holmes, Longfellow, Stowe, and Whittier. He drew contributions from Hawthorne, some fourteen pieces during Fields's editorship, and he solicited essays from Thoreau, providing a wider venue for this eccentric genius whose writings had been previously little known beyond Concord. These authors constituted an American literary canon, their works codified in keepsake editions by Houghton Mifflin. Bliss Perry, *Atlantic* editor at the end of the century, persuaded Houghton Mifflin to publish the journals of Emerson and Thoreau, considering this his most important accomplishment.[33] Horace Scudder, Houghton Mifflin's chief literary adviser and head of their trade department as well as an *Atlantic Monthly* editor (1890–1899), fulfilled his goal of preserving the New England authors in "Riverside Editions," handsome sets suitable for the nation's libraries and bourgeois family bookshelves. Furthermore, Scudder's interest in public education led to the adoption of these authors in public schools across the nation, defining Boston-based, *Atlantic Monthly*–Houghton Mifflin authors as canonical representatives of American literature into the mid-twentieth century.[34] By the end of the nineteenth century, a commentator could affirm with assurance the fertile relations between place and literary purpose in Greater Boston, focusing upon Emerson, Hawthorne, Longfellow, Whittier, Lowell, and Holmes. "Possibly no group of creative writers ever fitted more naturally and easily into their setting, than the authors of Concord, Cambridge, and Boston."[35]

Nathaniel Hawthorne, while a resident of Salem, the seaport some fifteen miles north of Boston, wove his hometown into his satirical romance on the city, but other famous members of his generation were turning their backs on Boston for Concord, "vaguely realizing westward," as Robert Frost would describe American migratory movements in "The Gift Outright." Concord, however, was hardly "unstoried, artless, unenhanced."[36] The transcendentalists and other writers of the mid-century who came to Concord would form the basis of the celebrated "American renaissance" in poems, memoirs, polemics, philosophical reflections, and other forms.[37] At various times this small market and farming town, located at the intersection of the Sudbury, Concord, and Assabet rivers, was the home of Ralph Waldo Emerson, Henry David Thoreau, Margaret Fuller, Nathaniel Hawthorne, Bronson Alcott, and his daughter Louisa May, creating what has been called an "American Bloomsbury."[38] Sleepy Hollow Cemetery's "Author's Ridge" is the burial site of many celebrated Concord literary figures, whose presence is marked in simple headstones—"Hawthorne," "Alcott," "Henry"— though the large slab of marble that stands over Emerson's grave emblemizes his unique eminence.

Young Louisa May Alcott would decry Concord as "one of the dullest little towns in Massachusetts"; Thoreau, her friend and teacher, would ask "What does our Concord culture amount to?"; but Concord became inextricably woven in the American mind with the writers who lived there and wrote about it.[39] Only twenty miles west of Boston, Concord for many became a haven, an idyll, an embodied realization of all that Boston had failed to become.

Ralph Waldo Emerson may have led the exodus of writers and thinkers from Boston, but he never cut his ties to the city where he was born in 1803. He was the son of Rev. William Emerson, pastor of the First Church of Boston, a man of principle and cultural purposes and one of the founders of the Boston Athenaeum and *The Monthly Anthology and Boston Review* (1804–1811). Young Waldo came of age as one of Boston's elect, defined by Boston's Unitarian-Federalist values that had rejected Puritan Congregationalism.

He was educated at Boston Public Latin School and Harvard College, after which he became minister of the Second Church of Boston. However, like many before and after him, Emerson felt constrained by Boston's propriety, presumption, and profit motives. While his father had defended John Winthrop for banishing Anne Hutchinson, Emerson identified with this antinomian rebel. Like Hawthorne, Emerson repudiated his Puritan ancestors who had preached the stern words of New England Calvinism. Even as a boy, after his eminent father's death, living in his mother's rooming house at the base of Beacon Hill, Emerson had recoiled from the public hangings he saw on Boston Common and the mounds of rubble left from the topping-off of Trimountain. As an adult, though well placed in his ministry at Second Church, even Boston's tolerant Unitarianism could not hold him, so Emerson resigned his pulpit in 1832 and moved west of the confining city, seeking greater space for his thoughts and transforming himself from a preacher into a philosopher, poet, and prophet.

Concord had been an alternative world for Emerson since he was a boy, when he paid extended visits to the house his grandfather had built beside the Concord River, near the site where farmers fought off British troops in April, 1775. After his beloved first wife, Ellen, died of tuberculosis, Emerson lived in what came to be called The Old Manse, where Sophia and Nathaniel Hawthorne would also dwell as newlyweds in the 1840s. There Emerson wrote his manifesto, *Nature* (1836), urging his readers to reject the getting-and-spending world of cities and to become "a transparent eyeball, . . . part and parcel of God"; there he recorded an epiphany that had seized him while "crossing a bare common," Boston Common. In the dark heart of the city, "in snow puddles, at twilight, under a clouded sky," Emerson had experienced a transforming pastoral vision that repudiated Boston. "In the woods is perpetual youth."[40]

In Concord Emerson distanced himself from Boston's religious turmoil. In 1838 he delivered his famous "Divinity School Address" at Harvard's Class Day, telling a graduating class of future ministers "to go alone; to refuse the good models, even those which are sacred in the imagination of men, and dare to love God without mediator or veil," an injunction that echoes those made by Anne Hutchinson two centuries earlier. The address outraged members of the faculty, and Emerson was not invited back to Harvard, then the center of New England Unitarianism, for nearly thirty years. In 1839 the Dexter Professor of Sacred Literature at Harvard Divinity

School, Andrews Norton, delivered an address describing Emerson's words as "The Latest Form of Infidelity."[41] Concord and Boston were not just twenty miles, but rather many worlds apart; however, each community needed the other to define itself.

Concord became a spacious pastoral retreat from congested, commercial Boston for Emerson and his disciples. As Winthrop and his colonists sought to convert the peninsula they would call Boston into a utopian theocracy, rejecting what they saw as the corruptions of London, so too would Emerson and other Concordians seek to make their village an outpost of free thought and association, an exemplary and cautionary option to Boston. Thoreau went further in expressing Emerson's ideal: he sought not a city upon a hill, not even a noble village of men, but found that a pond would serve as his symbolic center: his "earth's eye."[42]

Thoreau built his wood cabin—well made and small, suitable for a majority of one—on land owned by Emerson near Walden Pond, but Emerson reigned from his imposing colonial home on the Cambridge Turnpike, the route between Concord and Boston which he frequently took to maintain the connection between his two worlds. Indeed Emerson, having inherited Ellen Tucker's money and married Lydia (renamed Lydian) Jackson, was the financial backer of many members of the Concord literary community; he subsidized *The Dial*, hired Thoreau as a resident handyman and tutor for the Emerson children, arranged to have the just-wed Hawthornes reside in The Old Manse, continually supported the impoverished Alcott family, and, to Lydian's annoyance, invited the compelling Margaret Fuller to be a frequent house guest.[43] At the same time, Emerson was also a central figure in Boston's literary clubs: Town and Country, Atlantic, and the Saturday Club. If Concord, where he formed the Transcendental Club, was the personal, pastoral retreat which inspired his ideas, Boston was the urban, urbane place where he publicly tested his ideas in clubroom talks and lectures. In 1839 he noted in his journal: "For the last five years I have read each winter a new course of lectures in Boston, and each was my creed and confession of faith."[44]

Two poems—or, as he titled them, "hymns"—illustrate Emerson's differing visions of Concord and Boston, the symbolic and morally contrasting landscapes of his imagination. In "Concord Hymn: Sung at the Completion of the Battle Monument, July 4, 1837," Emerson commemorated the 1775 battle in stirring words that would be memorized by generations of Americans:

> By the rude bridge that arched the flood,
> Their flag to April's breeze unfurled,
> Here once the embattled farmers stood,
> And fired the shot heard round the world.[45]

His grandfather, William Emerson, family legend had it, heard that shot from his recently built manse beside the Concord River, so Ralph Waldo Emerson here placed himself in relation to American history, as would Hawthorne after him; but Emerson wrote to praise famous men, while Hawthorne satirized his infamous ancestors. Emerson embedded the event deep in history, in nature imagery, and in Concord consciousness. Emerson read his "Boston Hymn" at Boston's Music Hall on January 1, 1863, after President Lincoln's Emancipation Proclamation was declared. Henry James, age twenty, was there to hear him and long remembered "the immense effect with which this beautiful voice pronounced the lines."[46] (Two decades later, James would employ the Music Hall setting for far less celebratory purpose in his satirical novel *The Bostonians*.) Emerson characterized the Puritan founders as "Pilgrims" who sought freedom from the confining rule of British royalty and religious hierarchy. Two stanzas near the poem's end brought the audience, which included many escaped slaves, to their feet.

> Today unbind the captive
> So only are ye unbound;
> Lift up a people from the dust,
> Trump of their rescue, sound!
>
> Pay ransom to the owner,
> And fill the bag to the brim.
> Who is the owner? The slave is owner,
> And ever was. Pay him.[47]

Emerson continued to write occasional verse in celebration of Boston. On December 16, 1873, for example, in Faneuil Hall, on the 100th anniversary of the Boston Tea Party, he read "Boston." Again he praised the "happy town beside the sea" for its freedom, but concluded the poems on an ominous note, foreseeing that Boston would eventually be reduced to its natural origins:

> The sea returning day by day
> Restores the world-wide mart;

> So let each dweller on the Bay
> Fold Boston in his heart
> Till these echoes be choked with snows,
> Or over the town blue ocean flows.[48]

Emerson sustained his ambivalence about the city of his birth, only reluctantly acknowledging that Boston was still America's city upon a hill. "I do not speak with any fondness, but the language of coldest history, when I say that Boston commands attention as the town which was appointed in the destiny of nations to lead the civilization of North America."[49] He denounced Boston in 1850 after Daniel Webster supported the Fugitive Slave Act and the city's leading citizens remained silent. "It is now as disgraceful to be a Bostonian as it was hitherto a credit."[50] Though he was born and educated in Boston, though he there assumed the ministry, though he dined, lectured, and published in Boston, the commercial city that served the purpose as a counterpoint model in his arguments for spiritual and idealistic Concord, Emerson remained convinced that "the dear old Devil kept his state in Boston."[51] Boston, for Ralph Waldo Emerson, was a failed community, located east of his Eden—Concord.

Emerson refused to join the Brook Farm commune—Hawthorne did join, but quickly withdrew; Fuller stayed briefly; Thoreau also refused membership; instead he built a commune composed of himself alone at Walden Pond—but Emerson gathered a loose Concord colony of followers, self-determined exiles from Boston.

Bronson Alcott, the orphic educator and prophet, was the most dramatic example of those, stung by their Boston experiences, who sought pastoral calm and safety in Emerson's oracular orbit in placid Concord. In 1834 Alcott opened an experimental school in Boston's Masonic Temple, assisted first by Elizabeth Palmer Peabody, who would become Hawthorne's sponsor and sister-in-law, and later by Margaret Fuller, two brilliant women who would be in the forefront of Boston reformers. After some initial success, Alcott's methods of encouraging his students to speak freely about the gospels came under criticism. Criticism turned to shock when it became known, through the publication of his *Conversations with Children on the Gospels* (1836), that Alcott had used the story of the Virgin Mary to discuss the mysteries of birth with his impressionable students. His book and teaching methods were denounced in the popular press as "obscene" (*Boston Courier*) and by the high-table keepers of standards who agreed with that verdict. Andrews Norton, ever ready with a pithy denunciation for apostasy, called *Conversations* "one third absurd, one third blasphemous, and one third obscene." By 1839 Alcott's Boston experiment in educational freedom of expression had failed miserably. He and his growing family abandoned the city which, as he saw it, was ruled by Bacchus and the Prince of Devils, and sought sanctuary under Emerson's subsidizing aegis in Concord.[52] The Alcotts settled just down the road from Emerson's grand home, in modest Dovecote Cottage, where Alcott tried his hand at woodcutting and practiced his educational theories on his children, one of whom would chafe at his training and go on to express a mind and will of her own in her writings.[53]

However, even the anti-urban Alcott family would once again seek their fortune, or at least minimal subsistence, in Boston. After years of unsuccessful experiments in living in Concord and briefly in Harvard, a village a few miles to the west—at Fruitlands, a failed utopian community Louisa May would later mock in "Transcendental Wild Oats" (1873)—Bronson moved his family back to Boston in 1848, settling in humble quarters on Dedham Street, where he planned to hold "conversations" at the nearby West Street bookshop of the Peabodys. The Alcotts would remain in Boston for the next decade before again retreating to Concord for sanctuary.[54]

By the time Louisa May turned eighteen in 1850, family misfortunes pushed her to the decision to "go out into service," a scarring experience she later codified in *Work*, an 1872 novel about an alter ego, Christie, a young woman who tries to earn money as a maid, an actress, a nurse, a governess, a companion, and a seamstress, based upon Louisa May's various work experiences in the 1850s.[55] Christie was so frequently exploited and assaulted by employers that she attempted suicide before she found independence. In an essay, "How I Went Out to Service" (1874), Alcott tried to treat this painful period with a lighter touch, but her miseries at having to turn to service employment to support her family come through. If Louisa May Alcott's Concord life is preserved in the idyllic *Little Women* (1868) and other novels that sentimentalized her Dovecote Cottage years, her Boston years are recorded in these darker writings about demeaning work.

Though born in Concord (1817), Henry David Thoreau—Louisa May's teacher, Emerson's devoted day-worker, child-tender, and disciple—lived as a boy in Boston, where his father taught school. In *Walden* (1854) he records his own version of Emerson's "crossing a bare common" epiphany, in Thoreau's case a pilgrim's progress from destructive Boston to salvific Concord.

> When I was four years old, as I well remember, I was brought from Boston to this native town, through these very woods, and this field, to the pond. It is one of the oldest scenes in my memory. And now tonight my flute has waked the echoes over that very water. . . . I have at length helped to clothe that fabulous landscape of my infant dreams, and one of the results of my presence and influence is seen in these bean leaves, corn blades, and potato vines.[56]

Art, symbolized by the flute, nurtures both memories and plantings in Concord. However, Thoreau adds, "a huckleberry never reaches Boston; they have not been known there since they grew on her three hills."[57]

Words as well as huckleberries flourished in Concord. Conversations, journal-keeping, essay-writing and publication provided these transcendentalists and their fellow travelers an account of their existence and a record of their beliefs, just as such genres had for their Puritan ancestors. Margaret Fuller proved to be an adept and brilliant practitioner in all of these forms, from her Boston "conversations" to her Concord editing of *The Dial*, where, among other things, she initiated Thoreau's publishing career by accepting "Natural History of Massachusetts" (1842), an essay adapted from his journal. Born in Cambridgeport, schooled by a demanding father, a congressman who insisted that she be as well educated as any man, Fuller—tall, articulate, imposing—was an exotic in dress, manner, and thought, casting a spell composed of verbal brilliance and repressed sexuality over men around her, particularly enthralling Hawthorne and Emerson. She had briefly been a fellow utopian with Hawthorne at Brook Farm and continued to intrigue and provoke him well into his marriage. Fuller was drawn to Concord by Emerson, who took her into his home and, some say, his heart. She walked the Concord woods, exchanging ideas and stirring frissons alternately with Hawthorne and Emerson in the early 1840s. *The Dial*, founded in 1840 by Emerson and Fuller, was designed "to lift men to a higher platform," but it wore Fuller out after two years of editing duties, so she relinquished her post and turned to her own writing. She published "The Great Lawsuit. Man vs. Men. Woman vs. Women" in *The Dial* in 1843, an essay that led to her defining work, a feminist foundation text in 1845, *Woman in the Nineteenth Century*.

Margaret Fuller had long been working to lift women to a higher platform. She taught at Alcott's Temple School in Boston from 1837 to 1839, then in Providence, Rhode Island. In 1839 Fuller began organizing "conversations," discussions of wide-ranging topics and ideas among local women, in the parlor and bookstore of Elizabeth Peabody, at 13 West Street, Boston. These Saturday meetings, which lasted for five years, allowed women, who were not able to express their views from pulpits or classroom lecterns, to speak up on many subjects, but their conversations always returned to the issue of women's rights. Fuller set out to help women clarify their thoughts and gain a public voice.[58] Attending were Lydian Emerson, Lydia Maria Child, the Peabody sisters (Elizabeth, Mary, and Sophia), Lydia (Mrs. Theodore) Parker, and many other influential women of her day. These conversations initiated by Fuller, along with her editing of *The Dial*, inspired her own writings, from "The Great Lawsuit" to *Woman in the Nineteenth Century*. Traces of her electric presence and feminist independence appear in Hawthorne's radical women characters—Hester Prynne in *The Scarlet Letter* (1850) and Zenobia in *The Blithedale Romance* (1852), a satire of Brook Farm—and also in Olive Chancellor, the radical feminist Henry James holds up to early mockery and eventual sympathy in his satirical novel *The Bostonians* (1886). By inspiring women of Boston to find their own voices, Margaret Fuller set an example of just how far women could go, in and beyond the city, for she left Boston for a career in journalism in New York City, then in Italy.

Essayist Elizabeth Hardwick has argued that Margaret Fuller "was born in the wrong place, the place thought to be the only right one for an American intellectual in the nineteenth century. That is, Fuller was born in Cambridgeport, Massachusetts, around Harvard, Boston, Concord, and all the rest."[59] Hardwick was not happy when she lived in Boston in the late 1950s with her husband, Robert Lowell, and she wrote a scathing essay on the city before they returned to Manhattan, "Boston, a Lost Ideal," so it is consistent for her to see Greater Boston as a destructive milieu for Fuller.[60] Yet, while it is just of Hardwick to note that Fuller suffered from repressive patriarchal pressures in her own family and in the Greater Boston cultural community, which she eventually escaped for a freer life in New York and in Italy, it is also fair to ask where in the America of that period *other* than in the heady heights of Greater Boston could she have so flourished? A more balanced assessment of Fuller's relation to her home place is struck when Hardwick grants that "what the whole span of [Fuller's] life shows is that she got all from being around Boston at the transfiguring moment, and would have lost all had she not escaped."[61] Like others before and after her, Margaret Fuller got all she could from Boston, then got out before it stifled her expression.

Greater Boston at mid-century was indeed transfigured. As Van Wyck Brooks puts it, it was then "that the New England mind had crystallized, that there was a renaissance in Boston,—one of those 'heats and genial periods' of which Emerson spoke in *English Traits*, 'by which high tides are caused in the human spirit.'" All this "had not escaped the firm of Ticknor & Fields."[62] Through the agency of James T. Fields, the Boston literary community had spread north to Salem and west through Cambridge and Concord to the Berkshires to draw in contributors to Ticknor & Fields, to the *Atlantic Monthly*, and eventually to Houghton Mifflin, through which these Greater Boston writers were established in the American mind as canonical. Outside the city, idealists and utopians had set up communities that sought collectivist alternatives to Boston's commercial ways: Brook Farm, a miniature, Fourier-inspired "phalanx" established along the Charles River in West Roxbury in 1841; Fruitlands, the short-lived "consociate" community hatched out of the visionary but impractical mind of Bronson Alcott, located in Harvard, Massachusetts for a few months in 1843; a thriving Shaker community in the village of Harvard; and, most important, Emerson's loose, idea-grazing flock in Concord. Though these pastoral utopian communities—established as original arrangements in living which repudiated those found in Boston—came and went, a literary record of their existence endured, much of it gathered by James T. Fields.

Still, Boston remained the hub of the literary universe, for there, in nearby Cambridge, stood Harvard; there were located journal and book publishers; there the Saturday Club met. And there, at 148 Charles Street, stood the home of Annie and James T. Fields, a literary and cultural salon for half a century. Famous figures came to Ticknor & Fields's downtown offices in the Old Corner Bookstore to visit the affable editor, providing him a unique perspective on their lives and works, as he illustrates in his account of Hawthorne in *Yesterdays with Authors* (1882). These same figures came to

Charles Street to savor the company of James, of course, but remained because of the charm and wit of his young wife, Annie, who sustained the family tradition of high-minded hospitality for decades after her husband's death in 1881, as she illustrates in her loving and incisive memoir of Oliver Wendell Holmes and other literary luminaries in *Authors and Friends* (1896). Annie Fields possessed her own literary talents as well as considerable social charm. She read manuscripts and made shrewd publishing recommendations, particularly about women authors. With her support, Rebecca Harding Davis, Harriet Beecher Stowe, and Elizabeth Stuart Phelps were published in *Atlantic Monthly* while her husband was editor (1861–1871). After James died, Annie Fields extended her relations and influence to include Celia Thaxter, Louise Imogen Guiney, Rose Terry Cooke, Mary Wilkins Freeman, and other writers who were establishing women's perspectives in the discourse of the day. In 1916 Harriet Prescott Spofford described this group of Boston women writers in her aptly titled *A Little Circle of Friends*. Finally, Annie Fields published her own books: *Life and Letters of Harriet Beecher Stowe* (1897) and *Letters of Sarah Orne Jewett* (1911).[63]

The Fieldses' three-story, federal brick home on Charles Street, built in 1856, opened onto a garden and offered an unobstructed view of the Charles River from the first-floor dining room and the second-floor library, a "waterside museum" of memorabilia in the appreciative words of Henry James, a frequent visitor. Charles Dickens, among other notable guests, stayed in the Fieldses' third-floor guest bedroom. *Atlantic Monthly* editor Thomas Bailey Aldrich and contributor Oliver Wendell Holmes lived nearby, forming a literate urban community, an alternative to the pastoral literary community in Concord.[64]

Henry James drew on his memories of the Fieldses' home for the setting of Olive Chancellor's home in *The Bostonians* (1886). It is described through the wondering eyes of young Basil Ransom, a former Confederate officer who has come to Boston after the Civil War to seek his fortune through contact with wealthy and socially connected Olive, a distant cousin. Ransom's perspective on the city, at once envious and sardonic, is looked upon patronizingly by James's narrator, who has presumably seen the great cities of Europe, but both the narrator and the impressionable young man seem to agree that Boston is a symbolic city of culture, centered on Charles Street. Yet James remained coolly ironic about Boston, which he reconstructed in fiction from his new home, London.

In *The Bostonians* James set out "to write a very *American* tale" by centering upon "the condition of women, the decline of the sentiment of sex, the agitation on their behalf."[65] He focused on what has come to be known as a "Boston marriage," an intimate relationship between two women accepted by Boston society. James's sister, Alice, had just such a bond with her caretaker, Katharine Loring, and he saw such a "marriage" in the relationship between Annie Fields, then a widow, and Sarah Orne Jewett, a frequent *Atlantic Monthly* contributor who came to live on Charles Street for many months each year. "I verily remember being struck with the stretch of wings that the spirit of Charles Street could bring off," wrote James after visiting them.[66] James had found on Charles Street what he took to be the "most salient and peculiar point" in Boston's character and the key to *The Bostonians*, which he called "a "study of one of those friendships between women which are so common in New England."[67]

Young Willa Cather moved to Boston in 2007, assigned by *McClure's Magazine* to write a book on Mary Baker Eddy, founder of the Christian Science Church. Cather came to call on Annie Fields, then seventy-four, in 1908. Cather brought her own outsider's romantic perspective to the setting, as she later wrote in "148 Charles Street" (1936).

> At five o'clock in the afternoon the river was silvery from a half-hidden sun; over the great open space of water the western sky was dove-colored with little ripples of rose. The air was full of soft moisture and the hint of approaching spring. Against this screen of pale winter light were the two ladies: Mrs. Fields reclining on a green sofa, directly under the youthful portrait of Charles Dickens (now in the Boston Art Museum), Miss Jewett seated, the low tea-table between them.[68]

Cather carried no Jamesian irony into this setting, for she was seeking not fortune like Basil Ransom, but a little circle of friends, the encouraging company of women who gathered around Annie Fields. Cather's description, in the words of her biographer Sharon O'Brien, "is like a Mary Cassatt painting: the impressionist skyline, the soft air, the two ladies grouped around the tea table."[69] Coming of age in stark Red Cloud, Nebraska, where she read the Boston worthies published by *Atlantic Monthly* and Ticknor & Fields, Cather sought an enriching literary community and felt that she had found just that in Boston.

At 148 Charles Street—and at Thunderbolt Hill, the Fieldses' summer

home at Manchester by the Sea on the Massachusetts North Shore—Cather found a particular mentor in Annie Fields's partner, Sarah Orne Jewett.
Though Jewett died not long after this meeting, her brief encounters and
her correspondence with Cather brought about a transforming shock of recognition, similar to Melville's encounter with Hawthorne half a century before. In both cases the older, more established author inspired the younger
to her/his greatest works; in both instances a Fields served as the enabler.
Jewett would inspire Cather to give up writing articles for *McClure's* magazine and dedicate herself to fiction. Cather had associated literary achievement with Henry James, whose style she attempted to imitate in her early
novel, *Alexander's Bridge* (1912), set in Boston. But Annie Fields's memories
of the young Henry James gave Cather a less intimidating perspective on
"the Master" and Jewett offered a counter model of literary achievement.
Rather than reject American scenes as provincial, as James had, Jewett,
from South Berwick, Maine, showed Cather and other local-color women
writers how to focus on "simple scenes close at hand," as had Jewett in writing *The Country of the Pointed Firs* (1896). Jewett's advice to write about "the
parish" freed Cather from her strained effort to imitate James and gave her
license to record her own authentic experiences of coming of age in Nebraska. By 1909 Jewett was dead, but her influence, commencing with that
chance meeting on Charles Street in 1908, remained, as did Cather's friendship with Annie Fields until the death of "lady Juno herself" in 1915.[70]

Ralph Waldo Emerson was the magnetic center of the American literary renaissance, drawing fresh energies, new ideas, and extraordinary talents to
Concord, that watery pastoral village that rebuked paved, money-mad Boston. Yet Emerson and his followers needed Boston to represent all that they
repudiated—urban density, vanity, greed—in their construction of idyllic,
spiritual, poetic Concord. They needed Boston, as well, to serve as a market-
place for their ideas. James T. and Annie Fields represented a vital center for
the Greater Boston writers of the American renaissance and those who came
after, from their early gatherings in Boston, Cambridge, and Concord in mid-
century to their waning but enduring influence well into the twentieth century. Van Wyck Brooks notes that Harriet Beecher Stowe declared New England the "seed-bed" of the republic, for its people were "called and chosen for
some great work on earth." Brooks adds, that "if New England was the seed-
bed, Boston was its hothouse. There the rarer seedlings came to blossom."[71]

Henry Wadsworth Longfellow, "Paul Revere's Ride," written April 19, 1860, published in *Tales of a Wayside Inn* (1863)

Henry Wadsworth Longfellow (1807–1882), poet and Harvard professor, wrote and reigned in historic Craigie House, Cambridge, with his wife and children. Many of his poems celebrated an idealized New England past. His *Tales of a Wayside Inn*, published in the midst of the Civil War, reminded Americans of their common heritage.

> Listen my children and you shall hear
> Of the midnight ride of Paul Revere,
> On the eighteenth of April, in Seventy-five;
> Hardly a man is now alive
> Who remembers that famous day and year.
>
> He said to his friend, "If the British march
> By land or sea from the town to-night,
> Hang a lantern aloft in the belfry arch
> Of the North Church tower as a signal light,—
> One, if by land, and two if by sea;
> And I on the opposite shore will be,
> Ready to ride and spread the alarm
> Through every Middlesex village and farm,
> For the country folk to be up and to arm."
> Then he said "Good-night!" and with muffled oar
> Silently rowed to the Charlestown shore,
> Just as the moon rose over the bay,
> Where swinging wide at her moorings lay
> The Somerset, British man-of-war;
> A phantom ship, with each mast and spar
> Across the moon like a prison bar,
> And a huge black hulk, that was magnified
> By its own reflection in the tide.
>
> Meanwhile, his friend, through alley and street
> Wanders and watches, with eager ears,
> Till in the silence around him he hears

The muster of men at the barrack door,
The sound of arms, and the tramp of feet,
And the measured tread of the grenadiers,
Marching down to their boats on the shore.

Then he climbed the tower of the Old North Church,
By the wooden stairs, with stealthy tread,
To the belfry-chamber overhead,
And startled the pigeons from their perch
On the sombre rafters, that round him made
Masses and moving shapes of shade,—
By the trembling ladder, steep and tall,
To the highest window in the wall,
Where he paused to listen and look down
A moment on the roofs of the town,
And the moonlight flowing over all.
Beneath, in the churchyard, lay the dead,
In their night-encampment on the hill,
Wrapped in silence so deep and still
That he could hear, like a sentinel's tread,
The watchful night-wind, as it went
Creeping along from tent to tent,
And seeming to whisper, "All is well!"
A moment only he feels the spell
Of the place and the hour, and the secret dread
Of the lonely belfry and the dead;
For suddenly all his thoughts are bent
On a shadowy something far away,
Where the river widens to meet the bay,—
A line of black that bends and floats
On the rising tide, like a bridge of boats.

Meanwhile, impatient to mount and ride,
Booted and spurred, with a heavy stride
On the opposite shore walked Paul Revere.
Now he patted his horse's side,
Now he gazed at the landscape far and near,
Then, impetuous, stamped the earth,

And turned and tightened his saddle girth;
But mostly he watched with eager search
The belfry-tower of the Old North Church,
As it rose above the graves on the hill,
Lonely and spectral and sombre and still.
And lo! as he looks, on the belfry's height
A glimmer, and then a gleam of light!
He springs to the saddle, the bridle he turns,
But lingers and gazes, till full on his sight
A second lamp in the belfry burns!

A hurry of hoofs in a village street,
A shape in the moonlight, a bulk in the dark,
And beneath, from the pebbles, in passing, a spark
Struck out by a steed flying fearless and fleet;
That was all! And yet, through the gloom and the light,
The fate of a nation was riding that night;
And the spark struck out by that steed, in his flight,
Kindled the land into flame with its heat.
He has left the village and mounted the steep,
And beneath him, tranquil and broad and deep,
Is the Mystic, meeting the ocean tides;
And under the alders, that skirt its edge,
Now soft on the sand, now loud on the ledge,
Is heard the tramp of his steed as he rides.

It was twelve by the village clock,
When he crossed the bridge into Medford town.
He heard the crowing of the cock,
And the barking of the farmer's dog,
And felt the damp of the river fog,
That rises after the sun goes down.

It was one by the village clock,
When he galloped into Lexington.
He saw the gilded weathercock
Swim in the moonlight as he passed,
And the meeting-house windows, black and bare,

Gaze at him with a spectral glare,
As if they already stood aghast
At the bloody work they would look upon.

It was two by the village clock,
When he came to the bridge in Concord town.
He heard the bleating of the flock,
And the twitter of birds among the trees,
And felt the breath of the morning breeze
Blowing over the meadows brown.
And one was safe and asleep in his bed
Who at the bridge would be first to fall,
Who that day would be lying dead,
Pierced by a British musket-ball.

You know the rest. In the books you have read,
How the British Regulars fired and fled,—
How the farmers gave them ball for ball,
From behind each fence and farm-yard wall,
Chasing the red-coats down the lane,
Then crossing the fields to emerge again
Under the trees at the turn of the road,
And only pausing to fire and load.

So through the night rode Paul Revere;
And so through the night went his cry of alarm
To every Middlesex village and farm,—
A cry of defiance, and not of fear,
A voice in the darkness, a knock at the door,
And a word that shall echo forevermore!
For, borne on the night-wind of the Past,
Through all our history, to the last,
In the hour of darkness and peril and need,
The people will waken and listen to hear
The hurrying hoof-beats of that steed,
And the midnight message of Paul Revere.

Oliver Wendell Holmes, "Old Ironsides" (1831), "The Last Leaf" (1831)

Physician, poet, essayist, Oliver Wendell Holmes (1809–1894), the ironically self-described "Autocrat," was influential in the definition and creation of Boston as America's cultural center during the nineteenth century.

OLD IRONSIDES (1831)

Author's Note: This was the popular name by which the frigate Constitution was known. The poem was first printed in the *Boston Daily Advertiser*, at the time when it was proposed to break up the old ship as unfit for service. . . .

> Ay, tear her tattered ensign down!
>   Long has it waved on high,
> And many an eye has danced to see
>   That banner in the sky;
> Beneath it rung the battle shout,
>   And burst the cannon's roar;--
> The meteor of the ocean air
>   Shall sweep the clouds no more!
>
> Her deck, once red with heroes' blood,
>   Where knelt the vanquished foe,
> When winds were hurrying o'er the flood,
>   And waves were white below,
> No more shall feel the victor's tread,
>   Or know the conquered knee;—
> The harpies of the shore shall pluck
>   The eagle of the sea!
>
> O better that her shattered hulk
>   Should sink beneath the wave;
> Her thunders shook the mighty deep,
>   And there should be her grave;
> Nail to the mast her holy flag,
>   Set every thread-bare sail,
> And give her to the god of storms,—
>   The lightning and the gale!

The Last Leaf (1831)

Author's Note: This poem was suggested by the sight of a figure well known to Bostonians [in 1831 or 1832], that of Major Thomas Melville, "the last of the cocked hats," as he was sometimes called. The Major had been a personable young man, very evidently, and retained evidence of it in "the monumental pomp of age," which had something imposing and something odd about it for youthful eyes like mine. He was often pointed at as one of the "Indians" of the famous "Boston Tea Party" of 1774. His aspect among the crowds of the later generation reminded me of a withered leaf which has held its stem through the storms of autumn and winter, and finds itself still clinging to its bough while new the growths of spring are bursting their buds and spreading their foliage all around it. . . .

I saw him once before,
As he passed by the door,
    And again
The pavement stones resound,
As he totters o'er the ground
    With his cane.

They say that in his prime,
Ere the pruning-knife of Time
    Cut him down,
Not a better man was found
By the Crier on his round
    Through the town.

But now he walks the streets,
And he looks at all he meets
    Sad and wan,
And he shakes his feeble head,
That it seems as if he said,
    "They are gone!"

The mossy marbles rest
On the lips that he has pressed
    In their bloom,
And the names he loved to hear

Have been carved for many a year
    On the tomb.

My grandmamma has said—
Poor old lady, she is dead
    Long ago—
That he had a Roman nose,
And his cheek was like a rose
    In the snow;

But now his nose is thin,
And it rests upon his chin
    Like a staff,
And a crook is in his back,
And a melancholy crack
    In his laugh.

I know it is a sin
For me to sit and grin
    At him here;
But the old three-cornered hat,
And the breeches, and all that,
Are so queer!

And if I should live to be
The last leaf upon the tree
    In the spring,
Let them smile, as I do now,
At the old forsaken bough
    Where I cling.

Thomas Wentworth Higginson, from "Letter to a Young Contributor" (1862)

Thomas Wentworth Higginson (1823–1911) was a noted American minister; author of poems, essays, and memoirs, including *Army Life in a Black Regiment* (1869) and *Cheerful Yesterdays* (1898); an abolitionist, and a decorated soldier. During the Civil War, he served as colonel of the 1st South Carolina Volunteers, the first federally authorized African American regiment, in 1862–1864. He was, as well, the friend and mentor of Emily Dickinson, who answered his "Letter."

My dear young gentleman or young lady,—for many are the Cecil Dreemes [a gothic novel by Theodore Winthrop, a descendant of John Winthrop, published by Ticknor & Fields in 1862] of literature who superscribe their offered manuscripts with very masculine names in very feminine handwriting,—it seems wrong not to meet your accumulated and urgent epistles with one comprehensive reply, thus condensing many private letters into a printed one. And so large a proportion of "Atlantic" readers either might, would, could, or should be "Atlantic" contributors also, that this epistle will be sure of perusal, though Mrs. Stowe remain uncut and the Autocrat go for an hour without readers.

Far from me be the wild expectation that every author will not habitually measure the merits of a periodical by its appreciation of his or her last manuscript. I should as soon ask a young lady not to estimate the management of a ball by her own private luck in respect to partners. But it is worth while at least to point out that in the treatment of every contributor the real interests of editor and writer are absolutely the same, and any antagonism is merely traditional, like the supposed hostility between France and England, or between England and Slavery. No editor can ever afford the rejection of a good thing, and no author the publication of a bad one. The only difficulty lies in drawing the line. Were all offered manuscripts unequivocally good or bad, there would be no great trouble; it is the vast range of mediocrity which perplexes: the majority are too bad for blessing and too good for banning; so that no conceivable reason can be given for either fate, save that upon the destiny of any single one may hang that of a hundred others just like it. But whatever be the standard fixed, it is equally for the interest of all concerned that it be enforced without flinching.

Nor is there the slightest foundation for the supposed editorial prejudice against new or obscure contributors. On the contrary, every editor is always hungering and thirsting after novelties. . . .

Strive always to remember—though it does not seem intended that we should quite bring it home to ourselves—that "To-Day is a king in disguise," and that this American literature of ours will be just as classic a thing, if we do our part, as any which the past has treasured. There is a mirage over all literary associations. Keats and Lamb seem to our young people to be existences as remote and legendary as Homer, yet it is not an old man's life since Keats was an awkward boy at the door of Hazlitt's lecture room, and Lamb was introducing Talfourd to Wordsworth as his own only admirer. In reading Spence's "Anecdotes," Pope and Addison appear no farther off; and wherever I open Bacon's "Essays," I am sure to end at last with that one magical sentence, annihilating centuries, "When I was a child, and Queen Elizabeth was in the flower of her years."

And this imperceptible transformation of the commonplace present into the storied past applies equally to the pursuits of war and to the serenest works of peace. Be not misled by the excitements of the moment into over-rating the charms of military life. In this chaos of uniforms, we seem to be approaching times such as existed in England after Waterloo, when the splenetic Byron declared that the only distinction was to be a little undistinguished. No doubt, war brings out grand and unexpected qualities, and there is a perennial fascination in the Elizabethan Raleighs and Sidneys, alike heroes of pen and sword. But the fact is patent, that there is scarcely any art whose rudiments are so easy to acquire as the military; the manuals of tactics have no difficulties comparable to those of the ordinary professional text-books; and any one who can drill a boat's crew or a ball-club can learn in a very few weeks to drill a company or even a regiment. Given in addition the power to command, to organize, and to execute,—high qualities, though not rare in this community, and you have a man needing but time and experience to make a general. More than this can be acquired only by a exclusive absorption in this one art; as Napoleon said, that, to have good soldiers, a nation must be always at war.

If, therefore, duty and opportunity call, count it a privilege to obtain your share in the new career; throw yourself into it as resolutely and joyously as if it were a summer-campaign in the Adirondack, but never fancy for a moment that you have discovered any grander or manlier life than you might be leading every day at home. It is not needful here to decide which is intrinsically the better thing, a column of a newspaper or a column of attack, Wordsworth's "Lines on Immortality" or Wellington's Lines of Torres Vedras; each is noble, if nobly done, though posterity seems to remember literature the longest. The writer is not celebrated for having been the favorite of the conqueror, but sometimes the conqueror only for having favored or even for having spurned the writer. . . .

Once the poets and the sages were held to be pleasing triflers, fit for hours of relaxation in the lulls of war. Now the pursuits of peace are recognized as the real, and war as the accidental. It interrupts all higher avocations, as does the cry of fire: when the fire is extinguished, the important affairs of life are resumed. Six years ago the London "Times" was bewailing that all thought and culture in England were suspended by the Crimean War. "We want no more books. Give us good recruits, at least five feet seven, a good model for a floating-battery, and a gun to take effect at five thousand yards,—and Whigs and Tories, High and Low Church, the poets, astronomers, and critics, may settle it among themselves." How remote seems that epoch now! And how remote will the present soon appear! While art and science will resume their sway serene, beneath skies eternal. Yesterday I turned from treatises on gunnery and fortification to open Milton's Latin Poems, which I had never read, and there, in the "Sylvarum Liber," I came upon a passage as grand as anything in "Paradise Lost,"—his description of Plato's archetypal man, the vast ideal of the human race, eternal, incorrupt, coeval with the stars, dwelling either in the sidereal spaces, or among the Lethean mansions of souls unborn, or pacing the unexplored confines of the habitable globe. There stood the majestic image, veiled in a dead language, yet stilt visible; and it was as if one of the poet's own sylvan groves had been suddenly cut down, and opened a view of Olympus. Then all these present fascinating trivialities of war and diplomacy ebbed away, like Greece and Rome before them, and there seemed nothing real in the universe but Plato's archetypal man. . . .

Yet, if our life be immortal, this temporary distinction is of little moment, and we may learn humility, without learning despair, from earth's evanescent glories. Who cannot bear a few disappointments, if the vista be so wide that the mute inglorious Miltons of this sphere may in some other sing their Paradise as Found? War or peace, fame or forgetfulness, can bring no real injury to one who has formed the fixed purpose to live nobly day by day. I fancy that in some other realm of existence we may look back with some kind interest on this scene of our earlier life, and say to one another, "Do you remember yonder planet, where once we went to school?" And whether our elective study here lay chiefly in the fields of action or of thought will matter little to us then, when other schools shall have led us through other disciplines.

Ralph Waldo Emerson, "Concord Hymn" (1837), "Boston Hymn" (1863)

Ralph Waldo Emerson (1803–1882), poet, essayist, and philosopher, was the central figure of American transcendentalism. In "At the Saturday Club" (1884), Oliver Wendell Holmes described Emerson as the "Delphi" of Concord, its "chosen priest, prophet or poet, mystic, sage or seer."

HYMN: SUNG AT THE COMPLETION OF THE CONCORD MONUMENT, APRIL 19, 1836

By the rude bridge that arched the flood,
    Their flag to April's breeze unfurled,
Here once the embattled farmers stood,
    And fired the shot heard round the world.

The foe long since in silence slept;
    Alike the conqueror silent sleeps;
And Time the ruined bridge has swept
    Down the dark stream which seaward creeps.

On this green bank, by this soft stream,
    We set to-day a votive stone;
That memory may their deed redeem,
    When, like our sires, our sons are gone.

Spirit, that made those heroes dare
    To die, or leave their children free,

Bid Time and Nature gently spare
The shaft we raise to them and thee.

BOSTON HYMN

Emerson read "Boston Hymn" in Boston Music Hall on January 1, 1863,
after President Lincoln signed the Emancipation Proclamation.

The word of the Lord by night
To the watching Pilgrims came,
As they sat by the seaside,
And filled their hearts with flame.

God said, I am tired of kings,
I suffer them no more;
Up to my ear the morning brings
The outrage of the poor.

Think ye I made this ball
A field of havoc and war,
Where tyrants great and tyrants small
Might harry the weak and poor?

My angel,—his name is Freedom,—
Choose him to be your king;
He shall cut pathways east and west.
And fend you with his wing.

Lo! I uncover the land
Which I hid of old time in the West,
As the sculptor uncovers his statue
When he has wrought his best;

I show Columbia, of the rocks
Which dip their foot in the seas,
And soar to the air-borne flocks
Of clouds, and the boreal fleece.

I will divide my goods;
Call in the wretch and slave:

None shall rule but the humble,
And none but Toil shall have.

I will have never a noble,
No lineage counted great;
Fishers and choppers and ploughmen
Shall constitute a state.

Go, cut down trees in the forest,
And trim the straightest boughs;
Cut down trees in the forest,
And build me a wooden house.

Call the people together,
The young men and the sires,
The digger in the harvest field,
Hireling, and him that hires.

And here in a pine state-house
They shall choose men to rule
In every needful faculty,
In church, and state, and school.

Lo, now! if these poor men
Can govern the land and sea,
And make just laws below the sun,
As planets faithful be.

And ye shall succor men;
'T is nobleness to serve;
Help them who cannot help again;
Beware from right to swerve.

I break your bonds and masterships,
And I unchain the slave:
Free be his heart and hand henceforth
As wind and wandering wave.

I cause from every creature
His proper good to flow:
As much as he is and doeth,

So much he shall bestow.

But, lay hands on another
To coin his labor and sweat,
He goes in pawn to his victim
For eternal years in debt.

To-day unbind the captive
So only are ye unbound;
Lift up the people from the dust,
Trump their rescue, sound!

Pay ransom to the owner,
And fill the bag to the brim.
Who is the owner? The slave is owner,
And ever was. Pay him.

O North! give him beauty for rags,
And honor, O South! for his shame;
Nevada! coin thy golden crags
With Freedom's image and name.

Up! and the dusky race
That sat in darkness long,—
Be swift their feet as antelopes,
And as behemoth strong.

Come, East, and West, and North,
By races, as snow-flakes,
And carry my purpose forth,
Which neither halts nor shakes.

My will fulfilled shall be,
For, in daylight or in dark,
My thunderbolt has eyes to see
His way home to the mark.

Louisa May Alcott, from "How I Went Out to Service" (1874)

Louisa May Alcott (1832–1888), daughter of Abigail May Alcott and noted transcendentalist Amos Bronson Alcott, wrote of family life in Concord and Boston in many novels and essays, most notably in *Little Women* (1868). "How I Went Out to Service" was first published in *Independent* 26 (June 4, 1874). Here she converts a painful experience—working as a domestic for a family in Dedham, a Boston suburb, in the 1850s—into a "serio-comico experience." She also wrote a novel, *Work: An Experience* (1873), which shows a young woman seeking independence through service employment.

When I was eighteen I wanted something to do. I had tried teaching for two years, and hated it; I had tried sewing, and could not earn my bread in that way, at the cost of health; I tried story-writing and got five dollars for stories which now bring a hundred; I had thought seriously of going upon the stage, but certain highly respectable relatives were so shocked at the mere idea that I relinquished my dramatic aspirations.

"What *shall* I do?" was still the question that perplexed me. I was ready to work, eager to be independent, and too proud to endure patronage. But the right task seemed hard to find, and my bottled energies were fermenting in a way that threatened an explosion before long.

My honored mother was a city missionary that winter, and not only served the clamorous poor, but often found it in her power to help the decayed gentlefolk by quietly placing them where they could earn their bread without the entire sacrifice of taste and talent which makes poverty so hard for such to bear. Knowing her tact and skill, people often came to her for companions, housekeepers, and that class of the needy who do not make their wants known through an intelligence office.

One day, as I sat dreaming splendid dreams, while I made a series of little petticoats out of odds and ends sent in for the poor, a tall, ministerial gentleman appeared, in search of a companion for his sister. He possessed an impressive nose, a fine flow of language, and a pair of large hands, encased in black kid gloves. With much waving of those somber members, Mr. R. set forth the delights awaiting the happy soul who should secure this home. He described it as a sort of heaven on earth. "There are books, pictures, flowers, a piano, and the best of society," he said. "This person will be one of the family in all respects, and only required to help about the lighter work, which my sister has done herself hitherto, but is now a martyr to neuralgia and needs a gentle hand to assist her."

My mother, who never lost her faith in human nature, in spite of many impostures, believed every word, and quite beamed with benevolent interest as she listened and tried to recall some needy young woman to whom the charming home would be a blessing. I also innocently thought:

"That sounds inviting. I like housework and can do it well. I should have time to enjoy the books and things I love, and D—— is not far away from home. Suppose I try it."

So, when my mother turned to me, asking if I could suggest any one, I became red as a poppy and said abruptly:

"Only myself."

"Do you really mean it?" cried my astonished parent.

"I really do if Mr. R. thinks I should suit" was my steady reply, as I partially obscured my crimson countenance behind a little flannel skirt, still redder.

The Reverend Josephus gazed upon me with the benign regard which a bachelor of five and thirty may accord a bashful damsel of eighteen. A smile dawned upon his countenance, "sicklied o'er with the pale cast of thought," or dyspepsia; and he softly folded the black gloves, as if about to bestow a blessing as he replied, with emphasis:

"I am sure you would, and we should think ourselves most fortunate if we could secure your society and—ahem—services for my poor sister."

"Then I'll try it," responded the impetuous maid.

"We will talk it over a little first, and let you know tomorrow, sir," put in my prudent parent, adding, as Mr. R. arose: "What wages do you pay?"

"My dear madam, in a case like this let me not use such words as those. Anything you may think proper we shall gladly give. The labor is very light, for there are but three of us and our habits are of the simplest sort. I am a frail reed and may break at any moment; so is my sister, and my aged father cannot long remain; therefore, money is little to us, and any one who comes to lend her youth and strength to our feeble household will not be forgotten in the end, I assure you." And, with another pensive smile, a farewell wave of the impressive gloves, the Reverend Josephus bowed like a well-sweep and departed.

"My dear, are you in earnest?" asked my mother.

"Of course I am. Why not try the experiment? It can but fail, like all the others."

"I have no objection; only I fancied you were rather too proud for this sort of thing."

"I am too proud to be idle and dependent, ma'am. I'll scrub floors and take in washing first. I do housework at home for love; why not do it abroad for money? I like it better than teaching. It is healthier than sewing and surer than writing. So why not try it?"

"It is going out to service, you know, though you are called a companion. How does that suit?"

"I don't care. Every sort of work that is paid for is service; and I don't mind being a companion, if I can do it well. I may find it is my mission to take care of neuralgic old ladies and lackadaisical clergymen. It does not sound exciting, but it's better than nothing," I answered, with a sigh; for it was rather a sudden downfall to give up being a Siddons [Sarah Siddons, British actress] and become a Betcinder [maid]. . . .

Now all this was altogether romantic and sensational, and I felt as if about to enter one of those delightfully dangerous houses we read of in novels, where perils, mysteries, and sins freely disport themselves, till the newcomer sets all to rights, after unheard of trials and escapes.

I arrived at twilight, just the proper time for the heroine to appear; and, as no one answered my modest solo on the rusty knocker, I walked in and looked about me. Yes, here was the long, shadowy hall, where the ghosts doubtless walked at midnight. Peering in at an open door on the right, I saw a parlor full of ancient furniture, faded, dusty, and dilapidated. Old portraits stared at me from the walls and a damp chill froze the marrow of my bones in the most approved style.

"The romance opens well," I thought, and peeping in at an opposite door, beheld a luxurious apartment, full of the warm glow of firelight, the balmy breath of hyacinths and roses, the white glimmer of piano keys, and tempting rows of books along the walls.

The contrast between the two rooms was striking, and, after an admiring survey, I continued my explorations, thinking that I should not mind being "ministered to" in that inviting place when my work was done.

A third door showed me a plain, dull sitting room, with an old man napping in his easy-chair. I heard voices in the kitchen beyond, and entering there, beheld Puah the fiend. Unfortunately, for the dramatic effect of the tableaux, all I saw was a mild-faced old woman, buttering toast, while she conversed with her familiar, a comfortable gray cat.

The old lady greeted me kindly, but I fancied her faded blue eye had a weird expression and her amiable words were all a snare, though I own I was rather disappointed at the commonplace appearance of this humble Borgia.

She showed me to a tiny room, where I felt more like a young giantess than ever, and was obliged to stow away my possessions as snugly as in a ship's cabin. When I presently descended, armed with a blue apron and "a heart for any fate," I found the old man awake and received from him a welcome full of ancient courtesy and kindliness. Miss Eliza crept in like a timid mouse, looking so afraid of her buxom companion that I forgot my own shyness in trying to relieve hers. She was so enveloped in shawls that all I could discover was that my mistress was a very nervous little woman, with a small button of pale hair on the outside of her head and the vaguest notions of work inside. A few spasmodic remarks and many awkward pauses brought me to teatime, when Josephus appeared, as tall, thin, and cadaverous as ever. After his arrival there was no more silence, for he preached all suppertime something in this agreeable style.

"My young friend, our habits, as you see, are of the simplest. We eat in the kitchen, and all together, in the primitive fashion; for it suits my father and saves labor. I could wish more order and elegance; but *my* wishes are not consulted and I submit I live above these petty crosses, and, though my health suffers from bad cookery, I do not murmur. Only, I must say, in passing, that if you *will* make your battercakes green with saleratus, Puah, I shall feel it my duty to throw them out of the window. I am used to poison; but I cannot see the coals of this blooming girl's stomach destroyed, as mine have been. And, speaking of duties, I may as well mention to you, Louisa (I call you so in a truly fraternal spirit), that I like to find my study in order when I come down in the morning; for I often need a few moments of solitude before I face the daily annoyances of my life. I shall permit you to perform this light task, for you have some idea of order (I see it in the formation of your brow), and feel sure that you will respect the sanctuary of thought. Eliza is so blind she does not see dust, and Puah enjoys devastating the one poor refuge I can call my own this side of the grave. We are all waiting for you, sir. My father keeps up the old formalities, you observe; and I endure them, though my views are more advanced."

The old gentleman hastily finished his tea and returned thanks, when his son stalked gloomily away, evidently oppressed with the burden of his wrongs, also, as I irreverently fancied, with the seven "green" flapjacks he had devoured during the sermon. . . .

I was up betimes next morning and had the study in perfect order before the recluse appeared, enjoying a good prowl among the books as I worked and becoming so absorbed that I forgot the eggs, until a gusty sigh startled me, and I beheld Josephus, in dressing gown and slippers, languidly surveying the scene.

"Nay, do not fly," he said, as I grasped my duster in guilty haste. "It pleases me to see you here and lends a sweet, domestic charm to my solitary room. I like that graceful cap, that housewifely apron, and I beg you to wear them often; for it refreshes my eye to see something tasteful, young, and womanly about me. Eliza makes a bundle of herself and Puah is simply detestable."

He sank languidly into a chair and closed his eyes, as if the mere thought of his enemy was too much for him. I took advantage of this momentary prostration to slip away, convulsed with laughter at the looks and words of this bald-headed sentimentalist.

After breakfast I fell to work with a will, eager to show my powers and glad to put things to rights, for many hard jobs had evidently been waiting for a stronger arm than Puah's and a more methodical head than Eliza's.

Everything was dusty, moldy, shiftless, and neglected, except the domain of Josephus. Up-stairs the paper was dropping from the walls, the ancient furniture was all more or less dilapidated, and every hold and corner was full of relics tucked away by Puah, who was a regular old magpie. Rats and mice reveled in the empty rooms and spiders wove their tapestry undisturbed, for the old man would have nothing altered or repaired, and his part of the house was fast going to ruin.

I longed to have a grand "clearing up"; but was forbidden to do more than keep things in livable order. On the whole, it was fortunate, for I soon found that my hands would be kept busy with the realms of Josephus, whose ethereal being shrank from dust, shivered at a cold breath, and needed much cosseting with dainty food, hot fires, soft beds, and endless service, else, as he expressed it, the frail reed would break.

I regret to say that a time soon came when I felt supremely indifferent as to the breakage, and very skeptical as to the fragility of a reed that ate, slept, dawdled, and scolded so energetically. The rose that fell to pieces so suddenly was a good symbol of the rapid disappearance of all the romantic delusions I had indulged in for a time. A week's acquaintance with the inmates of this old house quite settled my opinion, and further developments only confirmed it. . . .

Alas! for romance and the Christian virtues, several pairs of boots were cleaned that night, and my sinful soul enjoyed the spectacle of the reverend bootblack at his task. I even found my "fancy work," as I called the evening job of paring a bucketful of hard russets with a dull knife, much cheered by the shoe brush accompaniment played in the shed.

Thunder-clouds rested upon the martyr's brow at breakfast, and I was as much ignored as the cat. And what a relief that was! The piano was locked up, so were the bookcases, the newspapers mysteriously disappeared, and a solemn silence reigned at table, for no one dared to talk when that gifted tongue was mute. Eliza fled from the gathering storm and had a comfortable fit of neuralgia in her own room, where Puah nursed her, leaving me to skirmish with the enemy.

It was not a fair fight, and that experience lessened my respect for mankind immensely. I did my best however—grubbed about all day and amused my dreary evenings as well as I could; too proud even to borrow a book, lest it should seem like surrender. What a long month it was, and how eagerly I counted the hours of that last week, for my time was up Saturday and I hoped to be off at once. But when I announced my intention such dismay fell upon Eliza that my heart was touched, and Puah so urgently begged me to stay till they could get some one that I consented to remain a few days longer, and wrote post-haste to my mother, telling her to send a substitute quickly or I should do something desperate.

That blessed woman, little dreaming of all the woes I had endured, advised me to be patient, to do the generous thing, and be sure I should not regret it in the end. I groaned, submitted, and did regret it all the days of my life.

Three mortal weeks I waited; for, though two other victims came, I was implored to set them going, and tried to do it. But both fled after a day or two, condemning the place as a very hard one and calling me a fool to stand it another hour. I entirely agreed with them on both points, and, when I had cleared up after the second incapable lady, I tarried not for the coming of a third, but clutched my property and announced my departure by the next train.

Of course, Eliza wept, Puah moaned, the old man politely regretted, and the younger one washed his hands of the whole affair by shutting himself up in his room and forbidding me to say farewell because "he could not bear it." I laughed, and fancied it done for effect then; but I soon understood it better and did not laugh.

At the last moment, Eliza nervously tucked a sixpenny pocketbook into my hand and shrouded herself in the little blanket with a sob. But Puah kissed me kindly and whispered, with an odd look: "Don't blame us for anything. Some folks is liberal and some ain't." I thanked the poor old soul for her kindness to me and trudged gayly away to the station, whither my property had preceded me on a wheelbarrow, hired at my own expense.

I never shall forget that day. A bleak March afternoon, a sloppy, lonely road, and one hoarse crow stalking about a field, so like Josephus that I could not resist throwing a snowball at him. Behind me stood the dull old house, no longer either mysterious or romantic in my disenchanted eyes; before me rumbled the barrow, bearing my dilapidated wardrobe; and in my pocket reposed what I fondly hoped was, if not a liberal, at least an honest return for seven weeks of the hardest work I ever did.

Unable to resist the desire to see what my earnings were, I opened the purse and beheld *four dollars*.

I have had a good many bitter minutes in my life; but one of the bitterest came to me as I stood there in the windy road, with the sixpenny pocketbook open before me, and looked from my poor chapped, grimy, chill-blained hands to the paltry sum that was considered reward for all the hard and humble labor they had done.

A girl's heart is a sensitive thing. And mine had been very full lately; for it had suffered many of the trials that wound deeply yet cannot be told; so I think it was but natural that my first impulse was to go straight back to that sacred study and fling this insulting money at the feet of him who sent it. But I was so boiling over with indignation that I could not trust myself in his presence, lest I should be unable to resist the temptation to shake him, in spite of his cloth.

No. I would go home, show my honorable wounds, tell my pathetic tale, and leave my parents to avenge my wrongs. I did so; but over that harrowing scene I drop a veil, for my feeble pen refuses to depict the emotions of my outraged family. I will merely mention that the four dollars went back and the reverend Josephus never heard the last of it in that neighborhood.

My experiment seemed a dire failure and I mourned it as such for years; but more than once in my life I have been grateful for that serio-comico experience, since it has taught me many lessons. One of the most useful of these has been the power of successfully making a companion, not a servant, of those whose aid I need, and helping to gild their honest wages with the sympathy and justice which can sweeten the humblest and lighten the hardest task.

James T. Fields, from "Hawthorne,"
Yesterdays with Authors (1871)

James T. Fields (1817–1881), a founder of *Atlantic Monthly*, was Boston's most important publisher of the nineteenth century and a central figure in the Greater Boston literary community.

When Mr. George Bancroft, then Collector of the Port of Boston, appointed Hawthorne weigher and gauger in the custom-house, he did a wise thing, for no public officer ever performed his disagreeable duties better than our romancer. Here is a tattered little official document signed by Hawthorne when he was watching over the interests of the country: it certifies his attendance at the unlading of a brig, then lying at Long Wharf in Boston. I keep this precious relic side by side with one of a similar custom-house character, signed "Robert Burns."

I came to know Hawthorne very intimately after the Whigs displaced the Democratic romancer from office. In my ardent desire to have him retained in the public service, his salary at that time being his sole dependence,—not foreseeing that his withdrawal from that sort of employment would be the best thing for American letters that could possibly happen,—I called, in his behalf, on several influential politicians of the day, and well remember the rebuffs I received in my enthusiasm for the author of the "Twice-Told Tales." One pompous little gentleman in authority, after hearing my appeal, quite astounded me by his ignorance of the claims of a literary man on his country. "Yes, yes," he sarcastically croaked down his public turtle-fed throat, "I see through it all, I see through it; this Hawthorne is one of them 'ere visionists, and we don't want no such a man as him round." So the "visionist" was not allowed to remain in office, and the country was better served by him in another way. In the winter of 1849, after he had been ejected from the custom-house, I went down to Salem to see him and inquire after his health, for we heard he had been suffering from illness. He was then living in a modest wooden house in Mall Street, if I remember rightly the location. I found him alone in a chamber over the sitting-room of the dwelling; and as the day was cold, he was hovering near a stove. We fell into talk about his future prospects, and he was, as I feared I should find him, in a very desponding mood. "Now," said I, "is the time for you to publish, for I know during these years in Salem you must have got something ready for the press." "Non-sense," said he; "what heart had I to write anything, when my publishers (M. and Company) have been so many years trying to sell a small edition of the 'Twice-Told Tales'?" I still pressed upon him the good chances he would have now with something new. "Who would risk publishing a book for <u>me</u>, the most unpopular writer in America?" "I would," said I, "and would start with an edition of two thousand copies of anything you write." "What mad-ness!" he exclaimed; "your friendship for me gets the better of your judg-ment. No, no," he continued; "I have no money to indemnify a publisher's losses on my account." I looked at my watch and found that the train would soon be starting for Boston, and I knew there was not much time to lose in trying to discover what had been his literary work during these last few years in Salem. I remember that I pressed him to reveal to me what he had been writing. He shook his head and gave me to understand he had produced nothing. At that moment I caught sight of a bureau or set of drawers near where we were sitting; and immediately it occurred to me that hidden away somewhere in that article of furniture was a story or stories by the author of the "Twice-Told Tales," and I became so positive of it that I charged him vehemently with the fact. He seemed surprised, I thought, but shook his head again; and I rose to take my leave, begging him not to come into the cold entry, saying I would come back and see him again in a few days. I was hurrying down the stairs when he called after me from the chamber, asking me to stop a moment. Then quickly stepping into the entry with a roll of manuscript in his hands, he said: "How in Heaven's name did you know this thing was there? As you have found me out, take what I have written, and tell me, after you get home and have time to read it, if it is good for anything. It is either very good or very bad,—I don't know which." On my way up to Boston I read the germ of "The Scarlet Letter"; before I slept that night I wrote him a note all aglow with admiration of the marvelous story he had put into my hands, and told him that I would come again to Salem the next day and arrange for its publication. I went on in such an amazing state of excitement when we met again in the little house, that he would not believe I was really in earnest. He seemed to think I was beside myself, and laughed sadly at my enthusiasm. However, we soon arranged for his appearance again before the public with a book.

This quarto volume before me contains numerous letters, written by him from 1850 down to the month of his death. The first one refers to "The Scarlet Letter," and is dated in January, 1850. At my suggestion he had altered the plan of that story. It was his intention to make "The Scarlet Letter" one of several short stories, all to be included in one volume, and to be called

"OLD TIME LEGENDS

TOGETHER WITH SKETCHES,

EXPERIMENTAL AND IDEAL."

His first design was to make "The Scarlet Letter" occupy about two hundred pages in his new book; but I persuaded him, after reading the first chapters of the story, to elaborate it, and publish it as a separate work. After it was settled that "The Scarlet Letter" should be enlarged and printed by itself in a volume he wrote to me:—

"I am truly glad that you like the Introduction, for I was rather afraid that it might appear absurd and impertinent to be talking about myself, when nobody, that I know of, has requested any information on that subject.

"As regards the size of the book, I have been thinking a good deal about it. Considered merely as a matter of taste and beauty, the form of publication which you recommend seems to me much preferable to that of the 'Mosses.'

"In the present case, however, I have some doubts of the expediency, because, if the book is made up entirely of 'The Scarlet Letter,' it will be too sombre. I found it impossible to relieve the shadows of the story with so much light as I would gladly have thrown in. Keeping so close to its point as the tale does, and no otherwise than by turning different sides of the same to the reader's eye, it will weary very many people and disgust some. Is it safe, then, to stake the fate of the book entirely on this one chance? A hunter loads his gun with a bullet and several buckshot; and, following his sagacious example, it was my purpose to conjoin the one long story with half a dozen shorter ones, so that, failing to kill the public outright with my biggest and heaviest lump of lead, I might have other chances with the smaller bits, individually and in the aggregate. However, I am willing to leave these considerations to your judgment, and should not be sorry to have you decide for the separate publication.

"In this latter event it appears to me that the only proper title for the book would be 'The Scarlet Letter,' for 'The Custom-House' is merely introductory,—an entrance-hall to the magnificent edifice which I throw open to my guests. It would be funny if, seeing the further passages so dark and dismal, they should all choose to stop there! If 'The Scarlet Letter' is to be the title, would it not be well to print it on the title-page in red ink? I am not quite sure about the good taste of so doing, but it would certainly be piquant and appropriate, and, I think, attractive to the great gull whom we are endeavoring to circumvent."

One beautiful summer day, twenty years ago, I found Hawthorne in his little red cottage at Lenox, surrounded by his happy young family. He had the look, as somebody said, of a banished lord, and his grand figure among the hills of Berkshire seemed finer than ever. His boy and girl were swinging on the gate as we drove up to his door, and with their sunny curls formed an attractive feature in the landscape. As the afternoon was cool and delightful, we proposed a drive over to Pittsfield to see Holmes, who was then living on his ancestral farm. Hawthorne was in a cheerful condition, and seemed to enjoy the beauty of the day to the utmost. Next morning we were all invited by Mr. Dudley Field, then living at Stockbridge, to ascend Monument Mountain. Holmes, Hawthorne, Duyckinck, Herman Melville, Headley, Sedgwick, Matthews, and several ladies, were of the party. We scrambled to the top with great spirit, and when we arrived, Melville, I remember, bestrode a peaked rock, which ran out like a bowsprit, and pulled and hauled imaginary ropes for our delectation. Then we all assembled in a shady spot, and one of the party read to us Bryant's beautiful poem commemorating Monument Mountain. Then we lunched among the rocks, and somebody proposed Bryant's health, and "long life to the dear old poet." This was the most popular toast of the day, and it took, I remember, a considerable quantity of Heidsieck to do it justice. In the afternoon, pioneered by Headley, we made our way, with merry shouts and laughter, through the Ice-Glen. Hawthorne was among the most enterprising of the merry-makers; and being in the dark much of the time, he ventured to call out lustily and pretend that certain destruction was inevitable to all of us. After this extemporaneous jollity, we dined together at Mr. Dudley Field's in Stockbridge, and Hawthorne rayed out in a sparkling and unwonted manner. I remember the conversation at table chiefly ran on the physical differences between the present American and English men, Hawthorne stoutly taking part in favor of the

American. This 5th of August was a happy day throughout, and I never saw Hawthorne in better spirits.

Annie Fields, from "Oliver Wendell Holmes: Personal Recollections and Unpublished Letters," *Authors and Friends* (1896)

Annie Fields (1834–1915) was a publishing adviser to her husband, an author, and a hostess for literary Boston.

Dr. Holmes's social nature, as expressed in conversation and in his books, drew him into communication with a very large number of persons. It cannot be said, however, in this age marked by altruisms, that he was altruistic; on the contrary, he loved himself, and made himself his prime study—but as a member of the human race, he had his own purposes to fulfill, his own self-appointed tasks, and he preferred to take men only on his own terms. He was filled with righteous indignation, in reading Carlyle, to find a passage where, hearing the door-bell ring one morning when he was very busy, he exclaimed that he was afraid it was "the man Emerson!" Yet Dr. Holmes was himself one of the most carefully guarded men, through his years of actual production, who ever lived and wrote. His wife absorbed her life in his, and mounted guard to make sure that interruption was impossible. Nevertheless, he was eminently a lover of men, or he could not have drawn them perpetually to his side. His writings were never aimed too high; his sole wish was to hit the heart, if possible; but if a shot hit the head also, he showed a childlike pride in the achievement. . . .

Our acquaintance and friendship with him lasted through many years, beginning with my husband's early association. I think their acquaintance began about the time when the doctor threatened to hang out a sign, "The smallest fevers gratefully received," and when the young publisher's literary enthusiasm led him to make some excuse for asking medical advice. . . .

The removal from Montgomery Place, where he had lived some years, to Charles Street was a matter of great concern. He says in the "Autocrat" that "he had no idea until he pulled up his domestic establishment what an enormous quantity of roots he had been making during the years he had been planted there." Before announcing his intention, he came early one morning, with his friend Lothrop Motley, to inspect our house, which was similar to the one he thought of buying. I did not know his intention at the time, but I was delighted with his enthusiasm for the view over Charles River Bay, which in those days was wider and more beautiful than it can ever be again. Nothing would satisfy him but to go to the attic, which he declared, if it were his, he should make his study.

Shortly after, the doctor took possession of his new house, but characteristically made no picturesque study in which to live. He passed many long days and evenings, even in summer, in a lower room opening on the street, which wore the air of a physician's office, and solaced his love for the picturesque by an occasional afternoon at his early home in Cambridge. Of a visit to this latter house I find the following description in my note-book: "Drove out in the afternoon and overtook Professor Holmes" (he liked to be called "Professor" then), "with his wife and son, who were all on their way to his old homestead in Cambridge. They asked us to go there with them, as it was only a few steps from where we were. The professor went to the small side door, and knocked with a fine brass knocker which had just been presented to him from the old Hancock House. It was delightful to see his pleasure in everything about the old house. There hung a portrait of his father, Abiel Holmes, at the age of thirty-one,—a beautiful face it was; there also a picture of the reverend doctor's first wife, fair, and perhaps a trifle coquettish, or what the professor called 'a little romantic,' the old chairs from France were still there; but no modern knickknacks interfered with the old-fashioned, quiet effect of the whole. He has taken for his writing-room the former parlor looking into the garden. He loves to work there, and he and his wife evidently spend a good deal of time at the old place. There is a legend that Washington spent three nights there, and that Dr. Bradshaw stepped from the door to make a prayer upon the departure of the troops from that point. Behind the house are some fine trees where we sat in the shade talking until the shadows grew long upon the grass." . . .

Any record of Dr. Holmes's life would be imperfect which contained no mention of the pride and pleasure he felt in the Saturday Club. Throughout the forty years of its prime he was not only the most brilliant talker of that distinguished company, but he was also the most faithful attendant. He was seldom absent from the monthly dinners either in summer or in winter, and he lived to find himself at the head of the table where Agassiz, Longfellow, Emerson, and Lowell had in turn preceded him. Could a shorthand writer have been secretly present at those dinners, what a delightful book of wise talk and witty sayings would now lie open before us! . . .

Soon after Dr. Holmes's removal to Charles Street began a long series of early morning breakfasts at his publisher's house—feasts of the simplest kind. Many strangers came to Boston in those days, on literary or historical errands—men of tastes which brought them sooner or later to the "Old Corner" where the "Atlantic Monthly" was already a power. Of course one of the first pleasures sought for was an interview with Dr. Holmes, the fame of whose wit ripened early—even before the days of the "Autocrat." It came about quite naturally, therefore, that they should gladly respond to any call which gave them the opportunity to listen to his conversation; and the eight-o'clock breakfast hour was chosen as being the only time the busy guests and host could readily call their own. Occasionally these breakfasts would take place as frequently as two or three times a week. The light of memory has a wondrous gift of heightening most of the pleasures of this life, but the conversation of those early hours was far more stimulating and inspiring than any memory of it can ever be. There were few men, except Poe, famous in American or English literature of that era who did not appear once at least. The unexpectedness of the company was a great charm; for a brief period Boston enjoyed a sense of cosmopolitanism, and found it possible, as it is really possible only in London, to bring together busy guests with full and eager brains who are not too familiar with one another's thought to make conversation an excitement and a source of development . . .

Who that heard him can ever forget the exquisite reading of "The Last Leaf" at the Longfellow memorial meeting. The pathos of it was then understood for the first time. The poem had become an expression of his later self, and it was given with a personal significance which touched the hearts of all his hearers.

Willa Cather, from "148 Charles Street," *Not Under Forty* (1936)

Willa Cather (1873–1947) came of age in Nebraska. Her best known works are set on the nineteenth-century American frontier: *O Pioneers!* (1913), *My Ántonia* (1918), and *Death Comes for the Archbishop* (1927). However, she arrived at her epiphany of authorial purpose in Boston, where she met her mentor, Sarah Orne Jewett, in the Charles Street home of Annie Fields.

Late in the winter of 1908 Mrs. Louis Brandeis conducted me along a noisy street in Boston and rang at a door hitherto unknown to me. Sometimes entering a new door can make a great change in one's life. That afternoon I had set out from the Parker House (the old, the real Parker House, before it was "modernized") to make a call on Mrs. Brandeis. When I reached her house in Otis Place she told me that we would go farther: she thought I would enjoy meeting a very charming old lady who was a near neighbor of hers, the widow of James T. Fields, of the publishing firm of Ticknor and Fields. The name of that firm meant something to me. In my father's bookcase there were little volumes of Longfellow and Hawthorne with that imprint. I wondered how the widow of one of the partners could still be living. Mrs. Brandeis explained that when James T. Fields was a man in middle life, a publisher of international reputation and a widower, he married Annie Adams, then a girl of nineteen. She had naturally survived him by many years.

When the door at 148 Charles Street was opened we waited a few moments in a small reception-room just off the hall, then went up a steep, thickly carpeted stairway and entered the "long drawing-room," where Mrs. Fields and Miss Jewett sat at tea. That room ran the depth of the house, its front windows, heavily curtained, on Charles Street, its back windows looking down on a deep garden. Directly above the garden wall lay the Charles River and, beyond, the Cambridge shore. At five o'clock in the afternoon the river was silvery from a half-hidden sun; over the great open space of water the western sky was dove-coloured with little ripples of rose. The air was full of soft moisture and the hint of approaching spring. Against this screen of pale winter light were the two ladies: Mrs. Fields reclining on a green sofa, directly under the youthful portrait of Charles Dickens (now in the Boston Art Museum), Miss Jewett seated, the low tea-table between them.

Mrs. Fields wore the widow's lavender which she never abandoned except for black velvet, with a scarf of Venetian lace on her hair. She was very slight and fragile in figure, with a great play of animation in her face and a delicate flush of pink on her cheeks. Like her friend Mrs. John Gardner, she had a skin which defied age. As for Miss Jewett—she looked very like the youthful picture of herself in the game of "Authors" I had played as a child, except that she was fuller in figure and a little grey. I do not at all remember what we talked about. Mrs. Brandeis asked that I be shown some of the treasures of the house, but I had no eyes for the treasures, I was too intent upon the ladies.

That winter afternoon began a friendship, impoverished by Miss Jewett's death sixteen months later, but enduring until Mrs. Fields herself died, in February 1915.

In 1922 M. A. De Wolfe Howe, Mrs. Fields' literary executor, published a book of extracts from her diaries under the title *Memories of a Hostess*, a book which delighted all who had known her and many who had not, because of its vivid pictures of the Cambridge and Concord groups in the '60s and '70s, not as "celebrities" but as friends and fellow citizens. When Mr. Howe's book appeared, I wrote for *The Literary Review* an appreciation of it, very sketchy, but done with genuine enthusiasm, which I here incorporate without quotation marks.

In his book made up from the diaries of Mrs. James T. Fields, Mr. De Wolfe Howe presents a record of beautiful memories and, as its subtitle declares, "a chronicle of eminent friendships." For a period of sixty years Mrs. Fields' Boston house, at 148 Charles Street, extended its hospitality to the aristocracy of letters and art. During that long stretch of time there was scarcely an American of distinction in art or public life who was not a guest in that house; scarcely a visiting foreigner of renown who did not pay his tribute there. . . .

Although Mrs. Fields was past seventy when I was first conducted into the long drawing-room, she did not seem old to me. Frail, diminished in force, yes; but, emphatically, not old. "The personal beauty of her younger years, long retained, and even at the end of such a stretch of life not quite lost," to quote Henry James, may have had something to do with the impression she gave; but I think it was even more because, as he also said of her, "all her implications were gay." I had seldom heard so young, so merry, so musical a laugh; a laugh with countless shades of relish and appreciation and kindness in it. And, on occasion, a short laugh from that same fragile source could positively do police duty! It could put an end to a conversation that had taken an unfortunate turn, absolutely dismiss and silence impertinence or presumption. No woman could have been so great a hostess, could have made so many highly developed personalities happy under her roof, could have blended so many strongly specialized and keenly sensitive people in her drawing-room, without having a great power to control and organize. It was a power so sufficient that one seldom felt it as one lived in the harmonious atmosphere it created—an atmosphere in which one seemed absolutely safe from everything ugly. Nobody can cherish the flower of social intercourse, can give it sun and sustenance and a tempered clime, without also being able very completely to dispose of anything that threatens it—not only the slug, but even the cold draught that ruffles its petals. . . .

When one was staying at that house the past lay in wait for one in all the corners; it exuded from the furniture, from the pictures, the rare editions, and the cabinets of manuscript—the beautiful, clear manuscripts of a typewriterless age, which even the printers had respected and kept clean. The unique charm of Mrs. Fields' house was not that it was a place where one could hear about the past, but that it was a place where the past lived on— where it was protected and cherished, had sanctuary from the noisy push of the present. In casual conversation, at breakfast or tea, you might at any time unconsciously press a spring which liberated recollection, and one of the great shades seemed quietly to enter the room and to take the chair or the corner he had preferred in life. . . .

It was at tea-time, I used to think, that the great shades were most likely to appear; sometimes they seemed to come up the deeply carpeted stairs, along with living friends. At that hour the long room was dimly lighted, the fire bright, and through the wide windows the sunset was flaming, or softly brooding, upon the Charles River and the Cambridge shore beyond. The ugliness of the world, all possibility of wrenches and jars and wounding contacts, seemed securely shut out. It was indeed the peace of the past, where the tawdry and cheap have been eliminated and the enduring things have taken their proper, happy places. . . .

I love to remember one charming visit in her summer house at Manchester-by-the-Sea, when Sarah Orne Jewett was there. . . . At Manchester, when there were no guests, Mrs. Fields had tea on the back veranda, overlooking a wild stretch of woodland. Down in this wood, directly beneath us, were a tea-table and seats built under the trees, where they used to have tea when the hostess was younger—now the climb was too steep for her. It was a little sad, perhaps, to sit and look out over a shrinking kingdom; but if she felt it, she never showed it. Miss Jewett and I went down into the wood, and she told me she hated to go there now, as it reminded her that much was already lost, and what was left was so at the mercy of chance! It seemed as if a strong wind might blow away that beloved friend of many years. We talked in low voices. Who could have believed that Mrs. Fields was to outlive Miss Jewett, so much the younger, by nearly six years, as she outlived Mr. Fields by thirty-four! She had the very genius of survival. She was not, as she once laughingly told me, "to escape anything, not even free verse or the Cubists!" She was not in the least dashed by either. Oh, no, she said, the Cubists weren't any queerer than Manet and the Impressionists were when they first came to Boston, and people used to run in for tea and ask her whether she had ever heard of such a thing as "blue snow," or a man's black hat being purple in the sun! . . . The next summer I was visiting Mrs. Fields at Manchester in a season of intense heat. We were daily expecting the arrival of Henry James, Jr., himself. One morning came a spluttery letter from the awaited friend, containing bitter references to the "Great American summer," and saying that he was "lying at Nahant," prostrated by the weather. I was very much disappointed, but Mrs. Fields said wisely: "My dear, it is just as well. Mr. James is always greatly put about by the heat, and at Nahant there is the chance of a breeze." . . .

Mrs. Fields' Journal tells us how in her young married days she always moved from Boston to Manchester-by-the-Sea in early summer, just as she still did when I knew her. I remember one characteristic passage in the Journal, written at Manchester and dated July 16, 1870:

It is a perfect summer day, she says. Mr. Fields does not go up to town but stays at home with a bag full of MSS. He and his wife go to a favorite spot in a pasture by the sea, and she reads him a new story which has just come in from Henry James, Jr., then a very young man—*Compagnons de Voyage*, in "execrable" handwriting. They find the quality good. "I do not know," Mrs. Fields wrote in her diary that evening, "why success in work should affect one so powerfully, but I could have wept as I finished reading, not from the sweet, low pathos of the tale, but from the knowledge of the writer's success. It is so difficult to do anything well in this mysterious world."

Yes, one says to oneself, that is Mrs. Fields, at her best. She rose to meet a fine performance, always—to the end. At eighty she could still entertain new people, new ideas, new forms of art. And she brought to her greeting of the new all the richness of her rich past: a long, unbroken chain of splendid contacts, beautiful friendships. . . .

Today, in 1936, a garage stands on the site of 148 Charles Street. Only in memory exists the long, green-carpeted, softly lighted drawing-room, and the dining-table where Learning and Talent met, enjoying good food and good wit and rare vintages, looking confidently forward to the growth of their country in the finer amenities of life. Perhaps the garage and all it stands for represent the only real development, and have altogether taken the place of things formerly cherished on that spot. If we try to imagine those dinner-parties which Mrs. Fields describes, the scene is certainly not to us what it was to her: the lighting has changed, and the guests seem hundreds of years away from us. Their portraits no longer hang on the walls of our academies, nor are their "works" much discussed there. The English classes, we are told, can be "interested" only in contemporary writers, the newer the better. A letter from a prep-school boy puts it tersely: "D. H. Lawrence is rather rated a back-number here, but Faulkner keeps his end up."

Not the prep-school boys only are blithe to leave the past untroubled: their instructors pretty generally agree with them. And the retired professors who taught these instructors do not see Shelley plain as they once did. The faith of the elders has been shaken.

Just how did this change come about, one wonders. When and where were the Arnolds overthrown and the Brownings devaluated? Was it at the Marne? At Versailles, when a new geography was being made on paper? Certainly the literary world which emerged from the war used a new coinage. In England and America the "masters" of the last century diminished in stature and pertinence, became remote and shadowy.

But Mrs. Fields never entered this strange twilight. She rounded out her period, from Dickens and Thackeray and Tennyson, through Hardy and Meredith to the Great War, with her standards unshaken. For her there was no revaluation. She died with her world (the world of "letters" which mattered most to her) unchallenged. Marcel Proust somewhere said that when he came to die he would take all his great men with him: since his Beethoven and his Wagner could never be at all the same to anyone else, they would go with him like the captives who were slain at the funeral pyres of Eastern potentates. It was thus Mrs. Fields died, in that house of memories, with the material keepsakes of the past about her.

III

POST–CIVIL WAR BOSTON

In 1838 Henry Adams was born "under the shadow of Boston State House," as he put it in the opening sentence of *The Education of Henry Adams* (1918), in a "little passage called Hancock Avenue" that rose from Beacon Street to Mount Vernon Street, near the summit of Beacon Hill. Thus, in two centuries had Boston been symbolically transformed from John Winthrop's city upon a hill, shining with promise, to Henry Adams's "little passage," shadowed by doubt. Adams, descendant of two presidents, came of age burdened by the city's long historical shadow and the Boston Brahmin clan's great expectations of noble public service, particularly for his exalted family, in an era when the city's political power was shifting into the hands of Irish immigrants. All of which ill prepared him for "starting a twentieth-century career from a nest of associations so colonial,—so troglodytic—as the First Church, the Boston State House, Beacon Hill, John Hancock and John Adams, Mount Vernon and Quincy, all crowding on ten pounds of unconscious babyhood." The modest hill on which he was born is the remaining remnant of three steep hills—Trimountain included Beacon Hill, Mount Vernon, and Pemberton Hill—two of which were cut down, leaving one, which was pared back to provide landfill and space for real estate development; also, the symbolic beacon that long stood atop the hill had been removed before Adams's birth. In Adams's parable of decline and fall, old Boston was on the make for the new, eager to toss its noble memories and founders' standards "into an ash-heap."[1]

In Adams's memorable myth of diminished person and place, Boston had dealt him a fortunate hand, but he was reluctant to play its crass game. Though educated in the matchless Adams library at his grandfather's Quincy home, at Boston Latin School, Harvard College, and the University of Berlin, Adams felt himself miseducated, unprepared to assume a role in the mercantile, expansionist era of the Gilded Age. His great-grandfather, John, had helped win the Revolution and had served as the new nation's second president. His grandfather, John Quincy, had helped shape the nation in his role as its sixth president and still ruled as the family patriarch at the Adams Quincy demesne. His father, Charles Francis, wrote for *North American Review*, served in the House of Representatives and as Ambassador to the Court of St. James during the Civil War. However, Henry became, as he insists in *Education*, an observer, a historian, a detached, spectatorial eye.

Adams found a redeeming alternative to constricted, cold Boston in spacious, sunny Quincy, at the Adams family dwelling and in its fields, where he spent his summers. "Town was restraint, law, unity. Country, only seven miles away, was liberty, diversity, outlawry, the endless delight of mere sense impressions given by nature for nothing, and breathed by boys without knowing it." Boston winters and Quincy summers contended in his character and represented a symbolic dialectic, so "the Bostonian could not help but develop a double nature. Life was a double thing."[2]

Adams's Boston was also a divided thing, particularly since the incoming flood of Irish Catholic immigration, following Ireland's Great Famine of the late 1840s, drove many Brahmin families away from the harbor, to the high ground of Beacon Hill, briefly to the grand townhouses of the South End, then to the "new land" of Back Bay, or to village havens outside the city; this immigrant influx and migratory movement led to Yankee-Celt tensions that defined the city for the next century. Boston's first families grew nostalgic for a lost era of wholeness, harmony, and radiance, the world of Anglo-Saxon Protestant dominance that had prevailed for two centuries. Early in the nineteenth century, in Nathaniel Hawthorne's youth, as Henry James strikingly describes it, "the tide of foreign immigration had scarcely begun to break upon the rural strongholds of the New England race; it had at most begun to splash them with the salt Hibernian spray."[3] In Adams's youth, long-established Bostonians felt the ominous Irish tide rising around them.

Adams was both drawn to and repelled by loyalties to his class, but his enduring sympathies remained with his own kind. Brahmin Boston, as he saw it, presumed that it had "solved the universe." Though Adams was not content with its solutions, he could not imagine that any other group might offer better answers. In a revealing passage from *Education*, Adams recalls a schoolboy snowball fight on Boston Common in 1850 as an illustrative example of the city's class and ethnic warfare and a foreshadowing of its future divisions and violence. On a winter afternoon his Latin School lads contended with West End intruders. At first they held off these sons of Irish immigrants, but as the day grew darker the battle shifted when Adams and his classmates were attacked by snowballs packed with stones. They were driven back to the Beacon Street Mall by "a swarm of blackguards from the slums, led by a grisly terror called Conky Daniels," who, "with a club and a hideous reputation, was going to put an end to the Beacon Hill crowd forever." This threat of class annihilation was rebuffed by the bravery of two classmates, Savage and Marvin, who turned back Daniels's rowdy crowd and saved the day for the boy Brahmins. The "obvious moral" Adams drew was "that blackguards were not so black as they were painted." A decade later Savage and Marvin were killed in the Civil War, leading Adams to speculate that they may have discovered their bravery and capacity for sacrifice in that boyhood fight on Boston Common.[4] However, Adams had nothing to say about the fate of Conky Daniels and his Irish gang, who also had been trained for courage, sacrifice, and death in battle. Many like them served valiantly in the 28th Massachusetts Volunteer Infantry, "The Irish Brigade." On Boston Common the representative young men from *both* tribes learned to battle each other in Boston before they joined the Union armies to fight the Confederacy. Adams saw Boston as a double thing, but he was sympathetic only to one side of its contending forces.

In his self-regarding and self-ironic memoir, Adams articulated his ambivalent sense of Boston as a city in conflict with itself: at once the inspiring center of culture, the museum of abandoned national ideals, and the betrayer of its own values. Adams determined "to prevent [himself] from becoming what of all things [he] despised, a Boston prig. . . . Anything which takes a man morally out of Beacon Street, Nahant and Beverly Farms, Harvard College and the Boston press, must be in itself a good."[5] In such critical reflections on the city of his birth, Adams joined a chorus of voices: writers and thinkers of his generation, most of them born elsewhere, who were drawn by Boston's cultural promises and thrived in its supportive society, but who then were repelled by its repressive propriety, and finally, like Adams, left the city for brighter prospects beyond this city. Mark Twain, born in Missouri three years before Adams; William Dean Howells, born in Ohio a year before Adams; and Henry James, born in New York City five years after Adams—each of these ambitious writers assumed the role of the young man from the provinces; each came to Boston, the Athens of America, to ascend its Acropolis and take his place amid its Parthenon of writers. Each, in the end, found his true home elsewhere. Adams moved to Washington, D.C., Twain settled in Hartford, Howells in Manhattan, and James in Rye, becoming an English citizen. Boston, once their destination of choice, eventually became a way-station on their journeys of discovery.

Mark Twain made his first Boston appearance as a public speaker, alongside George Washington Cable ("twins of genius"), on November 13, 1884, at the Music Hall. In the audience was his friend, *Atlantic Monthly* editor William Dean Howells, who later wrote to praise Twain's performance: "You simply straddled down to the footlights and took that house up in the hollow of your hand and *tickled* it."[6] Yet, despite Howells's reassurance, Twain was apprehensive while speaking before a Boston audience of "4,000 critics."[7] Boston did not tickle Twain's fancy, as is clear from a "Letter" he published five years later, "A First Visit to Boston," in San Francisco's *Alta California*. Twain mocked Boston's twisting streets, originally cow-paths, as well as its citizens, as "crooked." Yet, he quickly adapted to Boston's circuitous, if quaint charms. "The hard, straight, unrelenting lines one is used to in other cities, give way, in Boston, to graceful curves that go sweeping in and out in a pleasant and undulating way that impels a man to assume a luxurious waltz-step in place of the driving, forward-march movement he has learned in unswerving and unbending Broadway." Waltzing through winding, crooked Boston, Twain satirized the city's provincialism and its pride in "antiquities," particularly its exaggerated veneration of events, emblems, and figures from its over-celebrated past. He dismissed the importance of the Boston massacre ("who cares?"), the Old South Church, and Benjamin Franklin, whom Twain presumed to criticize because Franklin broke the Sabbath by flying his kite on Sundays! As for Boston's famed Tea Party, Twain thought tea "a poor insipid beverage," and went on to say, "it is a pity the Indians could not have lived forever to indulge their fancy for emptying it into the sea." He was intrigued to learn that the Battle of Bunker Hill was actually fought on *another* hill, thus, he suggested, sparing this celebrated site from carnage. He mockingly praised the view from atop the Bunker Hill Monument, but added that he never actually climbed up to see the city from its heights. Twain found Boston's citizens affable, but he could not persuade an Irishman to give him directions because "he was a distillery in disguise." The message of Twain's "Letter," then, was that Boston is a city of marginal curiosity with an inflated sense of its own importance and a newly arrived immigrant class whose spokesperson fulfills Twain's cultural stereotype of the drunken Irishman, though perhaps a more benign example than Huck Finn's Pap.[8]

At Howells's urging, Twain wrote a lyrical memoir of his youth, "Old Times on the Mississippi," which was serialized in seven issues of *Atlantic Monthly* in 1875, a work which gave Twain standing in literary Boston and allowed Howells to incorporate the vigorous vernacular of Twain's frontier voice into the staid diction of the magazine, though Twain told Howells that he felt like an imposter as a contributor to *Atlantic Monthly*. "Don't write *at* any supposed *Atlantic* audience," Howells reassured Twain, "but yarn it off as if into my sympathetic ear."[9] Howells and Twain became life-long friends who could yarn it off to each other in the loose, expansive manner of fellow westerners. They inspired each other to behave in Boston with playful impropriety, as in 1875, when Twain came up from Hartford to travel with Howells from Cambridge to Concord so that they might attend centennial celebrations of the American Revolution. Enjoying each other's company, they never arrived in Concord, though they concocted a story that they had, a tall tale which failed to persuade their unamused wives. Polite Howells took pleasure when playful Twain gave him license to become prankish in proper Boston. Twain, the loose-mannered westerner, found delight in mocking tight-mannered Bostonians, famously extending his japery to the changeable New England weather in an 1876 essay. "The people of New England are by nature patient and forbearing; but there are some things which they will not stand. Every year they kill a lot of poets for writing about 'Beautiful Spring.'"[10] The next year Twain would learn more about the patience of Bostonians and feel himself like one of those poets who risk their lives by misrepresenting the region's beliefs.

When Twain's behavior or words overstepped Boston's boundaries, Howells, who had worked so hard for acceptance in Boston, was embarrassed. At the celebratory dinner for John Greenleaf Whittier's seventieth birthday, held on December 17, 1877, at the Brunswick Hotel, a large gathering of *Atlantic Monthly* and Greater Boston worthies dined sumptuously (seven courses) and listened to tributes from literary luminaries. The last leaves of the mid-century flowering of writers from the Boston-Cambridge-Concord center of the American renaissance were represented by Ralph Waldo Emerson, who recited Whittier's "Ichabod" (1850); by Oliver Wendell Holmes, who read a poem written for the occasion; and by Charles Eliot Norton— considered the most cultivated man in America, Norton was a professor of art history at Harvard—who offered a toast. The Greater Boston literary community honored Whittier, the fabled "wood-thrush of Essex," and, in turn, celebrated itself. Howells, the evening's toastmaster, flattered the assembly by calling them "all naturalized Bostonians in the finest and highest sense." Then he introduced Twain and the evening turned sour.[11] Twain offered a fabulation in which three tramps, named Emerson, Longfellow, and Holmes, bamboozle an old western miner out of his liquor and boots! While he was yarning off his tall tale, Twain felt chilled by the audience's silence; they "seemed turned to stone with horror" at the insults directed at the three Boston literary icons, all present and apparently puzzled.[12] Actually, Twain's talk—delivered late in the evening to a food-and-speech-sated audience in a large, noisy hall—confused more than it offended. Emerson, age seventy-four, did not get it, perhaps did not even hear much of it; Longfellow, age seventy, and Holmes, age sixty-eight, brushed it off as a characteristic example of Twain's broad humor, but Howells, age forty, felt humiliated. From his perspective, Twain, at his invitation, had mocked the venerable figures of Boston letters, proving that neither man could ever wholly become a naturalized Bostonian. That speech haunted both men for the rest of their lives. They long felt or imagined the shadows of judgmental Boston upon them. Twain seldom returned, and Howells began to look for a way out of the city that had taken him in.

William Dean Howells first came to the city upon a hill in 1860 when he was twenty-three, a wide-eyed, ambitious pilgrim from Ohio who sought recognition, indeed sought sanctification, from Greater Boston's literary luminaries. This intensely bookish, largely self-taught son of a frontier printer became "the passionate pilgrim from the West [who] approached his holy land at Boston." This was his Mecca and he was a pilgrim who then believed, as he later recalled, that "there is no question but our literary centre was then in Boston."[13]

In Concord he met his hero, Hawthorne, who led the young man up a hill behind the Wayside, the Hawthorne home, where the romancer sat on a log, smoked a cigar, and talked with his disciple about the American West, which Hawthorne believed was embodied in Howells. For Hawthorne the West was the nation's energetic future and Boston was paralyzed in the past, while for Howells the West was a blank landscape from which to escape and Boston was the cultured center of America. So Hawthorne and Howells talked warmly, but at cross purposes, revealing their differing senses of place. Hawthorne also warned Howells that New Englanders possessed a cold character. After finding Howells "worthy," Hawthorne sent him on with a note of endorsement to a brief visit with the chilly Thoreau and a longer visit with august Emerson at his great manse on the Lexington Road, where Howells learned that the Sage of Concord did not admire the tales and romances of Hawthorne, which Howells revered. Thus did Howells receive quick confirmation of Hawthorne's assessment of the sternness and quirkiness of the New England character. In time he would recoil from Boston's Calvinism, chauvinism, and class superiority, but as a young man fresh from America's remote provinces, Howells was eager to emulate his Boston betters. "Boston is my destiny, so far as I can shape it," he wrote to Boston's premier cultural hostess, Annie Fields, in 1866, when he joined *Atlantic Monthly* as an editor.[14]

During his first visit, Howells found his dreams of Boston's literary majesty fulfilled when he met the grand figures whose *Atlantic Monthly* writings he had read in Ohio, as he recalled forty years later in *Literary Friends and Acquaintances* (1900). He met James Russell Lowell, famed satirist, memorialist, and the first editor of the *Atlantic Monthly*, at Elmwood, Lowell's grand Cambridge estate, overlooking the Charles River. Lowell invited Howells to what became a legendary luncheon at Boston's Parker House, site of the memorable mid-century Saturday Club gatherings, which included Emerson, Longfellow, Hawthorne, and Whittier. "What famous names its record boasts," proclaimed Howells, noting the Parker House's days of glory and recalling his sense that his Boston visit had released him from his frontier "exile." At Howells's 1860 luncheon, Lowell was present, along with Oliver Wendell Holmes, the esteemed "Autocrat of the Breakfast Table" and Dean of the Harvard Medical School. James T. Fields, Hawthorne's publisher, *Atlantic Monthly* owner and future editor, joined the party. It was on this occasion that Holmes both endowed and burdened Howells with a Boston Brahmin mission by jokingly, yet shrewdly, remarking to Lowell that they had found in this likely lad a devoted disciple: "this is something like the apostolic succession . . . the laying on of hands."[15] Thus was Howells ceremonially initiated into the celebratory priesthood in Boston's temple of high culture.

Eventually, Howells became editor of *Atlantic Monthly*, a worthy successor to the Bostonians who made the city America's literary center. As editor,

Howells was an innovator who opened the pages of the journal to new, younger voices from the far provinces—for example, to Sarah Orne Jewett, from Maine. Howells fostered democracy and realism in the pages of *Atlantic Monthly*. He published brilliant works by both Henry James and Mark Twain, though there is little evidence that James took much interest in Twain's writings and Twain told Howells that "I would rather be damned to John Bunyan's heaven than finish reading *The Bostonians*."[16] However, late in their lives, James recalled he found "sublimity" in reading Twain's *Life on the Mississippi*, and Twain acknowledged James as a "master."[17] Howells occupied the vital center between these radically dissimilar American geniuses; Boston and *Atlantic Monthly* constituted their common ground.

Most important, Howells added to Boston's library of literary treasures through his fiction and criticism. In a series of novels, particularly in *The Rise of Silas Lapham* (1885), and in his essays and reminiscences, Howells came to terms with the romantic, idealized Boston of his youthful imagination and reshaped it into the qualified vision and plain language of literary realism. His "Boston" was not circumscribed by the city's actual boundaries but was defined by the map of his imagination, so it included Cambridge, where he and his wife established a home for seven years, and Concord, where his literary heroes lived and wrote. When he explored beyond these boundaries, he felt as though he entered a foreign country, as he noted in *Suburban Sketches* (1872), after he toured "Dublin," a then remote region of North Cambridge on the Somerville line, where the Irish had settled to labor in the brickworks. Howells loved high-table literary talks with notable Cambridge literary figures: James Russell Lowell, Charles Eliot Norton, and Henry Wadsworth Longfellow. When Howells walked back to his North Cambridge home after a heady evening at Craigie House, where he had heard Longfellow read from his translation of Dante, "the richest moment of my life," this young man from the provinces felt himself among the elect, "in the Elysian fields with an agreeable eternity before me," though he would come to reject this landscape, as his imagery hints, of the living dead.[18]

When he came to write *The Rise of Silas Lapham* in the mid-1880s, Howells's views of Boston had grown complex and ambivalent. The novel portrays an outsider, Silas Lapham, a paint manufacturer who decides to build a splendid house in the Back Bay, a land-fill development undertaken after the Civil War to extend the boundaries of Boston and the reach of its best families, who had long since filled Beacon Hill and needed additional gracious living space because the South End, their first enclave of privilege beyond Beacon Hill, was being invaded by impoverished and unmannerly immigrants. Back Bay's broad boulevards, designed on a Parisian model, attracted gentry and social climbers to the "new land," contiguous with Beacon Hill, alongside the Charles River. Howells built and lived in just such a fine house on the water side of Beacon Street, but conflicted Lapham, lacking Howells's abilities to blend in with Boston's betters, to speak the adopted language of privilege as well as his native country vernacular, accidentally, perhaps half-intentionally, burned his own house to the ground and thus destroyed his dreams of social ascent.

Howells was able to incorporate a double perspective into *The Rise of Silas Lapham*, seeing the city both from the anxious angle of the Corey family, Beacon Hill Brahmins who were wary of upstart intruders crowding into their sanctuary, and through the envious eyes of the Lapham family, new-moneyed arrivals who were ambitious for status and acceptance. However, in Howells's cautionary tale, Silas Lapham lacked the culture and polish necessary to allow him to pass through the invisible yet impermeable class barrier, though one of his daughters makes the transit, at some cost, by marrying a Corey, though the couple then decide to abandon Boston. After the fire, Lapham's business fails, and he has to move to Lumberville, Vermont, back to the provinces from which he came. This novel illustrates the proposition best articulated by Howells's friend Twain, a fellow outsider in Boston's closed community: "Overreaching Don't Pay."[19]

In the opening pages of *The Rise of Silas Lapham*, the paint manufacturer is interviewed by Bartley Hubbard, an ambitious and unprincipled journalist who has left Equity, Maine, driven by the dream of success in Boston. In an earlier novel, *A Modern Instance* (1882), Howells portrayed Hubbard as a rake who, a few years after his encounter with Lapham, overreaches and comes to ruin in Boston. Thus, two decades after he first arrived, Howells composed fictional parables which portrayed Boston as a city of destruction for these formerly good country people who were drawn by its bright lights and false promises. During the interview for his newspaper's "Solid Men of Boston" series, Bartley joshes with Silas that he wants "your money or your life," and Lapham jokes in reply, "so you want my life, death and Christian sufferings, do you, young man?"[20] This exchange illustrates the moral underpinnings of Howells's realistic novel of manners. Bartley, Howells suggests, is willing to trade his soul for success in Boston, but Silas refuses to sell out.

Either way, both outlanders are destroyed in the city. In the end, all social-climbing ambitions lost, Silas Lapham realizes it is better to go home again than futilely to batter against Boston's class barriers, but Howells, far more adaptable than his up-country and down-east characters who sought success but failed to find it in the hub of the solar system, used the income generated from sale of this novel to pay for his own Back Bay, Beacon Street house, a fitting gesture of triumph for this once "passionate pilgrim" to the heavenly city of Boston.

By the time Howells wrote *The Rise of Silas Lapham* he had come to see his literary pilgrimage as a spiritual journey of discovery, and he was gradually deciding that Boston was not the final destination in his quest. In 1881 he resigned his editorship of *Atlantic Monthly* to turn his attention to full-time writing. The works of fiction he published in the 1880s illustrate his increasing disenchantment with Boston, where he felt constrained by its history and propriety. Eventually, Howells moved to Manhattan, where, revitalized by the shock of the new, he wrote his best realistic fiction, particularly *A Hazard of New Fortunes* (1890). There, he mentored young naturalists like Stephen Crane and Theodore Dreiser. He contributed to *Harper's*, the magazine that was fast overtaking the circulation and cultural ascendancy of *Atlantic Monthly*. In moving from Boston to New York City, it has been argued by devoted New Yorker Alfred Kazin, Howells took the nation's literary center with him.[21] That granted, a saving remnant of literary achievement remained in Boston, and Howells carried the visions and values of the city in his head for the rest of his life.

Boston was a very heaven to Howells when, as a young sub-editor at *Atlantic Monthly*, he took long walks along Cambridge country lanes to Fresh Pond accompanied by Henry James. Howells could see that James, seven years younger, was at the brink of a great literary career. Howells greatly assisted that career by publishing James's stories and by serializing several of his novels in his journal. James would later acknowledge this in a letter of tribute he wrote for Howells's seventy-fifth birthday. "You held out your open editorial hand to me at the time I began to write—and I allude especially to the summer of 1866—with a frankness and sweetness of hospitality that was really the making of me. . . . You showed me the way and opened me the door."[22] Yet, despite such occasions of literary fellowship, James never felt at home in Greater Boston, where his peripatetic family settled in 1860, eventually in a Cambridge house on Quincy Street, the present site of the Harvard Faculty Club. The local literary-cultural community did shape his consciousness, as he grants in his tribute to Howells, for there "we knew together what American life *was*—or thought we did, deluded though we may have been."[23] However, James was neither enthralled nor burdened by Boston's fabled history and daunting manners, as was Howells—and as had been Hawthorne, who inspired both young novelists—so James, who had spent many boyhood years in European cities, never took the Boston Brahmins' claims to cultural eminence seriously. Boston, for James, was always small and insular, a provincial outpost compared with Europe's grand cultural centers. While Howells was arriving *at* Boston, his destination, James was passing *through* Boston, moving toward what he would call his "siege" of Paris and London.

In *Hawthorne* (1879), a monograph written for the British audience he was courting, James describes Hawthorne's America as a presence of absence, a place of empty spaces, a cultural desert which challenged the artistic imagination. Contemplating Boston from his "initiated" European perspective, he described the literary gatherings of Elizabeth Peabody, Hawthorne's sister-in-law, as "the lonely frigidity which characterized most attempts at social recreation in the New England world some forty years ago." Yet James grants a saving grace: "the best of it was that the thing was absolutely American; it belonged to the soil, to the air; it came out of the very heart of New England."[24]

James made his separate peace with Boston before he turned forty, but he would return at key moments, and he would remember Boston more fondly near the end of his life. In Boston's Brunswick Hotel in late 1881, four years after the infamous Whittier dinner was held there, James declared his life's mission in a notebook entry. "My choice is the old world—my choice, my need, my life."[25] His first step toward realizing this choice, this mission to realize his talents in ways provincial Hawthorne or Howells never could, was to leave Boston behind. Indeed, his 1881 stay in Boston, never his home ground, made James homesick for England.

Boston would serve James as a subject of satire. In *The Europeans* (1878) he portrayed new arrivals from Europe looking down upon the crowded, dirty city from a Parker House hotel room window during a spring snowstorm. They contemplate "a narrow grave-yard in the heart of a bustling, indifferent city." Battered by sleet, "an assemblage of Bostonians were trampling about in the liquid snow. Many of them were looking up and down; they appeared to be waiting for something."[26] Whatever these sleet-buffeted pedestrians or James's contemplating characters were waiting for, they would not find it in Boston.

In *The Bostonians* (1886) James issues his sharpest satire on Boston-Cambridge culture. Indeed, he planned the novel as "a remorseless exploitation of Boston."[27] The novel takes on Boston's tradition of high-principled ideologues, in this instance its militant feminists, personified in the figure of straight-backed, stern, first-family Olive Chancellor, who righteously judges the city from her townhouse on Beacon Hill. Olive is portrayed largely through the quizzical, reactionary gaze of Basil Ransom, a Confederate veteran and lawyer who has come to seek his fortune, by any means necessary, in Boston. Ransom, on the make, even briefly considers marriage to rich Olive, but quickly realizes she is "unmarried by every implication of her being." Thus does James introduce the theme of the "Boston marriage," examining locally sanctioned bonds between women, a topic discussed in chapter 2.[28] For James, feminism and chaste lesbianism offered revealing material for a parable of place: "The whole thing [must be] as local, as American, as possible, and as full of Boston: an attempt to show that I can write an American story."[29] Here James equates Boston with America.

James is particularly hard in *The Bostonians* on a revered figure in Olive's circle of reformers, Miss Birdseye, a disheveled and dithery survivor of Boston's prewar glory days when the city led America in the abolitionist and feminist movements. Miss Birdseye was conceived as a parody of Elizabeth Peabody, the noted reformer and advocate of many noble causes, who still could be seen on Boston's streets in search of injustices. "She was heroic, she was sublime, the whole moral history of Boston was reflected in her displaced spectacles," wrote James of Miss Birdseye.[30] William James, reading early installments of the novel in *Century Magazine*, thought this caricature of Elizabeth Peabody a "bad business" and wrote to his brother in London to say that he and other prominent Bostonians were offended. Henry James was surprised that Bostonians who had applauded Howells for writing *Silas Lapham* would now fault him. "The 'Bostonians' is sugar-cake, compared with it."[31] Still, James bent to the will of Boston's criticism, or perhaps modified his thinking, when he granted Miss Birdseye heroic stature late in the novel as she dies, describing her as "a battered, immemorial monument" to the lost "heroic age of New England life."[32] Southerner Basil Ransom grows more willfully selfish, Bostonian Olive Chancellor becomes more nobly self-sacrificial, and the novel moves toward qualified tribute to Boston as a city which still preserves a saving remnant of its idealistic Puritan past. *The Bostonians* opens in mockery, but concludes in tentative reconciliation, finding some good in its old ways and much to reject in its ambitious, manipulative newcomers.

When James returned after an absence of twenty years, in 1904, not everything had changed in Boston, as he found it had in New York City. Climbing to the peak of Beacon Hill, he was pleased to find that in Ashburton Place "the pair of ancient houses" where he had lived in the mid-1860s still stood. There he had initiated his dedication to the art of fiction; there he had learned of the deaths of Hawthorne in 1864 and Lincoln in 1865, revered figures who taught him what it meant to be an American. The still-standing houses became his emblem of precious perseverance, "the history of something as against the history of nothing." James was gathering material for *The American Scene* (1907), a meditation on a nation vastly transformed since his youth, so he was reassured when he found that a symbol of old Boston had endured. He traveled for a month, but then made a "justly-rebuked mistake" and returned for a second look at Boston, where, to his shock, he saw that the two ancient houses *had* suddenly been leveled to make way for new Beacon Hill construction. James's "small homogeneous Boston" disappeared in a flash. Boston, he concluded, was off with the beloved old and on with the vulgar new: poor immigrants speaking foreign languages, new-moneyed social climbers, new "tall buildings."

> Boston, the bigger, braver, louder Boston, was "away," and it was quite, at that hour, as if each figure in my procession were there on purpose to leave me no doubt of it. Therefore had I the vision, as filling the sky, no longer of the great Puritan "whip," the whip for the conscience and the nerves, of the local legend, but that of a huge applied sponge, a sponge saturated with the foreign mixture and passed over almost everything I remembered and might still have recovered.[33]

James took refuge from modern Boston in the art-filled sanctuary of Isabella Stewart Gardner's newly opened, anachronistic, Venetian palazzo in Boston's Fens. Only there, amid her European art collection—much of it chosen by art historian Bernard Berenson, who immigrated to Boston as a boy and was educated at Boston Latin School—could James, paradoxically, sense something of his old, lost Boston. Mrs. Jack Gardner was an outsider, a Stewart from New York, who became an insider in Boston's cultural landscape; as Douglass Shand-Tucci notes in his biography, her gallery-home served as a meeting place for Bohemian and Brahmin Boston.[34] James, the former Boston-Cambridge insider who chose English exile, found a haven from the new, alienating Boston in her cultured company and in her art-filled Fenway Court, in which guests could look out from long windows and balconies not at Boston's teeming streets but onto an enclosed garden. Boston was never James's home, though the city had provided him with a nurturing culture, a lifelong friend and supporter in Howells, a journal in which to publish, and a subject for his satire, but it had not held fast against the destructive rush of the new. For James Boston was "away," and so was he.

For these writers Boston was transformed in their lifetimes from the midsummer flowering of the American renaissance to the autumnal decline of literary energies, even to an early winter of irrelevance. For Henry Adams Boston was shadowy, stiff, antiquated; for Mark Twain the city was stuffy and censorious; for William Dean Howells the city turned from sanctified to stifling; for Henry James Boston went from a provincial preserve to just another American commercial city with no respect for its storied past or its former values. Yet, for these writers, Boston served as a literary center of consciousness, a hub of publication, a subject worthy of literary consideration, and a defining, if transient period in their lives.

SELECTIONS

Henry Adams, from *The Education of Henry Adams* (1918)

Henry Adams (1838–1918), historian and novelist, descended from one of Boston's and the nation's most prominent families. His autobiography, *The Education of Henry Adams*, appeared in a limited edition in 1906. After several revisions it was published in a trade edition in 1918, after Adams's death. Here Adams writes of his Boston heritage, which he sees as poor preparation for life in the twentieth century.

Under the shadow of Boston State House, turning its back on the house of John Hancock, the little passage called Hancock Avenue runs, or ran, from Beacon Street, skirting the State House grounds, to Mount Vernon Street, on the summit of Beacon Hill; and there, in the third house below Mount Vernon Place, February 16, 1838, a child was born, and christened later by his uncle, the minister of the First Church after the tenets of Boston Unitarianism, as Henry Brooks Adams.

Had he been born in Jerusalem under the shadow of the Temple and circumcised in the Synagogue by his uncle the high priest, under the name of Israel Cohen, he would scarcely have been more distinctly branded, and not much more heavily handicapped in the races of the coming century, in running for such stakes as the century was to offer; but, on the other hand, the ordinary traveler, who does not enter the field of racing, finds advantage in being, so to speak, ticketed through life, with the safeguards of an old, established traffic. Safeguards are often irksome, but sometimes convenient, and if one needs them at all, one is apt to need them badly. A hundred years earlier, such safeguards as his would have secured any young man's success; and although in 1838 their value was not very great compared with what they would have had in 1738, yet the mere accident of starting a twentieth-century career from a nest of associations so colonial—so troglodytic—as the First Church, the Boston State House, Beacon Hill, John Hancock and John Adams, Mount Vernon Street and Quincy, all crowding on ten pounds of unconscious babyhood, was so queer as to offer a subject of curious speculation to the baby long after he had witnessed the solution. What could become of such a child of the seventeenth and eighteenth centuries, when he should wake up to find himself required to play the game of the twentieth?

Had he been consulted, would he have cared to play the game at all, holding such cards as he held, and suspecting that the game was to be one of which neither he nor any one else back to the beginning of time knew the rules or the risks or the stakes? He was not consulted and was not responsible, but had he been taken into the confidence of his parents, he would certainly have told them to change nothing as far as concerned him. He would have been astounded by his own luck. Probably no child, born in the year, held better cards than he. Whether life was an honest game of chance, or whether the cards were marked and forced, he could not refuse to play his excellent hand. He could never make the usual plea of irresponsibility. He accepted the situation as though he had been a party to it, and under the same circumstances would do it again, the more readily for knowing the exact values. To his life as a whole he was a consenting, contracting party and partner from the moment he was born to the moment he died. Only with that understanding—as a consciously assenting member in full partnership with the society of his age—had his education an interest to himself or to others . . .

The atmosphere of education in which he lived was colonial, revolutionary, almost Cromwellian, as though he were steeped, from his greatest grandmother's birth, in the odor of political crime. Resistance to something was the law of New England nature; the boy looked out on the world with the instinct of resistance; for numberless generations his predecessors had viewed the world chiefly as a thing to be reformed, filled with evil forces to be abolished, and they saw no reason to suppose that they had wholly succeeded in the abolition; the duty was unchanged. That duty implied not only resistance to evil, but hatred of it. Boys naturally look on all force as an enemy, and generally find it so, but the New Englander, whether boy or man, in his long struggle with a stingy or hostile universe, had learned also to love the pleasure of hating; his joys were few.

Politics, as a practice, whatever its professions, had always been the systematic organization of hatreds, and Massachusetts politics had been as harsh as the climate. The chief charm of New England was harshness of contrasts and extremes of sensibility—a cold that froze the blood, and a heat that boiled it—so that the pleasure of hating—one's self if no better victim offered—was not its rarest amusement; but the charm was a true and natural child of the soil, not a cultivated weed of the ancients. The violence of the contrast was real and made the strongest motive of education. The double exterior nature gave life its relative values. Winter and summer, cold and heat, town and country, force and freedom, marked two modes of life and thought, balanced like lobes of the brain. Town was winter confinement, school, rule, discipline; straight, gloomy streets, piled with six feet of snow in the middle; frosts that made the snow sing under wheels or runners; thaws when the streets became dangerous to cross; society of uncles, aunts, and cousins who expected children to behave themselves, and who were not always gratified; above all else, winter represented the desire to escape and go free. Town was restraint, law, unity. Country, only seven miles away, was liberty, diversity, outlawry, the endless delight of mere sense impressions given by nature for nothing, and breathed by boys without knowing it.

Boys are wild animals, rich in the treasures of sense, but the New England boy had a wider range of emotions than boys of more equable climates. He felt his nature crudely, as it was meant. To the boy Henry Adams, summer was drunken. Among senses, smell was the strongest—smell of hot pine-woods and sweet-fern in the scorching summer noon; of new-mown hay; of ploughed earth; of box hedges; of peaches, lilacs, seringas; of stables, barns, cow-yards; of salt water and low tide on the marshes; nothing came amiss. Next to smell came taste, and the children knew the taste of everything they saw or touched, from pennyroyal and flagroot to the shell of a pignut and the letters of a spelling-book:—the taste of A-B, AB, suddenly revived on the boy's tongue sixty years afterwards. Light, line, and color as sensual pleasures, came later and were as crude as the rest. The New England light is glare, and the atmosphere harshens color. The boy was a full man before he ever knew what was meant by atmosphere; his idea of pleasure in light was the blaze of a New England sun. His idea of color was a peony, with the dew of early morning on its petals. The intense blue of the sea, as he saw it a mile or two away, from the Quincy hills; the cumuli in a June afternoon sky; the strong reds and greens and purples of colored prints and children's picture-books, as the American colors then ran; these were ideals. The opposites or antipathies, were the cold grays of November evenings, and the thick, muddy thaws of Boston winter. With such standards, the Bostonian could not but develop a double nature. Life was a double thing. After a January blizzard, the boy who could look with pleasure into the violent snow-glare of the cold white sunshine, with its intense light and shade, scarcely knew what was meant by tone. He could reach it only by education.

Winter and summer, then, were two hostile lives, and bred two separate natures. Winter was always the effort to live; summer was tropical license. Whether the children rolled in the grass, or waded in the brook, or swam in the salt ocean, or sailed in the bay, or fished for smelts in the creeks, or netted minnows in the salt-marshes, or took to the pine-woods and the granite quarries, or chased muskrats and hunted snapping-turtles in the swamps, or mushrooms or nuts on the autumn hills, summer and country were always sensual living, while winter was always compulsory learning. Summer was the multiplicity of nature; winter was school.

The bearing of the two seasons on the education of Henry Adams was no fancy; it was the most decisive force he ever knew; it ran though life, and made the division between its perplexing, warring, irreconcilable problems, irreducible opposites, with growing emphasis to the last year of study. From earliest childhood the boy was accustomed to feel that, for him, life was double. Winter and summer, town and country, law and liberty, were hostile, and the man who pretended they were not, was in his eyes a schoolmaster—that is, a man employed to tell lies to little boys. Though Quincy was but two hours' walk from Beacon Hill, it belonged in a different world. For two hundred years, every Adams, from father to son, had lived within sight of State Street, and sometimes had lived in it, yet none had ever taken kindly to the town, or been taken kindly by it. The boy inherited his double nature. He knew as yet nothing about his great-grandfather, who had died a dozen years before his own birth: he took for granted that any great-grandfather of his must have always been good, and his enemies wicked; but he divined his great-grandfather's character from his own. Never for a moment did he connect the two ideas of Boston and John Adams; they were separate and antagonistic; the idea of John Adams went with Quincy. He knew his grandfather John Quincy Adams only as an old man of seventy-five or eighty who was friendly and gentle with him, but except that he heard his grandfather always called "the President," and his grandmother "the Madam," he had no reason to suppose that his Adams grandfather differed in character from his Brooks grandfather who was equally kind and benevolent. He liked the Adams side best, but for no other reason than that it reminded him of the country, the summer, and the absence of restraint. Yet he felt also that Quincy was in a way inferior to Boston, and that socially Boston looked down on Quincy. The reason was clear enough even to a five-year old child. Quincy had no Boston style. Little enough style had either; a simpler manner of life and thought could hardly exist, short of cave-dwelling. The flint-and-steel with which his grandfather Adams used to light his own fires in the early morning was still on the mantelpiece of his study. The idea of a livery or even a dress for servants, or of an evening toilette, was next to blasphemy. Bathrooms, water-supplies, lighting, heating, and the whole array of domestic comforts, were unknown at Quincy. Boston had already a bathroom, a water-supply, a furnace, and gas. The superiority of Boston was evident, but a child liked it no better for that. . . .

Thus already, at ten years old, the boy found himself standing face to face with a dilemma that might have puzzled an early Christian. What was he?—where was he going? Even then he felt that something was wrong, but he concluded that it must be Boston. Quincy had always been right, for Quincy represented a moral principle,—the principle of resistance to Boston. His Adams ancestors must have been right, since they were always hostile to State Street. If State Street was wrong, Quincy must be right! Turn the dilemma as he pleased, he still came back on the eighteenth century and the law of Resistance; of Truth; of Duty, and of Freedom. He was a ten-year-old priest and politician. He could under no circumstances have guessed what the next fifty years had in store, and no one could teach him; but sometimes, in his old age, he wondered—and could never decide—whether the most clear and certain knowledge would have helped him. Supposing he had seen a New York stock-list of 1900, and had studied the statistics of railways, telegraphs, coal, and steel—would he have quitted his eighteenth-century, his ancestral prejudices, his abstract ideals, his semi-clerical training, and the rest, in order to perform an expiatory pilgrimage to State Street, and ask for the fatted calf of his grandfather Brooks and a clerkship in the Suffolk Bank?

Sixty years afterwards he was still unable to make up his mind. Each course had its advantages, but the material advantages, looking back, seemed to lie wholly in State Street. . . .

Except for politics, Mount Vernon Street had the merit of leaving the boy-mind supple, free to turn with the world, and if one learned next to nothing, the little one did learn needed not to be unlearned. The surface was ready to take any form that education should cut into it, though Boston, with singular foresight, rejected the old designs. What sort of education was stamped elsewhere, a Bostonian had no idea, but he escaped the evils of other standards by having no standard at all; and what was true of school was true of society. Boston offered none that could help outside. Every one now smiles at the bad taste of Queen Victoria and Louis Philippe—the society of the forties—but the taste was only a reflection of the social slackwater between a tide passed, and a tide to come. Boston belonged to neither, and hardly even to America. Neither aristocratic nor industrial nor social, Boston girls and boys were not nearly as unformed as English boys and girls, but had less means of acquiring form as they grew older. Women counted for little as models. Every boy, from the age of seven, fell in love at frequent intervals with some girl—always more or less the same little girl—who had nothing to teach him, or he to teach her, except rather familiar and provincial manners, until they married and bore children to repeat the habit. The idea of attaching one's self to a married woman, or of polishing one's manners to suit the standards of women of thirty, could hardly have entered the mind of a young Bostonian, and would have scandalized his parents. From women the boy got the domestic virtues and nothing else. He might not even catch the idea that women had more to give. The garden of Eden was hardly more primitive.

To balance this virtue, the Puritan city had always hidden a darker side. Blackguard Boston was only too educational, and to most boys much the more interesting. A successful blackguard must enjoy great physical advantages besides a true vocation, and Henry Adams had neither; but no boy escaped some contact with vice of a very low form. Blackguardism came constantly under boys' eyes, and had the charm of force and freedom and superiority to culture or decency. One might fear it, but no one honestly despised it. Now and then it asserted itself as education more roughly than school ever did. One of the commonest boy-games of winter, inherited directly from the eighteenth-century, was a game of war on Boston Common. In old days the two hostile forces were called North-Enders and South-Enders. In 1850 the North-Enders still survived as a legend, but in practice it was a battle of the Latin School against all comers, and the Latin School, for snowball, included all the boys of the West End. Whenever, on a half-holiday, the weather was soft enough to soften the snow, the Common was apt to be the scene of a fight, which began in daylight with the Latin School in force, rushing their opponents down to Tremont Street, and which generally ended at dark by the Latin School dwindling in numbers and disappearing. As the Latin School grew weak, the roughs and young blackguards grew strong. As long as snow-balls were the only weapon, no one was much hurt, but a stone may be put in a snowball, and in the dark a stick or a slung-shot in the hands of a boy is as effective as a knife. One afternoon the fight had been long and exhausting. The boy Henry, following, as his habit was, his bigger brother Charles, had taken part in the battle, and had felt his courage much depressed by seeing one of his trustiest leaders, Henry Higginson— "Bully Hig," his school name—struck by a stone over the eye, and led off the field bleeding in rather a ghastly manner. As night came on, the Latin School was steadily forced back to the Beacon Street Mall where they could retreat no further without disbanding, and by that time only a small band was left, headed by two heroes, Savage and Marvin. A dark mass of figures could be seen below, making ready for the last rush, and rumor said that a swarm of blackguards from the slums, led by a grisly terror called Conky Daniels, with a club and a hideous reputation, was going to put an end to the Beacon Street cowards forever. Henry wanted to run away with the others, but his brother was too big to run away, so they stood still and waited immolation. The dark mass set up a shout, and rushed forward. The Beacon Street boys turned and fled up the steps, except Savage and Marvin and the few champions who would not run. The terrible Conky Daniels swaggered up, stopped a moment with his body-guard to swear a few oaths at Marvin, and then swept on and chased the flyers, leaving the few boys untouched who stood their ground. The obvious moral taught that blackguards were not so black as they were painted; but the boy Henry had passed through as much terror as though he were Turenne or Henri IV, and ten or twelve years afterwards when these same boys were fighting and falling on all the battle-fields of Virginia and Maryland, he wondered whether their education on Boston Common had taught Savage and Marvin how to die.

If violence were a part of complete education, Boston was not incomplete. The idea of violence was familiar to the anti-slavery leaders as well as to their followers. Most of them suffered from it. Mobs were always possible. Henry never happened to be actually concerned in a mob, but he, like every other boy, was sure to be on hand wherever a mob was expected, and whenever he heard Garrison or Wendell Phillips speak, he looked for trouble. Wendell Phillips on a platform was a model dangerous for youth. Theodore Parker in his pulpit was not much safer. Worst of all, the execution of the Fugitive Slave Law in Boston,—the sight of Court Square packed with bayonets, and his own friends obliged to line the streets under arms as State militia, in order to return a negro to slavery—wrought frenzy in the brain of a fifteen-year-old, eighteenth-century boy from Quincy, who wanted to miss no reasonable chance of mischief.

One lived in the atmosphere of the Stamp Act, the Tea Tax, and the Boston Massacre. Within Boston, a boy was first an eighteenth-century politician, and afterwards only a possibility; beyond Boston the first step led only further into politics. . . .

Mark Twain, "The Whittier Birthday Speech" (1877)

Mark Twain (1835–1910), nationally celebrated author, lecturer, and humorist, delivered "The Whittier Birthday Speech" at the *Atlantic Monthly* dinner in honor of John Greenleaf Whittier's seventieth birthday, held on December 17, 1877, at the Brunswick Hotel, Boston. After the speech, both he and William Dean Howells felt shame at Twain's broad satire of Greater Boston's literary luminaries.

Mr. Chairman: This is an occasion peculiarly meet for the digging up of pleasant reminiscences concerning literary folk; therefore I will drop lightly into history myself. Standing here on the shore of the Atlantic and contemplating certain of its largest literary billows, I am reminded of a thing which happened to me some fifteen years ago, when I had just succeeded in stirring up a little Nevadian literary ocean puddle myself, whose spume flakes were beginning to blow Californiawards. I started an inspection tramp through the southern mines of California. I was callow and conceited, and I resolved to try the virtue of my *nom de plume*. I very soon had an opportunity. I knocked at a miner's lonely log cabin in the foothills of the Sierras just at nightfall. It was snowing at the time. A jaded, melancholy man of fifty, barefooted, opened the door to me. When he heard my *nom de plume* he looked more dejected than before. He let me in—pretty reluctantly, I thought—and after the customary bacon and beans, black coffee and hot whiskey, I took a pipe. This sorrowful man had not said three words up to this time. Now he spoke up and said, in the voice of one who is secretly suffering, "You're the fourth—I'm going to move." "The fourth what?" said I. "The fourth littery man that has been here in twenty-four hours—I'm going to move." "You don't tell me!" said I; "who were the others?" "Mr. Long-fellow, Mr. Emerson, and Mr. Oliver Wendell Holmes—dad fetch the lot!"

You can easily believe I was interested. I supplicated—three hot whiskeys did the rest—and finally the melancholy miner began. Said he:

"They came here just at dark yesterday evening, and I let them in, of course. Said they were going to the Yosemite. They were a rough lot—but that's nothing—everybody looks rough that travels afoot. Mr. Emerson was a seedy little bit of a chap, red-headed. Mr. Holmes was as fat as a balloon—he weighed as much as three hundred, and had double chins all the way down to his stomach. Mr. Longfellow was built like a prize-fighter. His head was cropped and bristly—like as if he had a wig made of hair brushes. His nose lay straight down his face, like a finger with the end joint tilted up. They had been drinking—I could see that. And what queer talk they used! Mr. Holmes inspected this cabin, then he took me by the buttonhole, and says he:

> Through the deep caves of thought
> I hear a voice that sings;
> Build thee more stately mansions,
> O my Soul!

"Says I, 'I can't afford it, Mr. Holmes, and moreover I don't want to.' Blamed if I liked it pretty well, either, coming from a stranger, that way! However, I started to get out my bacon and beans, when Mr. Emerson came and looked on awhile, and then *he* takes me aside by the buttonhole and says:

> Give me agates for my meat;
> Give me cantharides to eat;
> From air and ocean bring me foods,
> From all zones and latitudes.

"Says I, 'Mr. Emerson, if you'll excuse me, this ain't no hotel.' You see it sort of riled me—I warn't used to the ways of littery swells. But I went on a-sweating over my work, and next comes Mr. Longfellow and buttonholes me, and interrupts me. Says he:

> Honor be to Mudjckeewis!
> You shall hear how Pau-Puk-Kee-wis—

"But I broke in, and says I, 'Begging your pardon, Mr. Longfellow, if you'll be so kind as to hold your yawp for about five minutes and let me get this grub ready, you'll do me proud.' Well, sir, after they'd filled up I set out the jug. Mr. Holmes looks at it, and then he fires up all of a sudden and yells:

> Flash out a stream of blood-red wine!
> For I would drink to other days.

"By George, I was getting kind of worked up. I don't deny it, I was getting kind of worked up. I turns to Mr. Holmes, and says I, 'Looky here, my fat friend, I'm a-running this shanty, and if the court knows herself, you'll take whiskey straight or you'll go dry.' Them's the very words I said to him. Now I don't want to sass such famous littery people, but you see they kind of forced me. There ain't nothing onreasonable 'bout me; I don't mind a passer of guests a-treadin' on my tail three or four times, but when it comes to *standin'* on it it's different, and if the court knows herself, you'll take whiskey straight or you'll go dry! Well, between drinks they'd swell around the cabin and strike attitudes and spout. Says Mr. Longfellow:

> This is the forest primeval.

"Says Mr. Emerson:

> Here once the embattled farmers stood,
> And fired the shot heard round the world.

"Says I, 'Oh, blackguard the premises as much as you want to—it don't cost you a cent.' Well, they went on drinking, and pretty soon they got out a greasy old deck and went to playing cutthroat euchre at ten cents a corner—on trust. I begun to notice some pretty suspicious things. Mr. Emerson dealt, looked at his hand, shook his head, says:

> I am the doubter and the doubt—

and calmly bunched the hands and went to shuffling for a new layout. Says he:

> They reckon ill who leave me out;
> They know now well the subtle ways
> I keep. I pass, and deal *again!*

"Hang'd if he didn't go ahead and do it, too! Oh, he was a cool one. Well, in a minute things were running pretty tight, but all of a sudden I see by Mr. Emerson's eye he judged he had 'em. He had already corralled two tricks, and each of the others one. So now he kind of lifts a little in his chair and says:

> I tire of globes and aces!—
> Too long the game is played!

—and down he fetched a right bower. Mr. Longfellow smiles as sweet as pie and says:

> Thanks, thanks to thee, my worthy friend,
> For the lesson thou has taught,

—and dog my cats if he didn't down with *another* right bower! Well, sir, up jumps Holmes a-war whooping, as usual, and says:

> God help them if the tempest swings
> The pine against the palm!

—and I wish I may go to grass if he didn't swoop down with *another* right bower! Emerson claps his hand on his bowie, Longfellow claps his on his re-volver, and I went under a bunk. There was going to be trouble; but that monstrous Holmes rose up, wobbling his double chins, and says he, 'Order, gentlemen; the first man that draws, I'll lay down on him and smother him!' All quiet on the Potomac, you bet you!

"They were pretty how-come-you-so by now, and they begun to blow. Emerson says, 'The bulliest thing I ever wrote was "Barbara Frietchie."' Says Longfellow, 'It don't begin with my "Biglow Papers."' Says Holmes, 'My "Thanatopsis" lays over 'em both.' They mighty near ended in a fight. Then they wished they had some more company—and Mr. Emerson pointed to me and says:

> Is yonder squalid peasant all
> That this proud nursery could breed?

"He was a-whetting his bowie on his boot—so I let it pass. Well, sir, next they took it into their heads that they would like some music; so they made me stand up and sing 'When Johnny Comes Marching Home' till I dropped—at thirteen minutes past four this morning. That's what *I've* been through, my friend. When I woke at seven, they were leaving, thank good-ness, and Mr. Longfellow had my only boots on, and his own under his arm.

Says I, 'Hold on, there, Evangeline, what are you going to do with *them?*' He says, 'Going to make tracks with 'em; because:

> Lives of great men all remind us
> We can make our lives sublime;
> And, departing, leave behind us
> Footprints on the sands of Time.

"As I said, Mr. Twain, you are the fourth in twenty-four hours—and I'm going to move—I ain't suited to a littery atmosphere."

I said to the miner, "Why, my dear sir, these were not the gracious singers to whom we and the world pay loving reverence and homage; these were impostors."

The miner investigated me with a calm eye for a while; then said he, "Ah! Impostors—were they?—are *you?*" I did not pursue the subject, and since then I haven't traveled on my *nom de plume* enough to hurt. Such was the reminiscence I was moved to contribute, Mr. Chairman. In my enthusiasm I may have exaggerated the details a little, but you will easily forgive me that fault, since I believe it is the first time I have ever deflected from perpendicular fact on an occasion like this.

William Dean Howells, from
Literary Friends and Acquaintance (1900)

William Dean Howells (1837–1920)—noted novelist, critic and advocate for literary realism—was an editor of and contributor to both *Atlantic Monthly* and *Harper's*. This excerpt shows Howells's retrospective account of his first encounter with Boston and its literary luminaries.

Among my fellow-passengers on the train from New York to Boston, when I went to begin my work there in 1866, as the assistant editor of the Atlantic Monthly, was the late Samuel Bowles, of the Springfield Republican, who created in a subordinate city a journal of metropolitan importance. I had met him in Venice several years earlier, when he was suffering from the cruel insomnia which had followed his overwork on that newspaper, and when he told me that he was sleeping scarcely more than one hour out of the twenty-four. His worn face attested the misery which this must have been, and which lasted in some measure while he lived, though I believe that rest and travel relieved him in his later years. He was always a man of cordial friendliness, and he now expressed a most gratifying interest when I told him what I was going to do in Boston. He gave himself the pleasure of descanting upon the dramatic quality of the fact that a young newspaper man from Ohio was about to share in the destinies of the great literary periodical of New England.

I do not think that such a fact would now move the fancy of the liveliest newspaper man, so much has the West since returned upon the East in a refluent wave of authorship. But then the West was almost an unknown quality in our literary problem; and in fact there was scarcely any literature outside of New England. Even this was of New England origin, for it was almost wholly the work of New England men and women in the "splendid exile" of New York. The Atlantic Monthly, which was distinctively literary, was distinctively a New England magazine, though from the first it had been characterized by what was more national, what was more universal, in the New England temperament. Its chief contributors for nearly twenty years were Longfellow, Lowell, Holmes, Whittier, Emerson, Doctor Hale, Colonel Higginson, Mrs. Stowe, Whipple, Rose Terry Cooke, Mrs. Julia Ward Howe, Mrs. Prescott Spofford, Mrs. Phelps Ward, and other New England writers who still lived in New England, and largely in the region of Boston. Occasionally there came a poem from Bryant, at New York, from Mr. Stedman, from Mr. Stoddard and Mrs. Stoddard, from Mr. Aldrich, and from Bayard Taylor. But all these, except the last, were not only of New England race, but of New England birth. I think there was no contributor from the South but Mr. M. D. Conway, and as yet the West scarcely counted, though four young poets from Ohio, who were not immediately or remotely of Puritan origin, had appeared in early numbers; Alice Cary, living with her sister in New York, had written now and then from the beginning. Mr. John Hay solely represented Illinois by a single paper, and he was of Rhode Island stock. It was after my settlement at Boston that Mark Twain, of Missouri, became a figure of world-wide fame at Hartford; and longer after, that Mr. Bret Harte made that progress Eastward from California which was telegraphed almost from hour to hour, as if it were the progress of a prince. Miss Constance F. Woolson had not yet begun to write. Mr. James Whitcomb Riley, Mr. Maurice Thompson, Miss Edith Thomas, Octave Thanet, Mr. Charles Warren Stoddard, Mr. H. B. Fuller, Mrs. Catherwood, Mr. Hamlin Garland, all whom I name at random among other Western writers, were then as unknown as Mr. Cable, Miss Murfree, Mrs. Rives Chanler, Miss Grace King, Mr. Joel Chandler Harris, Mr. Thomas Nelson Page, in the South, which they by no means fully represent.

The editors of the Atlantic had been eager from the beginning to discover any outlying literature; but, as I have said, there was in those days very little good writing done beyond the borders of New England. If the case is now different, and the best known among living American writers are no longer New-Englanders, still I do not think the South and West have yet trimmed the balance; and though perhaps the new writers now more commonly appear in those quarters, I should not be so very sure that they are not still characterized by New England ideals and examples. On the other hand, I am very sure that in my early day we were characterized by them, and wished to be so; we even felt that we failed in so far as we expressed something native quite in our own way. The literary theories we accepted were New England theories, the criticism we valued was New England criticism, or, more strictly speaking, Boston theories, Boston criticism.

Of those more constant contributors to the Atlantic whom I have mentioned, it is of course known that Longfellow and Lowell lived in Cambridge, Emerson at Concord, and Whittier at Amesbury. Colonel Higginson was still and for many years afterwards at Newport; Mrs. Stowe was then at Andover; Miss Prescott of Newburyport had become Mrs. Spofford, and was presently in Boston, where her husband was a member of the General Court; Mrs. Phelps Ward, as Miss Elizabeth Stuart Phelps, dwelt in her father's house at Andover. The chief of the Bostonians were Mrs. Julia Ward Howe, Doctor Holmes, and Doctor Hale. Yet Boston stood for the whole Massachusetts group, and Massachusetts, in the literary impulse, meant New England. I suppose we must all allow, whether we like to do so or not, that the impulse seems now to have pretty well spent itself. Certainly the city of Boston has distinctly waned in literature, though it has waxed in wealth and population. I do not think there are in Boston to-day even so many talents with a literary coloring in law, science, theology, and journalism as there were formerly; though I have no belief that the Boston talents are fewer or feebler than before. I arrived in Boston, however, when all talents had more or less a literary coloring, and when the greatest talents were literary.

These expressed with ripened fullness a civilization conceived in faith and brought forth in good works; but that moment of maturity was the beginning of a decadence which could only show itself much later. New England has ceased to be a nation in itself, and it will perhaps never again have anything like a national literature; but that was something like a national literature; and it will probably be centuries yet before the life of the whole country, the American life as distinguished from the New England life, shall have anything so like a national literature. It will be long before our larger life interprets itself in such imagination as Hawthorne's, such wisdom as Emerson's, such poetry as Longfellow's, such prophecy as Whittier's, such wit and grace as Holmes's, such humor and humanity as Lowell's.

The literature of those great men was, if I may suffer myself the figure, the Socinian graft of a Calvinistic stock. Their faith, in its various shades, was Unitarian, but their art was Puritan. So far as it was imperfect—and great and beautiful as it was, I think it had its imperfections—it was marred by the intense ethicism that pervaded the New England mind for two hundred years, and that still characterizes it. They or their fathers had broken away from orthodoxy in the great schism at the beginning of the century, but, as if their heterodoxy were conscience-stricken, they still helplessly pointed the moral in all they did; some pointed to more directly, some less directly; but they all pointed it. I should be far from blaming them for their ethical intention, though I think they felt their vocation as prophets too much for their good as poets. Sometimes they sacrificed the song to the sermon, though not always, nor nearly always. It was in poetry and romance that they excelled; in the novel, so far as they attempted it, they failed. I say this with the names of all the Bostonian group, and those they influenced, in mind, and with a full sense of their greatness. It may be ungracious to say that they have left no heirs to their peculiar greatness; but it would be foolish to say that they left an estate where they had none to bequeath. . . . New England, in Hawthorne's work, achieved supremacy in romance; but the romance is always an allegory, and the novel is a picture in which the truth to life is suffered to do its unsermonized office for conduct; and New England yet lacks her novelist, because it was her instinct and her conscience in fiction to be true to an ideal of life rather than to life itself. . . . But the New England literature of the great day was the blossom of a New England root; and the language which the Bostonians wrote was the native English of scholars fitly the heirs of those who had brought the learning of the universities to Massachusetts Bay two hundred years before and was of as pure a lineage as the English of the mother-country.

William Dean Howells, from
The Rise of Silas Lapham (1885)

The opening pages of *The Rise of Silas Lapham* contrast two men from northern New England who have come to Boston to seek fame and fortune: cynical journalist Bartley Hubbard and naïve, self-satisfied Silas Lapham, a socially ambitious paint-manufacturer.

When Bartley Hubbard went to interview Silas Lapham for the "Solid Men of Boston" series, which he undertook to finish up in "The Events," after he replaced their original projector on that newspaper, Lapham received him in his private office by previous appointment.

"Walk right in!" he called out to the journalist, whom he caught sight of through the door of the counting-room.

He did not rise from the desk at which he was writing, but he gave Bartley his left hand for welcome, and he rolled his large head in the direction of a vacant chair. "Sit down! I'll he with you in just half a minute."

"Take your time," said Bartley, with the ease he instantly felt. "I'm in no hurry." He took a note-book from his pocket, laid it on his knee, and began to sharpen a pencil.

"There!" Lapham pounded with his great hairy fist on the envelope he had been addressing. "William!" he called out, and he handed the letter to a boy who came to get it. "I want that to go right away. Well, sir," he continued, wheeling round in his leather-cushioned swivel-chair, and facing Bartley, seated so near that their knees almost touched, "so you want my life, death, and Christian sufferings, do you, young man?"

"That's what I'm after," said Bartley. "Your money or your life."

"I guess you wouldn't want my life without the money," said Lapham, as if he were willing to prolong these moments of preparation.

"Take 'em both," Bartley suggested. "Don't want your money without your life, if you come to that. But you're just one million times more interesting to the public than if you hadn't a dollar; and you know that as well as I do, Mr. Lapham. There's no use beating about the bush."

"No," said Lapham, somewhat absently. He put out his huge foot and pushed the ground-glass door shut between his little den and the book-keepers, in their larger den outside.

"In personal appearance," wrote Bartley in the sketch for which he now studied his subject, while he waited patiently for him to continue, "Silas Lapham is a fine type of the successful American. He has a square, bold chin, only partially concealed by the short reddish-grey beard, growing to the edges of his firmly closing lips. His nose is short and straight; his forehead good, but broad rather than high; his eyes blue, and with a light in them that is kindly or sharp according to his mood. He is of medium height, and fills an average arm-chair with a solid bulk, which on the day of our interview was unpretentiously clad in a business suit of blue serge. His head droops somewhat from a short neck, which does not trouble itself to rise far from a pair of massive shoulders."

"I don't know as I know just where you want me to begin," said Lapham.

"Might begin with your birth; that's where most of us begin," replied Bartley.

A gleam of humorous appreciation shot into Lapham's blue eyes.

"I didn't know whether you wanted me to go quite so far back as that," he said. "But there's no disgrace in having been born, and I was born in the State of Vermont, pretty well up under the Canada line—so well up, in fact, that I came very near being an adoptive citizen; for I was bound to be an American of *some* sort, from the word Go! That was about—well, let me see!—pretty near sixty years ago: this is '75, and that was '20. Well, say I'm fifty-five years old; and I've *lived* 'em, too; not an hour of waste time about *me*, anywheres! I was born on a farm, and—"

"Worked in the fields summers and went to school winters: regulation thing?" Bartley cut in.

"Regulation thing," said Lapham, accepting this irreverent version of his history somewhat dryly.

"Parents poor, of course," suggested the journalist. "Any barefoot business? Early deprivations of any kind, that would encourage the youthful reader to go and do likewise? Orphan myself, you know," said Bartley, with a smile of cynical good-comradery.

Lapham looked at him silently, and then said with quiet self-respect, "I guess if you see these things as a joke, my life won't interest you."

"Oh yes, it will," returned Bartley, unabashed. "You'll see; it'll come out all right." And in fact it did so, in the interview which Bartley printed.

"Mr. Lapham," he wrote, "passed rapidly over the story of his early life, its poverty and its hardships, sweetened, however, by the recollections of a devoted mother, and a father who, if somewhat her inferior in education, was no less ambitious for the advancement of his children. They were quiet, unpretentious people, religious, after the fashion of that time, and of sterling morality, and they taught their children the simple virtues of the Old Testament and Poor Richard's Almanac."

Bartley could not deny himself this gibe; but he trusted to Lapham's unliterary habit of mind for his security in making it, and most other people would consider it sincere reporter's rhetoric.

"You know," he explained to Lapham, "that we have to look at all these facts as material, and we get the habit of classifying them. Sometimes a leading question will draw out a whole line of facts that a man himself would never think of." He went on to put several queries, and it was from Lapham's answers that he generalised the history of his childhood. "Mr. Lapham, although he did not dwell on his boyish trials and struggles, spoke of them with deep feeling and an abiding sense of their reality." This was what he added in the interview, and by the time he had got Lapham past the period where risen Americans are all pathetically alike in their narrow circumstances, their sufferings, and their aspirations, he had beguiled him into forgetfulness of the check he had received, and had him talking again in perfect enjoyment of his autobiography.

Henry James, from *The Bostonians* (1886)

Henry James (1843–1916)—novelist, critic, dramatist, and autobiographer—composed such an impressive body of writings that he became known as "The Master." *The Bostonians* was published in thirteen monthly installments in *Century Magazine* from February 1885 to February 1886. It was published as a book first in England, then in New York by Macmillan in 1886. In this passage Basil Ransom, a Southerner, visiting Boston for the first time, encounters Olive Chancellor, his distant cousin, in her splendid

Beacon Hill home, which James based upon the Charles Street home of Annie and James T. Fields. James contrasts regional types—the conservative former Confederate officer and the Boston feminist—and satirizes both.

When he had told her that if she would take him as he was he should be very happy to dine with her, she excused herself a moment and went to give an order in the dining-room. The young man, left alone, looked about the parlor—the two parlors which, in their prolonged, adjacent narrowness, formed evidently one apartment—and wandered to the windows at the back, where there was a view of the water; Miss Chancellor having the good fortune to dwell on that side of Charles Street toward which, in the rear, the afternoon sun slants redly, from an horizon indented at empty intervals with wooden spires, the masts of lonely boats, the chimneys of dirty "works," over a brackish expanse of anomalous character, which is too big for a river and too small for a bay. The view seemed to him very picturesque, though in the gathered dusk little was left of it save a cold yellow streak in the west, a gleam of brown water, and the reflection of the lights that had begun to show themselves in a row of houses, impressive to Ransom in their extreme modernness, which overlooked the same lagoon from a long embankment on the left, constructed of stones roughly piled. He thought this prospect, from a city-house, almost romantic; and he turned from it back to the interior (illuminated now by a lamp which the parlor-maid had placed on a table while he stood at the window) as to something still more genial and interesting. The artistic sense in Basil Ransom had not been highly cultivated; neither (though he had passed his early years as the son of a rich man) was his conception of material comfort very definite; it consisted mainly of the vision of plenty of cigars and brandy and water and newspapers, and a cane-bottomed arm-chair of the right inclination, from which he could stretch his legs. Nevertheless it seemed to him he had never seen an interior that was so much an interior as this queer corridor-shaped drawing-room of his new-found kinswoman; he had never felt himself in the presence of so much organized privacy or of so many objects that spoke of habits and tastes. Most of the people he had hitherto known had no tastes; they had a few habits, but these were not of a sort that required much upholstery. He had not as yet been in many houses in New York, and he had never before seen so many accessories. The general character of the place struck him as Bostonian; this was, in fact, very much what he had supposed Boston to be. He had always heard Boston was a city of culture, and now there was culture in Miss Chancellor's tables and sofas, in the books that were everywhere, on little shelves like brackets (as if a book were a statuette), in the photographs and watercolors that covered the walls, in the curtains that were festooned rather stiffly in the doorways. He looked at some of the books and saw that his cousin read German; and his impression of the importance of this (as a symptom of superiority) was not diminished by the fact that he himself had mastered the tongue (knowing it contained a large literature of jurisprudence) during a long, empty, deadly summer on the plantation. It is a curious proof of a certain crude modesty inherent in Basil Ransom that the main effect of his observing his cousin's German books was to give him an idea of the natural energy of Northerners. He had noticed it often before; he had already told himself that he must count with it. It was only after much experience he made the discovery that few Northerners were, in their secret soul, so energetic as he. Many other persons had made it before that. He knew very little about Miss Chancellor; he had come to see her only because she wrote to him; he would never have thought of looking her up, and since then there had been no one in New York he might ask about her. Therefore he could only guess that she was a rich young woman; such a house, inhabited in such a way by a quiet spinster, implied a considerable income. How much? He asked himself; five thousand, ten thousand, fifteen thousand a year? There was richness to our panting young man in the smallest of these figures. He was not of a mercenary spirit, but he had an immense desire for success, and he had more than once reflected that a moderate capital was an aid to achievement. He had seen in his younger years one of the biggest failures that history commemorates, an immense national *fiasco*, and it had implanted in his mind a deep aversion to the ineffectual. It came over him, while he waited for his hostess to reappear, that she was unmarried as well as rich, that she was sociable (her letter answered for that) as well as single; and he had for a moment a whimsical vision of becoming a partner in so flourishing a firm. He ground his teeth a little as he thought of the contrasts of the human lot; this cushioned feminine nest made him feel unhoused and underfed. Such a mood, however, could only be momentary, for he was conscious at bottom of a bigger stomach than all the culture of Charles Street could fill.

Afterwards, when his cousin had come back and they had gone down to dinner together, where he sat facing her at a little table decorated in the middle with flowers, a position from which he had another view, through a window where the curtain remained undrawn by her direction (she called his attention to this—it was for his benefit), of the dusky, empty river, spotted with points of light—at this period, I say, it was very easy for him to remark to himself that nothing would induce him to make love to such a type as that. Several months later, in New York, in conversation with Mrs. Luna [Olive Chancellor's sister], of whom he was destined to see a good deal, he alluded by chance to this repast, to the way her sister had placed him at table, and to the remark with which she had pointed out the advantage of his seat.

"That's what they call in Boston being very 'thoughtful,'" Mrs. Luna said, "giving you the Back Bay (don't you hate the name?) to look at, and then taking credit for it."

This, however, was in the future; what Basil Ransom actually perceived was that Miss Chancellor was a signal old maid. That was her quality, her destiny; nothing could be more distinctly written. There are women who are unmarried by accident, and others who are unmarried by option; but Olive Chancellor was unmarried by every implication of her being. She was a spinster as Shelley was a lyric poet, or as the month of August is sultry. She was so essentially a celibate that Ransom found himself thinking of her as old, though when he came to look at her (as he said to himself) it was apparent that her years were fewer than his own. He did not dislike her, she had been so friendly; but, little by little, she gave him an uneasy feeling—the sense that you could never be safe with a person who took things so hard. It came over him that it was because she took things hard she had sought his acquaintance; it had been because she was strenuous, not because she was genial; she had had in her eye—and what an extraordinary eye it was!—not a pleasure, but a duty. She would expect him to be strenuous in return; but he couldn't—in private life, he couldn't; privacy for Basil Ransom consisted entirely in what he called "laying off." She was not so plain on further acquaintance as she had seemed to him at first; even the young Mississippian had culture enough to see that she was refined. Her white skin had a singular look of being drawn tightly across her face; but her features, though sharp and irregular, were delicate in a fashion that suggested good breeding. Their line was perverse, but it was not poor. The curious tint of her eyes was a living color; when she turned it upon you, you thought vaguely of the glitter of green ice. She had absolutely no figure, and presented a certain appearance of feeling cold. With all this, there was something very modern and highly developed in her aspect; she had the advantages as well as the drawbacks of a nervous organization. She smiled constantly at her guest, but from the beginning to the end of dinner, though he made several remarks that he thought might prove amusing, she never once laughed. Later, he saw that she was a woman without laughter; exhilaration, if it ever visited her, was dumb. Once only, in the course of his subsequent acquaintance with her, did it find a voice; and then the sound remained in Ransom's ear as one of the strangest he had heard.

She asked him a great many questions, and made no comment on his answers, which only served to suggest to her fresh inquiries. Her shyness had quite left her, it did not come back; she had confidence enough to wish him to see that she took a great interest in him. Why should she? He wondered. He couldn't believe he was one of *her* kind; he was conscious of much Bohemianism—he drank beer, in New York, in cellars, knew no ladies, and was familiar with a "variety" actress. Certainly, as she knew him better, she would disapprove of him, though, of course, he would never mention the actress, nor even, if necessary, the beer. Ransom's conception of vice was purely as a series of special cases, of explicable accidents. Not that he cared; if it were a part of the Boston character to be inquiring, he would be to the last a courteous Mississippian. He would tell her about Mississippi as much as she liked; he didn't care how much he told her that the old ideas in the South were played out. She would not understand him any the better for that; she would not know how little his own views could be gathered from such a limited admission. What her sister imparted to him about her mania for "reform" had left in his mouth a kind of unpleasant aftertaste; he felt, at any rate, that if she had the religion of humanity—Basil Ransom had read Comte, he had read everything—she would never understand him. He, too, had a private vision of reform, but the first principle of it was to reform the reformers. As they drew to the close of a meal which, in spite of all latent incompatibilities, had gone off brilliantly, she said to him that she should have to leave him after dinner, unless perhaps he should be inclined to accompany her. She was going to a small gathering at the house of a friend who had asked a few people, "interested in new ideas," to meet Mrs. Farrinder.

"Oh, thank you," said Basil Ransom. "Is it a party? I haven't been to a party since Mississippi seceded."

"No; Miss Birdseye doesn't give parties. She's an ascetic."

"Oh, well, we have had our dinner," Ransom rejoined, laughing.

His hostess sat silent a moment, with her eyes on the ground; she looked at such times as if she were hesitating greatly between several things she might say, all so important that it was difficult to choose.

"I think it might interest you," she remarked presently. "You will hear some discussion, if you are fond of that. Perhaps you wouldn't agree," she added, resting her strange eyes on him.

"Perhaps I shouldn't—I don't agree with everything," he said, smiling and stroking his leg.

"Don't you care for human progress?" Miss Chancellor went on.

"I don't know—I never saw any. Are you going to show me some?"

"I can show you an earnest effort towards it. That's the most one can be sure of. But I am not sure you are worthy."

"Is it something very Bostonian? I should like to see that," said Basil Ransom.

"There are movements in other cities. Mrs. Farrinder goes everywhere; she may speak to-night."

"Mrs. Farrinder, the celebrated—?"

"Yes, the celebrated; the great apostle of the emancipation of women. She is a great friend of Miss Birdseye."

"And who is Miss Birdseye?"

"She is one of our celebrities. She is the woman in the world, I suppose, who has labored most for every wise reform. I think I ought to tell you," Miss Chancellor went on in a moment, "she was one of the earliest, one of the most passionate, of the old Abolitionists."

She had thought, indeed, she ought to tell him that, and it threw her into a little tremor of excitement to do so. Yet, if she had been afraid he would show some irritation at this news, she was disappointed at the geniality with which he exclaimed:

"Why, poor old lady—she must be quite mature!"

It was therefore with some severity that she rejoined:

"She will never be old. She is the youngest spirit I know. But if you are not in sympathy, perhaps you had better not come," she went on.

"In sympathy with what, dear madam?" Basil Ransom asked, failing still, to her perception, to catch the tone of real seriousness. "If, as you say, there is to be a discussion, there will be different sides, and of course one can't sympathize with both."

"Yes, but every one will, in his way—or in her way—plead the cause of the new truths. If you don't care for them, you won't go with us."

"I tell you I haven't the least idea what they are! I have never yet encountered in the world any but old truths—as old as the sun and moon. How can I know? But *do* take me; it's such a chance to see Boston."

"It isn't Boston—it's humanity!" Miss Chancellor, as she made this remark, rose from her chair, and her movement seemed to say that she consented. But before she quitted her kinsman to get ready, she observed to him that she was sure he knew what she meant; he was only pretending he didn't.

"Well, perhaps, after all, I have a general idea," he confessed; "but don't you see how this little reunion will give me a chance to fix it?"

She lingered an instant, with her anxious face. "Mrs. Farrinder will fix it!" she said; and she went to prepare herself.

It was in this poor young lady's nature to be anxious, to have scruple within scruple and to forecast the consequences of things. She returned in ten minutes, in her bonnet, which she had apparently assumed in recognition of Miss Birdseye's asceticism. As she stood there drawing on her gloves—her visitor had fortified himself against Mrs. Farrinder by another glass of wine—she declared to him that she quite repented of having proposed to him to go; something told her that he would be an unfavorable element.

"Why, is it going to be a spiritual *séance*?" Basil Ransom asked.

"Well, I have heard at Miss Birdseye's some inspirational speaking." Olive Chancellor was determined to look him straight in the face as she said this; her sense of the way it might strike him operated as a cogent, not as a deterrent, reason.

"Why, Miss Olive, it's just got up on purpose for me!" cried the young Mississippian, radiant, and clasping his hands. She thought him very handsome as he said this, but reflected that unfortunately men didn't care for the truth, especially the new kinds, in proportion as they were good-looking. She had, however, a moral resource that she could always fall back upon; it had already been a comfort to her, on occasions of acute feeling, that she hated men, as a class, anyway. "And I want so much to see an old Abolitionist; I have never laid eyes on one," Basil Ransom added.

"Of course you couldn't see one in the South; you were too afraid of them to let them come there!" She was now trying to think of something she might say that would be sufficiently disagreeable to make him cease to insist on accompanying her; for, strange to record—if anything, in a person of that intense sensibility, be stranger than any other—her second thought with regard to having asked him had deepened with the elapsing moments into an unreasoned terror of the effect of his presence. "Perhaps Miss Birdseye won't like you," she went on, as they waited for the carriage.

"I don't know; I reckon she will," said Basil Ransom good-humouredly. He evidently had no intention of giving up his opportunity.

From the window of the dining-room, at that moment, they heard the carriage drive up. Miss Birdseye lived at the South End; the distance was considerable, and Miss Chancellor had ordered a hackney-coach, it being one of the advantages of living in Charles Street that stables were near. The logic of her conduct was none of the clearest; for if she had been alone she would have proceeded to her destination by the aid of the street-car; not from economy (for she had the good fortune not to be obliged to consult it to that degree), and not from any love of wandering about Boston at night (a kind of exposure she greatly disliked), but by reason of a theory she devotedly nursed, a theory which bade her put off invidious differences and mingle in the common life. She would have gone on foot to Boylston Street, and there she would have taken the public conveyance (in her heart she loathed it) to the South End. Boston was full of poor girls who had to walk about at night and to squeeze into horse-cars in which every sense was displeased; and why should she hold herself superior to these? Olive Chancellor regulated her conduct on lofty principles, and this is why, having to-night the advantage of a gentleman's protection, she sent for a carriage to obliterate that patronage. If they had gone together in the common way she would have seemed to owe it to him that she should be so daring, and he belonged to a sex to which she wished to be under no obligations. Months before, when she wrote to him, it had been with the sense, rather, of putting *him* in debt. As they rolled toward the South End, side by side, in a good deal of silence, bouncing and bumping over the railway-tracks very little less, after all, than if their wheels had been fitted to them, and looking out on either side at rows of red houses, dusky in the lamp-light, with protuberant fronts, approached by ladders of stone; as they proceeded, with these contemplative undulations, Miss Chancellor said to her companion, with a concentrated desire to defy him, as a punishment for having thrown her (she couldn't tell why) into such a tremor:

"Don't you believe, then, in the coming of a better day—in its being possible to do something for the human race?"

Poor Ransom perceived the defiance, and he felt rather bewildered; he wondered what type, after all, he *had* got hold of, and what game was being played with him. Why had she made advances, if she wanted to pinch him this way? However, he was good for any game—that one as well as another—and he saw that he was "in" for something of which he had long desired to have a nearer view. "Well, Miss Olive," he answered, putting on again his big hat, which he had been holding in his lap, "what strikes me most is that the human race has got to bear its troubles."

"That's what men say to women, to make them patient in the position they have made for them."

"Oh, the position of women!" Basil Ransom exclaimed. "The position of women is to make fools of men. I would change my position for yours any day," he went on. "That's what I said to myself as I sat there in your elegant home."

He could not see, in the dimness of the carriage, that she had flushed quickly, and he did not know that she disliked to be reminded of certain things which, for her, were mitigations of the hard feminine lot. But the passionate quaver with which, a moment later, she answered him sufficiently assured him that he had touched her at a tender point.

"Do you make it a reproach to me that I happen to have a little money? The dearest wish of my heart is to do something with it for others—for the miserable."

Basil Ransom might have greeted this last declaration with the sympathy it deserved, might have commended the noble aspirations of his kinswoman. But what struck him, rather, was the oddity of so sudden a sharpness of pitch in an intercourse which, an hour or two before, had begun in perfect amity, and he burst once more into an irrepressible laugh. This made his companion feel, with intensity, how little she was joking. "I don't know why I should care what you think," she said.

"Don't care—don't care. What does it matter? It is not of the slightest importance."

He might say that, but it was not true; she felt that there were reasons why she should care. She had brought him into her life, and she should have to pay for it. But she wished to know the worst at once. "Are you against our emancipation?" she asked, turning a white face on him in the momentary radiance of a street-lamp.

"Do you mean your voting and preaching and all that sort of thing?" He made this inquiry, but seeing how seriously she would take his answer, he was almost frightened, and hung fire. "I will tell you when I have heard Mrs. Farrinder."

They had arrived at the address given by Miss Chancellor to the coachman, and their vehicle stopped with a lurch. Basil Ransom got out; he stood at the door with an extended hand, to assist the young lady. But she seemed to hesitate; she sat there with her spectral face. "You hate it!" she exclaimed, in a low tone.

"Miss Birdseye will convert me," said Ransom, with intention; for he had grown very curious, and he was afraid that now, at the last, Miss Chancellor would prevent his entering the house. She alighted without his help, and behind her he ascended the high steps of Miss Birdseye's residence. He had grown very curious, and among the things he wanted to know was why in the world this ticklish spinster had written to him.

IV

"VIEWED IN BOSTON LIGHT": TURN-OF-THE-CENTURY BOSTON

After a decade of contention over slavery and immigration, Boston experienced its finest era during the Civil War, when the community came together with unified purpose to oppose slavery, fight Confederate secession, and preserve the Union. In this trial of national identity and values Bostonians were reunited by recalling the high purpose that John Winthrop had set for the city's founders—to be "knit together by every joint"—and by memories of the city's leading role in the Revolution. In the spring of 1861, writes Boston historian Thomas H. O'Connor, citizens "were of one mind and one spirit, mobilized first by the attack on Fort Sumter, and then solidly united by the news that their own boys [in the Massachusetts 6th and 8th Regiments] had been fired upon by hostile rebels [in Baltimore]—and that on the anniversary of the battles of Lexington and Concord, eighty-six years earlier."[1] Even Boston's merchants, who depended upon the supply of Southern cotton for their mills in Lowell and Lawrence, had opposed slavery before the war; after the firing on Sumter, they called for military action. Amos A. Lawrence, for example, assured his manufacturing partner, William Appleton, that "a unanimity of sentiment about sustaining the government" was felt by most citizens of Boston, and he urged President Lincoln to mobilize 500,000 troops. As abolitionist Wendell Phillips proudly noted, principle and patriotism prevailed over commercial lust for profit in Boston.[2]

Still, some Bostonians were slow to join this consensus, particularly the Irish Catholic immigrants whose sudden influx during and after Ireland's Great Famine of 1845–1850 tested the city's commitment to democratic inclusion. In 1847 alone some 37,000 immigrants arrived in Boston from Ireland, transforming the city. Crime, disease, and infant mortality grew in crowded Irish districts along the waterfront, and residents of long standing fled the West End and North End, "sacrificing other interests in order to avoid the decline in social status that resulted from remaining," as Oscar Handlin put it in *Boston's Immigrants* (1941). Most established Bostonians, descendants of the Puritan-English founders, turned away in disgust, so "the Irish remained unneeded and unabsorbed."[3] The American Party (nicknamed "Know-Nothing" for their conspiratorial secrecy) had formed in opposition to "foreign" influence, capturing the state government in 1854 and passing a slate of anti-Catholic legislation. Irish Catholic immigrants, in turn, viewed abolitionists (many of them Know-Nothing supporters) as hypocrites and, seeing themselves as excluded residents, felt little commitment to the cause of preserving the Union.[4] However, after Fort Sumter was captured, the Boston Irish backed the Union forcefully. As *The Pilot*, the newspaper of the Boston Catholic Church, put it in January 1861, "We Catholics have only one course to adopt, only one line to follow. Stand by the Union; fight for the Union; die by the Union."[5] In 1863, riots in New York City, led by draft-protesting Irish immigrants, lasted five days, during which some 1200 were killed. Conscription also brought protests in Boston, though there were no riots, in part because Bishop John Bernard Fitzpatrick, who had cultivated cooperative relations with Boston's ruling elite, called upon his flock for accommodation rather than demonstration. Early in the war the 28th Regiment was formed, largely composed of Irish immigrants, and the regiment joined the Irish Brigade, which went on to fight valiantly at Fredericksburg. Through their commitment and sacrifice during this war, the Boston Irish demonstrated their patriotism and assured their permanent place in the city.[6] The Irish became true Bostonians.

Robert Gould Shaw came to embody the ideals of the city through his heroic and idealistic actions during the Civil War, and afterward in legend and literature--from James Russell Lowell's "*Memoriae positum*" (1864) to Robert Lowell's "For the Union Dead" (1960). Shaw, born in 1837, was a member of a prominent, proud Beacon Hill family. His father had financially backed Brook Farm and was a committed reformer. Robert, of course, attended Harvard and absorbed his Brahmin class's commitment to civic duty. In 1861 he joined the 2nd Massachusetts Infantry (the "Harvard Regiment") and was wounded at the Battle of Antietam. When the 54th Regiment, composed of African American volunteers, was formed, Governor John Andrew offered its command to Shaw, whom he saw as a gentleman of "the highest tone and honor." In May 1863, Shaw, then age twenty-five, marched his 54th Regiment to the State House, down Beacon Street past his home and his applauding family, and cheering crowds, onto the Boston Common parade ground for review, then through Boston's streets to Battery Wharf, where they shipped out to South Carolina.[7] Two months later he led them in the attack on Fort Wagner, on Morris Island, and was killed, along with half of his men. Dishonored by Confederate troops, he was buried in a ditch with his men; in Boston his nobility became legendary.[8] This event, suggests Richard Powers, "has lived on in literature and art, inspiring and incriminating, a mirror held up to the best and worst in American national character."[9] Sacrificing his life in the cause of liberty, dying for an ideal, Robert Gould Shaw became Boston's most exemplary citizen, "the very type of the heroic Brahmin," writes Louis Menand.[10] For the next century, Shaw would stand, in memory as in monument, as the best and brightest embodiment of Boston's idealized vision of itself, as a standard of values and conduct to which it aspired, though from which it often lapsed.

Oliver Wendell Holmes, Jr. was another son of Boston—his father was the "Autocrat" and his mother, the former Amelia Lee Jackson, was a staunch abolitionist—who left Harvard to fight for the Union and for Boston principles. Lt. Holmes, fighting in one savage battle after another, was wounded three times: at Ball's Bluff, Antietam, and Fredericksburg. He emerged from the war critical of his father's provincial and providential views. No longer did he see Boston as the hub of the solar system; no longer did he believe that *any* beneficent "system" reigned in the moral or physical universe. After witnessing the bloodshed at Spotsylvania, he tried to make this clear in a blunt letter to his characteristically optimistic father. "I am not the same man (may not have quite the same ideas) & certainly am not so elastic as I was and I *will not acknowledge the same claims upon me under those circumstances* that existed formerly."[11] Brahmin Boston was the mold in which young Holmes was formed, but his experiences in the Civil War broke that mold, and he reshaped himself as a realist and a pragmatist, as Menand notes in *The Metaphysical Club* (2002), a study of post–Civil War Boston's intellectual history.

> Holmes had grown up in a highly cultivated, homogeneous world, a world of which he was, in many ways, the consummate product: idealistic, artistic, and socially committed. And then he had watched that world bleed to death at Fredericksburg and Antietam, in a war that learning and brilliance had been powerless to prevent. When he returned, Boston had changed, and so had American life.[12]

Wendell Holmes's vision reached beyond the boundaries and units of measure of his father's Boston-fostered mind to larger concepts of nation and universe. Yet Holmes remained something of a Boston Puritan, as Edmund Wilson has pointed out, for Holmes viewed the war as a "crusade" and saw fighting as an act of faith, as he explains in "The Soldier's Faith," a Memorial Day address he delivered at Harvard in 1895. He might not "know the meaning of the universe," but he did know "that the faith is true and adorable which leads a soldier to throw away his life in obedience to a blindly accepted duty, in a cause he little understands, in a plan of campaign of which he has no notion, under tactics of which he does not see the use."[13] The Brahmin lessons Wendell Holmes learned in Boston and modified into a kind of existential pragmatism on the Civil War's killing fields stayed with him throughout a brilliant legal career that brought him to the Supreme Court. After his death in 1935, two uniforms were discovered in his closet, with a note attached reading, "These uniforms were worn by me in the Civil War and the stains upon them are my blood."[14] As Wilson puts it, "there runs through all this the special ideal of the Brahmin, whose superiority is not merely social."[15] In his affirmation of service over security, idealism over opportunism, Oliver Wendell Holmes, Jr. was a true descendant of Winthrop and remained, despite their differences, his father's son.

In an address delivered for Memorial Day, May 30, 1884, in Keene, New Hampshire, at the John Sedgwick Post No. 4, Grand Army of the Republic, Wendell Holmes said of his Civil War experience, "in our youth our hearts were touched with fire." These words not only invoked fled glories of battle and victory, but also spoke to the waning spirit of Holmes's Brahmin class and the fading of Boston's importance and influence. By the 1880s, as Van Wyck Brooks puts it, New England had entered its "Indian Summer" of tranquility, self-satisfaction, and diminished capacities for creativity. "The heats and the rigours of the past were long forgotten, the passions of the war, the old crusades, and a mood of reminiscence possessed the people, for whom the present offered few excitements."[16] Three decades before, Hawthorne had looked back on Boston's Puritan past with anger at what Boston's founders had created; now, Holmes and others looked back on the region's noble Civil War past with wonder at the passion and purpose that had been lost.

Holmes carried the vision of savagery and danger into his distinguished legal career, insisting that free speech was essential to the protection of democracy, though he was not, like his father, an optimist.[17] Thomas Went-worth Higginson—descendant of a founding Puritan minister and, like Shaw and Holmes, a Harvard man—was another exemplary creation of Brahmin Boston; he too served in the Union Army and was wounded, but Higginson remained a committed optimist, as the title of his reminiscence indicates: *Cheerful Yesterdays* (1898). He was also an engaged abolitionist who helped to free escaped slaves and aided militant John Brown before the war. A captain in the 51st Massachusetts Volunteers, then a colonel, Higginson led the First South Carolina Volunteers, the first regiment recruited from former slaves, an experience he later described in *Army Life in a Black Regiment* (1870). As we have seen in chapter 2, Higginson's 1862 essay for *Atlantic Monthly*, "Letter to a Young Contributor," inviting "young ladies" and "young gentlemen" to send in contributions, elicited a reply from Emily Dickinson, which eventually led to his visits to the reclusive belle of Amherst and the publication of her poems under Higginson's editorship.[18] Higginson also drew writings from Rose Terry, Celia Thaxter, Helen Hunt, and other women who tempered the masculine tone of the journal.[19] Like Holmes, Higginson, the embodiment of Bostonian courage and commitment, carried the bold decisiveness he learned in the Civil War into his postwar work.

William James, Wendell Holmes's Harvard classmate and friend, did not serve in the Civil War; instead, William spent those years painting and studying at the Lawrence Scientific School of Harvard. Nor did his brother Henry enlist; instead, Henry devoted himself to refining his art of fiction. (One of Henry James's Civil War stories, "Poor Richard," published in 1867, portrays a version of Wendell Holmes as a survivor who has been brutalized by his war experience.) However, their brothers, Robertson (Bob) and Garth Wilkinson (Wilky), both served and were marked for life by the experience of war. Bob became an alcoholic after following Wilky's example and enlist-ing at age sixteen in an African American regiment (the Massachusetts 55th) and Wilky, who had been Col. Shaw's adjutant in the Massachusetts 54th, was badly wounded at Fort Wagner and had to be carried to his family home in Newport, Rhode Island, on a stretcher.

This scene is vividly recreated in Colm Toibin's novel about Henry James, *The Master* (2004). As Wilky lies suffering, fighting for his life, Henry real-izes that the serene New England world of their youth is gone, "that a public pact, a version of the civic order as ordained by history, had been cruelly broken." When their mother says that they "should dedicate themselves to

taking the pain from Wilky and suffering a small part of it in their own bodies," William nods in agreement, "as though something wise and practical
had been said."[20] William's response was to sketch his recovering brother.

Indeed, William James's response to the Civil War, like those of his non-
combatant brother Henry, would remain vicarious, refractory, and haunted.
Wilky was dead at thirty-eight and Bob led a life of repeated failures, but
William and Henry James lived long, productive lives, though they never
forgot the Civil War they missed. When World War I broke out in 1914,
Henry James, who was then living in Rye, on the southern coast of England,
was seized by memories of 1861: "the invasion of Belgium reproduced with
intensity the agitation of the New England air by Mr. Lincoln's call to arms,
and I went about for a short space as with the queer secret locked in my
breast of at least already knowing how such occasions helped and what a big
war was going to mean."[21] Wilky and Bob were left with their wounds from
the Civil War, while William and Henry were left with their memories and
impressions. Wilky and Bob had heeded the Boston call to duty, but, like
Shaw and Holmes, they paid a high price for it. William and Henry, non-
combatants, paid the Boston duty of lifelong guilty consciences and haunting images.

William James delivered the oration at the dedication and unveiling of
Augustus Saint-Gaudens's Shaw Memorial in May 1897. This bronze bas-
relief stands at the peak of Beacon Street, facing the State House; it portrays
Shaw leading his troops down Beacon Hill in 1863. James honored Shaw
not as a warrior, but, perhaps thinking also of Holmes, as someone who took
his "civic courage" of peacetime into battle. A nation needed such men to
lead it, those who commit "acts without external picturesqueness, by speaking, writing, voting reasonably; by smiting corruption swiftly; by good temper between parties; by the people knowing true men when they see them,
and professing them as leaders to rabid partisans or empty quacks."[22] James
held Shaw up as a model to emulate and as a repudiation of the self-seeking
citizenry of Gilded Age Boston. As historian Thomas Brown puts it, "for
James, as for Emerson, the ascendancy of the individual culminated in a
history shaped by principle and will rather than circumstances." Celebrating Shaw as "the sovereign individual," James invoked the promise that the
Memorial represented: the hope that "great historical lines, inextricably
national" might still emanate from Boston.[23] Trying to put the painful memories of the Civil War behind him, William James saw the event as "the last

wave of the war breaking over Boston."[24] The city's glory days were over, it seemed; its noble yesterdays and its finest men had passed.

Henry Adams, like the two famous James brothers, did not see battle in the Civil War, but did serve as secretary to his father, Charles Francis Adams, Lincoln's Minister to the Court of St. James. Had Henry not spent the war years in London, he might not have enlisted anyway, for young Adams, as he here recalls in his third-person memoir, showed a cool detachment when he returned from his studies in Germany in 1860 and observed the rising bellicosity in Boston and Quincy.

> The November of 1860 at Quincy stood apart from other memories as lurid beyond description. Although no one believed in civil war, the air reeked of it, and the Republicans organized their clubs and parades as Wide-Awakes in a form military in all things except weapons. Henry reached home in time to see the last of these processions, stretching in ranks of torches along the hill-side, file down through the November night; to the Old House, where Mr. Adams, their Member of Congress, received them, and, let them pretend what they liked, their air was not that of innocence.[25]

Service in the Civil War defined this generation of Boston's best and brightest young men. Some threw themselves into the conflict of convictions, while others kept their distance. Edmund Wilson speculates that the choice between commitment to battle or detachment from service shaped the minds and styles of these men and marked their age. Those who fought were "positive and disciplined, sometimes trenchant and always concise, as if they were sure of themselves, as if they knew exactly what to think." Those who did not enlist, particularly Henry Adams and Henry James, developed "the opposite qualities—ambiguity, prolixity, irony—that reflect a kind of lack of self-confidence, a diffidence and a mechanism of self-defense."[26]

Edith Wharton explored proper Bostonians' response to military service in a short story, "Lamp of the Psyche," written in the early 1890s, when memories of the Civil War weighed on the minds both of those who served and of those who did not. Wharton, born into New York City's exclusive "400," learned a good deal about Boston, a city she never liked, when she married Edward Robbins Wharton. "Teddy" was an idle, Harvard-educated Boston patrician whose family townhouse stood near the Shaw residence on Beacon Street. In Wharton's story Delia Corbett brings her husband,

Laurence, home to meet the proud and principled Bostonian aunt who reared her. When he admits, without shame, that he avoided war service, her aunt's silent disapproval of his cowardice is withering and Delia suddenly sees him through judgmental eyes; she realizes he "cannot survive being viewed in Boston light." It has been suggested that the character and conflict of Laurence Corbett may have been based upon the husband of Isabella Stewart Gardner, "Jack," who also avoided war service.[27] Corbett's character may also echo another friend of Edith Wharton's, Egerton Winthrop, a descendant of John Winthrop, a prominent member of New York society and a playboy with a taste for decoration, who went to Paris to avoid service in the Civil War.[28] In any case, Edith Wharton portrayed the commitment to moral courage and military service as a central test of the Boston character.

Boston's "Indian Summer" of fading purpose, nostalgia, and diminished creativity became increasingly evident late in the nineteenth century. In Brooks's words, "society had lost its vital interests, and the Boston mind was indolent and flaccid, as if the struggle for existence had passed it by."[29] The great writers of the region's mid-century renaissance had died off, their works codified, institutionalized, and shelved as American classics; the literary center of America had moved to Manhattan, along with William Dean Howells; and Boston had become associated in the American mind with propriety and sanctimoniousness. The New England Society for the Suppression of Vice, which held its first annual meeting in the Park Street Church in 1879, initiated obscenity charges against Walt Whitman's *Leaves of Grass* in 1882. The Watch and Ward Society in 1891 helped "Banned in Boston" become a catch-phrase that mocked the city as stuffy and fussy in the nation's mind. "We are vanishing into provincial obscurity," decried Barrett Wendell, influential Harvard professor and celebrator of Boston's Puritan past. "America has swept from our grasp. The future is beyond us."[30]

Yet this was also a great period of cultural consolidation in Boston, when prosperous citizens contributed to the city's expansion, beautification, and institutional representation. In 1872, the year of Boston's "Great Fire"—which consumed some 65 acres and 700 buildings in Boston's downtown, but then led to vast reconstruction of the city—the Museum of Fine Arts was established in Copley Square, on the grounds of Back Bay, the landfill that extended Boston's reach and provided space for the grand dwellings of the city's expanding gentry. That same year Henry Hobson Richardson was enlisted to build the Romanesque Trinity Church in Copley Square, an Episcopal church famous for its beautiful windows: four were designed by Edward Burne-Jones and executed by William Morris; another four by John La Farge in layers of opalescent glass. La Farge also did the "Battle Window" at Harvard's Memorial Hall. Between 1880 and 1895 Frederick Law Olmsted's "Emerald Necklace" was constructed: nine parks, parkways, and waterways that link Boston Common to Jamaica Pond, that run through the Arnold Arboretum to Franklin Park, adding sculptured pastoral settings to the city's landscape, Boston's answer to New York City's Central Park. In 1895 the firm of McKim, Mead, and White built the magnificent Boston Public Library in Copley Square, the first publicly supported municipal library in the United States, a model of civic art. McKim, Mead, and White also designed the matchless Symphony Hall, inaugurated in 1900. Stately Horticultural Hall also designed in the Beaux Arts manner, opened, across the street, in 1901. In 1903 Fenway Court, conceived in the style of a Venetian Renaissance palazzo, was erected by Isabella Stewart Gardner, a wealthy and eccentric patron of the arts. Nearby, in the Back Bay Fens, the Boston Museum of Fine Arts, moved from Copley Square, opened in 1909 along Huntington Avenue, Boston's "Avenue of the Arts." John Singer Sargent, who had created murals for the Boston Public Library, added designs that glorify the MFA rotunda, further consolidating Boston's claims to artistic primacy.

Yet Boston's "problem" persisted. In the critical reading of Martin Green's study of this period, *The Problem of Boston* (1966), the city remained committed to Winthrop's ideal of a city upon a hill throughout the century, dedicated to the goal "of achieving a high quality of life in a community as a whole, and of expressing that quality in a great literature." However, by 1900, "actual Boston had become widely separated from ideal Boston. . . . It became progressively more malformed and dysfunctional, a caricature of the earlier ideal."[31]

Henry Adams came to see the city that shaped him in similar terms. His *Life of George Cabot Lodge* (1911) is a biography in the form of a parable of the city's lost purpose. Lodge was the son of Henry Cabot Lodge, Adams's former student at Harvard who became a leading isolationist Republican senator who led the fight to restrict immigration. George Cabot Lodge turned from politics to the arts, a writer of sonnets who died young. In

Adams's reading, *fin-de-siècle* Boston was no more welcoming to artful literary expression than it was to bold political or religious purpose. Since Emerson's day, "the sense of poetry had weakened like the sense of religion." The city valued George Cabot Lodge no more than it had Henry Adams. "The Bostonian of 1900 differed from his parents and grandparents of 1850, in owning nothing the value of which, in the market, could be affected by the poet."[32] Adams wrote his requiem for Boston while living in exile, mainly as a citizen of Washington, D.C., in a state of detachment in which he composed political novels of manners and his *Education*, his way of saying good-bye to all that Boston had meant to him and his family. He even blamed Boston for his hatred of mankind. "Indeed Boston cankers our hearts."[33]

No Boston writer speaks to or illustrates this era's state of ennui and bitterness more dramatically than George Santayana. He was first a student of William James at Harvard and then his colleague, joining James and Josiah Royce as yet another distinguished philosopher on the Harvard faculty. Born in Madrid in 1863 to a Catalonian mother who had married into a prominent Boston family, the Sturgises, George was brought to Boston at age eight to be educated. He never felt at ease in the Brahmin Zion; indeed, he grew up to infantilize Boston in his "fragments of autobiography," *Persons and Places* (1944): Boston "was a moral and intellectual nursery, always busy applying first principles to trifles."[34] His Catholicism detached him from the remaining remnants of Boston Puritanism and he dismissed the New England literary heritage as a mere "harvest of leaves."[35]

Though Santayana taught philosophy at Harvard for twenty-three years and became a local celebrity, lecturing Bostonians and walking the Cambridge streets in a long cape, he remained "a stranger at heart."[36] He resigned his position and left Boston and Cambridge forever in 1912, at age forty-eight, but, like other exiles before him, he carried their images and standards of measure in his head, if not in his heart. In his autobiography Santayana looked back upon the Boston of the mid-nineteenth century less in anger than in amusement at its pious pretensions. For example, he mocked Concord-Boston worthies of the 1850s by portraying them in attendance at a Boston theater fittingly called "The Museum." "Emerson is said to have exclaimed, 'This is art!' To which Margaret Fuller replied with added rapture, 'Ah, Mr. Emerson, this is religion!'"[37] Santayana's detached aestheticism and patronizing perspective here turn Boston's august figures into actors in a farce.

Santayana developed the drama of Boston in the theater of his mind for some forty-five years before he completed and published *The Last Puritan: A Memoir in the Form of a Novel* in 1936, a work that became a best-seller in part because it confirmed prevailing myths of Brahmin Boston. Actually, Oliver Alden, the novel's tragic anti-hero, spent little time in the city, though his character and values were misshaped by the city's Brahmin class. He was marked by Boston's Puritan values, which had hardened into the repressive gentility of his uncle, Nathaniel Alden. Every Tuesday and Thursday morning Nathaniel Alden emerged from his Beacon Street townhouse and turned *left* toward King's Chapel, the church which had stood at the corners of Tremont and School Streets since 1754. In its Anglican rituals and its adaptation to Unitarianism, King's Chapel was the high church of Brahmin Boston. "He always turned to the left, for never, except to funerals, did Mr. Nathaniel Alden walk *down* Beacon Hill."[38] Had he done the unimaginable and turned *right* to walk *down* Beacon Street, he would have come to Charles Street, which separates Boston Common, the city's old grazing ground, from the Public Garden, its beautiful public park built upon land-fill. At that corner Mr. Nathaniel Alden might have risked encountering alien voices and behaviors which surely would have disturbed him.

> The corner of Beacon and Charles Streets was central and respectable. Indeed it formed a sort of isthmus, leaving the flood of niggerdom to the north and paddydom to the south, and connecting Beacon Hill with Back Bay—the two islands of respectability composing socially habitable Boston.[39]

Far safer, then, to turn left, to walk proudly past the State House and the Athenaeum, Brahmin Boston's private library, down the other side of Beacon Street toward King's Chapel, the sanctuary of latter-day Puritans who shaped an original theology, the place where parishioners could reaffirm their own safety and superiority within the closed doors of its pews. Santayana here satirizes late Brahmin Boston, constricted by prejudices. Oliver Alden inherited these debilitating values and thus became a model of "Puritanism Self-condemned. Oliver was THE LAST PRUITAN."[40]

Oliver dies young, as had previous models of unrealized Brahmin possibilities, Robert Gould Shaw and George Cabot Lodge. However, while Shaw died nobly and Lodge poignantly, Alden died absurdly—in a motorcycle accident after the armistice ended the Great War in which he served.

Oliver's father had already committed suicide, so his valediction marked the end of his line and implied the end of his class.

> I was born a moral aristocrat, able to obey only the voice of God, which means that of my own heart. My people first went to America as exiles into a stark wilderness to lead a life apart, purer and soberer than the Carnival life of Christendom. . . . We are not wanted. . . . I shan't shut myself up in Beacon Street or mince my steps or wear black gloves. But I can keep my thoughts inviolate, like Uncle Nathaniel, and not allow the world to override me. We will not accept anything cheaper or cruder than our own conscience. We have dedicated ourselves to the truth, to living in the presence of the noblest things we can conceive. If we can't live so, we won't live at all.[41]

Here Santayana bids farewell to all that Boston had meant to him, all that he had mocked, by killing off the city's Last Puritan.

Dead, but not forgotten, the Brahmin representative man lived on in myth and tale, even in film, only to die yet again in John P. Marquand's *The Late George Apley* (1937), a novel which enforced the era's theme of moral and spiritual attrition. Marquand, like Santayana, takes an ironic tack into Beacon Hill's lofty airs, but his work is far less bitter, much more forgiving. Marquand's satire dissolves into sentiment, perhaps because Apley's class had lost its choking grip on the city. Puritan judgmentalism has faded into fussiness and pettiness, inviting the reader's amusement rather than anger, but also revealing the honorable core values that so long had sustained these proper Bostonians. Both *The Last Puritan* and *The Late George Apley* became national best-sellers, suggesting that Santayana and Marquand, writing in the midst of the Great Depression, were not only providing rare glimpses into the lives behind the leaded glass windows of Beacon Hill's redbrick townhouses but also were offering ways of understanding the values that had been lost in the passing of this world of old Boston money, manners, and morality.

Santayana brushed off Marquand's novel with the same disdain he had dismissed Emerson's writings. "Mr. Marquand's hero seems to me not so much Bostonian as provincial."[42] To which Marquand might have justly replied, "Exactly!"—for provincial smugness and class defensiveness characterize his novel's narrator, Horatio Willing, a Beacon Hill stuffed shirt determined to bury George Apley in filiopietistic prose.

Marquand, a great-nephew of Margaret Fuller and married to Christina

Sedgwick, niece of Ellery Sedgwick, (*Atlantic Monthly* editor 1909–1938), had entry into Apley's Brahmin world, but he was detached from it, with roots on the Massachusetts North Shore and in an old Newburyport family. Thus Marquand, who had felt himself an outsider at Harvard, brought a whimsical eye to the manners of Boston's self-anointed saving remnant. When he moved to Beacon Hill in 1927, he joined the Tavern Club and became a member of the Athenaeum—which overlooks the Granary Burial Ground, resting place of the Boston elect—Brahmin preserves in which he could observe tribal rites as though he were Margaret Mead in Samoa. The Tavern Club, founded in 1884 in downtown Boston, became something of a literary center, with Henry James, William Dean Howells, Rudyard Kipling, and others as members. The Boston Athenaeum, founded in 1807 and first named the Anthology Club, has since 1850 stood in a grand building atop Beacon Street, its Reading Room and five galleried floors a cultural haven for cultured Bostonians. As Katherine Wolff puts this in her history of this private library, *Culture Club,* in the nineteenth century "the Athenaeum ethos was built upon Federalism and Unitarianism. The majority of the institution's leaders emphasized a restrained attitude toward popular democracy. Long after the Federalist Party was dead, Federalist sentiment held sway in Boston. In elite circles, men believed in a gradual uplifting of society through charity and enlightened leadership."[43] George Apley assumes his responsibilities as a Brahmin enlightened reader by campaigning to have the books of Sigmund Freud stored in the Athenaeum's Locked Room.

"Boston is the only city in America you could satirize," Marquand declared.[44] He was inspired to write his novel after reading the honorific tributes to Brahmin worthies by Mark A. De Wolfe Howe, Jr., a fellow club and library member, author of *Barrett Wendell and His Letters* (1924) and other flattering biographies of Boston worthies. In the pages of *Atlantic Monthly,* in 1903, Howe mounted his defense of the Boston cultural realm in "The Literary Centre," affirming Boston's centrality as an unarguable fact: "the assertion that Boston was the literary centre during the period in which American literature acquired a shelf of its own in the library of the race is hardly open to dispute."[45]

An outsider like Howells and Marquand, Howe, from Bristol, Rhode Island, came to view Boston as his heavenly city. He could trace his first family lineage back to James Howe, who arrived in Roxbury in 1637. Howe lived on Beacon Hill; he was a member of Harvard's Board of Overseers; he became a director of Atlantic Monthly Company, a trustee of the Boston Symphony Orchestra, a member of both the library committee of the Athenaeum and the vestry of Trinity Church. Howe, then, was the quintessential Solid Man of Boston, its reliable tribal memorialist and protector. When, for example, Annie Fields prepared to publish a volume of letters, Howe advised her to remove her sentimental nicknames ("Pinny," "Fluff") for Sarah Orne Jewett, lest Bostonians get the correct impression that they shared a "Boston marriage."[46] When Howe compiled *Memoirs of a Hostess* (1922), drawing upon Annie Fields's diaries, he drew a discreet veil over the actual Fields-Jewett relationship, describing it as a joining of "true *aristophiles*" who embodied "those lasting things that are more excellent"—more excellent, presumably, than the transient things so evident in the Irish-dominated, money-centered Boston of Howe's era.[47]

In Marquand's epistolary novel, John Apley, George's son, enlists Horatio Willing, "Boston's Dean of Letters," modeled upon Howe, to "take a hand in my father's notes and letters" after his death. Willing echoes Howe's insistently celebratory treatment of his subject in order to illustrate "the true spirit of our city and of our time, since Apley was so essentially a part of both."[48] However, out of respect for his father's memory, John urges Willing to reveal some of the compromising truths of George Apley's life. John knew and wanted his family and friends to understand that his father had been trapped in the confining persona of the Proper Bostonian. "Father was a frustrated man, but then I could see that he had been trying all his life to get through the meshes of a net, a net which he could never break, and in a sense it was a net of his own contriving."[49] Marquand's irony is evident in his artful presentation of contending perspectives, Willing's puffery and John's candor, on the life of George Apley, a Bostonian representative man.

Willing would have his readers see George, Harvard class of 1887, as "a type, perhaps, but a type of which Harvard may be definitely proud," though John prods Willing to affirm George's uniqueness by including a chapter on his brief passion for Mary Monahan, his "SWEET IRISH ROSE." Willing attempts to circumscribe this intense period in Apley's life by titling his chapter "Interlude," something transient, and adding a note: "Dealing with a Subject Which Would Not Ordinarily Be Discussed in a Work of This Nature," thus detaching himself from responsibility for including what he thinks constitutes embarrassing information on this Boston worthy. Willing reluctantly reports that young George was swept away by his feelings for

Mary because, as he wrote to her, "you took me away, just as I hope you will take me away forever from everything which binds and ties me."[50] However, when his shocked parents learn of his unthinkable dalliance with an Irish girl, it is George who is quickly taken away, swept off to Europe where they hoped he would forget her. While abroad, George has an epiphany of his limited life and resigns himself to his inherited role, as he expresses through an arresting, domestic image in a letter to a friend—a letter John insists that Willing include in his book.

> It seems to me that all this time a part of Boston has been with me. I am a raisin in a slice of pie which has been conveyed from one plate to another. I have moved; I have seen plate after plate; but all the other raisins have been around me in the same relation to me that they were when we were all baked.[51]

Though he treasured the memory of Mary Monahan, an emblem of his thwarted life of impulse and feeling, George married within his Brahmin caste (a Bosworth), became a dutiful, public man of Boston, and even urged his son to follow his example. "You can go to the uttermost ends of the earth but, in a sense, you will still be in Boston."[52] As a historical irony, Mark De Wolfe Howe, Jr.'s son, who became a distinguished Harvard law professor, shared his father's name but not his disdain for the Irish, if Marquand's portrayal of Horatio Willing accurately reflects the senior Howe's attitudes. The young Mark De Wolfe Howe, Jr. married Mary Manning, an Irish actress and playwright, who helped revitalize the Poet's Theater in Cambridge in the 1950s.[53]

John Apley did escape Boston, becoming a New Yorker, but his honest tribute to his father, which he allows to be modified by Willing's praise, shows that he too came to see Boston as a inescapable fate. (New York City expressiveness and Bostonian reticence war within John Apley.) Marquand wrote as much in praise of George Apley as in mockery—thus the artfully balanced, contending voices of the novel. "Every incident [in the novel] has repeated itself with small variations in Boston," Marquand insisted after complaints about the novel were registered by fellow club members. "I have a good deal of respect for Boston and a reluctant respect for George Apley. I have a good deal of Apley in myself."[54] At the end of his day, George Apley remained an honorable, if repressed man. Marquand's novel, which begins in satire, ends as a tribute to what was good in Boston's old ways.

T. S. Eliot knew all about Boston's old ways and affirmed that "a New England genius" linked Hawthorne with Henry James. "I mean whatever we associate with certain purlieus of Boston, with Concord, with Salem, and Cambridge, Mass.: notably Emerson, Thoreau, Hawthorne and Lowell."[55] Eliot saw these writers as composing a "literary aristocracy" with its cultural center in Greater Boston. Yet this literary aristocracy was at odds with the region's social aristocracy. "The society of Boston was and is quite uncivilized but refined beyond the point of civilization." The effect of this tension in Eliot's myth of place was the stunting of its writers, particularly of Hawthorne, justifying those, like James, who escaped its influence.[56] Eliot, after his years at Harvard, would follow James's example and move to England, becoming a British citizen, far from Boston's reach.

Eliot was born and reared in St. Louis, but his New England roots reached back to Andrew Eliot, who was one of the judges at the Salem witch trials. Tom Eliot was educated at Milton Academy and at Harvard, renewing his Boston family connections, about which he remained ambivalent. When Robert Lowell first met Eliot in April 1947, these two first-family Bostonians had much to discuss, though some thirty years separated them in age. As Lowell later recalled:

> Behind us Harvard's Memorial Hall with its wasteful, irreplaceable Victorian architecture and scrolls of the Civil War dead. Before us, the rush-hour traffic. As we got stuck on the sidewalk, looking for an opening, Eliot out of the blue sky said, "Don't you loathe being compared with your relatives?" Pause, as I put the question to myself, groping for what I really felt, for what I should decently feel and what I should indecently feel. Eliot: "I do. . . . I was reading Poe's reviews the other day. He took up two of my family and wiped the floor with them. . . . I was delighted."[57]

In "Portrait of a Lady" Eliot satirized a Bostonian grande dame at ease amid her bibelots. In "The Boston Evening Transcript" Eliot mocked the closed-minded Beacon Hill set. In "Cousin Nancy" he burlesqued the broken link between Boston society and the New England literary tradition. Miss Nancy Ellicott rode "to hounds/ Over the cow pastures," while "upon the glazen shelves kept watch / Matthew and Waldo, guardians of the faith, / The army of unalterable law."[58] In "The Love Song of J. Alfred Prufrock" Eliot casts his cold eye both on Boston drawing-room culture and upon himself. Eliot's poetic persona wandered "through certain half-deserted streets, . . . Streets that follow like a tedious argument / of insidious intent / To lead you to an overwhelming question." But the poem's speaker settles for the mannered chatter Eliot had heard in Beacon Hill drawing rooms, where "the women come and go / Talking of Michelangelo." For him the mermaids would not sing.[59] As an exile from Boston, Eliot would find a larger symbol in the winding streets of London, his urban center of paralysis, expressed in *The Waste Land* (1922). Even when Boston was part of Eliot's past, it remained a living presence in his poetry, where pious and proper Boston is reimagined as a modern landscape of anxiety and anomie.

Despite all the talk of decline and fall among Boston's writers, despite all their poignant remembrances of great things past, Boston became a vibrant, modern city after the Civil War. "Was New England really dying?" asks Van Wyck Brooks, principal proponent of the attrition thesis. "Or did it merely wish to think so?"[60] As we have seen, Boston was expanding its boundaries, extending its claims as an educational and financial center, and establishing its eminence in the erection of impressive cultural institutions. In the words of urban historian Sam Bass Warner, Jr., "no period in Boston's history was more dynamic that the prosperous years of the second half of the nineteenth century," when the city grew from two hundred thousand inhabitants to over a million. "In 1850 Boston was a tightly-packed seaport; by 1900 it sprawled over a ten-mile radius and contained thirty-one cities and towns."[61] By the early years of the twentieth century, old Boston, as we have seen Henry James decry in *The American Scene*, was long gone. Repressive Puritanism, the ideology on which the city was founded, had evolved into permissive Unitarianism and practical pragmatism; the social cohesion which was the creation of homogeneous settlers and their descendants had dissolved as the Irish, followed by other newcomers, registered their presence; the idealism evident in Bostonians' commitment to end slavery and preserve the Union had given way to less lofty, more commercial goals; and, as Warner points out, industrialization, immigration, and "ever more intense urbanization" transformed Boston into an alien country for many of its long-established residents.[62]

Edward Bellamy's best-selling utopian novel, *Looking Backward: 2000–1887*, published in 1888, illustrates the end-of-the-century anxieties felt among the Boston elite in facing this transformed city. Julian West, the narrator, a young Boston Brahmin tormented by the social chaos of the Gilded

Age, falls asleep in an underground chamber of his townhouse, only to awaken, to his amazement, in 2000 to find that all social conflicts have been resolved through the imposition of communist egalitarianism. Bellamy's use of a future setting for his utopian vision in *Looking Backward*, like Hawthorne's use of a past setting for his dystopian vision in *The Scarlet Letter*, written forty years before, dramatized the social and cultural failures of his day. Both novels call Boston back to its vision of a unified society, John Winthrop's place of "justice and mercy."[63] At the turn into the twentieth century, Boston had become for many of its first citizens and finest writers a nightmare from which they were trying to awake.

Bellamy's anxieties were well founded, but also exaggerated, for Boston would thrive throughout the twentieth century, despite its testing social, economic, and political trials. Boston retained a sense of itself as a city of position and purpose, even as it lost ground to New York City during what *Time* magazine publisher Henry Luce called the American Century. Boston's three centuries of rich history gave it a strong sense of the past, even when its writers looked back on that past with fond amusement, as did Cleveland Amory in *The Proper Bostonians* (1947), a work that celebrated the once-dominant but now increasingly marginalized class of Boston Brahmins as valuable contributors to the city's "charm," even while the city was being transformed utterly by the contributions of "other" Bostonians.[64]

Oliver Wendell Holmes, Jr., "Dead, Yet Living" (1884)

Oliver Wendell Holmes, Jr. (1841–1935), Civil War hero, author, and Supreme Court Justice, delivered this speech on Memorial Day, May 30, 1884, at Keene, New Hampshire, before John Sedgwick Post No. 4, Grand Army of the Republic. Holmes speaks of the time, twenty years before, when men and women were "touched by fire."

Not long ago I heard a young man ask why people still kept up Memorial Day, and it set me thinking of the answer. Not the answer that you and I should give to each other,—not the expression of those feelings that, so long as you live, will make this day sacred to memories of love and grief and heroic youth,—but an answer which should command the assent of those who do not share our memories, and in which we of the North and our brethren of the South could join in perfect accord.

So far as this last is concerned, to be sure, there is no trouble. The soldiers who were doing their best to kill one another felt less of personal hostility, I am very certain, than some who were not imperiled by their mutual endeavors. I have heard more than one of those who had been gallant and distinguished officers on the Confederate side say that they had had no such feeling. I know that I and those whom I knew best had not. We believed that it was most desirable that the North should win; we believed in the principle that the Union is indissoluable; we, or many of us at least, also believed that the conflict was inevitable, and that slavery had lasted long enough. But we equally believed that those who stood against us held just as sacred conviction that were the opposite of ours, and we respected them as every man with a heart must respect those who give all for their belief. The experience of battle soon taught its lesson even to those who came into the field more bitterly disposed. You could not stand up day after day in those indecisive contests where overwhelming victory was impossible because neither side would run as they ought when beaten, without getting at last something of the same brotherhood for the enemy that the north pole of a magnet has for the south—each working in an opposite sense to the other, but each unable to get along without the other. As it was then, it is now. The soldiers of the war need no explanations; they can join in commemorating a soldier's death with feelings not different in kind, whether he fell toward them or by their side.

But Memorial Day may and ought to have a meaning also for those who do not share our memories. When men have instinctively agreed to celebrate an anniversary, it will be found that there is some thought of feeling behind it which is too large to be dependent upon associations alone. The Fourth of July, for instance, has still its serious aspect, although we no longer should think of rejoicing like children that we have escaped from an outgrown control, although we have achieved not only our national but our moral independence and know it far too profoundly to make a talk about it, and although an Englishman can join in the celebration without a scruple. For, stripped of the temporary associations which gives rise to it, it is now the moment when by common consent we pause to become conscious of our national life and to rejoice in it, to recall what our country has done for each of us, and to ask ourselves what we can do for the country in return.

So to the indifferent inquirer who asks why Memorial Day is still kept up we may answer, it celebrates and solemnly reaffirms from year to year a national act of enthusiasm and faith. It embodies in the most impressive form our belief that to act with enthusiasm and faith is the condition of acting greatly. To fight out a war, you must believe something and want something with all your might. So must you do to carry anything else to an end worth reaching. More than that, you must be willing to commit yourself to a course, perhaps a long and hard one, without being able to foresee exactly where you will come out. All that is required of you is that you should go somewhither as hard as ever you can. The rest belongs to fate. One may fall—at the beginning of the charge or at the top of the earthworks—but in no other way can he reach the rewards of victory.

When it was felt so deeply as it was on both sides that a man ought to take part in the war unless some conscientious scruple or strong practical reason made it impossible, was that feeling simply the requirement of a local majority that their neighbors should agree with them? I think not: I think the feeling was right—in the South as in the North. I think that, as life is action and passion, it is required of a man that he should share the passion and action of his time at peril of being judged not to have lived.

If this be so, the use of this day is obvious. It is true that I cannot argue a man into a desire. If he says to me, Why should I seek to know the secrets of philosophy? Why seek to decipher the hidden laws of creation that are graven upon the tablets of the rocks, or to unravel the history of civilization that is woven in the tissue of our jurisprudence, or to do any great work, either of speculation or of practical affairs? I cannot answer him; or at least my answer is as little worth making for any effect it will have upon his wishes if he asked why I should eat this, or drink that. You must begin by wanting to. But although desire cannot be imparted by argument, it can be by contagion. Feeling begets feeling, and great feeling begets great feeling. We can hardly share the emotions that make this day to us the most sacred day of the year, and embody them in ceremonial pomp, without in some degree imparting them to those who come after us. I believe from the bottom of my heart that our memorial halls and statues and tablets, the tattered flags of our regiments gathered in the Statehouses, are worth more to our young men by way of chastening and inspiration than the monuments of another hundred years of peaceful life could be.

But even if I am wrong, even if those who come after us are to forget all that we hold dear, and the future is to teach and kindle its children in ways as yet unrevealed, it is enough for us that this day is dear and sacred.

Accidents may call up the events of the war. You see a battery of guns go by at a trot, and for a moment you are back at White Oak Swamp, or Antietam, or on the Jerusalem Road. You hear a few shots fired in the distance, and for an instant your heart stops as you say to yourself, the skirmishers are at it, and listen for the long roll of fire from the main line. You meet an old comrade after many years of absence; he recalls the moment that you were nearly surrounded by the enemy, and again there comes up to you that swift and cunning thinking on which once hung life and freedom—Shall I stand the best chance if I try the pistol or the sabre on that man who means to stop me? Will he get his carbine free before I reach him, or can I kill him first? These and the thousand other events we have known are called up, I say, by accident, and, apart from accident, they lie forgotten.

But as surely as this day comes round we are in the presence of the dead. For one hour, twice a year at least—at the regimental dinner, where the ghosts sit at table more numerous than the living, and on this day when we decorate their graves—the dead come back and live with us.

I see them now, more than I can number, as once I saw them on this earth. They are the same bright figures, or their counterparts, that come also before your eyes; and when I speak of those who were my brothers, the same words describe yours.

I see a fair-haired lad, a lieutenant, and a captain on whom life had begun somewhat to tell, but still young, sitting by the long mess-table in camp before the regiment left the State, and wondering how many of those who gathered in our tent could hope to see the end of what was then beginning. For neither of them was that destiny reserved. I remember, as I awoke from my first long stupor in the hospital after the battle of Ball's Bluff, I heard the doctor say, "He was a beautiful boy," and I knew that one of those two speakers was no more. The other, after passing through all the previous battles, went into Fredericksburg with strange premonition of the end, and there met his fate.

I see another youthful lieutenant as I saw him in the Seven Days, when I looked down the line at Glendale. The officers were at the head of their companies. The advance was beginning. We caught each other's eye and saluted. When next I looked, he was gone.

I see the brother of the last—the flame of genius and daring on his face— as he rode before us into the wood of Antietam, out of which came only dead and deadly wounded men. So, a little later, he rode to his death at the head of his cavalry in the Valley.

In the portraits of some of those who fell in the civil wars of England, Vandyke has fixed on canvas the type who stand before my memory. Young and gracious faces, somewhat remote and proud, but with a melancholy and sweet kindness. There is upon their faces the shadow of approaching fate, and the glory of generous acceptance of it. I may say of them, as I once heard it said of two Frenchmen, relics of the *ancien regime*, "They were very gentle. They cared nothing for their lives." High breeding, romantic chivalry—we who have seen these men can never believe that the power of money or the enervation of pleasure has put an end to them. We know that life may still be lifted into poetry and lit with spiritual charm.

But the men, not less, perhaps even more, characteristic of New England, were the Puritans of our day—for the Puritan still lives in New England, thank God! and will live there so long as New England lives and keeps her old renown. New England is not dead yet. She still is mother of a race of conquerors. Stern men, little given to the expression of their feelings, sometimes careless of their graces, but fertile, tenacious, and knowing only duty. Each of you, as I do, thinks of a hundred such that he has known. . . .

I have spoken of some of the men who were near to me among others very near and dear, not because their lives have become historic, but because their lives are the type of what every soldier has known and seen in his own company. In the great democracy of self-devotion private and general stand side by side. Unmarshalled save by their own deeds, the army of the dead sweep before us, "wearing their wounds like stars." It is not because the men I have mentioned were my friends that I have spoken of them, but, I repeat, because they are types. I speak of those whom I have seen. But you all have known such; you, too, remember!

It is not of the dead alone that we think on this day. There are those still living whose sex forbade them to offer their lives, but who gave instead their happiness. Which of us has not been lifted above himself by the sight of one of those lovely, lonely women, around whom the wand of sorrow has traced its excluding circle—set apart, even when surrounded by loving friends who would fain bring back joy to their lives? I think of one whom the poor of a great city know as their benefactress and friend. I think of one who has lived not less greatly in the midst of her children, to whom she has taught such lessons as may not be heard elsewhere from mortal lips. The story of these and her sisters we must pass in reverent silence. All that may be said has been said by one [Emily Bronte] of their own sex:

> But when the days of golden dreams had perished,
> And even despair was powerless to destroy;
> Then did I learn how existence could be cherished,
> Strengthened, and fed without the aid of joy.
>
> Then did I check the tears of useless passion,
> Weaned my young soul from yearning after thine;
> Sternly denied its burning wish to hasten
> Down to that tomb already more than mine.

Comrades, some of the associations of this day are not only triumphant, but joyful. Not all of those with whom we once stood shoulder to shoulder—not all of those whom we once loved and revered—are gone. On this day we still meet our companions in the freezing winter bivouacs and in those dreadful summer marches where every faculty of the soul seemed to depart one after another, leaving only a dumb animal power to set the teeth and to persist—a blind belief that somewhere and at last there was bread and water. On this day, at least, we still meet and rejoice in the closest tie which is possible between men—a tie which suffering has made indissoluble for better, for worse.

When we meet thus, when we do honor to the dead in terms that must sometimes embrace the living, we do not deceive ourselves. We attribute no special merit to a man for having served when all were serving. We know that if the armies of our war did anything worth remembering, the credit belongs not mainly to the individuals who did it, but to average human nature. We also know very well that we cannot live in associations with the past alone, and we admit that, if we would be worthy of the past, we must find new fields for action or thought, and make for ourselves new careers.

But, nevertheless, the generation that carried on the war has been set apart by its experience. Through our great good fortune, in our youth our hearts were touched with fire. It was given to us to learn at the outset that life is a profound and passionate thing. While we are permitted to scorn nothing but indifference, and do not pretend to undervalue the worldly rewards of ambition, we have seen with our own eyes, beyond and above the gold fields, the snowy heights of honor, and it is for us to bear the report to those who come after us. But, above all, we have learned that whether a man accepts from Fortune her spade, and will look downward and dig, or from Aspiration her axe and cord, and will scale the ice, the one and only success which it is his to command is to bring to his work a mighty heart.

Such hearts—ah me, how many!—were stilled twenty years ago; and to us who remain behind is left this day of memories. Every year—in the full tide of spring, at the height of the symphony of flowers and love and life—there comes a pause, and through the silence we hear the lonely pipe of death. Year after year lovers wandering under the apple trees and through the clover and deep grass are surprised with sudden tears as they see black veiled figures stealing through the morning to a soldier's grave. Year after year the comrades of the dead follow, with public honor, procession and commemorative flags and funeral march—honor and grief from us who stand almost alone, and have seen the best and noblest of our generation pass away.

But grief is not the end of all. I seem to hear the funeral march become a paean. I see beyond the forest the moving banners of a hidden column. Our dead brothers still live for us, and bid us think of life, not death—of life to which in their youth they lent the passion and joy of the spring. As I listen, the great chorus of life and joy begins again, and amid the awful orchestra of seen and unseen powers and destinies of good and evil our trumpets sound once more a note of daring, hope, and will.

Edith Wharton, from "The Lamp of Psyche" (1895)

Edith Wharton (1862–1937) authored many distinguished works of fiction, including *The House of Mirth* (1905), *Ethan Frome* (1912), and *The Age of Innocence* (1920). In this scene from "The Lamp of Psyche" Delia Corbett incorporates the Bostonian moral values of her proud Aunt Mary. Delia comes to feel shame because her husband, Laurence, avoided service in the Civil War, realizing that he "cannot survive being viewed in Boston light."

Two weeks later the Corbetts returned to Europe. Corbett had really been charmed with his visit, and had in fact shown a marked inclination to outstay the date originally fixed for their departure. But Delia was firm; she did not wish to remain in Boston. She acknowledged that she was sorry to leave her Aunt Mary; but she wanted to get home.

"You turncoat!" Corbett said, laughing. "Two months ago you reserved that sacred designation for Boston."

"One can't tell where it is until one tries," she answered, vaguely.

"You mean that you don't want to come back and live in Boston?"

"Oh, no—no!"

"Very well. But pray take note of the fact that I'm very sorry to leave. Under your Aunt Mary's tutelage I'm becoming a passionate patriot."

Delia turned away in silence. She was counting the moments which led to their departure. She longed with an unreasoning intensity to get away from it all; from the dreary house in Mount Vernon Street, with its stencilled hall and hideous drawing-room, its monotonous food served in unappetizing profusion; from the rarefied atmosphere of philanthropy and reform which she had once found so invigorating; and most of all from the reproval of her aunt's altruistic activities. The recollection of her husband's delightful house in Paris, so framed for a noble leisure, seemed to mock the aesthetic barrenness of Mrs. Hayne's environment. Delia thought tenderly of the mellow bindings, the deep-piled rugs, the pictures, bronzes, and tapestries; of the "first nights" at the Francais, the eagerly discussed *conferences* on art or literature, the dreaming hours in galleries and museums, and all the delicate enjoyments of the life to which she was returning. It would be like passing from a hospital-ward to a flower-filled drawing-room; how could her husband linger on the threshold?

Corbett, who observed her attentively, noticed that a change had come over her during the last two weeks of their stay in Mount Vernon Street. He wondered uneasily if she were capricious; a man who has formed his own habits upon principles of the finest selection does not care to think that he has married a capricious woman. Then he reflected that the love of Paris is an insidious disease, breaking out when its victim least looks for it, and concluded that Delia was suffering from some such unexpected attack.

Delia certainly was suffering. Ever since Mrs. Hayne had asked her that innocent question—"Why shouldn't your husband have been in the war?"— she had been repeating it to herself day and night with the monotonous iteration of a monomaniac. Whenever Corbett came into the room, with that air of giving the simplest act its due value which made episodes of his entrances she was tempted to cry out to him—"Why weren't you in the war?" When she heard him, at a dinner, point one of his polished epigrams, or smilingly demolish the syllogism of an antagonist, her pride in his achievement was chilled by the question—"Why wasn't he in the war?" When she saw him, in the street, give a coin to a crossing-sweeper, or lift his hat ceremoniously to one of Mrs. Hayne's maid-servants (he was always considerate of poor people and servants) her approval winced under the reminder— "Why wasn't he in the war?" And when they were alone together, all through the spell of his talk and the exquisite pervasion of his presence ran the embittering undercurrent, "Why wasn't he in the war?"

At times she hated herself for the thought; it seemed a disloyalty to life's best gift. After all, what did it matter now? The war was over and forgotten; it was what the newspapers call "a dead issue." And why should any act of her husband's youth affect their present happiness together? Whatever he might once have been, he was perfect now; admirable in every relation of life; kind, generous, upright; a loyal friend, an accomplished gentleman, and, above all, the man she loved. Yes—but why had he not been in the war? And so began again the reiterant torment of the question. It rose up and lay down with her; it watched with her through sleepless nights, and followed her into the street; it mocked her from the eyes of strangers, and she dreaded lest her husband should read it in her own. In her saner moments she told herself that she was under the influence of a passing mood, which would vanish at the contact of her wonted life in Paris. She had become over-strung in the high air of Mrs. Hayne's moral enthusiasms; all she needed was to descend again to regions of more temperate virtue. This thought increased her impatience to be gone; and the days seemed interminable which divided her from departure.

The return to Paris, however, did not yield the hoped-for alleviation. The question was still with her, clamoring for a reply, and reinforced, with separation, by the increasing fear of her aunt's unspoken verdict. That shrewd woman had never again alluded to the subject of her brief colloquy with Delia; up to the moment of his farewell she had been unreservedly cordial to Corbett; but she was not the woman to palter with her convictions.

Delia knew what she must think; she knew what name, in the old days, Corbett would have gone by in her aunt's uncompromising circle.

Then came a flash of resistance—the heart's instinct of self-preservation. After all, what did she herself know of her husband's reasons for not being in the war? What right had she to set down to cowardice a course which might have been enforced by necessity, or dictated by unimpeachable motives? Why should she not put to him the question which she was perpetually asking herself? And not having done so, how dared she condemn him unheard?

A month or more passed in this torturing indecision. Corbett had returned with fresh zest to his accustomed way of life, weaned, by his first glimpse of the Champs Elysees, from his factitious enthusiasm for Boston. He and his wife entertained their friends delightfully, and frequented all the "first nights" and "private views" of the season, and Corbett continued to bring back knowing "bits" from the Hotel Drouot, and rare books from the quays; never had he appeared more cultivated, more decorative and enviable; people agreed that Delia Benson had been uncommonly clever to catch him.

One afternoon he returned later than usual from the club, and, finding his wife alone in the drawing-room, begged her for a cup of tea. Delia reflected, in complying, that she had never seen him look better; his fifty-two years sat upon him like a finish which made youth appear crude, and his voice, as he recounted his afternoon's doings, had the intimate inflections reserved for her ear.

"By the way," he said presently, as he set down his tea-cup, "I had almost forgotten that I've brought you a present—something I picked up in a little shop in the Rue Bonaparte. Oh, don't look too expectant; it's not a *chef-d'oeuvre*; on the contrary, it's about as bad as it can be. But you'll see presently why I bought it."

As he spoke he drew a small flat parcel from the breast-pocket of his impeccable frock-coat and handed it to his wife.

Delia, loosening the paper which wrapped it, discovered within an oval frame studded with pearls and containing the crudely executed miniature of an unknown young man in the uniform of a United States cavalry officer. She glanced inquiringly at Corbett.

"Turn it over," he said.

She did so, and on the back, beneath two unfamiliar initials, read the brief inscription: "Fell at Chancellorsville, May 3, 1863."

The blood rushed to her face as she stood gazing at the words.

"You see now why I bought it?" Corbett continued. "All the pieties of one's youth seemed to protest against leaving it in the clutches of a Jew pawnbroker in the Rue Bonaparte. It's awfully bad, isn't it?—but some poor soul might be glad to think that it had passed again into the possession of fellow-country-men." He took it back from her, bending to examine it critically. "What a daub!" he murmured. "I wonder who he was? Do you suppose that by taking a little trouble one might find out and restore it to his people?"

"I don't know—I dare say," she murmured, absently.

He looked up at the sound of her voice. "What's the matter, Delia? Don't you feel well?" he asked.

"Oh, yes. I was only thinking"—she took the miniature from his hand. "It was kind of you, Laurence, to buy this—it was like you."

"Thanks for the latter clause," he returned, smiling.

Delia stood staring at the vivid flesh-tints of the young man who had fallen at Chancellorsville.

"You weren't very strong at his age, were you, Laurence? Weren't you often ill?" she asked.

Corbett gave her a surprised glance. "Not that I'm aware of," he said; "I had the measles at twelve, but since then I've been unromantically robust."

"And you—you were in America until you came abroad to be with your sister?"

"Yes—barring a trip of a few weeks in Europe."

Delia looked again at the miniature; then she fixed her eyes upon her husband's.

"Then why weren't you in the war?" she said.

Corbett answered her gaze for a moment; then his lids dropped, and he shifted his position slightly.

"Really," he said, with a smile, "I don't think I know."

They were the very words which she had used in answering her aunt.

"You don't know?" she repeated, the question leaping out like an electric shock. "What do you mean when you say that you don't know?"

"Well—it all happened some time ago," he answered, still smiling, "and the truth is that I've completely forgotten the excellent reasons that I doubtless had at the time for remaining at home."

"Reasons for remaining at home? But there were none; every man of your age went to the war; no one stayed at home who wasn't lame, or blind, or deaf, or ill, or—" Her face blazed, her voice broke passionately.

Corbett looked at her with rising amazement.

"Or—?" he said.

"Or a coward," she flashed out. The miniature dropped from her hands, falling loudly on the polished floor.

The two confronted each other in silence; Corbett was very pale.

"I've told you," he said, at length, "that I was neither lame, deaf, blind, nor ill. Your classification is so simple that it will be easy for you to draw your own conclusion."

And very quietly, with that admirable air which always put him in the right, he walked out of the room. Delia, left alone, bent down and picked up the miniature; its protecting crystal had been broken by the fall. She pressed it close to her and burst into tears.

An hour later, of course, she went to ask her husband's forgiveness. As a woman of sense she could do no less; and her conduct had been so absurd that it was the more obviously pardonable. Corbett, as he kissed her hand, assured her that he had known it was only nervousness; and after dinner, during which he made himself exceptionally agreeable, he proposed their ending the evening at the Palais Royal, where a new play was being given.

Delia had undoubtedly behaved like a fool, and was prepared to do meet penance for her folly by submitting to the gentle sarcasm of her husband's pardon; but when the episode was over, and she realized that she had asked her question and received her answer, she knew that she had passed a milestone in her existence. Corbett was perfectly charming; it was inevitable that he should go on being charming to the end of the chapter. It was equally inevitable that she should go on being in love with him; but her love had undergone a modification which the years were not to efface.

Formerly he had been to her like an unexplored country, full of bewitching surprises and recurrent revelations of wonder and beauty; now she had measured and mapped him, and knew beforehand the direction of every path she trod. His answer to her question had given her the clue to the labyrinth; knowing what he had once done, it seemed quite simple to forecast his future conduct. For that long-past action was still a part of his actual being; he had not outlived or disowned it; he had not even seen that it needed defending.

Her ideal of him was shivered like the crystal above the miniature of the warrior of Chancellorsville. She had the crystal replaced by a piece of clear glass which (as the jeweler pointed out to her) cost much less and looked equally well; and for the passionate worship which she had paid her husband she substituted a tolerant affection which possessed precisely the same advantages.

George Santayana, from *Persons and Places* (1963), including *The Background of My Life* (1944), *The Middle Span* (1945), and *My Host the World* (1953)

George Santayana (1863–1952)—philosopher, essayist, poet, novelist, and Harvard teacher—was born in Spain. His mother, Josefina Borrás, the daughter of a Spanish official, was the widow of George Sturgis, a first-family Boston merchant. After her husband's death, she took her three Sturgis children with her to live in Madrid, where she married Agustín Santayana in 1862. In 1869 George Santayana's mother returned to Boston with her children. Santayana studied at Boston Latin School and Harvard University, where he also taught until he left America in 1912. His detached, ironic perspective is evident in this passage on what he calls "the clan," or "Boston Society."

When in the year 1858 my mother heroically fulfilled her promise to her late husband and first went to live in Boston, she knew what she was doing, for she had spent some months there two years before and had made the acquaintance of all the Sturgises and their friends. And yet I think she had expectations that were never realized. If not for herself—since she had lost all interest in society—at least for her children, she pictured a perfect amalgamation with all that was best in Boston. The amalgamation never took place. I have described the difficult position that my sister Susana found herself in, and her ultimate return to Spain; and my brother Robert, though a thorough American in all externals, never made a place for himself in good Boston society. This society, in my time, was on the one hand clannish, and on the other highly moralized and highly cultivated. The clannishness was not one of blood: you might almost say that all the "old families" were new. It was a clannishness of social affinity and habit; you must live in certain places, follow certain professions, and maintain a certain tone. Any adaptable rich family could easily enter the charmed circle within one generation. Money was necessary, not in itself but as a means of living as everybody else did in good society; and those who became too poor fell out within one generations also. As to the other characteristic of being cultivated and high-principled, it was not indispensable for individuals already in the clan; but it was necessary to the clan as a whole, for a standard and a leaven. I suspect that the lack of those qualities may have dissolved the society that I speak of, and allowed it to become indistinguishable from the flowing mass of the rich and fashionable all the world over.

Conversation in society, for me at least, was almost exclusively with ladies; but whenever I found myself by chance among elderly men, as for a while after dinner, I became aware of living in a commercial community. Talk reverted from banter to business worries, if not to "funny stories." The leaders were "business men," and weight in the business world was what counted in their estimation. Of course there must be clergymen and doctors also, and even artists, but they remained parasites, and not persons with whom the bulwarks of society had any real sympathy. Lawyers were a little better, because business couldn't be safeguarded without lawyers, and they often were or became men of property themselves; but politicians were taboo, and military men in Boston non-existent. Such persons might be occasionally entertained, and lauded rhetorically in after-dinner speeches; but they remained strangers and foreigners to the inner circle, and disagreeable to the highly moralized and highly cultivated Bostonian.

My contacts with this society were neither those of a native nor those of a visiting foreigner; nor could they be compared with my relations to Harvard

College, where I was as much at home as anybody, with a perfectly equal and legal status. In order to have slipped no less automatically and involuntarily into Boston society, I should have had to go to a fashionable school, and my family would have had to occupy the position that I imagine my mother had dreamt of. As it was, I skirmished on the borders of the polite world, and eventually limited myself to a few really friendly families.

John P. Marquand, from *The Late George Apley: A Novel in the Form of a Memoir* (1937)

John P. Marquand (1893–1960), great-nephew of Margaret Fuller and descendant of a long line of New England families, was reared on the Massachusetts North Shore, in Newburyport. He attended Harvard, married into another Boston first family, the Sedgwicks, and became a successful novelist of manners, focusing satirical attention on New England's waning Brahmin class. In this chapter of *The Late George Apley* Horatio Willing, Apley's biographer and an apologist for his class, reluctantly follows the wishes of Apley's son, John, and recounts his subject's brief romance with Mary Monahan, before his marriage to Catharine Bosworth.

INTERLUDE

Dealing with a Subject Which Would Not Ordinarily
Be Discussed in a Work of This Nature

It should be stated at the outset that nothing which will be published regarding a youthful lapse discussed in this chapter reflects to the discredit of our subject. It serves rather to illustrate that anyone at a certain stage of life may be beset by vagaries which must not be considered seriously. It must be remembered that through it all George Apley remained an outstanding success, not only in his Harvard class, but in society. That he did so, speaks well for his tradition and for his self-control.

As one approaches the age for marriage there are many of both sexes who find it difficult to settle their lives finally in the direction where their real emotions and convictions should lead them. If it is so with George Apley, others of us have faced the same problem. The solicitude of his parents at this time is manifest by the correspondence which was kept intact—as may be illustrated by these extracts from a few letters.

EXTRACT FROM A LETTER FROM ELIZABETH APLEY.

You are probably too modest, George darling, and too preoccupied with your Club and your College activities to know what a swathe you are cutting here in Boston. This makes me very proud, within limits, but you must not use that attractiveness, George, as a means of playing fast and loose. I do not need to say any more, because I know that you will be the gallant knight.

I think it is time for you to realize, though, that you are in the middle of your Senior year, that there is a certain young thing, and a very sweet one, who is taking you quite seriously. Your father and I are very glad and very much approve, because the Bosworths are quite our type of person. Catharine Bosworth has what my dear Jane Austen would call both "sense and sensibility." She has been brought up as you have been, to know that true happiness in life, such as your dear father and I have shared, is not based on external show. I think it would be very nice if you were to pay Catharine some little particular attention the next time you come into town. You and she have so much in common.

LETTER FROM GEORGE APLEY TO CATHARINE BOSWORTH.

Dear Catharine:—

Mother is coming up to my room for tea on Thursday afternoon, after the meeting at the Hemenway gymnasium. She and I would like it very much if you and your mother would drop in afterwards at Gray's. . . .

LETTER FROM ELIZABETH APLEY.

Dear George:—

I enjoyed the little tea party. I thought that dear Catharine looked very beautiful. Mrs. Bosworth could help but say how well you two dear children looked walking across the Yard together. . . .

LETTER FROM THOMAS APLEY.

Dear George:—

The portion of your grandfather's estate which came to you under her will makes a small but comfortable sum that under certain circumstances is enough to start life on, modestly. I am holding it in trust for you, as the will directs, using the income for your further education. I am also conserving a part for another contingency, in case you wish to speak to me about it. . . .

These beginnings, so intimately connected with George Apley's happiness, had an unforeseen and erratic interruption. This takes the form to-day of a bundle of letters, taped and sealed, with a subscription in Thomas Apley's handwriting, which reads as follows: "To be given to my son, George, at my death, with my request that he burn them." It is the writer's opinion that they should have been burned, either by George Apley or by his son, and this suggestion was made when this work reached the present stage. The reply of John Apley to the writer's request, which is appended here, is his authority for delving into a painful and needless detail.

Dear Mr. Willing:—

I have been over these letters very carefully myself and cannot see the harm in them. That you do only makes me feel how different your and father's world must have been from mine. My one desire is to see Father depicted as a human being. Having read what you have written up to date, and it is phrased as only you yourself could phrase it, I think this business is a good deal to his credit. It must have required a good deal of initiative on his part to go as far as he did. . . .

We will, therefore, continue in the light of this advice. The letters begin on May 1, 1887.

LETTER TO MISS MARY MONAHAN.

Dear Mary:—

It is eleven o'clock at night. My roommate has gone to bed, so naturally I am sitting writing to you, because my mind keeps going back over every minute we have been together. I believe in fate now, I believe in destiny. Why should I have been in Cambridge Port, and why should you have been there? When I picked up your handkerchief and we looked at each other, I remember every shade of violet in your eyes and every light in the black of your hair. You called me a "Back Bay dude!" Do you remember? You said we shouldn't be seen together but you met me that Sunday on Columbus Avenue. You make me see things as I have never seen them. I am not what you think me, Mary, and now I am going to show you. I am going down to Worcester Square to call on you next Sunday. If your brother Mike doesn't like it, it's time he knew better. I'll be glad to see Mike any time. . . .

For reasons too obvious to be specified, any letters which George Apley may have received from this young woman, Mary Monahan, are not at present in existence, but information gathered from conversation and correspondence with members of the family and friends gives one a glimpse of this young woman who appears so abruptly in Apley's life. This glimpse, it must be admitted, reflects favorably on George Apley's taste, granting the impossible elements of this escapade. It appears that the Monahans, in their class, were respectable. The girl's grandfather, a small farmer who held title to his own land in County Galway, left hurriedly for America for political reasons during one of those abortive revolutionary efforts near the middle of the last century. The girl's father, a contractor, who had inherited his family's political proclivities, was in a position regarded as comfortable by many of his nationality in South Boston. There was, it appears, a sufficient amount of attractiveness in this family circle to appeal to some weakness in George Apley's makeup, for there is no doubt that on many occasions he found actual relaxation at this girl's home. It may have been that George Apley's athletic prowess furnished him an additional entrée, in that further correspondence reveals that the Monahans were personal friends of the notorious pugilist John L. Sullivan.

As for the girl herself, she appears to have been superior to her class, even to the extent of being sought after by a young attorney and by a son of a member of the City Council. Apley's classmate, Chickering, who once accidentally encountered the pair in a canoe, on the upper Charles River, gave the writer a description upon which he will draw, not having himself seen the young woman. According to Chickering, who at the time was something of a lady's man, Miss Monahan had many of the externals of a young person of a higher position. She was well and quietly dressed, and of a striking beauty that was more romantic than vulgar. Her figure was slender, as were her hands and ankles, her features delicate and interesting, her hair dark, her eyes deep violet. Her manners were quiet and polite; she was even mistaken once, when George Apley was seen walking with her on Commonwealth Avenue, for a visiting Baltimore belle. It need scarcely be pointed out that all these favorable attributes served to lend to the affair most serious complications.

LETTER TO MARY MONAHAN.

My sweet wild rose:—

I hope your people liked me as much as I liked them. Dearest, I had a very good time. Darling, I love you more than anything in the world. You give me something that makes me feel free for the first time in my life. Nothing, dear, has made me so happy as this sense of freedom. Will you let me read you Browning again sometime? Poetry itself is real when I read it to you. . . .

LETTER TO MARY MONAHAN.

Sweetheart:—

I am glad that Tim thinks I am all right, because think that Tim is the same. I suppose Tim thinks so because when I went out with him I did more than shake the hand that shook the hand of Sullivan. Of course it wasn't anything, my darling. It was very kind of big John to let me stand up to him for two minutes with the gloves on and something I won't forget in a hurry. When can I see you again? Nothing here amounts to anything. Everything is a travesty until I see you. . . .

LETTER TO MARY MONAHAN.

Darling:—

Once and for all I want you to know that I mean every word that I tell you. I never knew how dull existence was until I saw you. If your father is worried by my attitude toward you, I think I had better speak to him myself. I shall gladly tell him what I have told you, that I love you and want to marry you, that I shall try all my life to make you happy. If my own family were to see how sweet you are, how utterly beautiful, they would want it, too. Believe me, believe me, everything I say I mean. . . .

LETTER TO MARY MONAHAN.

I should not care what they say, there are other places beside Boston and we can go to them. There is the West, for instance.

LETTER TO MARY MONAHAN.

For the life of me I can't stop thinking of the sailboat we hired, and of the clearness of the day, so like your soul. Though I remember every minute of it, it all goes together into something delicately sweet like music, so that I cannot take one moment from another. You took me away, just as I hope you will take me away forever from everything which binds and ties me.

The language in which these letters are couched betrays only too clearly the seriousness of George Apley's infatuation. Many passages must be left out for delicacy, as they might probe too intimately into the secrets of a high-minded idealist. It is certain that his intentions in this direction were always of the most honorable, and if latitude was offered him by the young Monahan woman, that he took no advantage of it. This is the one pleasing aspect of an affair which obviously could not be of long duration. It was only natural that in the course of time George Apley's aspirations should come to Thomas Apley's attention. Much of the ensuing detail can now be supplied only by the imagination, but the following letter suggests how the truth may have found its was to Thomas Apley.

LETTERS TO MARY MONAHAN.

Mary, darling:—

Why do you always have in the back of your mind the feeling that this is not permanent? Nothing, I can tell you, nothing can stop my love for you. All the things you speak about mean nothing to me. If you could see you would know that I am right. I am tired of being brought up in this atmo-sphere of self-assurance. I am tired of everything but you.

That is why I do not worry about rumors. What if old Clarence Corcoran has seen me in your company and has expressed surprise? It is true that Clar-ence was my father's gardener just you say, and still calls me "Master George," but I don't see why this is alarming. I am proud to tell anyone that I love you. I am prouder still that you love me, because I do not deserve it. . . .

Poor, sweet darling:—

You must leave this to me. It is very dear of you to be afraid, but I am not in the least. If my father and mother were once to see you they would understand everything. Once they do, you'll find that the Apleys stick together, and that you will be one of us. . .

Darling:—

You must not be afraid. You are the only person I shall ever love. It has been very dreadful, but they cannot stop me, my sweet, and you cannot because I love you. . . . .

Since these letter are not dated, one is obliged to guess at their chronological sequence. It will be left to the reader to fill between the lines himself, and to draw his own conclusions regarding such events as these lines foreshadow. Since this correspondence comes to an abrupt end, it may be assumed that rumors finally reached the ear of Thomas Apley, but the natural reticence of a man of affairs and of a family confronted with such a problem leaves his exact reaction to it, and his methods of dealing with what must have been, to him, a shocking affair, considerably in the dark.

The reactions of the Monahan girl, who one suspects betrayed better sense than many another in her position and of her connections, lie also behind a blank wall of silence.

T. S. Eliot, *"The Boston Evening Transcript"* (1917) and *"Cousin Nancy"* (1917)

T. S. Eliot (1888–1965), distinguished poet, critic, and playwright, was awarded the Nobel Prize for Literature in 1948. His poetry includes *The Waste Land* (1922) and *Four Quartets* (1943). Though born and reared in St. Louis, the poet had extensive Greater Boston relations, and his family spent summers in Gloucester, on Cape Ann, north of Boston. "The river is within us, the sea is all about us," wrote Eliot in "The Dry Salvages." Though he was a successful Harvard student, taking two degrees, and his cousin, Charles William Eliot, was the college's president, Eliot cast a cold eye on Boston society.

The Boston Evening Transcript

The readers of the *Boston Evening Transcript*
Sway in the wind like a field of ripe corn.

When evening quickens faintly in the street,
Wakening the appetites of life in some
And to others bringing the *Boston Evening Transcript*,
I mount the steps and ring the bell, turning
Wearily, as one would turn to nod good-bye to Rochefoucauld
If the street were time and he at the end of the street,
And I say, "Cousin Harriet, here is the *Boston Evening Transcript*."

Cousin Nancy

Miss Nancy Ellicott
Strode across the hills and broke them,
Rode across the hills and broke them—
The barren New England hills—
Riding to hounds
Over the cow-pasture.

Miss Nancy Ellicott smoked
And danced all the modern dances;
And her aunts were not quite sure how they felt about it,
But they knew that it was modern.

Upon the glazen shelves kept watch
Matthew and Waldo, guardians of the faith,
The army of unalterable law.

Edward Bellamy, from *Looking Backward* (1888)

Edward Bellamy (1850–1898), novelist and Socialist, was born in Chicopee Falls, in western Massachusetts, the son of a Baptist minister and Calvinist mother. He carried their moral zeal into the writing of *Looking*

Backward, a utopian novel which is critical of the past-haunted and so-cially divided Boston of his day. *Equality* (1897) is a sequel. Here, in the opening chapter of *Looking Backward,* Bellamy portrays late nineteenth-century Boston as a city on the brink of revolution.

I first saw the light in the city of Boston in the year 1857. "What!" you say, "eighteen fifty-seven? That is an odd slip. He means nineteen fifty-seven, of course." I beg pardon, but there is no mistake. It was about four in the after-noon of December the 26th, one day after Christmas, in the year 1857, not 1957, that I first breathed the east wind of Boston, which, I assure the reader, was at that remote period marked by the same penetrating quality charac-terizing it in the present year of grace, 2000.

These statements seem so absurd on their face, especially when I add that I am a young man apparently of about thirty years of age, that no person can be blamed for refusing to read another word of what promises to be a mere imposition upon his credulity. Nevertheless I earnestly assure the reader that no imposition is intended, and will undertake, if he shall follow me a few pages, to entirely convince him of this. If I may, then, provisionally assume, with the pledge of justifying the assumption, that I know better than the reader when I was born, I will go on with my narrative. As every schoolboy knows, in the latter part of the nineteenth century the civiliza-tion of to-day, or anything like it, did not exist, although the elements which were to develop it were already in ferment. Nothing had, however, occurred to modify the immemorial division of society into the four classes, or nations, as they may be more fitly called, since the differences between them were far greater than those between any nations nowadays, of the rich and the poor, the educated and the ignorant. I myself was rich and also educated, and possessed, therefore, all the elements of happiness enjoyed by the most for-tunate in that age. Living in luxury, and occupied only with the pursuit of the pleasures and refinements of life, I derived the means of my support from the labor of others, rendering no sort of service in return. My parents and grandparents had lived in the same way, and I expected that my descen-dants, if I had any, would enjoy a like easy existence.

But how could I live without service to the world? You ask. Why should the world have supported in utter idleness one who was able to render ser-vice? The answer is that my great-grandfather had accumulated a sum of

money on which his descendants had ever since lived. The sum, you will
naturally infer, must have been very large not to have been exhausted in
supporting three generations in idleness. This, however, was not the fact.
The sum had been originally by no means large. It was, in fact, much larger
now that three generations had been supported upon it in idleness, than it
was at first. This mystery of use without consumption, of warmth without
combustion, seems like magic, but was merely an ingenious application of
the art now happily lost but carried to great perfection by your ancestors, of
shifting the burden of one's support on the shoulders of others. The man
who had accomplished this, and it was the end all sought, was said to live
on the income of his investments. To explain at this point how the ancient
methods of industry made this possible would delay us too much. I shall
only stop now to say that interest on investments was a species of tax in
perpetuity upon the product of those engaged in industry which a person
possessing or inheriting money was able to levy. It must not be supposed
that an arrangement which seems so unnatural and preposterous according
to modern notions was never criticized by your ancestors. It had been the
effort of lawgivers and prophets from the earliest ages to abolish interest, or
at least to limit it to the smallest possible rate. All these efforts had, however, failed, as they necessarily must so long as the ancient social organizations prevailed. At the time of which I write, the latter part of the nineteenth century, governments had generally given up trying to regulate the
subject at all.

By way of attempting to give the reader some general impression of the
way people lived together in those days, and especially of the relations of the
rich and poor to one another, perhaps I cannot do better than to compare
society as it then was to a prodigious coach which the masses of humanity
were harnessed to and dragged toilsomely along a very hilly and sandy road.
The driver was hunger, and permitted no lagging, though the pace was necessarily very slow. Despite the difficulty of drawing the coach at all along so
hard a road, the top was covered with passengers who never got down, even
at the steepest ascents. These seats on top were very breezy and comfortable.
Well up out of the dust, their occupants could enjoy the scenery at their leisure, or critically discuss the merits of the straining team. Naturally such
places were in great demand and the competition for them was keen, every
one seeking as the first end in life to secure a seat on the coach for himself
and to leave it to his child after him. By the rule of the coach a man could

leave his seat to whom he wished, but on the other hand there were many accidents by which it might at any time be wholly lost. For all that they were so easy, the seats were very insecure, and at every sudden jolt of the coach persons were slipping out of them and falling to the ground, where they were instantly compelled to take hold of the rope and help to drag the coach on which they had before ridden so pleasantly. It was naturally regarded as a terrible misfortune to lose one's seat, and the apprehension that this might happen to them or their friends was a constant cloud upon the happiness of those who rode. . . .

In 1887 I came to my thirtieth year. Although still unmarried, I was engaged to wed Edith Bartlett. She, like myself, rode on the top of the coach. That is to say, not to encumber ourselves further with an illustration which has, I hope, served its purpose of giving the reader some general impression of how we lived then, her family was wealthy. In that age, when money alone commanded all that was agreeable and refined in life, it was enough for a woman to be rich to have suitors; but Edith Bartlett was beautiful and graceful also.

My lady readers, I am aware, will protest at this. "Handsome she might have been," I hear them saying, "but graceful never, in the costumes which were the fashion at that period, when the head covering was a dizzy structure a foot tall, and the almost incredible extension of the skirt behind by means of artificial contrivances more thoroughly dehumanized the form than any former device of dressmakers. Fancy any one graceful in such a costume!" The point is certainly well taken, and I can only reply that while the ladies of the twentieth century are lovely demonstrations of the effect of appropriate drapery in accenting feminine graces, my recollection of their great-grandmothers enables me to maintain that no deformity of costume can wholly disguise them.

Our marriage only waited on the completion of the house which I was building for our occupancy in one of the most desirable parts of the city, that is to say, a part chiefly inhabited by the rich. For it must be understood that the comparative desirability of different parts of Boston for residence depended then, not on natural features, but on the character of the neighboring population. Each class or nation lived by itself, in quarters of its own. A rich man living among the poor, an educated man among the uneducated, was like one living in isolation among a jealous and alien race. When the house had been begun, its completion by the winter of 1886 had been expected. The spring of the following year found it, however, yet incomplete, and my marriage still a thing of the future. The cause of a delay calculated to be particularly exasperating to an ardent lover was a series of strikes, that is to say, concerted refusals to work on the part of the brick-layers, masons, carpenters, painters, plumbers, and other trades concerned in house building. What the specific causes of these strikes were I do not remember. Strikes had become so common at that period that people had ceased to inquire into their particular grounds. In one department of industry or another, they had been nearly incessant ever since the great business crisis of 1873. In fact it had come to be the exceptional thing to see any class of laborers pursue their avocation steadily for more than a few months at a time.

The reader who observes the dates alluded to will of course recognize in these disturbances of industry the first and incoherent phase of the great movement which ended in the establishment of the modern industrial system with all its social consequences. This is all so plain in the retrospect that a child can understand it, but not being prophets, we of that day had no clear idea what was happening to us. What we did see was that industrially the country was in a very queer way. The relation between the workingman and the employer, between labor and capital, appeared in some unaccountable manner to have become dislocated. The working classes had quite suddenly and very generally become infected with a profound discontent with their condition, and an idea that it could be greatly bettered if they only knew how to go about it. On every side, with one accord, they preferred demands for higher pay, shorter hours, better dwellings, better educational advantages, and a share in the refinements and luxuries of life, demands which it was impossible to see the way to granting unless the world were to become a great deal richer than it then was. Though they knew something of what they wanted, they knew nothing of how to accomplish it, and the eager enthusiasm with which they thronged about any one who seemed likely to give them any light on the subject lent sudden reputation to many would-be leaders, some of whom had little enough light to give. However chimerical the aspirations of the laboring classes might be deemed, the devotion with which they supported one another in the strikes, which were their chief weapon, and the sacrifices which they underwent to carry them out left no doubt of their dead earnestness.

As to the final outcome of the labor troubles, which was the phrase by which the movement I have described was most commonly referred to, the opinions of the people of my class differed according to individual temperament. The sanguine argued very forcibly that it was in the very nature of things impossible that the new hopes of the workingmen could be satisfied, simply because the world had not the wherewithal to satisfy them. It was only because the masses worked very hard and lived on short commons that the race did not starve outright, and no considerable improvement in their condition was possible while the world, as a whole, remained so poor. It was not the capitalists whom the laboring men were contending with, these maintained, but the iron-bound environment of humanity, and it was merely a question of the thickness of their skulls when they would discover the fact and make up their minds to endure what they could not cure.

The less sanguine admitted all this. Of course the workingmen's aspirations were impossible of fulfillment for natural reasons, but there were grounds to fear that they would not discover this fact until they had made a sad mess of society. They had the votes and the power to do so if they pleased, and their leaders meant they should. Some of these desponding observers went so far as to predict an impending social cataclysm. Humanity, they argued, having climbed to the top round of the ladder of civilization, was about to take a header into chaos, after which it would doubtless pick itself up, turn round, and begin to climb again. Repeated experiences of this sort in historic and prehistoric times possibly accounted for the puzzling bumps on the human cranium. Human history, like all great movements, was cyclical, and returned to the point of beginning. The idea of indefinite progress in a right line was a chimera of the imagination, with no analogue in nature. The parabola of a comet was perhaps a yet better illustration of the career of humanity. Tending upward and sunward from the aphelion of barbarism, the race attained the perihelion of civilization only to plunge downward once more to its nether goal in the regions of chaos.

This, of course, was an extreme opinion, but I remember serious men among my acquaintances who, in discussing the signs of the times, adopted a very similar tone. It was no doubt the common opinion of thoughtful men that society was approaching a critical period which might result in great changes. The labor troubles, their causes, course, and cure, took lead of all other topics in the public prints, and in serious conversation.

The nervous tension of the public mind could not have been more strikingly illustrated than it was by the alarm resulting from the talk of a small band of men who called themselves anarchists, and proposed to terrify the American people into adopting their ideas by threats of violence, as if a mighty nation which had but just put down a rebellion of half its own numbers, in order to maintain its political system, were likely to adopt a new social system out of fear.

As one of the wealthy, with a large stake in the existing order of things, I naturally shared the apprehensions of my class. The particular grievance I had against the working classes at the time of which I write, on account of the effect of their strikes in postponing my wedded bliss, no doubt lent a special animosity to my feeling toward them.

Cleveland Amory, "The Hub," from *The Proper Bostonians* (1947)

Cleveland Amory (1917–1998), himself a Proper Bostonian, was born in Nahant, the summer resort just north of Boston; he came of age in Milton, a gentry suburb just south of the city, and, after graduating from Harvard, took up a life of writing, focusing particularly upon the topics of Boston Brahmins and animal rights.

There is a story in Boston that in the palmy days of the twenties a Chicago banking house asked the Boston investment firm of Lee, Higginson & Co. for a letter of recommendation about a young Bostonian they were considering employing. Lee, Higginson could not say enough for the young man. His father, they wrote, was a Cabot, his mother a Lowell; farther back his background was a happy blend of Saltonstalls, Appletons, Peabodys, and other of Boston's First Families. The recommendation was given without hesitation.

Several days later came a curt acknowledgement from Chicago. Lee, Higginson was thanked for its trouble. Unfortunately, however, the material supplied on the young man was not exactly of the type the Chicago firm was seeking. "We were not," their letter declared, "contemplating using Mr._____ for breeding purposes."

The story is legendary but it is at the same time basic to an understanding of Boston and the Proper Bostonian. To the country at large the Proper

Bostonian is not always easily identifiable. He does not necessarily live in Proper Boston. He may still live in the Beacon Hill area of the city, but he is more likely to be found in such socially circumspect Boston suburbs as Brookline, Chestnut Hill, Milton, Wellesley, Needham, Dedham or Dover – and way stations from Pride's Crossing to Woods Hole. He is not especially individual in appearance. Although outside observers have claimed to be able to tell the Proper Bostonian male by waistcoat, and the Proper Bostonian female by hat, these marks are not foolproof. Neither is his speech an infallible sign. The actor, Leo Carroll, engaged in learning how to speak for his role of George Apley, in the play based on John P. Marquand's novel of latter-day Proper Bostonians, found no less than thirteen recognized Boston Brahmin accents. The broad "a" and the stern omission of the "r," generally regarded as typically Bostonian, is not an invariable rule. Actually the Proper Bostonian is more inclined to speak with a clipped "a." He says not Haa-vaard for the college he loves so well, but Hah-vud. He may leave out the "r" in a word like marbles, but he doesn't say mabbles. In a word like idea, he has even been known to add an "r."

Once identified, however, the Proper Bostonian is a very well-defined type—more so, it would seem, than the Proper Baltimorean, the Proper Philadelphian, or the Proper person of any other city. His basic character traits are almost unmistakable. This is undoubtedly because, as the Lee, Higginson story suggests, Boston Society has always devoted a great deal of attention to his breeding. The Proper Bostonian did not just happen; he was planned. Since he was from the start, in that charming Boston phrase "well connected," he was planned to fit into a social world so small that he could not help being well-defined. He is a charter member of a Society which more than one historian has called the most exclusive of that of any city in America, and which has charter members only. It used to be said that, socially speaking, Philadelphia asked who a person is, New York how much he is worth, and Boston what does he know. Nationally it has now become generally recognized that Boston Society has long cared even more than Philadelphia about the first point and has refined the asking of who a person is to the point of demanding to know who he was. Philadelphia asks about a man's parents; Boston wants to know about his grandparents. According to the Boston Chamber of Commerce, Boston is 2,350,000 people. Boston society, according to the Boston *Social Register*, is 8000 people. Yet to the strict Proper Bostonian this volume, which admits only one Jewish man and, in a city now 79 percent Catholic in population, less than a dozen Catholic families, is considered impossibly large. Too much attention to it is regarded as a mark of social insecurity, and several Boston Society leaders have never allowed their names to be listed at all. One Somerset Club bachelor always referred to the *Register* as a "damned telephone book" and regularly protested its size by making it a practice, upon receiving his annual copy, to tear it in half and return it to its New York headquarters.

Actually this man, in his rough division of the *Register*, was not going far enough. Operating on the basis of the Families which it has come to regard as First Families—only a few dozen in all—Boston Society is fundamentally far less than half its 8000 Social Registerites. Out of a total number of Bostonians, few are called and fewer still are chosen into this fundamental Boston Society. Not content with excluding some million Bostonians of Irish background, as well as many hundreds of thousands of Bostonians of Italian, Jewish, Polish and other backgrounds, it also cheerfully excludes another several hundred thousand or so of persons whose backgrounds are as undeniably Anglo-Saxon as its First Families' own and yet, because of imperfectly established connections with a First Family, can never hope to become Proper Bostonians.

This figurative handful, the First Family Society of the Proper Bostonian, would be interesting enough if it had done nothing more, through all the years of its existence, than hold its social fort against all comers. But it has done considerably more than this. Despite its numerical insignificance it has set its stamp on the country's fifth largest city so indelibly that when an outsider thinks of a Bostonian he thinks only of the Proper Bostonian. When Thomas Gould Appleton a century ago used the phrase "Cold Roast Boston," he was a Proper Bostonian speaking only of other Proper Bostonians. But the phrase has lasted, not alone for Appleton and his friends and their descendants, but for Boston itself. In the same way, one small poem which had its genesis in the social aspirations of just two Boston families has become what is probably the closets thing to a social folk song any city ever had. Originally patterned on a toast delivered by an anonymous "Western man" at a Harvard alumni dinner in 1905, it was refined in 1910 by Dr. John Collins Bossidy of Holy Cross to be recited, apparently for all time, as follows:

> And this is good old Boston
> The home of the bean and the cod,

Where the Lowells talk to the Cabots,
And the Cabots talk only to God.

The stamp of the Proper Bostonian on his city has stood the test of time. The personality of Boston remains the personality of the Proper Bostonian—not only to such alien critics as the editors of the *New Yorker* and *Time* magazines, and to countless authors of fiction from Worcester to Hollywood, but in fact, Boston's Irish population may be in control of the city's government, but not for nothing are they referred to as "the poor, downtrodden majority." Boston as a city still moves almost as it did in Emerson's day, when he described it as locomoting as cautiously as a Yankee gentleman "with his hands in his pockets." In 1945 an up-and-coming court removed the still existing ban imposed in 1637 on the "Boston Jezebel," Miss Anne Hutchinson, but only a year later, in 1946, as Boston was making elaborate plans to be the City of Tomorrow, the park commissioner, engaged in planning a modern parking space under Boston Common, noted rather sadly that if any of the old-time property owners of Beacon Hill wished to take advantage of the ancient and immutable statute permitting them to graze their cows on top of the Common, he would still be powerless to do anything about it.

To the Proper Bostonian such things are part and parcel of Boston's charm. He has always had much less interest in what he still firmly regards as "his Boston" becoming any City of Tomorrow than he has had in keeping it the City of Yesterday. . . .

If the Proper Bostonian has stamped on his city its stigma of narrow provinciality and general cold roastness, it seems to be also generally recognized that on his back still falls a large share of the burden of carrying on the cultural tradition which in various fields once made Boston known as the Athens of America.

V

THE "OTHER" BOSTONIANS:
NEW VOICES AND VISIONS

After the Civil War Boston's ascendancy class grew anxious that the city upon a hill was under siege, that they were being crowded out, invaded by immigrants. Bromfield Corey, the representative Brahmin in William Dean Howells's *The Rise of Silas Lapham* (1885), realized while walking toward Beacon Hill across the Common that he felt like an "alien" in his native city when he had to speak Italian to buy an apple from a fruit peddler who appeared to be quite at home in Boston. Corey "glanced up and down the facades and through the crooked vistas like a stranger, and the swarthy fruitier . . . was not surprised that the purchase be transacted in his own tongue."[1] In the serial publication of this novel in *Century* magazine, Howells also included a family exchange over Jews who were buying property and thus, the Laphams believed, lowering its value in the South End where they lived. "You see, they *have* got in—and pretty thick, too—it's no use denying it," says Mrs. Lapham to her husband. The Laphams aspired to join the Corey elite by building a house on the "New Land," the privileged enclave of Boston's Back Bay, but they first had to remove themselves from the company of aspiring Jews who wished to live near them in the no-longer-fashionable South End. When protests were registered about this passage, Howells at first defended it as irony to expose bigotry, but in the end he cut this and another anti-Semitic passage from the novel before book publication, apparently in agreement with the letters of complaint he had received from Cyrus L. Sulzberger, editor of *American Hebrew*, and others.[2]

Thomas Apley, George's father and owner of textile mills in Apley Falls (Lowell), might have told the Laphams that the South End's fashionable era was over. In John P. Marquand's *The Late George Apley* (1937), Thomas Apley had an epiphany the day he emerged from his South End home and was shocked to see a threatening stranger, an encounter that led him to decide to move his family to the safety of Beacon Hill. George, seven at the time, recalls his father's response,

> "Thunderation," Father said, "there is a man in his shirt sleeves on those steps." The next day he sold his house for what he had paid for it and we moved to Beacon Street. Father had sensed the approach of change; a man in his shirt sleeves had told him that the days of the South End were numbered.[3]

Swarthy fruitiers, moneyed Jews, men in shirtsleeves, not to mention the incoming Irish horde—all seemed to be pressing long-established Bostonians up to the heights of the Hill, out to the edges of the city and beyond to Brookline and other rich suburbs, but Beacon Hill and Back Bay remained "the two islands of respectability composing socially habitable Boston," linked by a narrow "isthmus," as George Santayana's representative elitist saw the all-but-walled city of Brahmins in *The Last Puritan* (1935).[4] Here the saving remnant of Boston's founding class of English Puritans, along with those of similar ethnic-religious background whose wealth, education, and manners qualified them to join it, could feel safe, secure from encroaching African Americans, many of whom lived on the "wrong" side of Beacon Hill; from the encircling Irish, who had seized the city's waterfront areas and were moving inland; from the late-arriving Italians, who had taken the North End away from the Irish whose presence after the Famine had driven out the founding Yankees; from the unwelcome Jews, who had arrived in the city in small numbers; and from others, symbolized by that man in shirt-sleeves—a homeowner with casual standards of dress? an Irish laborer? an anarchist?—whose presence marked the demise of the South End.

Boston's literature, though largely composed by Protestants descended from English founders and settlers, along with others adopted into their class, has nevertheless, from the beginning, been racially and ethnically various. Notably, the first Africans, brought as slaves to Boston in 1638, and their descendants made their voices and views known, and asserted themselves into the conversation concerning Boston's values and purpose. By 1705 over 400 slaves lived in Boston, and a free black community was forming in the North End. In 1773 Boston slaves petitioned officials for their liberty, a cry of the heart revealing their sorry state. "We have no property! We have no wives! No children! We have no city! No country!"[5] However, by the end of the American Revolution more free blacks than slaves lived in Boston. By 1790 Massachusetts was the only state in the Union to record no slaves. Between 1800 and 1900, most of the city's African Americans, free but poor, lived in the West End and on the North Slope of Beacon Hill.

The African Meeting House on Beacon Hill was built in 1806 in what once was the heart of Boston's nineteenth-century African American community. Before and after the Civil War, as Thomas H. O'Connor puts it, "Black Bostonians were . . . confined to their back-of-the-hill community along the slopes of 'Nigger Hill' . . . prevented from becoming apprentices in the skilled professions, and . . . denied the kind of social acceptance that was consistent with their civil rights."[6] The Joy Street Meeting House became the center of abolitionist action before the Civil War. There in 1832 William Lloyd Garrison founded the New England Anti-Slavery Society; there in 1860 Frederick Douglass delivered an anti-slavery speech after being run out of Tremont Temple; there in 1863 troops were recruited for the Massachusetts 54th Regiment. "The Black Faneuil Hall" remains a central reminder of the continuous contributory presence of African Americans in Boston. The African Meeting House, the oldest black church building still standing in America, is now fittingly the final stop on Boston's Black Heritage Trail. The equally fitting first stop is the Saint-Gaudens Memorial to Robert Gould Shaw and the black soldiers of the 54th Regiment. These two symbolic sites show that African Americans were an essential presence at the city's finest moments of renewed self-definition. Boston was by then less a city seeking salvation in the next world than one committed to ideals of freedom and justice in this world.[7] In Boston, African Americans both found and helped to define a city.

Even before Boston led a revolution for national independence, Phillis Wheatley had learned the lesson of the Boston mission and, in turn, wrote to remind the city that *all* men and women were equal in God's eyes: "Remember, *Chieftans, Negros,* black as *Cain,*/ May be refin'd and join th' angelic train."[8] Though it was never free from segregation, racial prejudice, and patronization, as the case of Wheatley illustrated, Boston was more receptive than other American cities to African Americans, though they remained a small percentage of Boston's population, in part because many of its citizens affirmed the ideal of equity that Wheatley had articulated. In 1700 Samuel Sewall, the only judge at the Salem witch trial of 1692 who recanted, wrote *The Selling of Joseph,* an anti-slavery tract which was based upon a Christian vision of equity. "These Ethiopians, as black as they are, seeing they are the sons and daughters of the first Adam, the brethren and sisters of the last Adam [Jesus Christ], and the offspring of God, they ought to be treated with a respect agreeable."[9] In *The Negro Christianized* (1706), Cotton Mather similarly argued that slave-owners must convert their slaves.

In 1770 Crispus Attucks, a former slave, became an emblem of colonial oppression when he, along with three white demonstrators, was shot down by British troops, an event memorialized as the Boston Massacre. Attucks's blood sacrifice made him a Boston hero to those, like Samuel Adams, who used the incident to rally forces against English oppression, though others, notably John Adams, saw Attucks and his fellow victims differently. When John Adams successfully defended the British troops involved in the "massacre" on the grounds of self-defense, he dismissed the demonstrators as "a mob . . . a motley rabble of saucy boys, negroes and molattoes, Irish teagues and outlandish jack tarrs."[10] Adams would come to learn that just such marginalized men of Boston, black and white, native and immigrant, would fight to drive the British army out of the city and found a nation. Yet, despite the revolution, slavery persisted in Boston, as Abigail Adams reminded her husband. "I wish most sincerely there was not a slave in the province; it always appeared a most iniquitous scheme to me to fight ourselves for what we are daily robbing and plundering from those who have as good a right to freedom as we do."[11] Abigail Adams's letter highlighted the central contradiction in Boston's culture: the gap between the city's idealistic claims of equity and justice under God and its actual toleration of injustices in its treatments of African Americans, immigrant laborers, and, as she particularly reminded her husband, women!

The African American writers of Boston who followed Wheatley reinforced her vision. Indeed, many of Boston's black citizens called attention to Boston's proffered promises at the same time they noted the city's failure to fulfill them. In *Freedom's Birthplace* (1914) John Daniels underscored the long-standing tension between the city's devotion to "spiritual freedom" and its tolerance first for slavery and later for demeaning prejudice against its black citizens. "It was a contradiction, moreover, which in modified degree and form has survived to the present, and which still troubles the Boston community" into the early years of the twentieth century.[12] This "contradiction" not only survived but thrived for another century in what has been called "liberty's chosen home," and it blew up into open racial confrontation over court-ordered integration of Boston's public schools in the mid-1970s, a bitter countering of the city's claim for "common ground."[13] However, this destructive racial tension would have a positive side. Boston infused its black citizens with religious and political ideals; in turn, Boston's blacks would testify to their painful existence, their social and political exclusion, inspiring some white Bostonians to live up to the city's assumed moral and political missions. Defined by this contradiction, many in Boston's black community took on the role of what William D. Pierson has called "black Yankees—a very special breed of Afro-American New Englanders." Though marginalized in Boston, these black Yankees created "a double identity, a positive sense of themselves within the larger Yankee community."[14]

Boston stood as a beacon of freedom for escaped slaves. William Wells Brown found his plain-style voice in Boston, where he wrote his *Narrative of W. W. Brown, a Fugitive Slave* (1847) and his novel, *Clotelle* (1852). Frederick Douglass also shaped his eloquent voice in Boston, under the tutelage of the city's abolitionists, who enlisted his testimony as a witness against slavery. His *Narrative of the Life of Frederick Douglass* (1845) was published under the imprint of the Anti-Slavery Office, with endorsements by Boston abolitionists William Lloyd Garrison and Wendell Phillips. It was Garrison's *Liberator* that inspired Douglass's polemical purpose. "The paper became my meat and drink. My soul was set on fire."[15] In those days, as Oliver Wendell Holmes, Jr. would later say, most Bostonians, black and white, were "touched by fire."

Former slave women also sought freedom and self-expression in Boston. Charlotte Forten (later Charlotte Forten Grimke) was schooled in Salem's strict abolitionist values. Boston embodied culture to Forten, who was inspired by the example of Phillis Wheatley to write poetry and essays. However, it is Forten's journal (1854–1889) that provides the best record of this Greater Bostonian's moving responses to her trying times. This is particularly evident in her record of the 1854 arrest of escaped slave Anthony Burns and his forced return to slavery under the Fugitive Slave Act. "To-day Massachusetts has again been disgraced; again she has showed her submissions to the Slave Power."[16] Harriet E. Wilson, author of *Our Nig*, a novel printed in Boston in 1859, satirized bourgeois racism in the North. Harriet A. Jacobs's *Incidents in the Life of a Slave Girl* (1861), an autobiography disguised as a novel, was also published in Boston, where, like so many escaped slaves before her, Jacobs had come to find freedom and support for her writing.

W. E. B. Du Bois was reared in a pastoral village in western Massachusetts, enlightened by his years in the South and became a central presence in the Harlem Renaissance. Though he is not usually associated with Boston, his experiences at Harvard and his encounters with Boston's black bourgeoisie were informing. He received a lesson in self-assertion from an assured black Boston aristocrat, "Mrs. Ruffin of Charles Street," who published many of his Harvard essays in the *Courant*, "a type of small colored weekly paper."[17] At Harvard, across the Charles River and Boston's racial divide, Du Bois worked on his prose under Barrett Wendell, guardian of the Brahmin Boston's exclusive world view. However, despite his class allegiances, Wendell praised Du Bois's fluid sentences and, as he proudly recalls, asked him to read aloud in class his essay on growing up in Great Barrington.[18] In 1934, Du Bois would remember that during his Harvard days he met William Monroe Trotter, publisher of the *Boston Guardian*, a newspaper that publicized racial injustices and strengthened the identity of Boston's black community, then spreading from the West End into the South End. Du Bois praised Trotter's "unflinching" fight against the argument for racial accommodation identified with Booker T. Washington and he honored Trotter's advocacy of the "separation and discrimination in church and school, and in professional and business life." But Du Bois saw things growing worse for Boston's black citizenry. "The free lance like Trotter is not strong enough. The mailed fist has got to be clenched."[19] Boston and Harvard thus provided invaluable literary training and lasting political lessons for W. E. B. Du Bois.

In *Contending Forces* (1900), a novel, Pauline E. Hopkins based two of her characters on Du Bois and Washington, incorporating their debate over black identity. Hopkins, educated in Boston's public schools, was inspired by William Wells Brown's fiction and was determined to preserve and celebrate black culture in her own works. "Fiction . . . is a record of growth and development from generation to generation. No one will do this for us."[20] Hopkins became a staff writer for *Colored American Magazine* (1900–1904), where she followed Trotter's example by publishing essays of protest and racial affirmation. Hopkins's black Bostonians would have to rely upon themselves, she argued, but she was also inspired by Boston's exemplary white leaders. Her novel's epigraph is taken from Emerson: "The civility of no race can be perfect whilst another race is degraded."[21] *Contending Forces* shows that Boston's contentious racial divisions were central to understanding its culture and conscience.

Three writers—a novelist, an autobiographer, and a poet—illustrate the range and creativity of African American Bostonians in the early decades of the twentieth century, a period when more Southern blacks moved into the city, resulting in cultural and economic tensions between the races and among members of the black community. Each of these authors adapted a literary form to demonstrate that Boston suffered a crisis of identity and a test of character in its treatment of African Americans.

In her novel *The Living Is Easy* (1948), Dorothy West dramatized the desperate efforts of the city's blacks to achieve respectability, a status conferred through acceptance by white Bostonians, during and after the Great War. West, who had been educated at Girls' Latin School and Boston University and had watched with dismay her mother's futile attempts to adopt Bostonian upper-class manners, abandoned the city as a provincial backwater. "I was just a little girl from Boston, a place of dull people with funny accents."[22] However, West, while becoming a leading light of the Harlem Renaissance, came to modify her anger with an understanding of her mother's desperate and failed efforts at social climbing and its poignant costs—the repudiation of her black heritage. Through the character of Cleo Judson, a version of her mother, West shows that hardening racial and territorial divisions were turning Boston, the supposed "city of neighborhoods," into a city of ghettos.

In his polemical memoir, *The Autobiography of Malcolm X* (written with Alex Haley, 1965), the former Malcolm Little recounted his coming-of-age and his realization of racial consciousness in Boston. He arrived, sitting in the back of a bus, in 1940, at age fifteen, to live with relatives in the Sugar Hill section of Roxbury, "the Harlem of Boston."[23] Boston came to mean two things to Malcolm: personal liberation, which he discovered in the city's bars and jazz clubs, and awareness of discrimination. At the Roseland Ballroom he heard the best jazz musicians of the day. On the streets of Roxbury he saw with amazement how blacks walked with pride: "neon lights, nightclubs, pool-halls, bars, the cars they drove!"[24] But he also witnessed, as had Dorothy West, many members of the black community who were "brainwashed" in their attempt to imitate white society.[25] Malcolm gravitated to Roxbury's lowlife, becoming a "cat," wearing zoot suits, eating soul food, until, as with West, the city became confining for him and he too abandoned Boston for the big time, New York City. "Within the first five minutes at Small's [Paradise, a Harlem club on Seventh Avenue], I had left Boston and Roxbury forever."[26] However, after World War II, Malcolm, by then a cocaine addict, returned to Boston, where he was arrested for burglary and sentenced to prison for eight to ten years. After a stay in Charlestown State Prison, he was transferred to Norfolk State Prison where he educated himself in an unusually large prison library. There he became a Muslim and a black militant, his unusual Boston education completed. In Boston, in the words of David Bradley, Malcolm "became a hustler, hipster, and purveyor who burned his hair straight with lye"; there he came of age and developed a consciousness that his personal story had large implications for America.[27] For the innocent Malcolm Little, who transformed himself into the wised-up Malcolm X, Boston remained, as it had for many other black Bostonians, a symbolic landscape in which they sought to discover their personal and racial identities, the place where they renamed themselves and reshaped their voices.

Martin Luther King, Jr. was an opponent of Malcolm X's call for black militancy during the 1960s. King too was shaped by his Boston experience when he studied at Boston University's School of Divinity (1951–1954). King, it has been noted, drew upon Boston's Phillips Brooks—famed preacher and Episcopal rector of Trinity Church, in Copley Square, where a Saint-Gaudens statue in his memory still stands—for inspiration and rhetorical formulation in his sermons.[28] Despite their differences, both Malcolm X and Martin Luther King drew upon the city's tradition of political and cultural idealism. "Both men," writes Marilyn Richardson, "went on to place their spiritual commitments at the service of the struggle to change secular history; like [Crispus] Attucks and [David] Walker [publisher of *Walker's Appeal* (1829), a political pamphlet which called for black action against slavery], they paid with their lives."[29] Both men, then, followed the example of noble sacrifice set by Col. Robert Gould Shaw and the black troops of his 54th Regiment.

In his poetry, criticism, and anthologies, William Stanley Braithwaite eschewed the sharp criticisms of Boston's white gentry class and black social climbers leveled by Dorothy West and Malcolm X, writers who abandoned the city. Braithwaite advocated cultural synthesis; his urban presence along with his urbane voice helped weave Boston's African American culture into the city's Brahmin literary tradition. He had to work his way up from poverty, becoming an errand boy and learning his way around the circuitous streets and the complex class structure of Boston, "my native city, the city that I loved, veined with memories."[30] As a typesetter for Ginn and Company in their Cambridge building, this ambitious young man could gaze across the Charles River and study the gracious homes on the slope of Beacon Hill. While setting type for Keats's "Ode on a Grecian Urn," Braithwaite experienced an "annunciation," his artistic calling, and devoted himself to the writing of the kind of poetry that might be appreciated in the homes he hoped to enter. In 1904 Braithwaite published *Lyrics of Life and Love* at his own expense, a poetry collection endorsed by Thomas Wentworth Higginson, the Civil War hero and Brahmin literary stalwart, who recommended the book to his friends, providing Braithwaite entry into a world of privilege and culture which he could previously only imagine. When he was invited into Higginson's Cambridge home, Braithwaite heard "the faint, subtle echoes of the mighty spirits that had glorified the environs of Cambridge, and Concord in the nineteenth century."[31] Braithwaite wrote for the *Boston Evening Transcript*, eventually becoming its literary editor. (T. S. Eliot mocked the stuffy respectability of this Brahmin newspaper of record: "The readers of the *Boston Evening Transcript*/ Sway in the wind like a field of ripe corn.")[32] Braithwaite also wrote articles, reviews, and poetry for many other periodicals and journals, including *Atlantic Monthly*, the *New York Times*, and the *New Republic*, establishing himself as a Boston man of letters without registering sharp racial consciousness in his works. He earned the respect of a range of Boston's cultural leaders, bridging the racial gap. W. E. B. Du Bois called him "the most prominent critic of poetry in America," and William Dean Howells praised him as "the most intelligent historian of contemporary poetry I know."[33]

As he grew more established in the culture of the city, Braithwaite did call attention to its black heritage. He described the journey of William Wells Brown from a slave in Kentucky to a celebrity in Boston as a more heroic version of his own quest, and he saw Du Bois's *The Souls of Black Folk* (1903)—"a quivering rhapsody of wrongs endured and hope to be fulfilled"—as a more direct and eloquent expression of his own literary mission.[34] In his autobiography Braithwaite recalled hearing Frederick Douglass lecture at the Park Street Church in 1888, when Braithwaite was ten. "I heard his thunderous voice go echoing upwards to vanish through the delicately beautiful Christopher Wren steeples on the church that pointed to heaven above the Old Granary Burial Ground where slept in eternal peace the parents of Benjamin Franklin."[35] Here, characteristically, Braithwaite fuses celebratory images of a powerful black presence (Douglass's "thunderous

voice") with the city's architectural expressions of piety (the Wren steeples that "pointed to heaven") and Boston's noble history (the Franklin
memorial).

Braithwaite would eventually leave Boston to teach in Atlanta and then
would live in Harlem, but he would always portray the city of his youth and
his first literary success in the most favorable terms, integrating a range of
color imagery into the black-and-white Brahmin cityscape, as he does in his
1904 poem "In the Public Garden."

> The illumined fountain flashed in the pond,
> It was purple, and green, and white,—
> You and I in the crowd, and beyond,
> The shining stars and night.
> And near was the fountain at play.
> —But ah, the dreams that have taken flight,
> And never come home to stay.[36]

Here Braithwaite's poignant sense of lost love is mixed into his metaphor of
Boston's tenuous promise—a medley of colors.

Boston offered its black citizens a double, divided identity. While practic-
ing discrimination and thus reneging upon its oft-stated noble values, the
city also provided a rich cultural heritage and offered noble models to emulate. By extending its mission to include African Americans, Boston renewed
its covenant as a city upon a hill during the Civil War era. In turn, as
William D. Pierson puts it, the presence of African Americans "influences
the lives of white Yankees as well, helping to mellow those rather puritani-
cal people."[37] In Boston many black writers, from Wheatley to Braithwaite,
learned to express themselves in polished literary forms which made their
writings more acceptable to the white power elite. However, these writers
also modified the image of the city, making Boston more inclusive, expanding its class hierarchy to include people of color. From Wheatley's cautionary poems to Malcolm X's denunciatory prose, these writers have added an
alternate, enriching perspective and a vigorous manner of expression, ranging from the polemic to the poetic, to the discourse of the city. Boston, a
city of the mind as well as a geographic area, has thus been reconceived and
renewed by its African American citizens.

The impact of the Irish on Boston, particularly during and after the Great

Famine in Ireland, was transforming and enduring. In 1847 alone, some 37,000 immigrants arrived, nearly all from Ireland, expanding the city's population by one-third and sending a shock wave of concern through the entrenched Yankee-Brahmin community. The impoverished Irish immigrants first settled along the city's waterfront—Batterymarch and Broad Streets, then in the North End and East Boston—packed into former Yankee dwellings which had been subdivided, often with no water, sanitation, ventilation, or access to daylight. Many Bostonians recoiled from their presence and the sight of their living conditions. A chastising Boston Committee of Internal Health, for example, described the Irish slum as "a perfect hive of human beings, without comforts and mostly without common necessaries—in many cases huddled together like brutes, without regard to age or sex or sense of decency. Under such circumstances self-respect, forethought, all the high and noble virtues soon die out, and sullen indifference and despair or disorder, intemperance, and utter degradation reign supreme."[38]

Boston did not welcome its new Irish Catholic citizens, though their labor was essential to expand the city, to sustain its businesses, and to service the great homes of Beacon Hill and Back Bay. While the Irish met hostility in other urban centers, particularly in New York City, historians agree that Boston provided a special challenge for Irish immigrants. Lawrence J. McCaffrey argues that Boston did not exemplify the representative Irish American experience. "The arrogance of the ancient vintage of its Anglo-Protestant upper class, the relatively static character of its economy, and the extremely slow mobility of its Irish population has resulted in an atypical rather than usual Irish American experience." The Boston Irish "were exceptionally disadvantaged," agrees Kevin Kenny in *The American Irish: A History* (2000).[39] For Catholic Irish immigrants, the Protestant Yankee-Brahmin ascendancy of Boston resembled the Protestant Anglo-Irish landowner and landlord class they had fled, intensifying animosities on both sides. Thus the Yankee-Celt passion play became *the* central Boston narrative for the next century, even after one of their own, John F. Kennedy, a man who combined his Irish heritage with a cultivated Brahmin manner, was elected president. Though this 1960 election symbolized the great American success saga of the Irish in Boston, it also ironically, as Daniel Patrick Moynihan put it, emblemized the "last hurrah" for Irish American politics, which had been shaped in Boston.[40]

Despite decades of overt and covert conflicts, Boston was renewed, revitalized, and redefined by the influx of Irish Americans, as it had been by the presence of African Americans. Bostonians, after all, were confined to a narrow, if expanding, strip of land, a peninsula that seemed at times a restrictive island—the "common ground" over which contending groups fought for living space and recognition. In time the Irish became loyal Bostonians and Boston became more Irish. "What is remarkable about the immigrant peoples—not only the Irish, but all," writes historian Thomas N. Brown, "is the readiness with which they have adopted the Yankee past as their own and have become attached to the old places."[41] For example, when he was a young man studying in Boston Latin School, John ("Honey Fitz") Fitzgerald, the future Boston mayor and grandfather of President John F. Kennedy, conducted tours through the North End, where he lived among Irish immigrants, explaining to visitors and tourists the noble deeds of Boston's founders and Revolution leaders in "these narrow old streets where history seemed to come alive."[42]

The Irish had their regional defenders. Ralph Waldo Emerson, for example, saw in them the possibilities of "a new race, a new religion, a new state, a new literature."[43] Thomas Wentworth Higginson, self-described "Protestant of the Protestants," had witnessed a mob burn down the Ursuline Convent in Charlestown in 1834, so he was sympathetic to these strangers in a strange land. However, the stronger voice of Puritan judgment against the Irish immigrants prevailed throughout the nineteenth century. Henry David Thoreau made a point in *Walden* of illustrating his belief that, "alas! the culture of an Irishman is an enterprise to be undertaken with a sort of moral boghoe." He had tried to teach the Protestant virtues of self-sufficiency, self-denial, and fishing to a representative Irishman, John Field, who was living near Walden Pond, but concluded that Field was unteachable, stuck as he was in "boggy ways."[44] The Irish constituted "a very undesirable addition" to the city, said Henry Cabot Lodge, celebrated scholar, statesman, and sponsor of immigration restriction in 1881, for they were "hard-drinking, idle, quarrelsome, and disorderly," a people "always at odds with the government."[45] Indeed, for some Bostonians the influx of immigrants, commencing with the Irish, along with the long-standing presence of African Americans, ensured the permanent division of the city. "But there is no point in using the term 'Boston' to include all the communities that then lived in the city; from our point of view they never made one community, because they never made one culture," argues Martin Green in *The Problem of Bos-*

ton (1966).[46] The Irish quickly got the Boston message: they "need not apply" for entry into the world of Brahmin culture. As a saying of the day went, the disillusioned Irish learned not only that the streets of Boston were not paved with gold, but also that many were not paved at all and, further, that they had been brought here only to pave them.

The "problem" of Boston was that the Irish immigrants had a far different view of "culture" than did the Yankee-Brahmin class. "The few Irishmen conscious of Boston's contemporary literature," writes Oscar Handlin, "were shocked and antagonized by its rational romanticism, regarding it as exclusively Protestant, overwhelmingly English, and suspect on both grounds."[47] However, John Boyle O'Reilly, the most distinguished writer and cultural presence to emerge from the Boston Irish community in the last decades of the nineteenth century, was an exceptional immigrant. O'Reilly took it upon himself to bridge the cultural gap between the Irish newcomers and the established Bostonians. He stressed themes of appreciation and patriotism in writings, speeches, and actions that were designed to present the Irish as more acceptable to hostile Brahmins, and he urged his own suspicious clan to accommodate to Boston's ways.

A Fenian rebel against British rule in Ireland, O'Reilly was banished to Australia, but he escaped to America, where he celebrated his Irish American identity with a passion he would impart to the Famine-era immigrants to Boston. "We can do Ireland more good by our Americanism than our Irishism."[48] To spread this view, in 1874 O'Reilly took over *The Pilot*, a newspaper for Irish immigrants, founded in 1829 by Bishop Benedict J. Fenwick; O'Reilly held the position of editor until his sudden death in 1890. Though *The Pilot* was committed to "the elevation of the Irish character in this country, the Independence of Ireland, and the overthrow of sectarian prejudice," O'Reilly played down the theme of cultural separation and stressed Irish American patriotism.[49] His poem "America" (1882) celebrated "two clasping hands," North and South, an image of post–Civil War reconciliation which offered a model of the cultural assimilation he urged on disputatious Bostonians. O'Reilly, who quickly became Boston's unofficial dedicatory poet, was supported by Brahmin elders Higginson and Holmes, and invited into their sanctuary, the Tavern Club.[50] "No treason we bring from Erin—nor bring we shame or guilt," he declared in "The Exile of the Gael," a message that reassured his Brahmin audience.[51]

Yet an anxiety ran beneath the celebratory surface of O'Reilly's writings, evident in "The Fame of the City" (1881), a poem which offers his sense of Boston as "a great rich city of power and pride" which needed a lesson: not to ignore its true riches, its poetic voice.[52] O'Reilly, Boston's representative Irish American of his era, was strained by cultural conflicts; he had to speak with one voice in *The Pilot* and another at the Tavern Club. The tensions he tried to resolve may have led to his early death, perhaps a suicide, at age forty-five. He was praised after his death by both communities: a megalithic-era rock marks his burial site at Brookline's Holyhood Cemetery, a place of honor for other deceased Irish Americans, and a massive memorial stands in Boston's Fenway, sculpted by Daniel Chester French and dedicated in 1896, which depicts Erin with her sons, Courage and Poetry. John Boyle O'Reilly is justly celebrated as an Irish American who broke into the Brahmin inner sanctum, achieved acceptance, and, in turn, taught his fellow immigrants to accept and be accepted by Boston.

Boston's Irish religious and political leaders also worked for acceptance, cultural independence, and power as their community gained in size and force. John Bernard Fitzpatrick, Bishop of Boston in 1846, tried to quiet prejudices against Famine-era immigrants at the same time he was enlarging the presence of the Catholic Church throughout New England. William Cardinal O'Connell, first as bishop, then as archbishop of the Boston diocese (1907–1944), revered Brahmins and their cultural values, but, at the same time, he stressed religious separation, enforcing a form of Catholic Puritanism on his flock. His successor, Richard Cardinal Cushing (1944–1970), born in South Boston, the son of Irish immigrants, was far more open to cultural exchanges and ecumenical ideas within his church and his community, while still retaining religious control of the Boston Irish. In 1964 Cardinal Cushing authorized the restoration of Saint Stephen's Church on Hanover Street in Boston's North End. Long a site of worship, it had been originally designed by Charles Bulfinch in 1804 as Boston's Second Church. The Irish took over the North End and the church by 1862, filling it with Catholic iconography, but Cardinal Cushing, in an ecumenical gesture, restored the building to its original Bulfinch design. Following upon Cardinal O'Connell's imperial manner, Cardinal Cushing's rough charm made him a more endearing and eminent Bostonian, as J. Anthony Lukas profiles him in *Common Ground* (1985). These Irish Catholic religious leaders worked to persuade both Yankees and Celts that Irish Catholics belonged in Boston.

Boston's early Irish-born political leaders followed the example of John Boyle O'Reilly by advocating accommodation with Brahmin Boston without sacrificing their ethnic identity. Hugh O'Brien, Boston's first Irish mayor (1884–1888), made significant gestures toward both constituencies; he raised money for the Boston Public Library, "a monument to our intelligence and culture," but he also closed Boston's libraries on Saint Patrick's Day. Patrick A. Collins, congressman and mayor (1902–1905), also spoke to cultural reconciliation, reassuring the wary Protestant community. "In American politics we are Americans, pure and simple."[53] However, as the Irish gained strength and assurance, a new breed of politicians took hold of Boston. Brash and Boston-born, they aggressively advanced Irish power against the Yankee establishment. John Fitzgerald emerged from the North End Irish ghetto to become mayor (1906–1908, 1910–1914), expanding mayoral powers, building a political machine, and establishing a tone of insouciant independence for the Boston Irish. He was defeated in 1914 by the even more aggressive and abrasive James Michael Curley, who dominated Boston politics for half a century, serving four terms as mayor, four terms in Congress, and one term as governor. Legendary rogue, Curley also served two terms in jail.

Curley was seen by Boston's former ruling elite and by many high-minded Boston Irish as a self-serving power-seeker, a man without a vision who fractured the community for his own advantage, but Boston's Irish American voters loved him, and Curley justified and rationalized his partisan and questionable legal acts as service to his community. After he was convicted of taking a civil service exam for a constituent in 1903, he based his future successful campaigns for office on the motto: "I did it for a friend," valuing loyalty over legality.[54] As Curley put it in his self-congratulatory autobiography, *I'd Do It Again* (1957), he was the "champion of the oppressed and underprivileged."[55] In time he and his era dissolved into legend—aided greatly by Edwin O'Connor's novel based upon Curley's career, *The Last Hurrah*, and John Ford's film version, which provided America with an idea of Boston—colorful, corrupt, endearing, polarized by Yankee-Celt conflict—that revised its previous image of stern Puritan unity. Thomas P. ("Tip") O'Neill, who commenced his career as a politician by imitating Curley, recalls that when he was Speaker of the House he was invited to visit President Ronald Reagan in the White House. Talk between these two Irish American politicians who took radically different political directions turned to the infamous former mayor. "Reagan, of course, asked me about James

Michael Curley, although he was about the only politician I ever met who hadn't actually read *The Last Hurrah*. But he had seen the movie, which was made in 1958 and featured Spencer Tracy as Curley."[56]

Curley's best biographer, Jack Beatty, conveys the complexity and ambivalence of his portrayal of the man in his title, *The Rascal King* (1992).[57] Curley's first biographer, Joseph F. Dineen, was far less ambivalent about his subject, saying in *The Purple Shamrock* (1949) that Curley "was the last of the political buccaneers, ungovernable, unmanageable, irrepressible, incorrigible, apparently indestructible."[58] Dineen's sympathy for Curley and scorn for the Boston Yankee-Brahmin class was based upon the record of mistreatment of Irish immigrants, a story he told in *Ward Eight* (1936), a novel which portrays the climb of the powerless immigrants to political authority by banding together in ward politics. "This is the story of a place and of the people in it. The place might be the slums of any American city, but it happens to be historic Boston, where Hancock, Adams, and Revere hallowed Ward Eight so that Big Tim O'Flaherty [based upon ward boss Martin Lomasney] could throw peppers at their tombstones."[59] Curley built his career on just such resentments.

Edwin O'Connor, an outsider, born in Woonsocket, Rhode Island in 1918 and educated at Notre Dame, was fascinated by the Boston passion play between Yankees and Celts, which he approached with the detachment of a cultural anthropologist. O'Connor, like John Boyle O'Reilly, charmed his way into the world of Brahmin clubs and culture. A third-generation Irish American, he rose from radio announcing and book reviewing for the *Boston Herald* to editing *Treadmill to Oblivion* (1953), a memoir of early radio days by Fred Allen, famed radio comedian, and he became an accepted member of the *Atlantic Monthly* family.[60] When he was living in furnished rooms on Marlborough Street, in Boston's Back Bay, O'Connor would make his way to the journal daily, spreading wit and cheer. "His patented daily entrance routine at the *Atlantic* offices on Arlington Street—the vaudeville shuffle, the jokes, a toss of a coin out of the window as if money was no concern—were ways of overcoming some of his inhibitions as 'an Irish mother's son,'" writes Charles F. Duffy in *A Family of His Own: A Life of Edwin O'Connor* (2003).[61] The publishers and editors of the *Atlantic Monthly* adopted O'Connor, just as their predecessors had taken in William Dean Howells, another talented, ambitious outsider, whose bust stood watch at the window of their office overlooking the Public Garden. Howells left Boston for New York. Though O'Connor lived—finally in a Marlborough Street mansion across from his old rooming house—and died in Boston in 1968, he too found great success but then grew restive with his red brick city.

O'Connor's fiction—*The Last Hurrah* (1956), *The Edge of Sadness* (1961), and *All in the Family* (1966)—shaped a telling and influential myth of Irish American experience in Boston. As Edmund Wilson put it, "the Irish Catholic world of Boston . . . had never before been exploited with this seriousness, intelligence and intimate knowledge."[62] Taken together, these works constitute a fictional record of his own kind: the saga of their religious and political seizure of the city and their eventual disillusionment. "I wanted to do for the Irish in America what Faulkner did for the South," he told a friend. "I wanted to do a novel on the whole Irish American business."[63] That "business" was vivid, poignant, and comic but, finally, too dirty for O'Connor. Like other Boston writers before and after him, he took the lesson of the city upon a hill to heart: worldly attainment was not enough; the search for spiritual transcendence was, in the end, what most mattered. His myth of Boston, a city he never names in his works, moves from celebration to renunciation.

The Last Hurrah presents O'Connor's sentimentalized version of James Michael Curley in the character of Frank Skeffington, the seventy-two-year-old mayor of "The City" during his last campaign. While Curley had possessed vindictive powers, Skeffington, an aging lion, no longer posed a threat and thus could be loved, particularly in his characterization by Spencer Tracy in John Ford's film version. In the novel and film Skeffington introduces his nephew, Adam Caulfield, to the bizarre but winning habits of the Boston Irish clan, particularly its raucous wakes, thus reconciling him (as O'Connor set out to reconcile his readers) to the charms and chicaneries of ethnic ways, which seemed distant, even endearing, in the cosmopolitan Kennedy era. The novel celebrates Skeffington and "his city, the wonderful, old, sprawling chaos of a city, whose ancient, tangled streets and red bricks and ugly piles of quarried stone had held his heart forever."[64] Yet the city had a destructive element, for Skeffington loses his election and then dies; the Irish, in turn, lose their power in the city and see their distinct identity fading into undifferentiated, American blandness. *The Last Hurrah*, then, is a muted Irish wake. Yet O'Connor's elegy also demonstrates the vitality of Irish Americans in this unnamed city, unmistakably Boston, just as he presents their achievements both as a comic triumph and poignant loss.

Skeffington enlisted Adam, the novel's narrator, in his last campaign so he would "know something about this . . . grand freak" of a city. As Skeffington put it, Boston

> changed overnight you know. A hundred years ago the loyal sons and daughters of the first white inhabitants went to bed one lovely evening, and by the time they woke up and rubbed their eyes, their charming old city was swollen to three times its size. The savages had arrived. Not the Indians, far worse. It was the Irish. They had arrived and they wanted in. Even worse than that, they got in. The story of how they did may not be a particularly pretty one on either side, but I doubt if anyone would deny that it was exciting and, I say, unique. Moreover, it's not quite over yet, though we're in its last stages now.[65]

Edwin O'Connor gave the Boston Irish an assured place in American literature, just at the point when they were losing their grip on the city. Boston, in O'Connor's fictional representation, makes and then unmakes Irish Americans. The city provided a new home and a noble vision but delivered less that it had promised, leaving its citizen-seekers in quest of a better place—a view of the city that echoes the aspirations of Boston's original Puritan settlers.

Writers who came after O'Connor added their perspectives to the Boston Irish story. In *Mortal Friends*, a 1978 novel, James Carroll presents Curley as a man who "embodied the Irish and loved them, but he would do anything in his pursuit of power, even hand over his own to Beacon Hill Brit bloodhounds."[66] However, politics, piety, and power were not the only subjects of Boston's Irish writers, for they extended the range of references, associations, and speech rhythms that define the city. During the Curley era, in the midst of the Great Depression, writes Robert Taylor in *Fred Allen: His Life and Wit* (1989), "the country's most popular Bostonian since the heyday of Ralph Waldo Emerson" was the popular radio personality, Fred Allen, born John Florence Sullivan in Cambridge, in 1894.[67] Allen conveyed his ambivalence about his Boston background in humorous terms, writing to Groucho Marx, for example, that he had "just returned from Boston. It is the only thing to do if you find yourself up there." Escape remained a powerful Boston theme.

Less humorous and more lethal were Boston's criminal Irish. In *The Friends of Eddie Coyle* (1972) George V. Higgins expanded the Boston landscape of imagination by exploring the dark side of urban experience, Boston's Irish and Italian criminal underground, in a novel which foreshadows the dramatic revelations that exposed the North End Italian Mafia and the Irish Winter Hill gang in the 1990s. Eddie Coyle, a low-level gun dealer, is caught between the demands of his profession and the pressures of the police, who, when Eddie faces prosecution for truck hijacking, squeeze him into informing on his customers who, in turn, seek revenge against him. With his command of vivid street dialogue and his insider's knowledge of gangsters, Higgins, a Special Assistant U.S. Attorney (1973–1974) before he became a novelist, extends our sense of the city into its margins and back alleys. Higgins wrote not only of the city's scruffy, criminal side, but also of what that city should stand for. In *A City on a Hill*, a 1975 novel, he invokes both the inspiring words of John Winthrop's speech aboard the *Arbella* and John F. Kennedy's pre-inauguration address of January 9, 1961 before a joint session of the Massachusetts legislature, in which the newly elected president said he had been "guided by the standard John Winthrop set before his shipmates 331 years ago, as they, too, faced the task of building a government on a new and perilous frontier."[68] George V. Higgins thus invoked the lows and highs of the Boston Irish experience in his fiction.

James "Whitey" Bulger was an infamous Boston criminal, topping the FBI's Most Wanted list when he went into hiding in 1994, after being tipped off by an FBI agent (for whom Bulger served as an informer on other gangsters) that he would soon be arrested for narcotics dealing and murder. Whitey Bugler's brother is William Michael Bulger, former president of the Massachusetts State Senate and former president of the University of Massachusetts. The Bulger brothers grew up in a South Boston public housing project and went in different directions, crime and public service, staking out the extremes of the Boston Irish experience. William Bulger memorialized his formative years and beloved community in a 1996 memoir, *While the Music Lasts*, a work which colorfully contrasts Boston's extremes: the "pale towers of Yankee Babylon" with "the warmth and color of the hanging garden of South Boston, where we lived."[69] Whitey Bulger remains in hiding, far from the hanging gardens of Southie, where he left many bodies buried.

Eddie Coyle, a petty crook trying to get by, was more a sad victim than a notorious victimizer like Whitey Bulger. When Eddie is taken by fellow mobsters to a Bruins-Rangers hockey game late in Higgins's novel, he realizes his time is running out, so his admiration for a young hockey star is particularly poignant. "'Beautiful,' Coyle said, 'Beautiful. Can you imagine being that kid? . . . Bobby Orr. What a future he's got.'"[70] Like *The Last Hurrah* before it, *The Friends of Eddie Coyle* was made into a fine film, starring a seedy Robert Mitchum and directed by Peter Yates, in 1973, adding to and enriching the representation of the Boston Irish, whose best days seem long gone in these works.

Other Greater Boston Irish crime novelists also extended the literary range of focus far beyond genteel Beacon Hill, Back Bay, and Cambridge, into the dark and mean streets at the edges of the city. In a series of popular novels, Robert Parker has portrayed a city rife with crime and punishment; his *Spenser* novels, about a Boston private investigator, have been adapted into a popular television series. Dennis Lehane, from Dorchester, has also seen his most impressive work of noir fiction, *Mystic River* (2001), translated into a memorable film (2003) that reveals Boston as gritty and graceless. Another Lehane novel, *Gone, Baby, Gone* (1998), also made into a film (2007), amplifies the themes of loss and regret set forth by Higgins in the Irish crime genre.

These writers show that the Boston Irish were divided against themselves as much as they were united in opposition to the Yankee-Brahmin elite. This became dramatically evident in 1974 when Judge J. Arthur Garrity ordered the integration of Boston's public schools, initiating an ethnic and racial explosion in the city that held the nation's attention for years. In *Common Ground* J. Anthony Lukas dramatized all sides of this sad struggle between the city's races and classes, tensions which were particularly bitter among the Irish. Lukas singled out the acrimonious exchange between Judge Garrity and James J. Sullivan, attorney for the Boston School Committee, which was resisting the integration order. For Lukas this encounter was an informing parable of Boston's divided Irish American community. Judge Garrity, who lived in the posh Boston suburb of Wellesley, represented Irish American middle-class aspirations, while attorney Sullivan remained loyal to "his clan, his turf, his blood," the working-class Irish of Dorchester and South Boston, whose schools were being integrated against their wishes. "Indeed, the struggle in Arthur Garrity's courtroom that year often resembled an Irish morality play, fought out between various conceptions of what it meant to be Irish in contemporary Boston."[71]

Michael Patrick MacDonald, born in 1966 and reared in a public housing project on Columbia Point, near the site on which the John F. Kennedy Library would be erected, published searing memoirs, *All Souls* (1999) and *Easter Rising* (2006). From his marginalized perspective, MacDonald portrayed South Boston, the center of Irish American resistance to "forced busing," as a killing field for its residents. MacDonald's neighborhood, separated by a canal and an expressway from downtown Boston, held fast to its Irish identity, particularly on Saint Patrick's Day, when they proudly paraded, but Southie also became famous for its insularity and defensiveness. Southie citizens had a look about them, MacDonald says, "as if they'd spent much of their time defying whatever shit had come their way."[72]

Caught in the crossfire of these forces, the MacDonald family was shattered. Michael's sister Mary had two children, but no husband; his brother Davey received shock treatments at fourteen; his brother Kevin dealt drugs for Whitey Bulger; later Davey, drugged, jumped off a roof and died; their brother Frankie had to join the Marines to keep from being prosecuted; their "Ma" was shot by a stray bullet; their sister Kathy, high on angel dust, either jumped or was pushed from a roof and was maimed for life; Kevin was arrested for stealing a car and told to keep his mouth shut by Whitey's men; then Kevin married, with Whitey serving as his best man; Frankie was shot during a Wells Fargo robbery and killed, most likely strangled by one of his fellow thieves; Kevin, arrested for a jewelry store heist, died by hanging in jail, probably murdered; their brother Stevie, at age thirteen, was charged with murder. So, for Michael MacDonald's family did Southie, "the best place in the world," an Irish American haven, become a free-fire zone that produced shocking instances of death by suicide, murder, or drugs.

> The hearses kept rolling down Dorchester Street, where in better days we'd watched the St. Patrick's Day parade and the anti-busing motorcades. And every time it was another Southie mother's turn to see her child off at Jackie O'Brien's [Funeral Home], it brought Ma right back to reality. She started going to all the wakes, even if she didn't know the family, and in about a year she counted that she'd been to thirty-two, all dead from suicide, drugs, or crime.[73]

In *All Souls*, then in *Easter Rising*, MacDonald gave a compelling account of his journey out of Southie, the Irish American ghetto and mind-set that had doomed many members of his family, just as South Side Chicago had for James T. Farrell, whose 1930s trilogy recorded Studs Lonigan's brief, sad life.[74] MacDonald escaped, finding a new life in New York City and in Ireland, but he returned to Boston, wrote his books, and worked to hold together what remained of his family and, as a community organizer, to redeem his Boston Irish community, Southie.

Lawrence J. McCaffrey, leading historian of Irish American experience, posed a haunting question in *The Irish Diaspora in America* (1976) when he reflected on the journey of Irish Catholics from their pastoral to American "urban neighborhoods," then to "suburban melting pots"; he asks if all this has "been a journey to achievement and contentment or an excursion from someplace to no place?"[75] Despite the many successes won by the Irish in Boston, their political victories and secure presence in the city, this is the daunting question posed by many of its writers, from John Boyle O'Reilly to Michael Patrick MacDonald.

Boston's Jewish writers, like its black and Irish authors, recorded their struggle for life, liberty, and the pursuit of happiness in the unwelcoming city upon a hill. Though a few Jews appeared in Puritan-era Boston, the city was differentiated from other American cities by their absence. Boston "projected an image of formidable homogeneity; for a time it held the dubious distinction of being America's most homogeneous city," writes Jonathan D. Sarna in *The Jews of Boston* (1975). Starkly put, Jews "were seen as latecomers and interlopers, . . . an alien presence in early Boston."[76] Those few who did settle there were largely conservative until the immigration of Eastern European Jews increased and diversified the Jewish population tenfold to 50,000 in the 1880s–'90 s, then to some 90,000 by World War I. Jews gained a foothold in a small section of the North End; then in East Boston, in the South End, Roxbury and the West End, where they were enlisted into the political constituency of Irish ward boss Martin Lomasney. "The Democratic Party welcomes you to America," one Jewish newcomer recalls being greeted at the East Boston dock. "Martin Lomasney welcomes you to Boston."[77]

Jewish immigrants were met with suspicion by most Bostonians. Emerson, for example, had been offended by the presence of Polish Jews in 1839 ("they degrade and animalize"), but reconciled in 1869 he wrote, "I hail every one with delight."[78] After the Civil War, James Russell Lowell, Henry Adams, and Henry James expressed open disdain for Jews, as they did for Irish and Italian immigrants. Despite Lomasney's welcome, the Irish, though themselves victims of Yankee-Brahmin prejudice, were largely hostile, first to blacks, then to Jewish immigrants who arrived after them. Suddenly, it seemed, formerly homogeneous Boston was a battleground where turf wars were fought, intensified by economic tensions and cultural differences. The city became a center of anti-Semitism during the Great Depression, when followers of Father Charles E. Coughlin, the famous "radio priest," joined with the Christian Front in attacks upon Jews. However, when Cambridge priest Father Leonard Feeney denounced Jews as "horrid, degenerate hook-nosed perverts," he was dismissed from the Jesuit order, under pressure from Cardinal Richard Cushing; Feeney was finally excommunicated from the Catholic Church in 1949.[79] Cardinal Cushing worked to change Boston's prejudice against Jews, particularly in his support of proposals at the Second Vatican Council, in 1964, where he declared his love for the Jews as "the blood brothers of Christ."[80]

In 1894, when she was thirteen, Mary Antin left Poltz (or Plotzk), Russia, and came with her family to Boston, where, as she later described it, she experienced a "second birth."[81] Though she lived in a tenement house, Mary learned to love the idea of Boston as a citadel of liberty and culture. Coming of age in Boston's ethnic slums, centered on Dover Street, she composed a narrative, *From Plotzk to Boston*, in 1899, an account of her journey from a Russian shtetl, written in Yiddish, then translated into English.[82] Her resulting autobiography, *Promised Land* (1912), serialized in *Atlantic Monthly* before it was published as a book, became a best-seller because it revealed the conditions of Jewish immigrants and because it was a reassuring parable of purpose and patriotism. "In Poltz we had supposed that 'America' was practically synonymous with 'Boston.'"[83] The profits and esteem that accrued from this work allowed her to enroll in an elite Boston public school, Girls' Latin; she also published poetry in the *Boston Herald* and essays in *Atlantic Monthly*. When she was only fifteen, Mary published a poem in praise of George Washington and won wide approval. "It is so simple in Boston," she exclaimed. There, like so many newcomers before her, Mary Antin found her voice and gained acceptance though both her account of hard times and her affirmation of gratitude to Boston, her promised land.

Other Jewish Bostonians were far less celebratory. Recalling his "Boston Boyhood" (1929), Isaac Goldberg rejected this provincial, prejudiced, and political city, identifying himself as an American. "I am too good an American to be a truly good Bostonian; too enamored of the American tradition to surrender to the administrative fervors of its political hetmen [command-ers]." He invoked "Bolsheviki" license for rebellion against "the cradle of liberty."[84] On the other hand, Charles Angoff's *When I Was a Boy in Boston* (1947) celebrated assimilation. During the first decades of the twentieth century the young newcomer Angoff "became Americanized in record time," reveling in American treats: ketchup, movies, and ice cream.[85]

Reporter and presidential campaign historian Theodore H. White recalled in his memoir, *In Search of History* (1981), his more painful assimi-lation to Boston, growing up after World War I on Eire Street, Dorchester. Surrounded by the hostile Irish gangs, White felt trapped, a Jewish "iso-lato." He then transcended his ethnic enclosure, like Mary Antin before him, at Boston Latin School, to which he walked four miles each day, from Dorchester to the Fenway, during the Depression. At Harvard he was a day student, an outsider, but there he became a successful "looter" of culture, which provided him a ticket out of Boston: a fellowship at the Harvard-Yenching Institute in 1938 and a career as a writer. The Jewish boy from Boston had risen from street battles with the Irish, reinventing himself in famed Boston-Cambridge schools to become "the creature of other people, of another past, beneficiary of all the Establishment had packed into the Harvard processing system."[86]

Nat Hentoff, journalist, jazz and culture critic, born a decade after White, set out to counter the false myths of Boston's civility in his memoir, *Boston Boy* (1986). "It was in this city—so admired by many who have never lived there—that I grew up."[87] Like White, Hentoff had to battle his way through hostile Irish gangs as he made his way from his Roxbury home to the citadels of culture and safety, the Boston Public Library and Boston Latin School. (Boston Latin School provided both an education and a preparation for transcending Boston's limits for other Boston Jewish boys who became famous, including art critic Bernard Berenson, composer-conductor Leon-ard Bernstein, and child psychiatrist Robert Coles.)[88] "I would be going to *their* school, in *their* part of town, and so I would be not only learning Latin and Greek, but learning about *them*," wrote Hentoff.[89] Jazz spots, like Bos-ton's fabled Savoy and High-Hat, provided a democratizing sanctuary of racial-ethnic tolerance for him, as it had for Malcolm Little.

> Those of us who came out onto Massachusetts Avenue from the Savoy Café to find our various ways home occasionally walked in jazz time. But

it was hard to sustain that pulse and good feeling in the heavy air of Boston, with its tribal hatreds, the anti-Catholics sometimes being almost as venomous as the anti-Semites, and all mocking the Negroes—which is why they loved listening to Amos and Andy on the radio. But behind the closed doors of the Savoy, I felt more at home than anywhere else I had ever been, including home.[90]

Like Malcolm Little, Nat Hentoff assembled his identity from proper Boston's marginal elements and energies, from Left-Jewish politics to black jazz. He even learned lessons from the Boston Irish, particularly from those who fought for education and against their own church's indifference to anti-Semitism. Hentoff found worthy models in Frances Sweeney, owner-editor of the *Boston City Reporter,* who exposed political corruption, and George Frazier, the stylish *Boston Globe* columnist. "Both those Boston Irish lit up the city as long as they were in it, and they put some of their fire in me. And some of their romanticism, too."[91]

The ambivalent relationship between Boston and its Jews is evident in the realm of education. While Boston Latin did not discriminate, Harvard did, establishing a quota system under the presidency of A. Lawrence Lowell in 1922. "Harvard came to serve as something of a barometer of Jewish social acceptance within the city as a whole." When this policy yielded to merit-based admission, Jews took their rightful place as Harvard students, faculty, and administrators.[92] Indeed, Jewish commitment to the life of the mind and culture has made them worthy successors to the formerly ethnically exclusive Boston Brahmins as defined by Oliver Wendell Holmes. Louis Brandeis, the first Jewish appointment to the U.S. Supreme Court, was the model Jewish Boston Brahmin, notes Douglass Shand-Tucci.

> Like so many leading Bostonians over the years, Brandeis was an adopted rather than a native Bostonian, further evidence of how true it is that natives with half a brain usually get out of town as quickly as possible, while those from elsewhere in the world with brains enough to win their way to school in Boston very often fall in love with the place, especially the ones like Brandeis who value cosmopolitanism.[93]

In 1948 a great secular university, "a kind of Jewish Harvard," was founded just outside Boston and named after Brandeis in "the ultimate synthesis . . . of American and Jew."[94]

Despite its open anti-Semitism and ethnic tensions, Boston taught its Jewish citizens a great deal by providing both cultural traditions and educational opportunities that prepared them for success. As these memoirs show, the Jews of Boston, in turn, taught their fellow citizens the cost they paid for prejudice. Antin, White, Hentoff, Brandeis, and others were infused with the Bostonian ideal of justice, which gave them a critical perspective on Boston's prejudices. Like the African Americans and the Irish before them, Boston's Jews traveled a long way from marginality to centrality in Boston culture.

Leonard P. Zakim emblemizes the triumph of the Boston Jewish experience. For twenty years he served as director of the Anti-Defamation League of New England; he worked closely with Cardinal Bernard Law to oppose bigotry and increase understanding between Jews and Catholics. The Leonard P. Zakim–Bunker Hill Memorial Bridge, finished in 2003, a gorgeous, cable-stayed span across the Charles River, commemorates this Boston civic leader and civil rights activist who championed "building bridges between peoples" and honors the Battle of Bunker Hill.[95] As Thomas H. O'Connor puts it, "perhaps no more dramatic and tangible demonstration of the way in which Jews have taken on the flavor of Boston without losing their own distinctive identity came with the completion" of this bridge. Linking "the colonial heritage of Boston with the cause of religious liberty," the Leonard P. Zakim–Bunker Hill Memorial Bridge serves as "an appropriate symbol of the way in which Jews of Boston themselves have bridged the gap between the old and the new, between . . . the values of the Brahmins and of the Jews."[96] Boston's African Americans, Irish, and Jews shattered the city's homogeneity and challenged its Yankee-Brahmin hegemony, but, more important, they provided the city with the opportunity to live up to the words and great expectations of unity and purpose set for it by John Winthrop.

African American Bostonians and the descendants of Irish and Jewish immigrants left full and compelling literary records of their presence and redefined the image of the city, but Boston is now composed of people from an even wider range of ethnic representation. Though remarkably homogeneous during its first two hundred years, Boston has grown dramatically more various since the middle of the nineteenth century, particularly so in the late twentieth century. It has been estimated that only half of Boston's population in the early twenty-first century is white, with citizens of Irish and Italian origins composing the largest percentage, while less than 10 percent of the city is African American; Asian Americans, Hispanics or Latinos, Vietnamese, and Dominican Americans make up most of the rest.[97]

Boston's North End, once the home of Paul Revere and the starting-point of the famous midnight ride that instigated the American Revolution, has served as a model of ethnic-cultural transition. This "most historic part of the city" was the Puritans' first dwelling site and long remained a Yankee stronghold.[98] Boston's ruling class fled the area for Beacon Hill and later for Back Bay when the North End was taken over by Famine-era Irish immigrants, including "Honey" Fitzgerald, who would become the city's mayor and the grandfather of a president. Jewish immigrants in small numbers, then Italian immigrants in larger numbers crowded out most of the Irish by 1900. Soon the North End became home to nearly all of the city's Italian population and remained so for the rest of the twentieth century.[99] For much of that century, Boston, which liked to think of itself as a city of neighborhoods, became a city of ethnic enclaves in which groups led distinct lives, separated by bridges, bodies of water, rail lines, streets, and animosities. Construction of the Central Artery, which opened in 1959, sliced the city with a north-south highway and drove out many Italian families, obliterating the West End and further isolating the North End community until the Big Dig project of the 1990s converted this north-south throughway into a tunnel and reconnected the North End with the rest of the city. Long-established separation yielded to assimilation and gentrification, as former ethnic enclaves like the Italian North End, Irish South Boston, Jewish Roxbury, and Black Roxbury eventually, often reluctantly, welcomed diversity. Boston has been enriched by the incorporation of its once marginalized citizenry. Thomas M. Menino, for example, was elected the city's first Italian mayor in 1993, and he has become the longest occupant of that office, exemplifying the centrality of the Italian American presence in Boston.

Though African Americans, Irish Americans, and Jewish Americans have contributed more ample records of their impressions of Boston, Italian Americans have developed their own local literature, configuring the city from another informing perspective. The saga of Italian immigrants' struggle from painful settlement to hard-won acceptance and political success, "a story of pride, perseverance, and *Paesani*," is recounted in *The Boston Italians* (2007), by Stephen Puleo. The richness of the Greater Boston experience and its emerging literary expression can be seen in the opening chapter of Roland Merullo's novel *In Revere, in Those Days* (2002).[100] Through such compelling books, these "other," once marginalized Bostonians have made themselves central to the story, told in many voices, of Boston.

James Carroll, novelist, essayist, and columnist for the *Boston Globe*, though born in Chicago and raised in Washington, D.C., eloquently sums up his sense of the city, hints at its multiple meanings, grants that the city has problems, but points up its possibilities, realized and unrealized.

> The Boston of the American imagination exists only on the poster-sized map of the mind, with its border of oval-framed faces of patriots, politicians, preachers, and poets. The map is titled, variously, Athens of America, Brimstone Corner, City on a Hill, All Politics Is Local, Ireland West, Berkeley East, Race War North, Birthplace of Bio-Tech, and Banned in Boston. The features of the map include painted-brick footpaths through early America, prickly borders of tribal neighborhoods, the squared-off glass steeples of faith in financial services, a yawning harbor through which funnel ever fewer fish and a constant current of immigrants, stars marking the desks and workbenches of Nobel laureates, tidal charts of a seasonally shifting student population, the white needles of old churches, the compass rose of politics, and notations for the bus stops of the tourist trolleys. . . . Boston is precious because it lives in the national imagination and, increasingly, the world's, just so—as a tattered but still brilliant map of America's good hope.[101]

As the African Americans, the Irish Americans, and the Jewish Americans made their painful ways up the slopes of the city upon a hill, seeking acceptance, leaving a compelling literary record of their journeys, and redefining the city, so too followed Italian Americans; so too will follow representatives of still other "other Bostonians" who will leave their own literary record and reshape the city to the contours of their imaginations.

Charlotte Forten Grimke, from her Journal (1854)

Charlotte Forten Grimke (1838–1914)—anti-slavery activist, poet, and educator—kept a journal which provides a unique perspective on the activities of African American abolitionists and educators. Here she registers her dismay at the arrest in Boston of escaped slave Anthony Burns, who was returned to slavery in Virginia, despite protests by abolitionists, under the Fugitive Slave Act, a component of the Compromise of 1850.

Friday, June 2, 1854: Our worst fears are realized; the decision was against the poor [Anthony] Burns, and he has been sent back to a bondage worse, a thousand times worse than death. Even an attempt at rescue was utterly impossible; the prison was completely surrounded by soldiers with bayonets fixed, a canon loaded, ready to be fired at the slightest sign. Today Massachusetts has again been disgraced; again has she showed her submissions to the Slave Power; and Oh! with what deep sorrow do we think of what will doubtless be the fate of that poor man, when he is again consigned to the horrors of slavery. With what scorn must that government be regarded which cowardly assembles thousands of soldiers to satisfy the demands of slaveholders; to deprive of his freedom a man, created in God's own image, whose sole offense is the color of his skin! And if resistance is offered to this outrage, these soldiers are to shoot down American citizens without mercy; and this by express orders of a government which proudly boasts of being the freest in the world; this on the very soil on which the Revolution of 1776 began; in sight of the battlefield, where thousands of brave men fought and died in opposing British tyranny, which was nothing compared with the American oppression of today. In looking over my diary, I perceive that I did not mention that there was on the Friday night after the man's arrest, an attempt made to rescue him, but although it failed, on account of there not being men enough engaged in it, all honor should be given to those who bravely made the attempt. I can write no more. A cloud seems hanging over me, over all our persecuted race, which nothing can dispel.

Sunday, June 4, 1854: A beautiful day. The sky is cloudless, the sun shines warm and bright, and a delicious breeze fans my cheeks as I sit by the window writing. How strange it is that in a world so beautiful, there can be so much wickedness, on this delightful day, while many are enjoying themselves in their happy homes, not poor Burns only, but millions beside are suffering in chains; and how many Christian ministers to-day will mention him, or those who suffer with him? How many will speak from the pulpit against the cruel outrage on humanity which has just been committed, or against the many, even worse ones, which are committed in this country every day? Too well do we know that there are but very few, and these few alone deserve to be called the ministers of Christ, whose doctrine was "Break every yoke, and let the oppressed go free."—During the past week, we have had a vacation, which I had expected to enjoy very much, but it was, of course, impossible for me to do so. To-morrow school commences [the Higginson Grammar School in Salem, Massachusetts, where she was the only non-white student in a class of 200], and although the pleasure I shall feel in again seeing my beloved teacher, and in resuming my studies will be much saddened by recent events, yet they shall be a fresh incentive to more earnest study, to aid me in fitting myself for labor-ing in a holy cause, for enabling me to do much towards changing the condi-tion of my oppressed and suffering people. Would that those with whom I shall recite to-morrow could sympathize with me in this; would that they could look upon all God's creatures without respect to color, feeling that it is character alone which makes the true man or woman! I earnestly hope that the time will come when they feel thus.—I have several letters to write to-day to send my Aunt Harriet who leaves for Philadelphia tomorrow. Father left yesterday, he has not yet decided to come here to live; he will write and tell me what he has determined to do, as soon as he has consulted mother. I fear he has not now a very favorable opinion of Massachusetts; still I hope they will come; I long to see the children again.

W. E. B. Du Bois, from "A Negro Student at Harvard at the End of the Nineteenth Century" (1960)

W. E. B. Du Bois (1868–1963) was the most influential African Ameri-can of his generation: a civil rights activist, a leader of the Harlem Renaissance, an educator, historian, editor, scholar, and writer of note.

His most famous work is *The Souls of Black Folk* (1903). Here he recalls the education he received at Harvard and in Boston.

Harvard University in 1888 was a great institution of learning. It was two hundred and thirty-eight years old and on its governing board was Alexander Agassiz, Phillips Brooks, Henry Cabot Lodge, and Charles Francis Adams; and a John Quincy Adams, but not the ex-President. Charles William Eliot, a gentleman by training and a scholar by broad study and travel, was president. Among its teachers emeriti were Oliver Wendell Holmes and James Russell Lowell. Among the active teachers were Francis Child, Charles Eliot Norton, Justin Winsor, and John Trowbridge; Frank Taussig, Nathaniel Shaler, George Palmer, William James, Francis Peabody, Josiah Royce, Barrett Wendell, Edward Channing, and Albert Bushnell Hart. In 1890 arrived a young instructor, George Santayana. Seldom, if ever, has any American university had such a galaxy of great men and fine teachers as Harvard in the decade between 1885 and 1895.

To make my own attitude toward the Harvard of that day clear, it must be remembered that I went to Harvard as a Negro, not simply by birth, but recognizing myself as a member of a segregated caste whose situation I accepted. But I was determined to work from within that caste to find any way out.

The Harvard of which most white students conceived I knew little. I had not even heard of Phi Beta Kappa, and of such important social organizations as the Hasty Pudding Club, I knew nothing. I was in Harvard for education and not for high marks, except as marks would insure my staying. I did not pick out "snap" courses. I was there to enlarge my grasp of the meaning of the universe. We had had, for instance, no chemical laboratory at Fisk; our mathematics courses were limited. Above all I wanted to study philosophy! I wanted to get hold of the bases of knowledge, and explore foundations and beginnings. I chose, therefore, Palmer's course in ethics, but since Palmer was on sabbatical that year, William James replaced him, and I became a devoted follower of James at the time he was developing his pragmatic philosophy.

Fortunately I did not fall into the mistake of regarding Harvard as the beginning rather than the continuing of my college training. I did not find better teachers at Harvard, but teachers better known, who had wider facilities for gaining knowledge and lived in a broader atmosphere for approaching truth.

I hoped to pursue philosophy as my life career, with teaching for support. With this program I studied at Harvard from the fall of 1888 to 1890, as an undergraduate. I took a varied course in chemistry, geology, social science, and philosophy. My salvation here was the type of teacher I met rather than the content of the courses. William James guided me out of the sterilities of scholastic philosophy to realistic pragmatism; from Peabody's social reform with a religious tinge I turned to Albert Bushnell Hart to study history with documentary research; and from Taussig, with his reactionary British economics of the Ricardo school, I approached what was later to become sociology. Meantime, Karl Marx was mentioned, but only incidentally and as one whose doubtful theories had long since been refuted. Socialism was dismissed as unimportant, as a dream of philanthropy, or as a will-o-wisp of hotheads.

When I arrived at Harvard, the question of board and lodging was of first importance. Naturally, I could not afford a room in the college yard in the old and venerable buildings which housed most of the well-to-do students under the magnificent elms. Neither did I think of looking for lodgings among white families, where numbers of the ordinary students lived. I tried to find a colored home, and finally at 20 Flagg Street I came upon a neat home of a colored woman from Nova Scotia, a descendant of those black Jamaican Maroons whom Britain had deported after solemnly promising them peace if they would surrender. For a very reasonable sum I rented the second story front room and for four years this was my home. . . .

Following the attitudes I had adopted in the South, I sought no friendships among my white fellow students, nor even acquaintanceships. Of course I wanted friends, but I could not seek them. My class was large—some three hundred students. I doubt if I knew a dozen of them. I did not seek them, and naturally they did not seek me. I made no attempt to contribute to the college periodicals since the editors were not interested in my major interests. But I did have a good singing voice and loved music, so I entered the competition for the Glee Club. I ought to have known that Harvard could not afford to have a Negro in the Glee Club traveling about the country. Quite naturally I was rejected.

I was happy at Harvard, but for unusual reasons. One of these was my acceptance of racial segregation. Had I gone from Great Barrington High School directly to Harvard, I would have sought companionship with my white fellows and been disappointed and embittered by a discovery of social limitations to which I had not been used. But I came by way of Fisk and the South and there I had accepted color caste and embraced eagerly the companionship of those of my own color. This was of course no final solution. Eventually, in mass assault, led by culture, we Negroes were going to break down the boundaries of race; but at present we were banded together in a great crusade, and happily so. Indeed, I suspect that the prospect of ultimate full human intercourse, without reservations and annoying distinctions, made me all too willing to consort with my own and to disdain and forget as far as was possible that outer, whiter world.

In general, I asked nothing of Harvard but the tutelage of teachers and the freedom of the laboratory and library. I was quite voluntarily and willingly outside its social life. I sought only such contacts with white teachers as lay directly in the line of my work. I joined certain clubs, like the Philosophical Club; I was a member of the Foxcroft Dining Club because it was cheap. James and one or two other teachers had me at their homes at meal and reception. I escorted colored girls to various gatherings, and as pretty ones as I could find to the vesper exercises, and later to the class day and commencement functions. Naturally we attracted attention and the *Crimson* noted my girl friends. Sometimes the shadow of insult fell, as when at one reception a white woman seemed determined to mistake me for a waiter.

In general, I was encased in a completely colored world, self-sufficient and provincial, and ignoring just as far as possible the white world which conditioned it. This was self-protective coloration, with perhaps an inferiority complex, but with belief in the ability and future of black folks.

My friends and companions were drawn mainly from the colored students of Harvard and neighboring institutions, and the colored folk of Boston and surrounding towns. With them I led a happy and inspiring life. There were among them many educated and well-to-do folk, many young people studying or planning to study, many charming young women. We met and ate, danced and argued, and planned a new world.

Towards whites I was not arrogant; I was simply not obsequious, and to a white Harvard student of my day a Negro student who did not seek recognition was trying to be more than a Negro. The same Harvard man had much the same attitude toward Jews and Irishmen.

I was, however, exceptional among Negroes at Harvard in my ideas on voluntary race segregation. They for the most part saw salvation only in integration at the earliest moment and on almost any terms in white culture; I was firm in my criticism of white folk and in my dream of a self-sufficient Negro culture even in America.

This cutting of myself off from my white fellows, or being cut off, did not mean unhappiness or resentment. I was in my early manhood, unusually full of high spirits and humor. I thoroughly enjoyed life. I was conscious of understanding and power, and conceited enough still to imagine, as in high school, that they who did not know me were the losers, not I. On the other hand, I do not think that my white classmates found me personally objectionable. I was clean, not well-dressed but decently clothed. Manners I regarded as more or less superfluous and deliberately cultivated a certain brusquerie. Personal adornment I regarded as pleasant but not important. I was in Harvard, but not of it, and realized all the irony of my singing "Fair Harvard." I sang it because I liked the music, and not from any pride in the Pilgrims.

With my colored friends I carried on lively social intercourse, but necessarily one which involved little expenditure of money. I called at their homes and ate at their tables. We danced at private parties. We went on excursions down the Bay. Once, with a group of colored students gathered from surrounding institutions, we gave Aristophanes' *The Birds* in a Boston colored church. The rendition was good, but not outstanding, not quite appreciated by the colored audience, but well worth doing. Even though it worked me to death, I was proud of it.

Thus the group of professional men, students, white-collar workers, and upper servants, whose common bond was color of skin in themselves or in their fathers, together with a common history and current experience of discrimination, formed a unit that, like many tens of thousands of like units across the nation, had or were getting to have a common culture pattern which made them an interlocking mass, so that increasingly a colored person in Boston was more neighbor to a colored person in Chicago than to a white person across the street.

Mrs. Ruffin of Charles Street, Boston, and her daughter, Birdie, were often hostesses to this colored group. She was the widow of the first colored judge appointed in Massachusetts, an aristocratic lady, with olive skin and high-piled masses of white hair. Once a Boston white lady said to Mrs. Ruffin ingratiatingly: "I have always been interested in your race." Mrs. Ruffin flared: "Which race?" She began a national organization of colored women and published the *Courant,* a type of small colored weekly paper which was then spreading over the nation. In this I published many of my Harvard daily themes.

Naturally in this close group there grew up among the young people friendships ending in marriage. I myself, outgrowing the youthful attractions of Fisk, began serious dreams of love and marriage. There were, however, still my study plans to hold me back and there were curious other reasons. For instance, it happened that two of the girls whom I particularly liked had what to me was then the insuperable handicap of looking like whites, while they had enough black ancestry to make them look like "Negroes" in America. I could not let the world even imagine that I had married a white wife. Yet these girls were intelligent and companionable. One went to Vassar College, which then refused entrance to Negroes. Years later when I went there to lecture I remember disagreeing violently with a teacher who thought the girl ought not to have "deceived" the college by graduating before it knew of her Negro descent! Another favorite of mine was Deenie Pindell. She was a fine, forthright woman, blonde, blue-eyed and fragile. In the end I had no chance to choose her, for she married Monroe Trotter.

Trotter was the son of a well-to-do colored father and entered Harvard in my first year in the Graduate School. He was thick-set, yellow, with close-cut dark hair. He was stubborn and strait-laced and an influential member of his class. He organized the first Total Abstinence Club in the Yard. I came to know him and joined the company when he and other colored students took in a trip to Amherst to see our friends Forbes and Lewis graduate in the class with Calvin Coolidge.

Lewis afterward entered the Harvard Law School and became the celebrated center rush of the Harvard football team. He married the beautiful Bessie Baker, who had been with us on that Amherst trip. Forbes, a brilliant, cynical dark man, later joined with Trotter in publishing the *Guardian,* the first Negro paper to attack Booker T. Washington openly. Washington's friends retorted by sending Trotter to jail when he dared to heckle Washington in a public Boston meeting on his political views. I was not present nor privy to this occurrence, but the unfairness of the jail sentence led me eventually to form the Niagara movement, which later became the NAACP. . . .

Harvard of this day was a great opportunity for a young man and a young American Negro and I realized it. I formed habits of work rather different from those of most of the other students. I burned no midnight oil. I did my studying in the daytime and had my day parceled out almost to the minute. I spent a great deal of time in the library and did my assignments with thoroughness and with prevision of the kind of work I wanted to do later. From the beginning my relations with most of the teachers at Harvard were pleasant. They were on the whole glad to receive a serious student, to whom extracurricular activities were not of paramount importance, and one who in a general way knew what he wanted.

Dorothy West, from *The Living Is Easy* (1948)

Dorothy West (1907–1998), was a Boston short story writer and novelist who became an important figure in the Harlem Renaissance. In her final four decades she lived on Martha's Vineyard, where she wrote journalism and her last novel, *The Wedding* (1995). In this passage Cleo Judson, based upon West's mother, attempts to leap social boundaries by moving her family from South Boston to Brookline.

Cleo sailed up Northampton Street with Judy in tow. Dark, unshaven faces split in wide grins, and low, lewd whistles issued from between thick lips. This was her daily cross to bear in this rapidly deteriorating section of Boston. The once fine houses of the rich were fast emptying of middle-class whites and filling up with lower-class blacks. The street was becoming another big road, with rough-looking loungers leaning in the doorways of decaying houses and dingy stores. Coarse conversations balanced like balls in mouths stretched wide to catch the dirty pellets and toss them into other agile word jugglers along the way.

They kept on the lookout for Cleo because she walked proud with her eyes on a point above their bullet heads. They had sworn to a man to make her smile.

"Look away, look away," moaned an ogling admirer. "The yeller sun has took up walking like a nachal woman."

Roars of appreciative guffaws greeted this attempt at wit. As the laughter subsided, a falsetto voice implored, "Lawd, take me to heaven while I'm happy. You done open my eyes and I done see a host of angels coming at me. She look like fire, and she ack like ice. I'm hot, I's cold. Oh, Lawd, have mercy on my soul."

Twin spots glowed in Cleo's cheeks. A stream of white-hot words erupted inside her, but did not pass the thin line of her lips. She swallowed them down and felt the spleen spread to the pit of her stomach. Men were her enemies because they were male.

The trolley wires began to hum. "Here comes the trolley," said Cleo, with an expelled breath of profound relief. "Pick up your feet and don't you dare fall down. If you get yourself dirty before we get to Brookline, I'll give you to a Chinaman to eat."

The trolley halted, and she boosted Judy aboard. She dropped a single fare into the slot—Judy was small for going on six—asked for a transfer, guided Judy down the aisle of the swaying car, and shuttled her into a window seat. She sank down beside her and fanned herself elegantly with one gloved hand, stirring no air whatever.

She looked herself now, gay and earth-rooted and intensely alive. Her gray eyes sparkled at Judy, at the slyly staring passengers, at the streets that grew cleaner and wider as the trolley left the Negro neighborhood, at the growing preponderance of white faces.

Judy's nose was pressed against the glass. Cleo nudged her and whispered, "Judy, what do I tell you about making your nose flat?"

Judy sighed and straightened up. The exciting street scene was a whole inch farther away. She withdrew into an injured silence and studied her reflection in the glass. It was not very clear, but she knew what she looked like. She looked like Papa.

The people on the streetcar did not know that. They regarded her in a way that she was quite used to. They were wondering where Cleo got her. They carefully scrutinized Cleo, then they carefully scrutinized her, and raised their eyebrows a little.

She was dark. She had Papa's cocoa-brown skin, his soft dark eyes, and his generous nose in miniature. Cleo worked hard on her nose. She had tried clothespins, but Judy had not known what to do about breathing. Now Cleo was teaching her to keep the bridge pinched, but Judy pinched too hard, and the rush of dark blood made her nose look larger than ever.

A little white dog with a lively face and a joyful tail trotted down the street. Judy grinned and screwed to follow him with her eyes.

Cleo hissed in her ear: "Don't show your gums when you smile, and stop squirming. You've seen dogs before. Sit like a little Boston lady. Straighten your spine."

The trolley rattled across Huntington Avenue, past the fine granite face of Symphony Hall, and continued up Massachusetts Avenue, where a cross-street gave a fair and fleeting glimpse of the Back Bay Fens, and another cross-street showed the huge dome of Christian Science. At the corner of Boylston Street, within sight of Harvard Bridge and the highway to Cambridge, Cleo and Judy alighted to wait for the Brookline Village trolley.

Cleo saw with satisfaction that she was already in another world, though a scant fifteen-minute ride away from the mean streets of the Negro neighborhood. There were white people everywhere with sallow-skinned, thin, austere Yankee faces. They had the look that Cleo coveted for her dimpled daughter. She was dismayed by Judy's tendency to be a happy-faced child, and hoped it was merely a phase of growth. A proper Bostonian never showed any emotion but hauteur. Though Cleo herself had no desire to resemble a fish, she wanted to be able to point with pride of ownership to someone who did.

The Village trolley came clanging up Boylston Street, and Judy clambered up the steps, pushed by her mother and pulled by the motorman. Cleo was pleased to see that there were no other colored passengers aboard. The occupants of the half-filled car were mostly matrons, whose clothes were unmodish and expensive. All of them had a look of distinction. They were neither Cabots nor Lowells, but they were old stock, and their self-assurance sat well on their angular shoulders.

They did not stare at Cleo and Judy, but they were discretely aware of the pair, and appreciative of their neat appearance. Boston whites of the better classes were never upset nor dismayed by the sight of one or two Negroes exercising equal rights. They cheerfully stomached three or four when they carried themselves inconspicuously. To them the minor phenomenon of a colored face was a reminder of the proud role their forebears had played in the freeing of the human spirit for aspirations beyond the badge of house slave.

The motorman steered his rocking craft down a wide avenue and settled back for the first straight stretch of his roundabout run. Cleo looked at the street signs, and her heart began to pound with excitement. This was Brookline. There wasn't another colored family she knew who had beaten her to it. She would be the first to say, "You must come to see us at our new address. We've taken a house in Brookline."

She began to peer hard at house numbers. A row of red-brick houses began, and Cleo suddenly pulled the bell cord.

"We get off here," she said to Judy, and shooed her down the aisle.

Cleo walked slowly toward the number she sought, taking in her surroundings. Shade trees stood in squares of earth along the brick-paved sidewalk. Each house had a trim plot of grass enclosed by a wrought-iron fence. The half-dozen houses in this short block were the only brick houses within immediate sight except for a trio of new apartment houses across the way, looking flat-faced and ugly as they squatted in their new cement sidewalk.

In the adjoining block was a row of four or five weathered frame houses with wide front porches, big bay windows, and great stone chimneys for the spiraling smoke of logs on blackened hearths. The area beyond was a fenced-in field, where the sleek and beautiful firehorses nibbled the purple clover and frisked among the wild flowers. Near-by was the firehouse with a few Irish heads in the open windows, and a spotted dog asleep in a splash of sun.

Directly opposite from where Cleo walked was a great gabled mansion on a velvet rise, with a carriage house at the end of a graveled drive. The house was occupied, but there was an air of suspended life about it, as if all movement inside it was slow. Its columned porch and long French windows and lovely eminence gave the house grandeur.

A stone's-throw away was the winding ribbon of the Riverway Drive, over which the hooves of carriage horses clip-clopped and shiny automobiles choked and chugged. Beyond were the wooded Fens, at the outset of their wild wanderings over the city to Charlesgate.

Cleo was completely satisfied with everything she saw. There were no stoop-sitters anywhere, nor women idling at windows, nor loose-lipped loiterers passing remarks. Her friends who lived in Dorchester, or Cambridge, or Everett had nice addresses, of course. But Brookline was a private world.

She stopped and glanced down at her daughter to see if her ribbed white stockings were still smooth over her knees, and if the bright ribbons on the ends of her bobbing braids were as stiff and stand-out as they had been when she tied them. She scanned the small upturned face, and a rush of protective tenderness flooded her heart. For a moment she thought she had never seen anything as lovely as the deep rich color that warmed Judy's cheeks. She herself had hated being bright-skinned when she was a child. Mama had made her wash her face all day long, and in unfriendly moments her playmates had called her yaller punkins. Now her Northern friends had taught her to feel defensive because Judy was the color of her father.

"Don't speak unless you're spoken to," Cleo warned Judy, and mounted the steps of the house before which they stood.

In a moment or two a colored maid responded to her ring. She looked at Cleo with open-mouthed surprise, then her look became sly and secret. "Y'all come see about the house?" she asked in a conspiratorial whisper.

"I beg your pardon," Cleo said coolly. "I've come to see Mr. Van Ryper."

The maid's face froze. She knew these stuck-up northern niggers. Thought they were better than southern niggers. Well, all of them looked alike to the white man. Let this high-yaller woman go down South and she'd find out.

"Step inside," she said surlily. "You're letting in flies."

"I'm sorry," Cleo said sweetly. "I see a big black fly got in already." With a dazzling smile she entered the house, and instantly drew a little breath at sight of the spacious hall with its beautiful winding stairway.

"What's the name?" the maid asked briefly. If this woman wanted to be treated like white folks, at least she wasn't going to be treated like quality white folks.

"The name is Mrs. Judson," Cleo said readily. She had been asked a proper question, however rudely, and she was perfectly willing to answer it. This peevish incivility was much less insulting than the earlier intimacy. If she had wanted to gossip with the servant before seeing the master, she would have used the back door.

"Wait here," the woman said, and began a snail-pace ascent of the stairs, with her rocking buttocks expressive of her scorn.

"Always remember," said Cleo loudly and sweetly to Judy, "that good manners put you in the parlor and poor manners keep you in the kitchen." The maid's broad back seemed to swell the seams of her uniform. "That's what I'm paying good money to your governess for," Cleo added impressively. "So you won't have to wear an apron."

Judy stared down at her shoes, feeling very uncomfortable because Cleo's voice was carrying to the woman on the stairs. Miss Binney always said that a lady must keep her voice low, and never boast, and never, never say anything that might hurt somebody's feelings.

"She heard you," said Judy in a stricken voice.

Cleo gave her a look of amiable impatience. "Well, I expected her to hear. Who do you think I was talking to? I certainly wasn't talking to you."

Her eyes grew lively with amusement as she studied her daughter's distress. Sometimes she wondered where she had got Judy. Judy had no funny bone. Thea was probably responsible. She had no funny bone either. Their diversions were so watery. What was the sense in Judy's taking delight in a dog's wagging tail if she was going to miss the greater eloquence of that woman's wagging rear, and then look shocked her when her mother talked back at it? You really had to love Bostonians to like them. And the part of Cleo that did love them was continually at war with the part of her that preferred the salt flavor of lusty laughter.

Her eyes clouded with wistfulness. The more the years increased between the now and the long ago, the more the broad A's hemmed her in, the more her child grew alien to all that had made her own childhood an enchanted summer, so in like degree did her secret heart yearn for her sisters. She longed for the eager audience they would have provided, the boisterous mirth she would have evoked when she flatfooted up an imaginary flight of stairs, agitating her bottom. Who did she know in the length and breadth of Boston who wouldn't have cleared an embarrassed throat before she got going good on her imitation?

Sometimes you felt like cutting the fool for the hell of it. Sometimes you hankered to pick a bone and talk with your mouth full. To Cleo culture was a garment that she had learned to get into quickly and out of just as fast.

She put on her parlor airs now, for Mr. Van Ryper was descending the stairs. Her eyebrows arched delicately, her luscious mouth pursed primly, and a faint stage smile ruffled her smooth cheeks. These artifices had no effect on Mr. Van Ryper, who was elderly.

He reached the bottom of the step and peered at her. "Carrie should have shown you in here," he said fussily, piloting Cleo and Judy into the parlor.

He waved at a chair. "Sit down, Mrs.—uh—Jenkins, and you, young lady. What's your name, Bright Eyes or Candy Kid? Let's see if it's Candy Kid. Look in that box on the table, and mind you don't stick up yourself or the furniture."

Judy murmured her thanks and retired. She had learned to dissolve when grown-ups were talking. They forgot you and said very interesting things.

"Now, then, Mrs.—uh—Jordan," said Mr. Van Ryper. "I expect you've come about the house."

Cleo looked about the gracious room. The lacquered floors were of fine hardwood, the marble above the great hearth was massive and beautiful. The magnificent sliding doors leading into the dining room were rich mahogany, the wallpaper was exquisitely patterned. From the center of the high ceiling the gas chandelier spun its crystal tears.

"It's a beautiful house," said Cleo with awe.

"Best house on the block. Sorry to leave it, but I'm too old to temper my prejudices."

Cleo looked startled and felt humiliated. Were there colored people next door? Was that why Mr. Van Ryper was moving away? Should her pride make her rise and exit with dignity, or should she take the insult in exchange for this lovely house? Who were the people next door? If they were anybody Miss Binney would have known them. They must be old second-class niggers from way down South, whom she wouldn't want to live next to herself.

"Do you happen to know what part of the South the family came from?" she asked delicately.

Mr. Van Ryper looked startled now. "What family?" he asked testily, peering hard at Cleo with the intent of reading her foolish feminine mind.

"The colored family you're prejudiced at," Cleo said belligerently.

Mr. Van Ryper rose to his feet. His face purpled with anger. "Madame my father was a leader in the Underground Movement. I was brought up in an Abolitionist household. Your accusation of color prejudice is grossly impertinent. I believe in man's inalienable right to liberty. Let me lecture you a bit for the enlightenment of your long-eared child, who is probably being brought up in cotton batting because she's a little colored Bostonian who must never give a backward look at her beginnings.

"We who are white enslaved you who are—to use a broad term madam—black. We reduced your forebears to the status of cattle. It must be our solemn task to return their descendants to man's estate. I have been instrumental in placing a good many southern Negroes in the service of my friends. My maid Carrie is lately arrived from the South. She is saving her wages to send for her family. They will learn here. They will go to night school. Their children will go to day school. Their grandchildren will go to high school, and some of them will go to college.

"Negroes are swarming out of the South. The wheat and the chaff are mixed. But time is a sifting agent. True, the chaff will forever be our cross to bear, but one fine day the wheat will no longer be part of the Negro problem."

Cleo looked unimpressed. She had lent an unwilling ear to this long speech, and had stubbornly closed her mind every time Mr. Van Ryper used the word Negro, because colored Bostonians were supposed to feel scandalized whenever they heard this indecent appellation. This fancy talk was just to cover up his saying he didn't like niggers.

"Well, it's nice when people aren't prejudiced," Cleo said politely.

"Madame, I am distinctly prejudiced against the Irish," Mr. Van Ryper said wearily, thinking that colored women, for all they had to endure, were as addlepated as their fairer-skinned sisters. "The Irish present a threat to us entrenched Bostonians. They did not come here in chains or by special invitation. So I disclaim any responsibility for them, and reserve the right to reject them. I do reject them, and refuse to live in a neighborhood they are rapidly overrunning. I have decided to rent my house to colored. Do you or don't you want it?"

"I do," said Cleo faintly, thinking this was the oddest white man she had ever met. It would take an educated person like Miss Binney to understand how his mind worked.

"And is the rent within your means? Thirty-five dollars, but it struck me as a fair sum. There are ten rooms. I hope you won't mind if I don't show them to you now. The parish priest is waiting upstairs in the sitting room. Seems some neighbors have complained about my attitude. He's a man of taste and intelligence. Pity he has to be Irish, but I understand that some of his blood is English."

Cleo rose, with a little nod at Judy, who came as obediently as a puppy trained to heel. There was a ring of chocolate around her mouth that made her look comical, and a smudge of it on one of her gloves. Cleo sighed a little. Children made a mess with chocolate candy. Any fool ought to know that. What did this old man think lollipops were invented for?

"About the rent, Mr. Van Ryper," she said, wiping Judy's mouth with the cotton handkerchief and taking this opportunity to glare in her eye, "thirty dollar would suit me better. And you wouldn't have to wait for it. You'd have it every month on the dot. My husband told me to tell you that."

Mr. Van Ryper gestured toward the dining-room doors. His voice was patient and instructive. "Madam, each one of those doors cost two hundred dollars. The staircase cost a small fortune. There is a marble bowl in the master bedroom. The bathtub is porcelain, and so is the—ah—box. But if thirty dollars is all you can afford, I hope you will make up the difference in appreciation."

"Indeed I will," Cleo promised fervently. "It's been my dream to live in Brookline."

"This isn't Brookline," Mr. Van Ryper said crossly. "The other side of the street is Brookline. This side is Roxbury, which that thundering herd of Irish immigrants have overrun. They have finally pushed their boundary to here. Time was when Roxbury was the meeting place of great men. Now its fine houses are being cut up into flats for insurrectionists. I'm moving to Brookline within a few days. Brookline is the last stronghold of my generation."

Cleo swallowed her disappointment. Several colored families were already living in Roxbury. They didn't talk about the Irish the way Mr. Van Ryper did. They called them nice white people. They said they lived next door to such nice white people, and made you feel out of fashion because your neighbors were colored.

She opened her purse, taking great care that its contents were not wholly revealed to Mr. Van Ryper.

"Just one other thing first," he said. "Your reference. That is to say your husband's employer."

"My husband's in business," Cleo explained. "He has a wholesale place in the Market. All kinds of fruit, but mostly bananas."

Mr. Van Ryper's eyes filled with interest. "Bart Judson? The Black Banana King? Never met him, but I hear he's pretty amazing. Well, well. I'm happy to rent my house to him. I like to do business with a businessman. Tell you what. We'll settle on a rental of twenty-five dollars. Ah, that pleases you, doesn't it? But there's a condition to it. I'd want your husband to take care of minor repairs. You see, I'm a tired old man, quite unused to being a landlord. I'd hate to be called out of bed in the middle of the night to see about a frozen water pipe."

The matter was settled at once and Cleo handed over the money. Mr. Van Ryper found a scarp of paper and a stub of pencil in his pocket, and paused in the writing of the receipt to make an inquiry. Did Mrs. Judson want it in ink? Cleo answered hastily and heartily that pencil was fine.

———— ∞∞∞ ————

Malcolm X and Alex Haley, from *The Autobiography of Malcolm X* (1965)

Malcolm X (1925–1965), born Malcolm Little, rose from life as a petty criminal to become an important African American leader as a Black Muslim. Arriving from Michigan in 1941, Malcolm came of age in Boston, where he discovered social stratification and self-expression.

All praise is due to Allah that I went to Boston when I did. If I hadn't, I'd probably still be a brainwashed black Christian. . . .

About my second day there in Roxbury, Ella [Ella Little Collins, Malcolm's half-sister] told me that she didn't want me to start hunting for a job right away, like most newcomer Negroes did. She said that she had told all those she'd brought North to take their time, to walk around, to travel the buses and the subways, to get the feel of Boston, before they tied themselves down working somewhere, because they would never again have the time to really see and get to know anything about the city they were living in. Ella said she'd help me find a job when it was time for me to go to work.

So I went gawking around the neighborhood—the Waumbeck and Humboldt Avenue Hill section of Roxbury, which is something like Harlem's Sugar Hill, where I'd later live. I saw those Roxbury Negroes acting and living differently from any black people I'd ever dreamed of in my life. This was the snooty-black neighborhood; they called themselves the "Four Hundred," and looked down their noses at the Negroes of the black ghetto, or so-called "town" section where Mary, my other half-sister, lived.

What I thought I was seeing there in Roxbury were high-class, educated, important Negroes, living well, working in big jobs and positions. Their quiet homes sat back in their mowed yards. These Negroes walked along the sidewalks, looking haughty and dignified, on their way to work, to shop, to visit, to church. I know now, of course, that what I was really seeing was only a big-city version of those "successful" Negro bootblacks and janitors back in Lansing. The only difference was that the ones in Boston had been brainwashed even more thoroughly. They prided themselves in being incomparably more "cultured," "cultivated," "dignified," and better off than their black brethren down in the ghetto, which was no further away than you could throw a rock. Under the pitiful misapprehension that it would make them "better," these Hill Negroes were breaking their backs trying to imitate white people.

Any black family that had been around Boston long enough to own the home they lived in was considered among the Hill elite. It didn't make any difference that they had to rent out rooms to make ends meet. Then the native-born New Englanders among them looked down upon recently migrated Southern homeowners who lived next door, like Ella. And a big percentage of the Hill dwellers were in Ella's category—Southern strivers and scramblers, and West Indian Negroes, whom both the New Englanders and the Southerners called "Black Jews." Usually it was the Southerners and the West Indians who not only managed town the places where they lived, but also at least one other house which they rented as income property. The snooty New Englanders usually owned less than they. . . .

Soon I ranged out of Roxbury and began to explore Boston proper. Historic buildings everywhere I turned, and plaques and markers and statues for famous events and men. One statue in the Boston Commons astonished me: a Negro named Crispus Attucks, who had been the first man to fall in the Boston Massacre. I had never known anything like that.

I roamed everywhere. In one direction, I walked as far as Boston University. Another day, I took my first subway ride. When most of the people got off, I followed. It was Cambridge, and I circled all around in the Harvard University campus. Somewhere, I had already heard of Harvard—though I didn't know much more about it. Nobody that day could have told me I would give an address before the Harvard Law School Forum some twenty years later.

I also did a lot of exploring downtown. Why a city would have *two* big railroad stations—North Station and South Station—I couldn't understand. At both of the stations, I stood around and watched people arrive and leave. And I did the same thing at the bus station where Ella had met me. My wanderings even led me down along the piers and docks where I read plaques telling about the old sailing ships that used to put in there. . . .

On Massachusetts Avenue . . . was the huge, exciting Roseland State Ballroom. Big posters out in front advertised the nationally famous bands, white and Negro, that had played there. "COMING NEXT WEEK," when I went by that first time, was Glenn Miller. I remember thinking how nearly the whole evening's music at Mason High School had been Glenn Miller's records. What wouldn't that crowd have given, I wondered, to be standing where Glenn Miller's band was actually going to play? I didn't know how familiar with Roseland I was going to become.

Ella began to grow concerned, because even when I had finally had enough sight-seeing, I didn't stick around very much on the Hill . . . I didn't want to disappoint or upset Ella, but despite her advice, I began going down into the town ghetto section. That world of grocery stores, walk-up flats, cheap restaurants, poolrooms, bars, storefront churches, and pawnshops seemed to hold a natural lure for me.

Not only was this part of Roxbury more exciting, but I felt more relaxed among Negroes who were being their natural selves and not putting on airs. Even though I did live on the Hill, my instincts were never—and still aren't—to feel myself any better than any other Negro.

I spent my first months in town with my mouth hanging open. The sharp-dressed young "cats" who hung on the corners and in the poolrooms, bars and restaurants, and who obviously didn't work anywhere, completely entranced me. I couldn't get over marveling at how their hair was straight and shiny like white men's hair; Ella told this was called a "conk." I had never tasted a sip of liquor, never even smoked a cigarette, and here I saw little black children, ten or twelve years old, shooting craps, playing cards, fighting, getting grown-ups to put a penny or a nickel on their number for them, things like that. And these children threw around swear words I'd never heard before, even, and slang expressions that were just as new to me, such as "stud" and "cat" and "chick" and "cool" and "hip." Every night as I lay in bed I turned these new words over in my mind. It was shocking to me that in town, especially after dark, you'd occasionally see a white girl and a Negro man strolling arm in arm along the sidewalk, and mixed couples drinking in the neon-lighted bars—not slipping off to some dark corner, as in Lansing . . .

Most of Roseland's dances [where Malcolm worked as a "shoeshine boy"] were for whites only, and they had white bands only. But the only white band ever to play there at a Negro dance to my recollection, was Charlie Barnet's. The fact is that very few white bands could have satisfied the Negro dancers. But I know that Charlie Barnet's "Cherokee" and his "Redskin Rhumba" drove those Negroes wild. They'd jampack that ballroom, the black girls in way-out silk and satin dresses and shoes, their hair done in all kinds of styles, the men sharp in their zoot suits and crazy conks, and everybody grinning and greased and gassed.

Some of the bandsmen would come up to the men's room at about eight o'clock and get shoeshines before they went to work. Duke Ellington, Count Basie, Lionel Hampton, Cootie Williams, Jimmie Lunceford were just a few of those who sat in my chair. I would really make my shine rag sound like someone had set off Chinese firecrackers. Duke's great alto saxman, Johnny Hodges . . . still owes me for a shoeshine I gave him. He was in the chair one night, having a friendly argument with the drummer, Sonny Greer, who was standing there, when I tapped the bottom of his shoes to signal that I was finished. Hodges stepped down, reaching his hand in his pocket to pay me, but then snatched his hand out to gesture, and just forgot me, and walked away. I wouldn't have dared to bother the man who could do what he did with "Daydream" by asking him for fifteen cents. . . . Musicians never have had, anywhere, a greater shoeshine-boy fan than I was. I would write to Wilfred and Hilda and Philbert and Reginald back in Lansing, trying to describe it.

William Stanley Braithwaite, from "I Saw Frederick Douglass" (1948), and "Quiet Has a Hidden Sound" (1948)

William Stanley Braithwaite (1878–1962), poet, critic, and editor, was an influential literary figure in Boston and New York City for half a century. He served as literary editor for the *Boston Evening Transcript* and wrote articles, reviews, and poetry for many other periodicals and journals, including *Atlantic Monthly, The New York Times,* and *The New Republic.* For a decade he taught literature courses at Atlanta University; then he moved with his family in 1945 to Sugar Hill, Harlem, New York, where he continued to write and publish.

From "I Saw Frederick Douglass"

How long ago it is, looking back from this mid-twentieth century, to that night in 1888, when my boyish eyes and ears were focused upon that giant of a man, and being swept by him still further backward through time over southern plantations and swamplands, across turbulent seas into the dim, mysterious African centuries, of racial anguish!

I had seen Frederick Douglass!—heard him lecture at the Park Street Church! Heard his thunderous voice go echoing upwards to vanish through the delicately beautiful Christopher Wren steeple on the church that pointed to heaven above the Old Granary Burial Ground where slept in eternal peace the parents of Benjamin Franklin.

My great-grandmother's husband, Mr. Overman, took me to hear the great man speak. He was her second husband, and everyone in the family, elders as well as children, addressed or referred to him as Mr. Overman. I don't think I ever heard his wife call him Sandy, which was his given name. He was a tall, gaunt man, with a laugh that was pointed with arrows of derision. He had known bondage, and strangely enough, freedom had not tempered him graciously, but made him brittle with arrogance. He seemed always wrapped in memories which made up, I have since surmised, a parcel of retributions he could not deliver. He made of every anti-slavery hero a god, but Frederick Douglass was *the* Divinity, the word made flesh of a conquering freedom, for to Mr. Overman, he was not simply the symbol of successful revolt against injustice but the foundation rock upon which was built a new citadel of human brotherhood.

Mr. Overman had an eloquence of his own when he expressed himself in worship of his hero, and he filled my young ears with Frederick Douglass' exploits as we walked along the Common malls, dimly lighted with gaslamps, on our way to the Park Street Church.

We found seats in the balcony, the church being completely filled with members of both races. The balcony had a vantage point that gave me great satisfaction—I could look down on the great figure of the man. When he raised his leonine head with its shock of white hair, as he often did in dramatic gesture, I could look full into his face as he poured forth his eloquence. That exciting moment brought a thrill never to be forgotten, as I have not forgotten in during the intervening sixty years.

I have no recollection of Frederick Douglass being introduced to the audience by some eminent citizen. My remembered impression is that he simply walked onto the platform and stood briefly facing the multitude, for there still echoes the thunderous applause that greeted him. . . .

There were titans in those days of the young Republic: there had to be titans if the Republic was to survive its internal ills, the civil, the political and industrial ills, which were the growing pains of the young nation. And the times produced them, the titans, William Lloyd Garrison, John Brown, and Frederick Douglass, upon whose shoulders was draped the mantle of an inspired new concept of government and society.

I cannot now recall the words that Frederick Douglass spoke that night in delivering his discourse. That is too much to expect, after all these years, of a boy in his ninth year. But there was something more important which make, in retrospection, the experience rare and momentous. It was the emanation of an oratory vitalized with the living mythology of a personality that had scaled a modern Olympus in pursuit of the North Star of Freedom. It was the sound of his voice, saturating my memory, that began like a murmur floating from the springs at the foot of Olympus, gathering force and color as it ascended to the crest where with volcanic power it broke into a roar of thunder, pouring out a message of wrongs and hopes. . . .

Mr. Overman and I left the church, in my spirit eternally woven the image of Frederick Douglass, and crossed the gas-lit Common homewards. The Common was silent and spectre-like, and the surrounding streets, Boylston, Tremont, Park, and Beacon, yet untouched with the modernity that has since altered their aspects. Up the sloping mall on the northern side where hilly Beacon Street rose to its crest, stood the State House with its famous Bullfinch front and golden dome. And opposite, on the Common side of the street, was the site where ten years later they were to place the great St. Gaudens monument which in bas-relief immortalized Col. Robert Gould Shaw leading his Negro troops (the 54th Massachusetts Regiment, which Frederick Douglass had been instrumental in organizing) against the ramparts of Fort Wagner. Its beauty and historical significance could not exist without a related tribute to the heroic memory and figure of Frederick Douglass, whose living greatness I had that night of my boyhood seen and heard.

"QUIET HAS A HIDDEN SOUND"

BEACON HILL

Quiet has a hidden sound
Best upon a hillside street,
When the sunlight on the ground
Is luminous with heat.

Something teases one to peek
Behind the summer afternoon
And watch the shadowy legends leak
Off Time's unscaled tune.

Just a common city street
Running up a city hill,
Filled with nothing but the heat
And houses standing still!

But where is silence castled,
Or stranger, the sunlight magic,
Than on this hillside, where the tread
Of summertime is tragic!

John Boyle O'Reilly, from "The Exile of the Gael" (1887) and "The Fame of the City" (1881)

John Boyle O'Reilly (1844–1890), essayist and poet, went from being an Irish rebel against English rule, sent to Australia for imprisonment, to the most respected Irish American of his generation in Boston.

From "The Exile of the Gael"

Read at the 150th anniversary of the Irish Charitable Society, Boston, March 17, 1887.

"What have ye brought to our Nation-building, Sons of the Gael?
What is your burden or guerdon from old Innisfail?"
Here build we higher and deeper than men ever built before;
And we raise no Shinar tower, but a temple forevermore.
What have ye brought from Erin your hapless land could spare?
Her tears, defeats, and miseries? Are these, indeed, your share?
Are the mother's *caoine* and the *banshee's* cry your music for our song?
Have ye joined our feast with a withered wreath and a memory of
    wrong?

With a broken sword and treason-flag from your Banba of the Seas?
O, where in our House of Triumph shall hang such gifts as these?"

O, Soul, wing forth! What answer across the main is heard?
From burdened ships and exiled lips,—write down, write down the
    word!

"No treason we bring from Erin—nor bring we shame nor guilt!
The sword we hold may be broken, but we have not dropped the hilt!
The wreath we bear to Columbia is twisted with thorns, not bays;
And the song we sing are saddened by thoughts of desolate days.
But the hearts we bring for Freedom are washed in the surge of tears;
And we claim our right by a People's fight outliving a thousand years!"

"What bring ye else to the Building?"
O, willing hands to toil;
Strong natures turned to the harvest-song, and bound to the kindly
    soil;
Bold pioneers for the wilderness, defender in the field,—
The sons of a race of soldiers who never learned to yield.
Young hearts with duty brimming—a faith makes sweet the due;
Their truth to me their witness they cannot be false to you!"

"What send ye else, old Mother, to raise our mighty wall?
For we must build against Kings and Wrongs a fortress never to fall!"

"I send you in cradle and bosom, wise brain and eloquent tongue,
Whose crowns should engild my crowning, whose songs for me
should be sung.
O, flowers unblown, from lonely fields, my daughters with hearts
    aglow,
With pulses warm with sympathies, with bosoms pure as snow,—
I smile through tears as the clouds unroll—my widening river that
    runs!
My lost ones grown in radiant growth—proud mothers of free-born
    sons!
My seed of sacrifice ripens apace! The Tyrant's cure is disease:
My strength that was dead like a forest is spread beyond the distant
    seas!"

"It is well, aye well, old Erin! The sons you give to me
Are symbolled long in flag and song—your Sunburst on the Sea!
All mine by the chrism of Freedom, still yours by their love's belief;
And truest to me shall the tenderest be in a suffering mother's grief.
Their loss is the change of the wave to a cloud, of the dew to the
 river and main;
Their hope shall perish through the sea and the mist, and thy
 streams shall be filled again.
As the smolt of the salmon go down to the sea, and as surely come
 back to the river,
Their love shall be yours while your sorrow endures, for God guardeth
 His right forever!"

"The Fame of the City"

A great rich city of power and pride,
With streets full of traders, and ships on the tide;
With rich men and workmen and judges and preachers,
The shops full of skill and the schools full of teachers.

The people were proud of their opulent town:
The rich men spent millions to bring it renown;
The strong men built and the tradesmen planned;
The shipmen sailed to every land;
The lawyers argued, the schoolmen taught,
And a poor shy Poet his verses brought,
And cast them into the splendid store.

The tradesmen stared at his useless craft;
The rich men sneered and the strong men laughed;
The preachers said it was worthless quite;
The schoolmen claimed it was theirs to write;

But the songs were spared, though they added naught
To the profit and praise the people sought,
That was wafted at last from distant climes;
And the townsmen said: "To remotest times
We shall send our name and our greatness down!"

The boast came true; but the famous town
Had a lesson to learn when all was told:
The nations that honored cared naught for its gold,
Its skill they exceeded an hundred-fold;
It had only been one of a thousand more,
Had the songs of the Poet been lost to its store.

Then the rich men and tradesmen and schoolmen said
They had never derided, but praised instead;
And they boast of the Poet their town has bred.

J. Anthony Lukas, from *Common Ground: A Turbulent Decade in the Lives of Three American Families* (1985)

J. Anthony Lukas (1933–1997) was a noted American journalist and author, best known for this study of racial tensions dividing Boston in the 1970s. The appointment by Pope Paul VI of Humberto Sousa Medeiros, the son of immigrants from the Portuguese Azores, to be Archbishop of Boston in 1970 broke the long hold Irish Americans held over the Boston Catholic Church. Medeiros replaced Boston's beloved Archbishop Richard Cardinal Cushing, who was dying. In *Common Ground* Lukas portrays Cardinal Cushing, who was exemplary in his efforts to reconcile both Irish-Yankee and Irish-black tensions in the city.

During those early years, Cushing seemed torn by conflicting impulses—at times pulled toward a new ecumenical openness, at times an irascible ghetto Catholicism. What resolved that tension, putting a distinctive stamp on his regime, was the powerful influence of "the two Johns"—John Fitzgerald Kennedy and Pope John XXIII—the first redefining what it meant to be Catholic in America, the second what it meant to be Catholic at all.

Cushing performed other services—raising campaign funds for Jack and bringing influence to bear on his behalf with the Catholic governor of Pennsylvania. But his most important contribution was his endorsement of Jack's political catechism. "I am not the Catholic candidate for President,"

Kennedy told Protestant ministers in Houston. "I am the Democratic Party's candidate for President who happens also to be Catholic. . . . I believe in an America where the separation of Church and state is absolute—where no Catholic prelate would tell the President (should he be a Catholic) how to act." Cushing—the prelate everyone had in mind—emphatically agreed. "Senator Kennedy would resent absolutely having a Cardinal, a bishop, or a priest telling him how to act. I don't know anyone who would try to tell him." Jack rewarded his "spiritual advisor" with an invitation to deliver the inaugural invocation, which he did at stentorian volume and mind-boggling length.

While his celebrity grew from association with John Kennedy, Cushing owed his rise in the Church to Pope John. Pius XII had been in no hurry to elevate the outspoken American, but the round peasant's son who became John XXIII immediately recognized a kindred spirit and, within six weeks of mounting the Throne of Peter in November 1958, made Cushing a Cardinal. . . .

Two events in the spring of 1964 profoundly affected the Cardinal and his advisors. The first occurred on St. Patrick's Day. Distressed by the refusal of white working-class Bostonians to support its challenge of *de facto* segregation, the NAACP, for the first time, entered the South Boston parade. Its float bore a large portrait of the recently assassinated John Kennedy and beside it, in bold green letters, "From the fight for Irish Freedom to the Fight for U.S. Equality." As it lumbered onto Dorchester Street near St. Augustine's Church, four teenagers leaped into the street brandishing their own homemade banner, decorated with shamrocks, reading: "Go home, nigger. Long live the spirit of independence in segregated Boston." Tomatoes, eggs, cherry bombs, bottles, and beer cans rained down on the float. A brick shattered the windshield and broke the driver's glasses, Police moved in, escorting the float to safety. The next day, the NAACP likened the incident to "the viciousness you would expect in New Orleans and the backwoods of Mississippi."

The second incident took place eight days later when two priests from St. Bridget's in Lexington—Father Tom MacLeod and Father John Fitzpatrick—were arrested trying to integrate a restaurant in Williamston, North Carolina. The Shamrock Café—the name rang ironically back in Boston—was just a few yards down the road from the spot where the Protestant clergymen had been arrested six months before. MacLeod and Fitzpatrick were the first American priests ever to be arrested for civil rights activity. . . . Cushing—annoyed because the pair hadn't consulted him—wasn't so pleased at first, but as congratulatory telegrams poured into the Chancery, the Cardinal came to see some merit in their actions.

Widespread condemnation of the St. Patrick's Day incident and praise for the young priests encouraged the Cardinal to speak out. On Pentecost Sunday in April, he delivered his strongest statement yet on the race issue; "I call this city and it citizens to justice. I call them to see in their Negro neighbors the face of Christ himself. I call them to change their hearts and to raise their hands, before the evils that we are tolerating call down the wrath of God upon his forgetful people. . . . To every believer, I say love all men and especially love Negroes, because they have suffered so much from lack of love." Only three months later, after rioting in Harlem and Rochester, Cushing sounded a more passionate note. Denouncing "the monstrous evil of racism," he said, "It is time we were disturbed, it is time we were shaken! We have been content to do things the easy way, to console with soft words and promises, to temporize and be patient in the face of inexcusable social evils. . . . In this hour, if men of God are silent, the very stones will cry out!"

The voice was Cushing's, the sentiments largely his, but the passion, the commitment, the words themselves came from Monsignor Francis J. Lally, Cushing's ghostwriter and conscience on such matters. Lally was an unusual churchman: a Boston Irish priest who had risen from an insular background to serve on the executive board of the National Council of Christians and Jews and the national committee of UNESCO. Cushing made him editor of the *Pilot,* the archdiocesan newspaper, a pulpit from which he inveighed weekly against narrow parochialism and racial injustice. . . . Lally was custodian of one side of Cushing's nature and the Cardinal relied on him to give it expression. . . .

[Cardinal Cushing caused furor within the Catholic Church in 1968 by] condoning Jackie Kennedy's marriage to Aristotle Onassis. The Vatican held that by marrying a divorced man, the President's widow had "knowingly violated the law of the Church" and was ineligible to receive the sacraments. But Cushing staunchly defended her: "What a lot of nonsense! Only God knows who is a sinner and who is not. Why can't she marry whomever she wants?" That brought him an avalanche of abusive mail, apparently the covert resentment many Boston Catholics felt for the privi-

'leged Kennedys. In a moment of intense depression, Cushing talked of re-
signing. "If they don't understand me after thirty years," he said, "they'll
never understand me." . . .

By 1969, the diseases which had gnawed at him for years—asthma, em-
physema, bleeding ulcers, cancer of the prostate and kidneys—were taking
a terrible toll. . . . [By 1970, with Humberto Sousa Medeiros appointed
Archbishop of Boston, Cushing was near death.] For nearly a decade, the
Vatican had been seeking to break up ethnic monopolies in American dio-
ceses, and nowhere had one ethnic group dominated the Church so long
and so thoroughly as in Boston. If O'Connell spoke for the lace-curtain
Irish and Cushing for the Irish working class, so Boston dissident priests and
laymen hoped Medeiros would be Archbishop of the dispossessed non-Irish.
Father Tom Corrigan, a founder of the Association of Boston Urban Priests,
welcomed him as "a unique and exciting choice." The Catholic Interracial
Council said Medeiros gave "every indication of being a spiritual leader of
distinction." But Cushing himself wasn't so sure. After sizing up his tiny, be-
spectacled successor, he began referring to him as "Birdy." One day, as he sat
with an aide gazing out of his residence window toward the statue of Our
Lady of Fatima, the dying Cardinal mused, "Birdy's going to take his rosary
beads and trot around that statue out there saying his prayers. Then he'll
come back and find his problems are still here."

Edwin O'Connor, from The Last Hurrah *(1956)*

Edwin O'Connor (1918–1968) wrote several popular and respected
novels, particularly *The Last Hurrah,* which describe the social rise and
moral disillusionment of Irish Americans in Boston. He amplified this
saga in *The Edge of Sadness* (1961) and *All in the Family* (1966). In this
scene from *The Last Hurrah,* Mayor Frank Skeffington introduces his
nephew Adam Caulfield (and the reader) to a fading tribal ritual, the
Irish wake.

At 7:30, Adam was waiting; Skeffington, on the other hand, was not. His
unpunctuality inviolable, he was fifteen minutes late, and as the long official

car pulled up he said genially, "Hop in. As a taxpayer, you're entitled to. Try the comforts of the vehicle you thoughtfully provided for me."

Adam got in. Determined to remove all mystery from the outset, he said, "By the way, when we were talking this afternoon I completely forgot to ask you where we were going."

"So you did," Skeffington said. "I took it as a rare mark of confidence; now I find it was only a lapse of memory. One more illusion lost." He chuckled and said, "Actually, we're going to a wake. Knocko Minihan's wake."

"A *wake?*"

"Surprised? I had an idea you might be: there was just the possibility that you weren't in the habit of spending your free evenings in visiting deceased strangers. But I felt that tonight it might be useful for you to come along. In its way, a wake can be quite an occasion."

"You may be underestimating me," Adam said. "I've been to a few wakes. Not many, but a few."

"I don't doubt it. Probably not exactly like this one, however. Not that poor Knocko's will be unique, but it might be a little different from those you've been to."

Adam was not prepared to dispute this. The car drove on, and he said, "His name wasn't Knocko, surely?"

"No, it was Aram. The mother was part French, and he was named for an uncle in Quebec. The old gentleman had some money, and the Minihans cherished the fond hope that one happy day it would fall into the lap of little Aram. Unfortunately there was a tragic development. The uncle went crazy and gave away all of his money to a convent outside Montreal; two months later he went to a Canadian lunatic asylum where he subsequently died. The Minihans naturally tried to prove that he'd been a madman before he gave the money to the convent. It seemed a reasonable assumption, especially when you consider that the old man suffered from the delusion that he was an air rifle and went around spitting BB's at squirrels. But as anyone can tell you who's ever tried to recover a bequest from an order of nuns in Quebec, the assumption wasn't quite reasonable enough. So no legacy was forthcoming for the little Aram. Meanwhile, of course, he'd been stuck with the name: I don't think he ever forgave his parents for that. It was a terrible start in life for a boy in this city. That's why he gladly became Knocko.

"And how did he make out after this terrible start?"

"Not too well. Save in one respect, that is. He married a grand woman who was a close friend of my wife's—you aunt's," he said. "In every other way he was a failure. He had a hardware store that he ran into the ground almost before the opening-day sale was over. Then he tried several other businesses, all of which petered out in no time at all. I don't know that people trusted him especially, and they certainly didn't like him. And neither," he said, rather surprisingly, "did I. However, *de mortuis* . . ."

"If nobody liked him," Adam said, "I imagine we'll run into a fairly slim attendance tonight."

"Not al all," said Skeffington. "The place'll be crowded to the doors. A wake isn't quite the same as a popularity contest. There are other factors involved. Ah, here we are."

They had arrived in front of a two-story frame tenement house which was in need of paint; the door on the left held a wreath with a large purple ribbon. Skeffington placed a hand just beneath this ornament and then, before pushing the door open, paused to regard the unlovely premises. He shook his head. "Charming," he said. "Come on, let's go in."

A heavy-set woman, dressed in black, and with a face of some large and extremely suspicious bird, came out of the darkness to greet them.

"Hello Frank," she said.

"Hello Agnes. Mrs. Burns, my nephew, Adam Caulfield, Mary's boy." There were nods, and exchange of greetings; Skeffington asked, "How's Gert taking it?"

"Pretty good. She cries a little," said the woman. Adam could not help but observe that she was herself noticeably dry of eye. In explanation she added, "She remembers all the nice things he done."

"She has a remarkable memory," Skeffington said dryly.

Mrs. Burns accepted this with a short nod of agreement, then pointed to a door on the right of the narrow hall. "He's in the parlor," she said. "I think there's no one in there now; it's still a little bit early. Go right in, Frank. He looks lovely."

Adam followed Skeffington into the parlor: he saw a tall, glum room which might have been designed specifically with this melancholy event in mind. Heavy dull plush furniture had been pushed back against the walls; stretching from side to side across the room were rows of thin metal chairs, of the kind furnished by catering services. At the moment these were empty; looking at them through the gloom Adam wondered whether this was indeed due to the hour of their arrival, or rather to the simple fact that Knocko Minihan had not been widely loved.

At the far end of the parlor, decorated with wreaths and floral sprays, was a gray coffin; to Adam it seemed huge, a sarcophagus fit for a giant. He advanced upon it with his uncle; they knelt by the side of the coffin and Adam saw Knocko in death. He lay stiffly among billows of white satin, a diminutive man lost in the recesses of his mighty container. Across the top of his head occasional strands of yellowish-white hair had been combed strategically; a taut, grudging smile, which somehow fell short of suggesting an interior peace, had been worked into position. His small hands were folded across his chest, clasping a rosary, and over the coffin a large crucifix, heavily studded with rhinestones, had been suspended. Someone of ingenious mind—undoubtedly the undertaker, thought Adam—had fixed a baby spotlight so that it played full upon the crucifix; high above Knocko's final, alien smile, the rhinestones glittered and danced.

Adam said a prayer for this man he had not known. Skeffington, after a moment, got to his feet slowly, looking about him, at the coffin, at the crucifix. "A lavish display," he said. "And you couldn't get the man near a theater in his life." He put his hand lightly on Adam's shoulder and said, "Will you do me a favor and stay here a moment? I have to go in and say a word to the widow."

Adam looked up, surprised; he rose quickly. "You mean wait *here?*"

Skeffington smiled slightly. "I'm afraid I do; it seems to be about the only place. You could wait in the car, but I've sent the chauffeur on an errand. In any event, it won't be too bad; I'll be back directly. Why don't you just sit down in one of those chairs in back? People will be coming in shortly, and anyway the whole thing is an experience you ought to have; it's a custom that's dying out. Besides, you can regard it as a meritorious act; you'll be keeping poor Knocko company."

Adam nodded reluctantly. There seemed nothing to do but agree, although he was scarcely happy over the prospect of the solitary vigil. Feeling vaguely that he had once again been out-generaled all along the line, he moved towards the back of the room, as far as possible from the dead Knocko, the rhinestones, and the baby spotlight. Here in the dim light of the evening, he sat down to away the return of his uncle.

In the first few minutes of his wait, the quiet, as well as the gloom, became increasingly uninviting. All light from the outside seemed to fade; the macabre cruciform dazzle above the coffin dominated the room. From somewhere there came the sound of a banging door; no one entered. Adam had indeed, as he had said earlier to Skeffington, attended a few wakes, but his memory of them was obscure. Now in this silent gloom he had a disquieting recollection of a story of Synge's about a wake in the Aran Islands: the long procession of shawled and sobbing women gathering at the bier, rocking back and forth to the wail of the keen. That such a scene could be duplicated in the parlor of Knocko Minihan tonight was wildly improbable; nevertheless, Adam found himself speculating upon it in some detail. Suddenly, from somewhere to his right, there came a sound. "*Ssss!*" it hissed.

He jumped, startled. He turned and at first saw no one; then, in a corner which was darker than the rest of the room because of the shadow of a partially opened door, he saw a small, puckered woman, peering out at his with lively eyes.

"Did I *scare* you?" she said. The possibility seemed to delight her.

"No," Adam lied stoutly. "You startled me. I didn't see you come in."

"Ah, I *was* in," she said. "I was here in my corner when you come in with Frank. Are you the nephew?"

Adam nodded. It seemed to him that with the discovery of this silent little watcher of the shadows a new dimension of eeriness had entered the room. She had spoken of "*my* corner" with a proud possessiveness, almost as if she had come in with the coffin and would remain in her appointed place, firm, open-eyed and irremovable, until it was taken away.

"I'm Delia Boylan," she said. "I knew you pa and I knew your ma and I knew you when you was a baby." Pepper-and-salt eyebrows rose as she considered him now. "You was homely as spit," she said.

"Ah," said Adam. How did one respond more fully to such frankness? He had no idea. He said, changing the subject hopefully, "I'm surprised there are so few people here to see Mr. Minihan."

'Ah, they'll be in," she said confidently. "They'll all want to get a good last look at old Knocko. There's them that's been waiting for it for a long time. We're early. I always like to be a bit early." She raised herself to a half-standing posture and gazed critically at the coffin. "He looks grand with the cheeks all puffed out, don't he?" she asked.

She spoke of the corpse with the nonchalant detachment possible only to those who have had vast experience with death. "He looks very nice,"

Adam said. He was painfully aware of his own lack of the special vocabulary of compliment appropriate to just such an occasion; he was sure than one existed. "Of course," he added, "I didn't know him when he was alive."

This, too, was maladroit; but Mrs. Boylan did not appear to mind. Her narrow little shoulders shrugged in contempt and she said, "A little runt of a man. Thin as a snake and no color to him at all. He was part French, you know."

"I know."

"That makes all the difference," she said mysteriously, "*Aram.* Ah well, that's small matter now." She spoke as one forgiving him the injury of his ancestry. "God be good to the man," she said. "He was mean as a panther, but good luck to him."

Adam said nothing. Once more, there seemed to be nothing to say. The silence was broken by the entrance of a trio of mourners who came in, looked slowly about the room, nodded to Delia, then filed up to the coffin.

"The Carmichael girls," Delia explained, "with the brother Tim. *They* come early, as a general rule." She moved abruptly in her chair, stretching out to face the door. "*Sssst!*" she hissed.

Adam followed her glance. He saw a stout, balding young man, spruce and smooth in the discreet clothing of his profession, moving with purposeful yet superlatively respectful steps toward the coffin.

"*Sssst!*" Delia said again. "Johnnie."

The young man paused and looked in their direction; Adam thought he appeared to be annoyed. In response to Delia's fanatically beckoning hand he came over to them with an obvious reluctance.

"Johnnie Degnan," Delia said to Adam, adding unnecessarily, "the undertaker. We always like to have our little talk."

"Good evening, Mrs. Boylan," the undertaker said unenthusiastically.

"Ah, Johnnie," Delia said. She introduced Adam. "Frank Skeffington's nephew, Johnnie. The sister's boy."

The undertaker brightened; he made a short, formal bow. "Very pleased to meet you, sir," he said. "I've always been a great admirer of your uncle, although I've never had the pleasure of making his acquaintance. I hope that will be remedied tonight. Ah . . . was there anything in particular, Mrs. Boylan?"

"He looks grand, Johnnie," she said, waving toward the coffin. "Just grand. Did he take a lot of doing?"

An expression of slight strain appeared on the undertaker's round face; clearly, thought Adam, questions from the laity were not encouraged. "Mr. Minihan was in remarkable condition, Mrs. Boylan, for one of his advanced years," he said. He spoke in a low voice and with extraordinary rapidity, as if in the hope that by a sudden sprint through his words he might bring this interview to a close. It was a forlorn hope; Delia had reached out and grabbed the sleeve of his coat.

"Ah, Johnnie," she said, "you laid him out in the *big* coffin! Ah, you rascal, you!" She rolled her eyes and released a little whoop of laughter; down by the coffin the Carmichael triumvirate turned in unison to stare. The undertaker made a swift, imploring pass with his hands, and Delia lowered her voice to a stage whisper. "My God," she said delightedly, "wouldn't it kill the man if he knew!"

The undertaker gave her a look of pain. "Mr. Minihan has a very fine casket," he said, emphasizing the final word. "As I'm sure he would have wished it."

"Ah," Delia said, "but the cost of it all! The cost, Johnnie!"

"Mr. Minihan," said the undertaker swiftly, "was a very prominent figure in the community. Very prominent."

Delia nodded agreeably. "He was the cheapest old devil that ever lived," she said. "And you know it. Well, he's gone now, poor man, and you done an elegant job on him, Johnnie." As a grace note she added, "No matter what you charge."

"Ah ha ha ha," said the undertaker tonelessly, giving Adam a nervous smile, presumably meant to imply that they both were familiar with the irrepressible Mrs. Boylan. "Well, I must go now, Mrs. Boylan. Many duties. A pleasure to have met you sir. I hope to meet your uncle." He bowed again and hurried away on muted feet.

"There's a great rogue," Delia said approvingly. "Only thirty years old and he'd steal the skin off your bones. Just give him the chance and it's the big coffin, ten limousines, and the Holy Name Choir to sing you good-by."

"And is he responsible for the crucifix?" Adam asked, pointing to the dazzling object above the coffin.

"The pride and joy," she assured him. "It all goes with the bill." She shook with a sudden rusty flutter of reminiscent mirth. "I says to him one day, I says, 'Don't you dare stick that big sparkler over me when I'm gone, Johnnie Degnan! Don't you dare!' And he damn well won't; he knows he won't get a ten-cent piece out of me. Ah, he's a sly one," she said, "but he knows I'm on to him. *Sssst!*"

The sound, while no longer unfamiliar, was unexpected; Adam jumped again. An angular woman of forbidding aspect had come into the room and was now engaged in making hand signals to Delia.

"Aggie Gormley," Delia said. "I wonder has she news about the will? I'd best go see. I'll be back in a minute."

She hustled away with jerky, efficient steps, and Adam was alone once more. He looked at Delia, conversing with her newsy friend; he looked at the Carmichaels, talking quietly with Johnny Degnan; he looked at the coffin and the jewelry above it. He looked, too, at his watch, and wondered absently when his uncle would return. Rather to his surprise, he did not greatly care, for he discovered to his horror that here in this presepulchral room, reserved for mourning, and in the appalling company of Delia Boylan, he was undoubtedly enjoying himself. . . .

[Skeffington] came into the parlor to discover that the crowd had begun to arrive. The rows of chairs, empty before, were now rapidly being filled; as he entered the room the heads turned towards him at once. He looked for Adam and signaled to him; Adam approached, only slightly behind Delia Boylan.

"Ah now, Frank," she said eagerly, "how is she taking it back there?"

His reply was brief. "As well as could be expected." He added dryly, "I'm happy to see that you're bearing up under the strain, Delia."

Once more Adam heard the derisive whoop of laughter; it rang through the gloomy room; heads turned; at his position of duty down by the coffin Johnnie Degnan frowned reprovingly and did a plump little dance step of despair. "I'll live," Delia said. "Well, me and the nephew has been having a lovely talk about poor Knocko, the old devil."

"I wish I'd been here to join you," Skeffington said. Turning to Adam he added, "Mrs. Boylan's pious reflections on the faithful departed never fail to uplift the spirit. She has a splendid attendance record at the deathbed of her many friends."

"I go to them all," she said proudly. "I don't miss a one."

"Everybody has to have a hobby," Skeffington said. "Now if you'll excuse us, Delia, I want to take my nephew into the next room and introduce him to some people. Give my best to Tom and the family."

"I will, Frank." The sharp little eyes glinted maliciously and she said,

"And I will tell them you wouldn't mind hearing from them come Election Day?"

"I always treasure the Boylan vote," Skeffington said, "and yours in particular, Delia. Every time I get thinking about the wisdom of giving the women the vote I think of you and my fears become quiet."

She crowed with delight. "Ah, that's all mush, Frank. But you know we're with you every single time. The whole family."

"I do, Delia. I appreciate it. And now," he said, with no change of expression, "we'll leave you to your prayers. Good-by, Delia."

Out in the hall he drew Adam aside and said, "I hope you see how things work out for the best. If I hadn't left you alone in there, you wouldn't have met Mrs. Boylan and had your little devotional chat. Your field of experience has been immeasurably widened in the space of but a few minutes."

"I won't deny it," Adam said. I've certainly never met anyone quite like her before. She's a fantastic woman."

"I suppose she is," Skeffington said carelessly. "I'm so used to her I don't notice any more. It takes a fresh eye to fully appreciate Delia. I may add that she's a woman it's fat better to have with you than against you. She has the tongue of a cobra."

"And does she really spend all of her time going to wakes?"

"Apart from a few hours of sleep each night, I believe she does. As she said, she doesn't miss a one. You must remember that she's a singularly devout woman. Also," he said reflectively, "it's somewhat cheaper than going to the movies." . . .

"You see, [Skeffington] said, "my position is slightly complicated because I'm not just an elected official of the city; I'm a tribal chieftain as well. It's a necessary kind of dual officeholding, you might say; without the second, I wouldn't be the first."

"The tribe," said Adam, "being the Irish?"

"Exactly."

Fred Allen, Letters, from Robert Taylor, *Fred Allen: His Life and Wit* (1989)

Fred Allen (1894–1956), born John Florence Sullivan, was one of the most popular and revered radio personalities of his day. His radio program (1934–1949) featured "Allen's Alley," a collection of ethnic characters: among them were Beauregard Claghorn, the inflated Southern senator; Pansy Nussbaum, the opinionated Jewish housewife; Titus Moody, the caustic New England farmer; and Ajax Cassidy, the sharp-tongued Irishman. In Allen's hands these stereotypes, drawn from his experience growing up in Greater Boston and from vaudeville characterizations, were made endearing. Here Robert Taylor, his biographer, presents Allen's ironic, absurdist perspective on Boston.

In May 1935, [Allen] announced: "I have been to Boston with disastrous results." . . . Boston in his letters began to sound like the radio small town version of Bedlam. For Joe Kelly, Fred struck to fustian circus-barker pose of *Town Hall Tonight*.

> I am not the type of man who enters a metropolis in ferret-like fashion, to slink around its outskirts playing my predatory profession under the mantle of darkness. I am not the sort who, groundhog fashion, sticks his head out of the Boston end of the East Boston tunnel on the first warm day for the questionable pleasure of seeing my shadow and returning to my lair. I am not the type of man given to tip-toeing around the Public Garden, after the first frost, awaiting an opportunity to slip my pet toads into the Frog Pond so that they may live at the city's expense over the winter.
>
> [On] the contrary, when I visit a city, bands meet me at the station. They are but bands of relatives, to be sure, but bands nevertheless. Abattoirs start full-blast, slaughtering fatted calves. Children rush from their toys and games to tag along following me as I march through the middle of stately thoroughfares with steady tread. Dogs howl, cats meow, camels at the zoo give off a rare odor which is often blamed on me for no apparent reason. Chameleons change their colors. Birds start south, knowing that my reception will chill the entire city. Laws are hurriedly passed, the key of the city is hidden in its municipal vault, mendicants rush to my side to match tatters . . . and chaos is king, sir.
>
> These are the things that happen when I come to Boston, and until

such time as you look out of your window to find the peace of Mason Street profaned by oaths and catcalls of a motley throng fleeing North Stationwards, you will know that I am missing. The day you do not see the entire population of the capital of Massachusetts rushing to the North Station, then you will know that I am arriving at either the Back Bay or the South Station.

   If you have seen a man there who looks like . . . Fred Allen . . . give him my sincerest sympathy.

As the fall radio season of 1936 opened, Allen, with twenty million listeners, was probably the country's most popular Bostonian since the heyday of Ralph Waldo Emerson. (Lanky college freshman John F. Kennedy, who would become Allen's successor in this role, had just entered Harvard.)

George V. Higgins, from *The Friends of Eddie Coyle* (1972)

George V. Higgins (1939–1999)—lawyer, essayist, and novelist—wrote a series of compelling works of fiction about the Boston Irish criminal and political classes: in particular see *The Digger's Game* (1973), *Cogan's Trade* (1974), and *A City on a Hill* (1975). In this chapter of *The Friends of Eddie Coyle,* Eddie has a brief vision of the fulfilled life he missed when he watches the young Boston Bruins star Bobby Orr skate in a Boston Garden hockey game; however, watching with Eddie are the men who will soon kill him so he won't inform on them to the police. Higgins intersects Boston criminality and sports, catching the slangy speech rhythms of Bostonians who lived at the city's margins.

In the course of the evening Coyle had several drinks. He drank beer with Dillon during the first period. Bobby Orr swung the Bruins net and faked three Rangers into sprawls. He quartered across the New York goal, faked low and left, shot high and right, and Coyle rose up with Dillon and fourteen thousand, nine hundred and sixty-five others to howl approval. The announcer said: "Goal to Orr, number four." There was another ovation.

   Next to Coyle there was an empty seat. Dillon said: "I can't understand where the fuck he is. That friend of mine, I was telling you about? He gives me both his tickets. I invited my wife's nephew. I can't understand where he is. Loves hockey, that kid. I don't know how he stays in school. He's always down here, scrounging for tickets. Twenty years old. But a bright kid."

The kid arrived during the intermission between the first and second periods. He apologized for his tardiness. "I get home," he said, "I get the message all right, but then I have to go and borrow a car. I though I was gonna miss the goddamn game."

"You couldn't take the trolley or something?" Coyle said.

"Not to fucking Swampscott," the kid said seriously. "You just can't get to Swampscott after nine o'clock. I mean it."

"Hey," Dillon said, "who wants a beer?"

"I'll have a beer," Coyle said. The kid had a beer, too. Dillon had a beer.

In the second period the Rangers opened with a goal on Cheevers. Sanderson went off for roughing. Sanderson came back on. Esposito went off for an elbow check. Sanderson fed Dallas Smith for a shorthanded goal. Orr fed Esposito who fed Bucyk for a goal.

Between the second and third periods, Coyle had trouble following the conversation between Dillon and his wife's nephew. Coyle went to the men's room. As he got up, Dillon observed that he might ask if anybody wanted a beer. Coyle returned with three beers, carried carefully before him. There was beer on his trousers. "Hard to carry beer in a crowd like this," he said.

"You're not supposed to have beer at the seats," the kid said.

"Look," Coyle said, "you want some beer or not?"

During the third period the Rangers got another goal. Sanderson drew a five minute major for fighting. The Bruins won, three to two.

"Beautiful," Coyle said. "Beautiful. Can you imagine being that kid? What is he, about twenty-one? He's the best hockey player inna world. Christ, number four, Bobby Orr. What a future he's got."

"Hey look," Dillon said, "I forgot to tell you. I got some girls."

"Jesus," Coyle said, "I don't know, it's pretty late."

"Come on," Dillon said, "Let's make a night of it."

"Hey," the kid said, "hey, I can't. I gotta get this car back. I got to go home."

"Where's your car?" Dillon said to Coyle.

"Cambridge," Coyle said. "I was over there and I take the trolley in, when I came to your place. I never got back for it."

"Shit," Dillon said. "These girls, I mean, they're absolutely all right. But there isn't any way. I mean, they're in Brookline."

"Well, look," the kid said. "I could drive you to his car, and then go home. I got a test tomorrow, so I can't hang around much."

They had a drink in the tavern on the concourse of the Boston Garden, to let the traffic thin out. Dillon had trouble walking when they got outside. Coyle had more trouble. "You two old bastards," the kid said. "I don't know where you'd be without the youth to help you along." They stumbled over the trolley tracks.

The kid had a 1968 Ford Galaxie, a white sedan. He opened the front passenger door. Dillon and Coyle stood there, weaving back and forth. "Look," Dillon said, "you ride inna front. I'll ride inna back. Okay?"

"Okay," Coyle said. He slid into the passenger seat.

Dillon walked quickly around the back of the car. The kid opened the driver's door, then reached in and unlocked the left rear door.

Dillon got in and sat down behind the driver. Coyle's head lay back on the top of the seat. He was breathing heavily.

"You sure you're gonna be all right to drive," Dillon said.

"Oh yeah," Coyle said, his eyes shut, "Absolutely perfectly all right. No sweat. Beautiful night so far."

"More to come," Dillon said. He reached down to the floor and groped around. On the mat on the right rear passenger side, he found a twenty-two magnum Arminius revolver, fully loaded. He picked it up and put it in his lap.

"I don't know where you want me to go," the kid said. He was backing the car around over the trolley tracks.

"You tell him," Dillon said to Coyle. Coyle snored.

"Go around the front of the Garden," Dillon said. "Go out past the Registry and head for Monsignor O'Brien Highway, in case he wakes up. You just drive now."

"I know what's going on," the kid said.

"Good," Dillon said, "I'm glad to hear that. You just drive. I was you, I'd drive to Belmont and I'd pick roads where I could go pretty fast without making anybody suspicious. I'd come out on Route 2, and I'd look for a gray Ford convertible in the parking lot of the West End Bowling Alleys. I wouldn't let nothing disturb me. When I got to the alleys, I'd pull up beside the Ford and get out and get in the Ford and wait for me, and then I'd head back to Boston.

"Somebody said something about some money," the kid said.

"If I was you," Dillon said. "I'd look hard for the convertible. You drive that convertible back to Boston and let me off and if I was you I'd look in that glove compartment for about a thousand bucks before I dropped that car off in the nigger district."

"Is it gonna be hot?" the kid said.

"Does a bear shit in the woods?" Dillon said.

The traffic thinned out rapidly when they got across the river into Cambridge. They proceeded north, following the Route 91 signs. Three miles onto 91 north, they were hitting sixty-five. "You're gonna turn off pretty soon here," Dillon said.

"I know, I know," the kid said.

When the Ford was alone on the road, Dillon brought the revolver up and held it an inch behind Coyle's head, the muzzle pointing at the base of the skull behind the left ear. Dillon drew the hammer back. The first shot went in nicely. Dillon continued firing, double-action. The revolver clicked on a spent round at last. Coyle lay thrust up against the frame between the door of the Ford. The speedometer read eighty-five.

'Slow down, you stupid shit," Dillon said. "You want to get arrested or something?"

"I got nervous," the kid said. "There were so many of them."

"There was nine of then," Dillon said. The car stank of gunpowder.

"It was loud in here," the kid said.

"That's why I use a twenty-two," Dillon said. "I ever let off a thirty-eight two-incher in here, youd've gone right off the road."

"Is he dead," the kid said.

"If he isn't," Dillon said, "he's never gonna be. Now slow down and get off this road."

The bowling alley was dark. The kid pulled the sedan in next to the Ford convertible. "Hey," he said, "that looks a lot like this car, in this light."

"You're learning," Dillon said, "that's the idea. Cops've been seeing that car all night. Now they're gonna see another one that looks almost like it. They won't search it for a couple of hours. Help me stuff him down there."

They crammed Coyle down onto the floor of the right passenger compartment. They got out of the Ford. "Lock it," Dillon said. "Keeps the volunteers out of it."

They got back into the convertible. It started at once. "Not a bad car," the kid said.

"Not a bad car at all," Dillon said. "Now go back Memorial Drive and take the Mass. Ave bridge, I gotta get rid of this gun."

Michael Patrick MacDonald, from *All Souls: A Family Story from Southie* (1999)

Michael Patrick MacDonald (1966–) was born and grew up in South Boston public housing projects, set within an insular and poor Irish Catholic neighborhood. His community opposed public school integration, and his family was ravaged by drugs and crime. MacDonald's autobiographical narratives also include *Easter Rising: An Irish American Coming Up from Under* (2006). He has become an activist, working to heal his community. In the opening section of *All Souls*, he writes of his return to South Boston after a four-year absence.

I was back in Southie, "the best place in the world," as Ma used to say before the kids died. That's what we call them now, "the kids." Even when we want to say their names, we sometimes get confused about who's dead and who's alive in my family. After so many deaths, Ma just started to call my four brothers "the kids" when we talked about going to see them at the cemetery. But I don't go anymore. They're not at the cemetery; I never could find them there. When I accepted the fact that I couldn't feel them at the graves, I figured it must be because they were in heaven, or the spirit world, or whatever you want to call it. The only thing I kept from the funerals were the mass cards that said, "Do not stand at my grave and weep, I am not there, I do not sleep. I am the stars that shine through the night," and so on. I figured that was the best way to look at it. There are seven of us kids still alive, and sometimes I'm not even sure if that's true.

I came back to Southie in the summer of 1994, after everyone in my family had either died or moved to the mountains of Colorado. I'd moved to downtown Boston after Ma left in 1990, and was pulled one night to wander through Southie. I walked from Columbia Point Project, where I was born, to the Old Colony Project where I grew up, in the "Lower End," as we called it. On that August night, after four years of staying away, I walked the streets of my old neighborhood, and finally found the kids. In my memory of that night I can see them clear as day. *They're right here,* I thought, and it was an ecstatic feeling. I cried, and felt alive again myself. I passed by the outskirts of Old Colony, and it all came back to me—the kids were joined in my mind by so many others I'd last seen in caskets at Jackie O'Brien's Funeral Parlor. They were all here now, all my neighbors and friends who had died young from violence, drugs and from the other deadly things we'd been taught didn't happen in Southie.

We thought we were in the best place in the world in this neighborhood, in the all-Irish housing projects where everyone claimed to be Irish even if his name was Spinnoli. We were proud to be from here, as proud as we were to be Irish. We didn't want to own the problems that took the lives of my brothers and of so many others like them: poverty, crime, drugs—those were black things that happened in the ghettos of Roxbury. Southie was Boston's proud Irish neighborhood.

On this night in Southie, the kids were all here once again—I could feel them. The only problem was no one else in the neighborhood could. My old neighbors were going on with their nightly business—wheeling and dealing on the corners, drinking on the stoops, yelling up to windows, looking for a way to get by, or something to fight for. Just like the old days in this small world within a world. It was like a family reunion to me. That's what we considered each other in Southie—family. There was always this feeling that we were protected, as if the whole neighborhood was watching our backs for threats, watching for all the enemies we could never really define. No "outsiders" could mess with us. So we had no reason to leave, and nothing ever to leave for. It was a good feeling to be back in Southie that night, surrounded by my family and neighbors; and I remember hating to have to cross over the Broadway Bridge again, having to leave the peninsula neighborhood and go back to my apartment in downtown Boston.

Mary Antin, from *The Promised Land* (1912)

Mary Antin (1881–1949), author and immigration-rights activist, became famous and influential after publishing this autobiography, which reflects

her immigrant experiences in Boston. In this passage from *The Promised
Land,* Antin shows her determination to succeed in Boston, despite her
family's poverty.

> What happened next was Dover Street.
> And what was Dover Street?

Ask rather, What was it not? Dover Street was my fairest garden of girl-
hood, a gate of paradise, a window facing on a broad avenue of life. Dover
Street was a prison, a school of discipline, a battlefield of sordid strife. The
air in Dover Street was heavy with evil odors of degradation, but a breath
from the uppermost heavens rippled through, whispering of infinite things.
In Dover Street the dragon poverty gripped me for a last fight, but I over-
threw the hideous creature, and sat on his neck as on a throne. In Dover
Street I was shackled with a hundred chains of disadvantage, but with one
free hand I planted little seeds, right there in the mud of shame, that blos-
somed into the honeyed rose of widest freedom. In Dover Street there was
often no loaf on the table, but the hand of some noble friend was ever in
mine. The night in Dover Street was rent with the cries of wrong, but the
thunders of truth crashed through the pitiful clamor and died out in prophetic silences.

Outwardly, Dover Street is a noisy thoroughfare cut through a South End
slum, in every essential the same as Wheeler Street. Turn down any street
in the slums, at random, and call it by whatever name you please, you will
observe there the same fashions of life, death, and endurance. Every one of
those streets is a rubbish heap of damaged humanity, and it will take a powerful broom and an ocean of soapsuds to clean it out.

Dover Street is intersected, near its eastern end, where we lived, by Harrison Avenue. That street is to the South End what Salem Street is to the
North End. It is the heart of the South End ghetto, for the greater part of its
length; although its northern end belongs to the realm of Chinatown. Its
multifarious business bursts through the narrow shop doors, and overruns
the basements, the sidewalk, the street itself, in pushcarts and open-air
stands. Its multitudinous population bursts through the greasy tenement
doors, and floods the corridors, the doorsteps, the gutters, the side streets,
pushing in and out among the pushcarts, all day long and half the night
besides.

Rarely as Harrison Avenue is caught asleep, even more rarely is it found clean. Nothing less than a fire or flood would cleanse this street. Even Passover cannot quite accomplish this feat. For although the tenements may be scrubbed to their remotest corners, on this one occasion, the cleansing stops at the curbstone. A great deal of the filthy rubbish accumulated in a year is pitched into the street, often through the windows; and what the ashman on his daily round does not remove is left to be trampled to powder, in which form it steals back into the houses from which it was so lately removed.

The City Fathers provide soap and water for the slums, in the form of excellent schools, kindergartens, and branch libraries. And there they stop: at the curbstone of the people's life. They cleanse and discipline the children's minds, but their bodies they pitch into the gutter. For there are no parks and almost no playgrounds in the Harrison Avenue district,—in my day there were none,—and such as there are have been wrenched from the city by public-spirited citizens who have no offices in City Hall. No wonder the ashman is not more thorough: he learns from his masters.

It is a pity to have it so, in a queen of enlightened cities like Boston. If we of the twentieth century do not believe in baseball as much as in philosophy, we have not learned the lesson of modern science, which teaches, among other things, that the body is the nursery of the soul; the instrument of our moral development; the secret chart of our devious progress from worm to man. The great achievement of recent science, of which we are so proud, has been the deciphering of the hieroglyphic of organic nature. To worship the facts and neglect the implications of the message of science is to applaud the drama without taking the moral to heart. And we certainly are not taking the moral to heart when we try to make a hero out of the boy by such foreign appliances as grammar and algebra, while utterly despising the fittest instrument for his uplifting—the boy's own body.

We had no particular reason for coming to Dover Street. It might just as well have been Applepie Alley. For my father had sold, with the goods, fixtures, and good-will of the Wheeler Street store, all his hopes of ever making a living in the grocery trade; and I doubt if he got a silver dollar the more for them. We had to live somewhere, even if we were not making a living, so we came to Dover Street, where tenements were cheap; by which I mean that rent was low. The ultimate cost of life in those tenements, in terms of human happiness, is high enough.

Our new home consisted of five small rooms up two flights of stairs, with the right of way through the dark corridors. In the "parlor" the dingy paper hung in rags and the plaster fell in chunks. One of the bedrooms was absolutely dark and air-tight. The kitchen windows looked out on a dirty court, at the back of which was the rear tenement of the estate. To us belonged, along with the five rooms and the right of way aforesaid, a block of upper space the length of a pulley line across this court, and the width of an arc described by a windy Monday's wash in its remotest wanderings.

The little front bedroom was assigned to me, with only one partner, my sister Dora. A mouse could not have led a cat much of a chase across this room; still we found space for a narrow bed, a crazy bureau, and a small table. From the window there was an unobstructed view of a lumberyard, beyond which frowned the blackened walls of a factory. The fence of the lumberyard was gay with theatre posters and illustrated advertisements of tobacco, whiskey, and patent baby foods. When the window was open, there was a constant clang and whirr of electric cars, varied by the screech of machinery, the clatter of empty wagons, or the rumble of heavy trucks.

There was nothing worse in all this than we had had before since our exile from Crescent Beach; but I did not take the same delight in the propinquity of electric cars and arc lights that I had till now. I suppose the tenement began to pall on me.

It must not be supposed that I enjoyed any degree of privacy, because I had half a room to myself. We were six in the five rooms; we were bound to be always in each other's way. And as it was within our flat, so it was in the house as a whole. All doors, beginning with the street door, stood open most of the time; or if they were closed, the tenants did not wear out their knuckles knocking for admittance. I could stand at any time in the unswept entrance hall and tell, from an analysis of the medley of sounds and smells that issued from doors ajar, what was going on in the several flats from below up. That guttural, scolding voice, unremittent as the hissing of a steam pipe, is Mrs. Rasnosky. I make a guess that she is chastising the infant Isaac for taking a second lump of sugar in his tea. *Spam! Bam!* Yes, and she is rubbing in her objections with the flat of her hand. That blubbering and moaning, accompanying an elephantine tread, is fat Mrs. Casey, second floor, home drunk from an afternoon out, in fear of the vengeance of Mr. Casey; to propitiate whom she is burning a pan of bacon, as the choking fumes and outrageous sizzling testify. I hear a feeble whining, interrupted by long silences. It is that scabby baby on the third floor, fallen out of bed again, with nobody home to pick him up.

To escape from these various horrors I ascend to the roof, where bacon and babies and child-beating are not. But there I find two figures in calico wrappers, with bare red arms akimbo, a basket of wet clothes in front of each, and only one empty clothes-line between them. I do not want to be dragged in as a witness in a case of assault and battery, so I descend to the street again, grateful to note, as I pass, that the third-floor baby is still.

In front of the door I squeeze through a group of children. They are going to play tag, and are counting to see who should be "it":—

"My-mother-and-your-mother-went-out-to-hang-clothes;
My-mother-gave-your-mother-a-punch-in-the-nose."

If the children's couplet does not give a vivid picture of the life, manners, and customs of Dover Street, no description of mine can ever do so.

Frieda was married before we came to Dover Street, and went to live in East Boston. This left me the eldest of the children at home. Whether on this account, or because I was outgrowing my childish carelessness, or because I began to believe, on the cumulative evidence of the Crescent Beach, Chelsea, and Wheeler Street adventures, that America, after all, was not going to provide for my father's family,—whether for any or all of these reasons, I began at this time to take bread-and-butter matters more to heart, and to ponder ways and means of getting rich. My father sought employment wherever work was going on. His health was poor; he aged very fast. Nevertheless he offered himself for every kind of labor; he offered himself for a boy's wages. Here he was found too weak, here too old; here his imperfect English was in the way, here his Jewish appearance. He had a few short terms of work at this or that; I do not know the name of the form of drudgery that my father did not practise. But all told, he did not earn enough to pay the rent in full and buy a bone for the soup. The only steady source of income, for I do not know what years, was my brother's earnings from his newspapers.

Surely this was the time for me to take my sister's place in the workshop. I had had every fair chance until now: school, my time to myself, liberty to run and play and make friends. I had graduated from grammar school; I was of legal age to go to work. What was I doing, sitting at home and dreaming?

I was minding my business, of course; with all my might I was minding my business. As I understood it, my business was to go to school, to learn everything there was to know, to write poetry, become famous, and make the family rich. Surely it was not shirking to lay out such a programme for myself. I had boundless faith in my future. I was certainly going to be a great poet; I was certainly going to take care of the family.

Thus mused I, in my arrogance. And my family? They were as bad as I. My father had not lost a whit of his ambition for me. Since Graduation Day, and the school-committeeman's speech, and half a column about me in the paper, his ambition had soared even higher. He was going to keep me at school till I was prepared for college. By that time, he was sure, I would more than take care of myself. It never for a moment entered his head to doubt the wisdom or justice of this course. And my mother was just as loyal to my cause, and my brother, and my sister.

It is no wonder if I got along rapidly: I was helped, encouraged, and upheld by every one. Even the baby cheered me on. When I asked her whether she believed in higher education, she answered, without a moment's hesitation, "Ducka-ducka-da!" Against her I remember only that one day, when I read her a verse out of a most pathetic piece I was composing, she laughed right out, a most disrespectful laugh; for which I revenged myself by washing her face at the faucet, and rubbing it red on the roller towel.

It was just like me, when it was debated whether I would be best fitted for college at the High or the Latin School, to go in person to Mr. Tetlow, who was principal of both schools, and so get the most expert opinion on the subject. I never send a messenger, you may remember, where I can go myself. It was vacation time, and I had to find Mr. Tetlow at his home. Away out to the wilds of Roxbury I found my way—perhaps half an hour's ride on the electric car from Dover Street. I grew an inch taller and broader between the corner of Cedar Street and Mr. Tetlow's house, such was the charm of the clean, green suburb on a cramped waif from the slums. My faded calico dress, my rusty straw sailor hat, the color of my skin and all bespoke the waif. But never a bit daunted was I. I went up the steps to the porch, rang the bell, and asked for the great man with as much assurance as if I were a daily visitor on Cedar Street. I calmly awaited the appearance of Mr. Tetlow in the reception room, and stated my errand without trepidation.

And why not? I was a solemn little person for the moment, earnestly seeking advice on a matter of great importance. That is what Mr. Tetlow saw, to judge by the gravity with which he discussed my business with me, and the courtesy with which he showed me to the door. He saw, too, I fancy, that I was not the least bit conscious of my shabby dress; and I am sure he did not smile at my appearance, even when my back was turned.

A new life began for me when I entered the Latin School in September. Until then I had gone to school with my equals, and as a matter of course. Now it was distinctly a feat for me to keep in school, and my schoolmates were socially so far superior to me that my poverty became conspicuous. The pupils of the Latin School, from the nature of the institution, are an aristocratic set. They come from refined homes, dress well, and spend the recess hour talking about parties, beaux, and the matinée. As students they are either very quick or very hard-working; for the course of study, in the lingo of the school world, is considered "stiff." The girl with half her brain asleep, or with too many beaux, drops out by the end of the first year; or a one and only beau may be the fatal element. At the end of the course the weeding process has reduced the once numerous tribe of academic candidates to a cosey little family.

By all these tokens I should have had serious business on my hands as a pupil in the Latin School, but I did not find it hard. To make myself letter-perfect in my lessons required long hours of study, but that was my delight. To make myself at home in an alien world was also within my talents; I had been practising it day and night for the past four years. To remain unconscious of my shabby and ill-fitting clothes when the rustle of silk petticoats in the schoolroom protested against them was a matter still within my moral reach. Half a dress a year had been my allowance for many seasons; even less, for as I did not grow much I could wear my dresses as long as they lasted. And I had stood before editors, and exchanged polite calls with school-teachers, untroubled by the detestable colors and archaic design of my garments. To stand up and recite Latin declensions without trembling from hunger was something more of a feat, because I sometimes went to school with little or no breakfast; but even that required no special heroism,—at most it was a matter of self-control. I had the advantage of a poor appetite, too; I really did not need much breakfast. Or if I was hungry it would hardly show; I coughed so much that my unsteadiness was self-explained.

Everything helped, you see. My schoolmates helped. Aristocrats though they were, they did not hold themselves aloof from me. Some of the girls who came to school in carriages were especially cordial. They rated me by my scholarship, and not by my father's occupation. They teased and admired me by turns for learning the footnotes in the Latin grammar by heart; they never reproached me for my ignorance of the latest comic opera. And it was more than good breeding that made them seem unaware of the incongruity of my presence. It was a generous appreciation of what it meant for a girl from the slums to be in the Latin School, on the way to college. If our intimacy ended on the steps of the school-house, it was more my fault than theirs. Most of the girls were democratic enough to have invited me to their homes, although to some, of course, I was "impossible." But I had no time for visiting; school work and reading and family affairs occupied all the daytime, and much of the night time. I did not "go with" any of the girls, in the school-girl sense of the phrase. I admired some of them, either for good looks, or beautiful manners, or more subtle attributes; but always at a distance. I discovered something inimitable in the way the Back Bay girls carried themselves; and I should have been the first to perceive the incongruity of Commonwealth Avenue entwining arms with Dover Street. Some day, perhaps, when I should be famous and rich; but not just then. So my companions and I parted on the steps of the school-house, in mutual respect; they guiltless of snobbishness, I innocent of envy. It was a graciously American relation, and I am happy to this day to recall it.

The one exception to this rule of friendly distance was my chum, Florence Connolly. But I should hardly have said "chum." Florence and I occupied adjacent seats for three years, but we did not walk arm in arm, nor call each other nicknames, nor share our lunch, nor correspond in vacation time. Florence was quiet as a mouse, and I was reserved as an oyster; and perhaps we two had no more in common fundamentally than those two creatures in their natural state. Still, as we were both very studious, and never strayed far from our desks at recess, we practiced a sort of intimacy of propinquity. Although Florence was of my social order, her father presiding over a cheap lunch room, I did not on that account feel especially drawn to her. I spent more time studying Florence than loving her, I suppose. And yet I ought to have loved her; she was such a good girl. Always perfect in her lessons, she was so modest that she recited in a noticeable tremor, and had to be told frequently to raise her voice. Florence wore her light brown hair brushed flatly back and braided in a single plait, at a time when pompadours were six inches high and braids hung in pairs. Florence had a pocket in her dress for her handkerchief, in a day when pockets were repugnant to fashion. All these things ought to have made me feel the kinship of humble circumstances, the comradeship of intellectual earnestness; but they did not.

The truth is that my relation to persons and things depended neither on social distinctions nor on intellectual or moral affinities. My attitude, at this time, was determined by my consciousness of the unique elements in my character and history. It seemed to me that I had been pursuing a single adventure since the beginning of the world. Through highways and byways, underground, overground, by land, by sea, ever the same star had guided me, I thought, ever the same purpose had divided my affairs from other men's. What that purpose was, where was the fixed horizon beyond which my star would not recede, was an absorbing mystery to me. But the current moment never puzzled me. What I chose instinctively to do I knew to be right and in accordance with my destiny. I never hesitated over great things, but answered promptly to the call of my genius. So what was it to me whether my neighbors spurned or embraced me, if my way was no man's way? Nor should any one ever reject me whom I chose to be my friend, because I would make sure of a kindred spirit by the coincidence of our guiding stars.

When, where in the harum-scarum life of Dover Street was there time or place for such self-communing? In the night, when everybody slept; on a solitary walk, as far from home as I dared to go.

I was not unhappy on Dover Street; quite the contrary. Everything of consequence was well with me. Poverty was a superficial, temporary matter; it vanished at the touch of money. Money in America was plentiful; it was only a matter of getting some of it, and I was on my way to the mint. If Dover Street was not a pleasant place to abide in, it was only a wayside house. And I was really happy, actively happy, in the exercise of my mind in Latin, mathematics, history, and the rest; the things that suffice a studious girl in the middle teens.

Still I had moments of depression, when my whole being protested against the life of the slum. I resented the familiarity of my vulgar neighbors. I felt myself defiled by the indecencies I was compelled to witness. Then it was I took to running away from home. I went out in the twilight and walked for hours, my blind feet leading me. I did not care where I went. If I lost my way, so much the better; I never wanted to see Dover Street again.

But behold, as I left the crowds behind, and the broader avenues were spanned by the open sky, my grievances melted away, and I fell to dreaming of things that neither hurt nor pleased. A fringe of trees against the sunset became suddenly the symbol of the whole world, and I stood and gazed and asked questions of it. The sunset faded; the trees withdrew. The wind went by, but dropped no hint in my ear. The evening star leaped out between the clouds, and sealed the secret with a seal of splendor.

A favorite resort of mine, after dark, was the South Boston Bridge, across South Bay and the Old Colony Railroad. This was so near home that I could go there at any time when the confusion in the house drove me out, or I felt the need of fresh air. I liked to stand leaning on the bridge railing, and look down on the dim tangle of railroad tracks below. I could barely see them branching out, elbowing, winding, and sliding out into the night in pairs. I was fascinated by the dotted lights, the significant red and green of signal lamps. These simple things stood for a complexity that it made me dizzy to think of. Then the blackness below me was split by the fiery eye of a monster engine, his breath enveloped me in blinding clouds, his long body shot by, rattling a hundred claws of steel; and he was gone, with an imperative shriek that shook me where I stood. So would I be, swift on my rightful business, picking out my proper track from the million that cross it, pausing for no obstacles, sure of my goal.

After my watches on the bridge I often stayed up to write or study. It is late before Dover Street begins to go to bed. It is past midnight before I feel that I am alone. Seated in my stiff little chair before my narrow table, I gather in the night sounds through the open window, curious to assort and define them. As, little by little, the city settles down to sleep, the volume of sound diminishes, and the qualities of particular sounds stand out. The electric car lurches by with silent gong, taking the empty track by leaps, humming to itself in the invisible distance. A benighted team swings recklessly around the corner, sharp under my rattling window panes, the staccato pelting of hoofs on the cobblestones changed suddenly to an even pounding on the bridge. A few pedestrians hurry by, their heavy boots all out of step. The distant thoroughfares have long ago ceased their murmur, and I know that a million lamps shine idly in the idle streets.

My sister sleeps quietly in the little bed. The rhythmic dripping of a faucet is audible through the flat. It is so still that I can hear the paper crackling on the wall. Silence upon silence is added to the night; only the kitchen clock is the voice of my brooding thoughts,—ticking, ticking, ticking.

Suddenly the distant whistle of a locomotive breaks the stillness with a long-drawn wail. Like a threatened trouble, the sound comes nearer, piercingly near; then it dies out in a mangled silence, complaining to the last.

The sleepers stir in their beds. Somebody sighs, and the burden of all his trouble falls upon my heart. A homeless cat cries in the alley, in the voice of a human child. And the ticking of the kitchen clock is the voice of my troubled thoughts.

Many things are revealed to me as I sit and watch the world asleep. But the silence asks me many questions that I cannot answer; and I am glad when the tide of sound begins to return, by little and little, and I welcome the clatter of tin cans that announces the milkman. I cannot see him in the dusk, but I know his wholesome face has no problem in it.

It is one flight up to the roof; it is a leap of the soul to the sunrise. The morning mist rests lightly on chimneys and roofs and walls, wreathes the lamp-posts, and floats in gauzy streamers down the streets. Distant buildings are massed like palace walls, with turrets and spires lost in the rosy clouds. I love my beautiful city spreading all about me. I love the world. I love my place in the world.

Nat Hentoff, from *Boston Boy* (1986)

Nat Hentoff (1925–) is a noted critic, essayist, and civil rights advocate. Here he explores the lessons, intellectual and social, he learned from attending Boston Latin School, the oldest public school in the United States, founded in 1635; among its many distinguished students were Cotton Mather, Benjamin Franklin, Sam Adams, Ralph Waldo Emerson, and Leonard Bernstein. Girls Latin School opened in 1878; Boston Latin School became coeducational in 1972.

I knew only one other [than Boston Public Library] neutral ground when I was growing up a Boston boy. Under the purple-and-white flag of Boston Latin School, we were all united—the Irish, the Italians, the Jews, the Greeks, the Scots, the Armenians, the relatively few Yankees who still went there (the others no longer applied because all the rest of us were there), and the far fewer blacks.

Whatever part of the city we came from, each of us, because we were going to Boston Latin School, was a special kid on his own street. The other kids, going to ordinary high schools, might well growl that we were snooty beyond words, but they knew we had already gone a few laps around the success track while they hadn't finished one. So to be thrown out of Latin School would mean being put back into the common pool of common students—much to the delight of the common pool, and to the everlasting shame and humiliation of our parents, let alone us.

A lot of Latin School kids did get thrown back to the neighborhood high schools. As Theodore H. White, the chronicler of presidential campaigns and an alumnus of BLS, said in his memoirs, *In Search of History:* "The Latin School was a cruel school. . . . It accepted students without discrimination, and it flunked them—Irish, Italian, Jewish, Protestant, black—with equal lack of discrimination."

Accordingly, the survivors, so long as they did survive, felt they had much, perilously, in common. It mattered more that we were long-distance runners under our purple-and-white colors than that we were Jews or Christians. (In school, anyway.) For the six years I was there, my closest friends were a Greek and an Irish lad. It took me a long time to believe that was possible.

The masters, moreover, paid no attention to where we came from, to whether our parents worked in grocery stores or were State Street bankers. The only thing that counted was whether we were willing to do the work, the incessant work, it took to stay in this place. If you stuck it out at Latin School, where, after all, eight signers of the Declaration of Independence had gone, you knew there was really nothing you couldn't accomplish from then on—if you really put your mind to it.

This unrelentingly serious place is the oldest public school in America, in a three-story red-brick building with formidable Corinthian columns on the broad Avenue Louis Pasteur in the Fenway. There were masters so cold that a kind word from them seemed to be a terrifying trap. There was a sardonic, sharpshooting math teacher who kept a supply of small pieces of chalk on his desk from which he would select messengers to peg hard at a scholar's head to quicken his attention. I do not recall his ever having missed. Other masters were somewhat more amiable, but no master allowed for much familiarity. As Robert Wernick, an alumnus, wrote in the April 1985 *Smithsonian* on the occasion of the school's three hundred fiftieth anniversary: "Even today when old graduates reminisce, you will rarely hear them say of any teacher, 'He really understood me.' They are more apt to say, 'He certainly taught me trigonometry and the ablative absolute.'"

After I left Boston Latin, I would occasionally complain about how un-caring most of the masters had been about our sensibilities, our souls. Final-ly, however, it occurred to me that they gave us something a good deal more important—respect. Whatever our backgrounds, we were in the school because we had shown that we could do the work. The masters, therefore, expected at least that much of us, and that was why we came to expect even more from ourselves.

There were some fierce and suspicious Jews in my neighborhood who dis-approved of Jewish boys discovering their potential in such a distant place. Distant not so much geographically, though Avenue Louis Pasteur was a far piece from Roxbury. But distant from Judaism. The whole point of this elite Latin School, these Jews said, was to produce one-hundred-and-fifty-per-cent-American boys. "So, if you send a Jewish boy there, he will forget what it is to be Jewish."

They might have been right if Boston Latin School had been all the world we knew. But on the trolley cars coming home, some of the parochial school boys growling reminded us we were Jewish, and back in Roxbury, at night, it was still foolish to go out in the dark alone. Back home, it still made a big difference where, in the old country, your parents came from.

Roland Merullo, from *In Revere, in Those Days* (2002)

Roland Merullo (1953–) came of age in Revere, a seaside city five miles north of Boston that served as a cultural extension of the city for work-ing-class Italians, just as Cambridge had for Yankee-Brahmins. Merullo graduated from Phillips Exeter Academy and Brown University. His writings include other works on Greater Boston: *Revere Beach Boule-vard* (1998) and *Revere Beach Elegy* (2002).

The story [takes place] in a small city called Revere, Massachusetts, which lies against the coastline just north of Boston. Three miles by two miles, with a salt marsh along its northern edge and low hills rising like welts in an irregular pattern across its middle, Revere must seem to the outside eye like an uninspiring place. The houses stand very close to each other and close to the street—plain, wood-frame houses with chain-link fences or low brick walls surrounding front yards you can walk across in six steps. These days the city has a crowded, urban feeling to it: sirens in the air, lines of automobiles and trucks at the stoplights and intersections, thin streams of weeds in the tar gutters.

But forty years ago, Revere was a different place. There were amusements and food stands along its curve of sandy beach, making it a sort of slightly less famous Coney Island. And there were still some open lots pocking the narrow streets, blushes of wildness on the tame city skin. Not far from where I lived, a mile west of the beach, was a large tract of undeveloped land we called "the Farms," though nothing had been cultivated there since before the Korean War. For my friends and me, for city kids like us, the Farms was a landscape from a childhood fable: pastures, boulders, half-acre ponds, fallow fields where we turned over stones and planks and pieces of corrugated metal and reached down quick and sure as hunters to take hold of dozing snakes—brown, green, black. The snakes would slither and writhe along our bare wrists, and snap their toothless gums against the sides of our fingers, and end up imprisoned in mayonnaise jars with holes banged into the metal tops. We carried them home like bounty from a war with the wilderness, and sold them to younger boys for ten or fifteen cents apiece.

The automobile had not yet quite been elevated to the position of worship it now holds. The streets were freer and quieter. Hidden behind the shingled, painted houses were backyards in the European style, with vegetable gardens given preference over lawns, with fruit trees and grape arbors, and ceramic saints standing watch over a few square feet of flower bed.

Revere is a thoroughly modern place now, a corner of blue-collar America with chain stores and strip malls and yellow busses lined up in front of flat-roofed schools. A hundred new homes have been squeezed onto the Farms, streets cut there, sewer and electric lines brought in. But in some way I have never really understood, the city had a mysterious quality to it in those days, as if it lay outside time, beyond the range of vision of the contemporary American eye. *Provincial* is a word you might have used to describe it. But *provincial* means that a community believes itself to be living at the center of the universe, that it refuses to make an idol of the metropolis. Revere was provincial then, in that way. And, I suppose, proud of it.

Even in the days when Juniper Street was quiet enough for nine uninterrupted innings of a local game called blockball, even then there was an underside to the life we believed we were living. The collection of bad characters known as the underworld, or the mafia, or the mob, had a number of nests in Revere. Those people, in my experience, in the experience of almost everyone in the city, had little in common with the fantasy underworld you see these days on movie and television screens. For most of us, the face of the mafia was found in nothing more terrifying than a coterie of local bookmakers—neighbors, family friends, the guy beside you in the pew at nine o'clock Mass—men who made their living from the yearning of their neighbors toward some higher, softer life. In this way perhaps they were not so different from the modern-day suburban portfolio managers.

The people in our neighborhood did not have executive jobs, did not commute into the city in suits and nice dresses, reading newly-folded copies of the *Wall Street Journal,* did not have parents and grandparents who had gone to college, and, with one or two exceptions, did not go to college themselves. They road the subway into offices and warehouses in Boston, or drove their five-year-old Chevies to the factories in Lynn—where my father worked, in fact—and spent their lives in bland cubicles or hot, loud workrooms, performing the same few tasks again and again as their youth dribbled away. On Fridays they took a dollar from their pay envelope, walked down to the butcher shop on Park Avenue, and had a quiet conversation there with a man we called "Zingy." Zingy would take the money, record the lucky number—a wife's birthday, a father's license plate—then sell his loyal customer half a pound of mortadella and a package of Lucky Strikes. And the workingman would go home to his cluttered life in his drafty house and fall asleep clutching a tendril of a dream that he might "hit," that "the number" would come in for him and his family that one time, and then all the world's harsher edges would be rubbed smooth.

Of course, in Revere and elsewhere, one of the things that has changed in the last forty years is that the government has taken over Zingy's job. Now people walk down to a corner store and print out their lucky number on a blue-edged lottery form, and carry away the receipt (something that, after certain highly-publicized arrests, Zingy stopped offering). But they go to sleep holding tight to the same dream. Only now, a portion of the profits goes to the state, to be spent by bureaucrats and politicians, whereas in earlier times the money went from the bookies upward—or, more accurately, downward—to a handful of violent, sly men in smoky private clubs, to be spent on jewelry for their girlfriends and vacations in Los Vegas.

The bookmakers were the mob's menial laborers, though, and didn't have exotic girlfriends or take exotic trips. Without exception, the ones I knew were affable, modest men who had stumbled into their profession by accident, or taken it up as a second job, the way someone else might put in a few hours delivering lost airport luggage or standing the night watch at an office building. But they were part of the fabric of Revere, too.

Occasionally, the ugly side of the fabric was turned to the light. In the 1960s there was a turf war going on in Greater Boston among different factions of the underworld—the Irish, the Jews, the various bands of Italians. This was closer to the movie version, to the brutal, hateful way of life modern moviegoers seem so attracted to—as if it isn't quite real and could never affect them. We would be listening to the news in our kitchen at breakfast and hear that a body had been found in a nearby city, or in Revere, a mile or two away—in the trunk of a car, on a street corner, behind a liquor store. Shot once in the back of the head, never any witnesses. Whenever those reports were broadcast, my mother would turn the radio off. I remember her bare freckled arm reaching up to the windowsill and twisting the nickel-sized black dial on the transistor radio, as though she might keep that aspect of Revere from my father and me, and maybe from herself as well. As if protecting us from life's unpleasant truths was as simple as slicing away the mealy sections of overripe cantaloupe and bringing to the table only the juicy golden heart of it. "That's not Revere," she would say. As if she was insisting: that is not cantaloupe, that part we scrape into the metal bowl and carry out to the garbage pail.

I understand why she did that. Like most of the people in Revere, she and my father went about their lives in a straightforward, honest fashion, and didn't much appreciate the fact that the Boston newspapers and TV stations gave so much attention to the mafia, and so little to the ordinary heroism of the household, the factory and the street. I've inherited some of my parents' attitudes. I don't much appreciate, to this day, that the Italian-American way of life has been reduced to a television cliché: thugs with pinkie rings slurping spaghetti and talking tough. My story has nothing to do with that cliché. Almost nothing.

But the mob was part of Revere in those days; it's pointless to deny that. The Martoglios shouting at each other at the top of Hancock Street when I delivered the *Revere Journal* on Wednesday afternoons was part of Revere. The dog track, the horse track, the hard guys and losers in the bars behind the beach, the crooked deals worked out near City Hall, the lusts, hatreds, feuds, petty boasts—it was all as much a part of that place as the neighbor who shoveled away the snow the city plow had left at the bottom of the driveway on the night of the storm, when you were off visiting your mother or sister or friend in the hospital; or the happy shouts of young families on the amusements rides; or my grandparents' neighbor Rafaelo Losco, who once, in the middle of a conversation with my mother, when I was five or six years old, broke from his cherry tree a yard-long branch heavy with ripe fruit, and handed it across the back fence to me.

Though I sometimes want to, I cannot paint a place, or a family, or a life—my place, my family, my life—in the pretty hues of cheap jewelry. I can't give only one-half of the truth here, because what I want to say to my daughter is not: Life is a sweet cantaloupe, honey; smile and be glad, eat. But: Life can be bitter and unfair and mean, and most people rise part of the way above that, and some people transcend it completely and have enough strength left over to reach out a hand to someone else, light to light, goodness to good, and I grew up among people like that—not in sentimental novels or on the movie screen, but in fact. They were imperfect people, who struggled to see the decency and hope in each other, and if I can be like them, even partly like them, I will, and so should you. A road across the territory between two extremes, a middle way—that's what I want to offer her. Between denial on the one hand and despair on the other, between sappiness and cynicism. A plain road, across good land.

VI

"THERE IT WAS":
BOSTON, CITY OF SELF AND SPIRIT

Conscience and self-consciousness, the habits of mind carried across the Atlantic to New England in the early seventeenth century by the Puritan settlers of Boston, dissipated but never entirely disappeared over the next four centuries. "New England was founded consciously, and in no fit of absence of mind," observed historian Samuel Eliot Morison on the establishment of the Bay Colony in 1630.[1] The Puritans' conscience-driven presence of mind persisted and evolved while the city expanded, transformed, and redefined itself. Bostonians often lost or altered their sense of mission, but periodically renewed and reshaped their original covenant, the quest for salvation through an errand into the wilderness. Puritan righteousness evolved into self-awareness and political passion. Yet moral purpose remained second nature to Bostonians and self-examination remained their primary literary impulse. "It was customary for Puritans to keep a strict daily accounting of their faults and failings, as well as their deeds and accomplishments, in order to better assess their position in the eyes of the Almighty," Thomas H. O'Connor notes.[2] Journal-keeping, autobiography, and biography—along with their poetic and fictional variations—have remained the most characteristic and revealing modes for Greater Boston writers. In such forms these writers have held up for moral measurement their days and ways against the highest standards of God's law as they saw it and against personal conscience, and they have registered a permanent record of their findings.

The first entry in Henry David Thoreau's journal, written on October 22, 1837, begins "'What are you doing now?,' he [Ralph Waldo Emerson] asked. 'Do you keep a journal?'—So I make my first entry today."[3] Emerson makes clear to his young disciple that journal-keeping constitutes a meaningful means of doing, while failing to keep a journal indicates suspect idleness and thoughtlessness. Articulation is worthy action. Thoreau's journal served as the source for all of his published writings and may be seen as his primary

literary achievement. In his journal Thoreau wrote his observations, opinions, reflections on readings, meditations, and inspirations—filling his verbal sketch book with entries which then were subject to reconsiderations
and revisions, observations he then recorded in notebooks and eventually
packed into a yellow pine box to contain his life's work. When a long-miss-
ing notebook was discovered, it fit exactly into the box he had carefully car-
pentered.[4] Form fit function.

In Thoreau's hands the journal became a sustained work of art, his prose
Leaves of Grass. Thoreau's journal shows, as well, that self-examination is a
means of self-dramatization, of validating the unique perspective of the
upright, outspoken I, for, as he reminds us on the opening page of *Walden*,
"it is, after all, always the first person that is speaking," and "every writer,
first and last" should be required to offer "a simple and sincere account of his
own life."[5]

Samuel Sewall, prominent Puritan judge and civic leader, notably contributed to this regional habit of expressive self-reflection by keeping an
extensive diary between 1673 and 1729, making vivid entries that range
from professions of conscience to confessions of concupiscence, shaping a
record, as historian Kenneth B. Murdock said, that presents "New England
life more fully and in truer colors than any other single document."[6] Sewall,
from jottings in his pocket notebooks, comments on passing moments, to
considered entries in his office journal on rights for slaves and women,
showed the flexibility and range of the form; he recorded his responses to
the "witches" he judged at the Salem Witch Trials of 1692 (judgments he
repented in a 1697 speech at Boston's Old South Church), to the widows he
courted, even to the hailstones that broke windows in Boston's new meet-
inghouse. Married three times, father of fourteen children, poet and essayist, successful businessman as well as Chief Justice, Sewall was a man fully
immersed in his historical moment and dedicated to recording it—the
"Puritan Pepys," as Henry Cabot Lodge called him.[7] Sewall saw the world in
a grain of sand and espied the universe beyond the scrim of the actual. As
his biographer Eve LaPlante puts it, "this diary, an internal record of his
spiritual career, was truly a memoir in that he wished to remember and find
meaning in his life."[8] Sewall was a worldly, modern man who could change
his mind, laugh at his own expense, and understand the perspective of the
victims of Puritan wrath—the misjudged "witches" of Salem, the persecuted
slaves and suppressed women of Boston—though he was enough of a Puri-

tan to believe that the apocalypse was near and that New England, the New Jerusalem, represented the last chance for salvation. Finally, though, he put his faith in the features and creatures of nature to redeem its citizens. "So long as Plum Island shall faithfully keep the command post, notwithstanding all the hectoring words and hard blows of the proud and boisterous ocean; so long as any salmon or sturgeon shall swim in the stream of the Merrimack, . . . so long as Christians be born there," then all would be well in the new world.[9]

Sewall's observational and reflective habit of mind endured in the letters of John and Abigail Adams, the autobiography of Benjamin Franklin, the diaries of John Quincy Adams, the journals of Emerson, Thoreau, and Hawthorne, and in the ironic self-examination of Henry Adams in his *Education*—works that link Puritans, patriots, abolitionists, and post–Civil War Bostonians in a tradition of conscience-driven expression. These writers, centered in Boston, shaped what Perry Miller and Thomas H. Johnson call a "true New England tradition," in works which undertook "no more than countless Puritans had done when they had at any time found that vision of the unity and meaning of the universe which they call regeneration."[10]

New England is a "place where the Lord will create a new Heaven, and a new Earth," wrote Puritan visionary Edward Johnson in his *Wonder-Working Providence of Sions Savior* (1659).[11] Boston's Puritan settlers saw the new world through their typological imagination: present actions were prefigured in the past—for example, their crossing of the Atlantic to the New Jerusalem replicated the Red Sea crossing by Moses and the Israelites; New Testament events were foreshadowed, preordained in the Old Testament. Past is prologue, literally. Further, the world around them was a symbolic terrain, God's composed text, which they read for its meaning, seeking His purpose in the language of landscape, in the weather, in encounters, indeed in every leaf that falls—which they noted, then faithfully recorded and glossed.

John Cotton, the colony's most revered minister, wanted his parishioners to *feel* the presence of God's mystery and grace. However, when his disciple Anne Hutchinson testified in 1637 that she heard God's voice without the required intermediary presence of congregation or ministerial intercession, she was denounced as a heretic. Though Hutchinson would later be celebrated, in the words of her twenty-first-century biographer, as "an American visionary, pioneer, and explorer who epitomized the religious freedom and tolerance that are essential to the nation's character," in her day Hutchinson was judged "the instrument of Satan," the "enemy of the chosen people," and "this *American Jezebel*" by Governor John Winthrop when he addressed the Massachusetts General Court.[12]

In the judgmental eyes of congregational Puritans, Hutchinson was a horrible example, her life a cautionary tale illustrating the sins of willful individualism. However, her spiritual independence, deemed "Antinomianism" by Puritans because they believed that she set herself against God's law, marked the moment, as historian of the Puritan era Andrew Delbanco argues, when "the idea of a suprarational spirit was beginning to be beaten down in New England."[13] Antinomianism—along with a parallel heresy, Armenianism, which held that salvation is conditional upon faith—made free will central to the moral and religious life, ideas that contributed to the creation of an American Adam and Eve.[14]

Hutchinson's faith in personal vision was eventually vindicated by those, like Thoreau, who celebrated the mystic, rapturous, American self, at ease in the sumptuous nature of the new world's Zion. "The Emersonian, or antinomian, critique of rationalized Puritanism is everywhere in our literature, though it has naturally been especially acute within the New England tradition itself," writes Delbanco.[15] The neo-antinomianism of the transcendentalists, then, rejected Puritan typology by denying the power of the past to prefigure and thus to determine the present, just as they rejected the coercions of Puritan congregationalism, and even the milder dictates of Unitarianism, for the opportunities of radical individualism. Winthrop sought salvation through the congregation; Emerson sought transcendence through "an original relation to the universe."[16]

From Anne Bradstreet's "To My Dear Children" (1656) to John Berryman's *Homage to Mistress Bradstreet* (1956), to Anne Sexton's *The Death Notebooks* (1974), the characteristic product of the New England mind, particularly its more intensely localized Greater Boston consciousness, remains the spiritual autobiography. In this mode, in poetry or prose, the writer or the writer's surrogate stands as a witness, as one who evokes the vision of a new life in a lay sermon. Puritan historian Sacvan Bercovitch has suggested that the "jeremiad"—a lament over sins, a prophecy of impending doom, mitigated by a faint prospect of salvation—was the central impulse of expression for Puritans, and it has persisted in the writings of those who followed them.[17] Writing in the 1830s, Alexis de Tocqueville concluded that "the whole destiny of America [is] contained in the first Puritan who landed on these shores, as that of the human race is in the first man."[18] At once self-assured and self-critical, the voice of that first Puritan has long echoed in and around Boston, even among those who repudiated Puritanism.

However, at least one diligent, modern-era Boston diarist set himself against the grain of moral uplift that characterized regional journal-keepers; he advanced the old-time religious theme of degeneration. Arthur Crews Inman (1895–1963) had no vision of any "unity and meaning of the universe" and he scorned Boston in the scabrous diaries—155 volumes, 17 million words—he kept from 1919 until his death. A wealthy and neurotic recluse, a bigot and misanthrope, a semi-invalid, and ultimately a suicide, Inman cast himself as the hero of his imagination by soliciting marginal Bostonians to come to his rooms, where he induced them to confess their sordid secrets and to submit to his sexual advances. He cruised the city in his chauffeur-driven Pierce-Arrow or Cadillac in search of "diary fodder," and he sent both his long-suffering wife and members of his "staff" into the streets of Boston to recruit "talkers."[19] Inman then scrupulously recorded his dark reflections on what he saw as the failed American character—denouncing the "unspeakable Jews," the "filthy Irish," and the city's blacks—and he mocked those who passed below his windows in the aptly named Garrison Hall, a run-down apartment hotel in the Back Bay.[20] Inman's Boston is a perverse metropolis witnessed by a Dostoevskian sick soul—a Boston version of the narrator in *Notes from Underground*. The Inman *Diary* is a distortion of the Puritan form of self-examination as a means of seeking salvation, written by an ingrown Bostonian who flaunted his spiritual degradation. That said, Inman's diary did provide, as he intended, a "Boston overview" of his era, and it can be justly placed within the Greater Boston tradition of focused and candid self-examination for presumed noble purposes, which he claimed to be his goal, though he failed miserably to reach it: "to be absolutely honest and do it within the bounds of social palatability and artistic acceptability."[21]

Inman's preening, bitter invectives represent an exception to the prevailing pattern of Boston autobiographies, in which the city serves as a fitting site for education in distinctions of social status and conflict, as well as the proper place for spiritual realization. Telling examples include Samuel Eliot Morison's *One Boy's Boston* (1962), Robert Lowell's *Notebooks* (1970), May Sarton's *Journal of Solitude* (1973) and *The House by the Sea* (1977), Anne

Sexton's *Death Notebooks* (1974), Dan Wakefield's *Returning: A Spiritual Journey* (1988), and John Updike's *Self-Consciousness* (1989). Self-expression remained a regional obsession.

Samuel Eliot Morison's *One Boy's Boston, 1887–1901* countered the prevailing myth—enforced by John P. Marquand's *The Late George Apley* and George Santayana's *The Last Puritan*—that Boston Brahmins were bloodless, pitiable snobs, tottering on their last legs in a city that had seen better days. From the first family comforts of Beacon Hill, Morison could look across Boston with satisfaction, celebrating the city's democratic vistas, though at the other end of the city, as we have seen in chapter 5, Nat Hentoff in *Boston Boy* would remember Boston as "the most anti-Semitic city in the nation."[22] However, for both the Brahmin from Beacon Hill and the Jew from Roxbury, Boston stood as a city of moral purpose, and their autobiographies, while demonstrating the form's range, exemplify the characteristic Boston theme of cultural and spiritual quest.

Brahmin Boston for Morison was both benign and benighted. Born in 1887 on Brimmer Street, at the landfilled base of Beacon Hill, amidst the city's ruling elite, Morison looked back some seventy years and recalled or reconceived a Boston in which, amazingly, "there were no distinctions of wealth" and ancestry did not count! His Boston was not, as critics had claimed, composed of "bigoted Protestants, nasty to the Irish"; rather, it was an open, democratic, idealistic city, held together by its best and brightest, its people of character and standing. A "solid core of nobility and bourgeois" families endowed Harvard, the Museum of Fine Arts, the Opera House, Massachusetts General Hospital, and many other Greater Boston cultural institutions whose presence affirmed their collective faith in the community. In Morison's eyes Boston remained nothing less than that "city upon a hill" envisioned by its founders. "Despite all the sneers and jeers at 'Proper Bostonians,' 'Boston Brahmins' and the like, there was a remarkable pattern of living here that existed nowhere else in the United States."[23] The differing perspectives upon the city registered by Morison, Hentoff, and Inman show that "Boston" remained a creation of the imagination, shaped by radically different experiences.

Five writers usefully illustrate Morison's and other autobiographers' insistence that Boston was a symbolic city and a unique community devoted to spiritual inquiry and to social standing from its founding right up to today. Robert Lowell, perhaps Boston's most important twentieth-century writer, left a rich record of reflections on the city of his birth in prose and poetry, particularly in his most memorable poetic expression of place and purpose, "For the Union Dead" (1960). Dan Wakefield, journalist and novelist from Indiana, by way of Manhattan and Los Angeles, recorded his willed recovery of health and faith in *Returning: A Spiritual Journey* (1988), a quest that culminated in a characteristically Bostonian spiritual renewal. John Updike, who also came to the city from elsewhere, a small town in western Pennsylvania—first as a Harvard student, then after an interlude in Manhattan, as a sometime resident of the city and a longtime resident of towns north of Boston—illustrates in his stories, novels, and essays that New England remains not only a fertile territory for imagining fiction, but also a proper place for furthering a spiritual quest, particularly in his autobiography, *Self-Consciousness* (1989). In writing his celebrated essay on baseball, "Hub Fans Bid Kid Adieu" (1960), Updike also showed that devotion to local sports teams had replaced evangelical purpose as a means of fusing Boston into a united community. Eve LaPlante, journalist and historian, shows that Boston's seventeenth-century past still lives in the twenty-first century in writings on her family connections to the city's founders and in her reinterpretations of their importance in her biographies of seventeenth-century Greater Boston worthies, Anne Hutchinson in *American Jezebel* (2004) and Samuel Sewall in *Salem Witch Judge* (2007). Finally, Patricia Powell, novelist and essayist, shows that Boston remains a city upon a hill worth seeking in "A Literary Landscape: From Jamaica to Boston" (2004).

The burden of the city's history weighed heavily upon Robert Lowell, born "high on Beacon Hill," at the heart of Brahmin Boston.[24] "He was so completely *Bostonian*," wrote Peter Davison, poet and *Atlantic Monthly* poetry editor, of Lowell in *The Fading Smile* (1994), a poignant account of the Boston-Cambridge poetic revival of the 1950s, largely inspired by Lowell.

> This flawed titan of the famed Lowell family was born in his grandfather Winslow's (his mother's father's) house on March 1, 1917, on Chestnut Street, the most beautiful street in Boston, at number 18, near the top of Beacon Hill, across from the former residence of Julia Ward Howe and from that of Ralph Adams Cram; one long block from where his great granduncle James Russell Lowell had lived and from the former residence

of Francis Parkman; and three blocks from the Massachusetts State House and the site, opposite, of Saint-Gaudens' noble monument to Robert Gould Shaw (another remote kinsman) and his Civil War regiment.[25]

Lowell looked back with tortured ambivalence upon a long line of Lowells and Winslows who had shaped the city. Edward Winslow arrived on the Mayflower and served as governor of Plymouth Plantation. James Russell Lowell—poet, editor, professor, public servant—provided a poetic precedent, as did Amy Lowell, local eccentric and fellow Boston poet; she was his cousin, as was her brother, A. Lawrence Lowell, president of Harvard. Small wonder, then, that Robert Lowell came to speak with what Seamus Heaney has called "a dynastic as well as an artistic voice, recalling how both sides of his family had a long history of service in the *rem publicam*, and this preoccupation with ancestry was a constant one." Lowell turned for inspiration to Henry Adams, another descendant of first family Bostonians, who expressed a love-hatred relationship with what Lowell called "the unforgivable landscape" of the city.[26] Like Henry Adams, Robert Lowell, as he put it, "too, was born under the shadow of the Boston State House," in another era when Boston's ruling class felt threatened by the growing influence of the Irish. Lowell saw this transformation through ironic, patrician eyes. "James Michael Curley was out of jail and waiting for a mandate from the people to begin the first of his many terms as Mayor of Boston. Nothing from now on was going quite as expected—even downhill."[27]

Boston remained a city divided against itself in Lowell's imaginative reconstruction, particularly in "91 Revere Street," an essay from *Life Studies* (1959), a resonant embodiment of Boston as both an actual and an emblematic place. He sought separation from his mother's snobbery. She, feeling disenfranchised from the line of Lowells who were enriched by money from the cotton mills in Lowell and Lawrence, believed that their Beacon Hill home was located "on the outer rim of the hub of decency," though, as her son bitterly put it, their townhouse in geographic fact stood "less than fifty yards from Louisburg Square, the cynosure of old historic Boston's plainspoken, cold roast elite—the hub of the Universe. Fifty yards!"[28]

Lowell found his fitting emblem of divided Boston in the contrast between the Boston Common and the Public Garden, parks separated by Charles Street and, in Lowell's youth, by contrasting types of Bostonians. He recalls his younger self, strolling with other Brimmer School students on a sunny spring afternoon, "on the polite, landscaped walks of the Public Garden."

Something made him break away and go to the heavy iron fence that enclosed the Garden and symbolically hemmed in his class. Beyond the fence, across Charles Street, he gazed upon another side of the city, one which stirred his imagination "the historic Boston Common, a now largely wrong-side-of the-track park."

> On the Common there were mossy bronze reliefs of Union soldiers, and a captured German tank filled with smelly wads of newspapers. Everywhere there were grit, litter, gangs of Irish, Negroes, Latins. On Sunday afternoons orators harangued about Sacco and Vanzetti, while others stood about heckling and blocking the sidewalks. Keen young policemen, looking for trouble, lolled on the benches. At nightfall a police lieutenant on horseback inspected the Common. In the Garden, however, there was only officer Lever, a single, white-haired and mustached dignitary, who had once been the doorman at the Union Club. He now looked more like a member of the club.[29]

Lowell would cross the line that separated the rigid, repressive Public Garden world from the raffish, expressive world of Boston Common.

Lowell, born a Boston insider, voiced an outsider's perspective on the city when he read "For the Union Dead"—a poem first published for the 103rd anniversary issue of *Atlantic Monthly* in November 1959—in the Public Garden at the Arts Festival held in June 1960, telling his audience that he, as a boy, had been ejected from the Garden by Officer Lever for fighting, but adding that his presence there "tonight partly makes up for it."[30] Lowell's poem honors Colonel Robert Gould Shaw and the monument that celebrates both Shaw and the black soldiers of his 54th Massachusetts Regiment, sculpted by Augustus Saint-Gaudens, dedicated in 1897. Erected across Beacon Street from the Golden Dome of the Massachusetts State House, at the peak of Beacon Hill, the Shaw Memorial stands as an embodiment of Boston's ideal self-image. Just after Shaw's death in July 1863, James Russell Lowell wrote *Memoriae Positum R.G.S.*, a poem which celebrated Shaw as a "saintly shape of fame," but also expressed fears that Bostonians would become "heedless" of Shaw's noble example, a theme Robert Lowell stressed nearly a century later in his tribute to Shaw.[31]

In "For the Union Dead" Boston is an arid wasteland, emblemized by the abandoned South Boston Aquarium, which had delighted Robert as a boy but now stood "in a Sahara of snow," its "airy tanks" dry. Boston Common no longer represented his raffish alternative to the staid Public Garden; it had been transformed into a raw, gouged construction site; its undulant landscape, once a setting for Puritan-era cattle grazings and sinner hangings, was now being hollowed out for the construction of an underground parking garage. "A girdle of orange, Puritan-pumpkin colored girders/ braces the tingling Statehouse." In this vulgar, mercenary, heritage-free Boston, Shaw is "out of bounds now" because he died for honor and principle, a fallen embodiment of the city's lost rectitude. Just as Shaw, in life and in Saint-Gaudens's beautiful bas relief "cannot bend his back," so too does Lowell stand stiff against backsliding Boston, where "giant finned cars nose forward like fish;/ a savage servility/ slides by on grease."[32] Lowell's great poem, according to Helen Vendler, portrays "a struggle between corruption and virtue," a traditional Puritan tension, "each aesthetically imagined," each balanced and fused in this poem about a city divided against itself. "Lowell's poem is a reconstruction rite intending to resuscitate both Shaw and his monument" for Bostonians who have betrayed their noble past.[33]

Soon after Lowell read his tribute to Shaw before a Boston audience whose approval surprised him, he moved from his Marlborough Street home to New York City with his wife, Elizabeth Hardwick, who had already published an essay that declared Boston's glory days done, "Boston: The Lost Ideal" (1959): "Boston—wrinkled, spindly-legged, depleted of nearly all her spiritual and cutaneous oils, provincial, self-esteeming—has gone on spending and spending her inflated bills of pure reputation decade after decade. Now, one supposes it is over at last."[34] Peter Davison suggests that "Boston's common ground was leveled twice in the late 1950s: once literally, when the Boston Common itself was excavated to house an underground garage, and once figuratively, when the 'shrill verve of [Elizabeth Hardwick's] invective,' as Robert Lowell's poem described it, pinned Boston's 'mysteriously enduring reputation' to the ground in 1959," when her essay was published in Harper's.[35] Lowell's first wife, Jean Stafford, had earlier satirized the piety, prudery, and pretension of Boston's first families in her novel Boston Adventure (1944), which portrays a city emblemized by the Beacon Hill home of Miss Pride, in which the novel's young heroine feels imprisoned as a servant, while "the sun, hidden elsewhere by the city's smoke, shone brilliantly on white doorways and their brass trimmings."[36]

Though Lowell, his wives, and the poets he taught—Anne Sexton, Sylvia Plath, and others who met with him when he led a poetry seminar at Boston University in the 1950s—saw Boston with a cold, critical eye, he could never wholly free himself from the city's influence any more than James Joyce could fly past the nets of his dear, dirty Dublin by becoming an exile. At the end of his life Lowell was still brooding upon Boston, the "myth of New England," and the writers it produced. By the mid-nineteenth century, Lowell wrote, "the great imaginative minds first clearly saw their heritage as something both to admire and fear." Hawthorne and Emerson "were anti-Puritans, conscious and deliberate about it, yet sure they had inherited its essence."[37] As had Lowell.

Robert Lowell was a Boston insider who worked his way out from under the bell-jar of Beacon Hill. Dan Wakefield was an outsider who came to climb the Hill, literally and symbolically. He too lived on Revere Street, not far from Louisburg Square, and he too left Boston: *au revoir* Revere. In the end, these two very different writers arrived at the same point—seeing Boston as a symbolic site for spiritual autobiography—though their assessments of the city were very different. Wakefield wrote three novels in which Greater Boston was treated as a moral landscape, as the implications of their titles indicate: *Starting Over* (1973), *Home Free* (1977), and *Selling Out* (1985).[38] In his autobiography, *Returning* (1988), he learns by going where he has to go, discovering his place and purpose in God's design—in Boston.

When Wakefield first lived in Boston in the 1960s, he was drawn to "the special solace of *place*," particularly present for him on Beacon Hill. At the time "the Hill was rather like a happily down-at-the-heels dowager, with a nice mix of Brahmin and hippie-bohemian flavors." After he left and then returned to Boston in 1972, Wakefield bought a townhouse on Revere Street, just up the Hill from the former Lowell residence. Wakefield finally felt "rooted." "Boston and the Hill became the real thing for me."[39] However, in 1980 Wakefield again found himself away from Boston and in crisis—the result of drinking, broken relationships, and professional failures—in Hollywood, writing unproduced film scripts, so he came "home" yet again to Boston, where he had once been happy. "Walking the brick streets of my old neighborhood on Beacon Hill, I felt in balance again with the universe, and a further pull to what seemed the center of it, the source of something I was searching for, something I couldn't name that went far beyond the satisfaction of scenery or local color."[40] His Hollywood had been a setting for physical and emotional collapse; his rediscovered Boston represented sanctuary, physical and spiritual recovery.

Wakefield came to an epiphany in King's Chapel, the Anglican-Unitarian church that has stood at the corner of Tremont and School Streets since 1688; the current church structure, built of Quincy granite, was opened in 1754. "It was there that for the first time I began to understand how my life could be viewed as a spiritual journey as well as a series of secular adventures of accomplishment and disappointment, personal and professional triumph and defeat."[41] Wakefield found his personal and spiritual *place* in Boston, particularly in King's Chapel. He even discovered that one of his ancestors, John Wakefield, was buried in the adjacent Old Granary Burial Ground, founded in 1660. "Knowing that the ancestors of my genealogical family were in the very ground of the place to which I had been so naturally drawn seemed part of the whole intricate pattern of my journey and return."[42] Boston became Dan Wakefield's symbolic and actual home ground, which he testified to in *Returning*, a memoir of his successful spiritual quest.

John Updike, from Shillington, Pennsylvania, claimed no New England heritage. However, when he came to Harvard as an undergraduate (A.B., 1954), the region's attractions opened for him. He responded to the muted landscape—the adjacent sea, the small mountains, the large literary tradition—and the region's private people, as he notes in *Self-Consciousness*, an account of his growth of awareness. "There are distances in New England, hard to see on the map, that come from the variousness of the regions set within a few miles of one another, and from a tact in the people which wordlessly acknowledges another's right to an inner life and private strangeness."[43] Though Updike lived only briefly in Boston—locating himself and his family in coastal towns along the North Shore—he defined himself within the tradition of Greater Boston's literary concerns and modes of expression. As had W. D. Howells, a writer Updike admired, a century before, Updike claimed his place among Greater Boston's writers, but while Howells departed for New York City, Updike returned after spending several years in New York City, where he wrote for *The New Yorker*, and he remained a Greater Bostonian until his death in 2009. When asked in 1999 "by a fledgling journal called *The Improper Bostonian*" why he lives in New England, Updike reflected on other tale tellers of his two adopted cities. "When William Dean Howells left Boston for Manhattan in the 1890s, he took the last slant ray of the Emersonian heyday with him, but, in the century since, Boston has retained the aura of a place where civilization, if not dynamically generated, is affectionately regarded."[44] In *Self-Consciousness* Updike places himself at the heart of the region's matter and meaning.

Echoing John Winthrop, he envisions a moral mission in a local landscape that resonates with universal implications. "Wherever there is a self, it may be, whether on Earth or in the Andromeda Galaxy, the idea of God will arise."[45]

Updike's sense of New England place grew over the years he lived north of Boston. He based a trilogy of novels on Hawthorne's *The Scarlet Letter—A Month of Sundays* (1975), *Roger's Version* (1986), and *S* (1988)—the second of which is set in Boston-Cambridge, the other two also containing his reflections on New England towns and the region's Puritan heritage. Updike's version of Hawthorne's Roger Chillingworth is Roger Lambert, a tortured Harvard Divinity School professor who seeks God's presence in illicit sex, an affair with his half-sister's daughter. Eventually Lambert renounces sin and the world that offers such enticements—Boston, that tempting allegorical landscape on which this representative Everyman is tested. "This city spread so wide and multiform around and beneath us: it was more than the mind could encompass, it overbrimmed the eye; but was it all? Was it enough? It did not appear to be."[46] Updike had incorporated Hawthorne's themes of imprisonment and transcendence in his parables of place. In "Hawthorne's Creed," Updike praises his romancer predecessor for his portrayal of the thick "social surround" of his characters, "solidly composed of ancient Boston's communal righteousness." Yet Updike believes, like Hawthorne, "with his Puritan ancestors" before him, "that man's spirit matters; that the soul can be distorted, strained and lost; that the impalpable exerts force against the material."[47]

Updike as a boy was first drawn to the *idea* of Boston not by Nathaniel Hawthorne but by Ted Williams, star of the Boston Red Sox, the premier hitter of his generation, perhaps in Major League history. In the fall of 1946 the fourteen-year-old Updike listened to the final game of the World Series, between the Red Sox and the St. Louis Cardinals, on his father's car radio in the Shillington High School parking lot. When the Red Sox lost he was stunned and felt "something lost forever, . . . a blissful innocence."[48] Thus did Updike learn the Boston lesson of earthly transience long before he became a Greater Bostonian.

When Updike moved his family to Massachusetts in the late 1950s, Williams was part of the local attraction. "I wanted to keep Ted Williams company while I could."[49] Updike was among a small crowd (10,454) in Fenway Park to say farewell to Williams, who played his last game for the Red Sox and concluded his brilliant career on September 28, 1960, on a characteristically chill, overcast Boston afternoon. Updike's essay on that occasion, "Hub Fans Bid Kid Adieu," is at once a great tribute to Williams, an exemplary piece of sports literature, and an insightful treatment of symbolic Boston.

"Fenway Park, in Boston, is a lyric little bandbox of a ballpark. Everything is painted green and seems in curiously sharp focus, like the inside of an old-fashioned peeping-type Easter egg." This striking opening sentence establishes Fenway Park as an apt symbol for the modern city—no longer the steep, stark mount of spiritual aspiration, but rather a colorfully enclosed playground for its citizenry. Yet even Fenway Park reflects Puritan tensions between absolutes and deviations. "It was built in 1912 and rebuilt in 1934, and offers, as do most Boston artifacts, a compromise between Man's Euclidean determinations and Nature's beguiling irregularities."[50]

Williams had been a Red Sox star since 1939, so he represented for Updike both Boston tradition and transformation. "In the two decades since Williams had come to Boston, his status had imperceptibly shifted from that of a naughty prodigy to that of a municipal monument."[51] Williams had undergone a conversion experience in his attitude toward the city, describing before his final game his "years in Boston" as "the greatest thing in my life."[52] This outsider from California, once scorned for his petulance and pride, had earned, through examples of character and heroic deeds, the city's respect. Williams's courage as hitter and war hero—he served as a decorated combat pilot in both World War II and the Korean War—made him into an exemplary Bostonian. Traces of earlier Boston heroines and heroes, from scorned Hester Prynne to celebrated Robert Gould Shaw, mix in the myth of Ted Williams, who, decades later, would later have named in his honor a tunnel linking downtown Boston with Logan Airport.

Updike parallels Williams's saga with classic mythic models—Jason, Achilles, and Nestor—and describes his final home run in epic terms: fitting emblems of descent and ascent. It was the eighth inning and Jack Fisher of the Baltimore Orioles was pitching.

> Williams swung mightily and missed. The crowd grunted, seeing that classic swing, so long and smooth and quick, exposed. Fisher threw the third time, Williams swung again, and there it was. The ball climbed on a diagonal line into the vast volume of air over center field. From my angle, behind third base, the ball seemed less an object in flight than the tip of a towering, motionless construct, like the Eiffel Tower or the Tappan Zee Bridge. It was in the books while it was still in the sky.[53]

Through John Updike's consummate view of this culminating deed, Fenway Park is transformed from a lyric little Boston bandbox into an epic emblem, a vision of transcendence. This storied Boston moment embodied a fulfillment of faith, a realization of possibilities recorded and celebrated by an adopted Bostonian. It was in Boston's books while it was still in the sky.

While Ted Williams's talents lifted him into mythic realms, the Boston Red Sox stumbled, winning their last World Series of the twentieth century in 1918. Speculations upon the team's failures flourished in this city devoted to interpretation. John Updike wondered if the Puritan-shaped Boston fans risked punishment by ever expecting such worldly success, which seemed so easily and frequently available to buoyant, bountiful New York fans and their swaggering Yankees in worldly Gotham. Red Sox president Larry Luchino jokingly referred to the Yankees as "the Evil Empire" in 2002, an epithet that at once cleverly parodied and intensified the century-old Yankees–Red Sox rivalry.[54] Updike:

> What makes Boston—little old Boston up here among the rocky fields and empty mills—think it deserves championship teams all the time? Having the Celtics may be miracle enough, not to mention a Patriots team that finally won in Miami. The founding Puritans left behind a lingering conviction that divine election is reflected in earthly success, and that this so-called city built upon a hill has hosies on a prime share.[55]

If far from elect, perhaps Boston was damned, or at least cursed, as some suggested. Near misses and seemingly inevitable failures haunted the Red Sox during the twentieth century. In 1946 Ted Williams's team lost the World Series to the St. Louis Cardinals on a late relay throw to home plate. Barely missing chances to go to the Series after losses in the final games of the 1948 and 1949 seasons, the Red Sox made it in 1967 only to lose again to the Cardinals, and in 1975, only to be defeated by the Cincinnati Reds. Most painfully, in game six of the 1986 World Series, Boston took a 5–3 lead against the New York Mets. In the top of the tenth inning they were one out away from winning the World Series when a ground ball skittered through the legs of Boston first baseman Bill Buckner; the deciding run scored for the Mets, who went on to win the Series, plunging the city yet again into gloom and talk of doom. "Casey at the Bat" (1888), written by Ernest Thayer, who grew up in nearby Worcester, seemed an appropriate poem for Bostonians, for yet again the mighty Red Sox had struck out and there was no joy in Boston, another "Mudville."

Boston seemed to suffer "The Curse of the Bambino," a phrase made famous when *Boston Globe* sports writer Dan Shaughnessy used it as the title of his 1990 book on the seemingly doomed Red Sox.[56] The "Bambino," of course, was one of the many honorific nicknames for the legendary Babe Ruth, who, after a brilliant career as a star pitcher and hitter for the Red Sox (1914–1919), was traded before the 1920 season to the team's hated rivals, the Yankees, where his home-run hitting—by then he was "the Sultan of Swat"—transformed the game and led the team to a series of championships; in all, the Yankees won twenty-six World Series championships and thirty-nine American League pennants in the twentieth century. Before Ruth left Boston, the Red Sox won five World Series titles, but after he was gone it took them eighty-six years to win another. However, magically, in 2004 the curse was lifted when the resurgent Red Sox came back from an 0–3, best-of-seven, deficit to beat the proud Yankees in the American League Championship Series and then went on to sweep their long-standing National League enemies, the St. Louis Cardinals, to win the World Series. This prompted Shaughnessy to write another book, *Reversing the Curse* (2005), which revised the dark myth of inevitable defeat that generations of Bostonians had long lived and died believing.[57] When Boston swept the Colorado Rockies to win the World Series again in 2007, Boston's new-found identity as a twenty-first century providential city, at least in the world of sports, was confirmed.

The New England Patriots (formerly the Boston Patriots before they moved to a suburban stadium) won three National Football League Super Bowls in four years between 2001 and 2005. In 2008 the Boston Celtics climaxed the city's success saga by winning the National Basketball Association Championship, their seventeenth. Community in Boston, once established through common origin, belief, and purpose was now, in the new, strikingly various and intensely sports-centered city, celebrated through its professional teams.

The new Boston, confident and freed from the memory of defeats, was further confirmed in 2005 when the Boston Red Sox began offering official citizenship in "Red Sox Nation." Bostonians may no longer gather in congregations of the elect, but they do meet in sold-out stadiums where they express their faith, fidelity, and cohesion. Indeed "Red Sox Nation" has become not only a regional but a national phenomenon, since fans in the Boston diaspora—ranging from snow-bird retirees to former students from Boston's many universities who live across the nation, many wearing Red Sox red-and-blue jerseys and caps, sporting a bright "B"—attend or watch on television in great numbers the road games their team plays, not only in Ft. Myers, Florida, the team's spring training site, but during the season in parks across the country, in Canada, and by website links around the world. Boston, it seems, has become a moveable feast.

In the twenty-first century Boston, however much it has expanded and grown in diversity, retains its sense of place and purpose. Its population has been enriched by newcomers who have brought new languages, rituals, and experiences into the community; they will be extending and revising the literary record of the city as Boston approaches its four hundredth anniversary. But there is little likelihood that Boston will lose its sense of the past. Nathaniel Hawthorne established Boston's literary heritage by setting *The Scarlet Letter* in the Puritan era, a century and a half before he wrote his romance in 1850. Eve LaPlante follows this pattern by looking back from the early twenty-first century to the mid-to-late seventeenth to inquire into the lives of Anne Hutchinson and Samuel Sewall, emblematic family figures from the Puritan era. LaPlante grew up in Greater Boston, hearing frightening stories about the Puritan founders. She was shocked when her Aunt Charlotte May Wilson told her that they were descendants of these righteous, persecuting Puritans. "I was really horrified by these people—Anne Hutchinson, Samuel Sewall, Simon Bradstreet, John Cotton," she said during an interview held near Sewall's tomb in Boston's Old Granary Burying Ground. "They sounded creepy. One was a heretic. One was a judge who hanged people. I thought, Why would anyone want to be associated with these people?"[58]

Aunt Charlotte was the proprietor of the Red Inn, located in Provincetown near the spot where Puritan separatists landed in 1620, so her vivid tales of the early settlers took on a living presence for young Eve, who liked to trace the routes of her ancestors—a network that included Louisa May Alcott, Harvard College graduates, as well as many ministers and civic leaders who shaped the history of Greater Boston. As an adult writer, LaPlante made these stories of the lives of her ancestors the subject of her inquiry. Just as Hawthorne had dug into the dark history of his ancestry, which reached back both to the original Boston settlement of the 1630s and to the Salem Witch Trials of the 1690s, so too did LaPlante trace family members who were rooted in the same eras. Anne Hutchinson was excommunicated as a heretic from the Church of Boston and banished in 1638. (In 1922 a statue of Hutchinson was erected on the grounds of the Massachusetts State House. In 1945 the legislature voted to revoke her banishment.) LaPlante came to see her great-grandmother, ten generations back, much as Hawthorne did: as a free-thinking heroine who set herself against the righteous, repressive powers of the Puritan theocracy. After writing *American Jezebel* (2004) on Anne Hutchinson, LaPlante went on to rehabilitate the reputation of another distant ancestor, Samuel Sewall, one of the nine judges—along with Nathaniel Hawthorne's ancestor John Hathorne—who condemned thirty citizens to death for witchcraft in Salem in 1692. In *Salem Witch Judge* (2007) LaPlante celebrates Sewall's Boston repentance in 1697, his rich journal, and his powerful essays advocating the rights of women, native Americans, and slaves. Hawthorne took shame upon himself for the misdeeds of his Puritan ancestors, and LaPlante offers praise for her forebears who testified against Puritan repression. As her prefaces to these biographies, a kind of spiritual autobiography, show, Anne Hutchinson and Samuel Sewall were not the dark Puritans many imagined them to be. They remain living presences, even models of rectitude, particularly for Greater Bostonians, into the twenty-first century. Indeed Boston has been continually reimagined, reconfigured, and replenished since its settlement in 1630. Boston, then, remains an open book in which the city's story continues to be written.

As Boston changes, so too is it continually transformed in our imaginations. In "Night Watch in the City of Boston," a poem commemorating the American Bicentennial, Archibald MacLeish, Harvard Boylston Professor of Rhetoric and Oratory, saw Boston as the "City of God" transformed into the "City of Man." It has also been reimagined and renamed "The Good City" because, in the words of Paul S. Grogan, president and CEO of the Boston Foundation, "Boston is wonderfully, dynamically alive. And it is alive above all else because the city understood how to restore and replenish what is special and distinctive about the urban experience."[59] Other than a fixed city upon a hill, Boston has been a city in constant flux, subject to transformation and redefinition. In *The Paradise of All These Parts* (2008), naturalist

John Hanson Mitchell imagines Boston as "an unreal city, a mere illusion that rises on this glacier-battered coast with false self-assurance, as if it were the hub of a great wheel and permanent in its centrality. I knew enough of geology by then to know that all is flux and that the land is as shifting and fluid as a wisp of morning mist."[60]

As we have seen, Boston has stood as the city upon a hill, the hub of the solar system, and other, less flattering images. The city and the region have been reshaped in "a continual process of invention and reinvigoration," as Joseph A. Conforti puts it in *Imagining New England.* Yet Boston remains, as it was at its founding, a city of aspiration, particularly for its writers.[61] As Patricia Powell puts it in "A Literary Landscape: From Jamaica to Boston," this is "the city where I have met, one by one, all of the people who would propel me in the direction of a literary life, the city where I would develop all the tools necessary to live out the writer's life."[62] Powell arrived in Boston from Jamaica at age sixteen, in the early 1980s, alone and "terrified." She could not then realize that she was reenacting a passage that linked her with other newcomers to Boston, a transit that reaches back to Anne Bradstreet, whose "heart rose" when in 1630 she saw the stark, unpromising landscape that would become Boston. Bradstreet accommodated herself to the new land, made the city her own, and, like so many after her, moved away and wrote about it. Powell too accepted that "this wintry city was to be my home and the place where another phase of my life was beginning, and I felt that my only choice was to settle down into the new existence, in this unknown city that was said by everyone to be a place full of opportunities."[63] Though most of her fiction is set in Jamaica, Powell remains in Greater Boston, writing and teaching creative writing at Massachusetts Institute of Technology. So Boston, this wintry city, this city made famous through its writings, remains, as it has for nearly four centuries, a place of opportunity, a home.

Boston, set on an exposed peninsula in a harsh climate, has been a stern city, as Nathaniel Hawthorne reminds us in the opening pages of *The Scarlet Letter,* when he portrays a hard-faced, judgmental crowd awaiting a terrified "sinner" to emerge from the prison and receive her punishment. Despite John Winthrop's statement of Boston's noble mission and the periodic restatement of that ideal over four centuries, Bostonians have continued to ban those they deemed heretics, as they have continued to persecuted and discriminate against those of different races, ethnic groups, and religions.

Perhaps the city's low point came on April 5, 1976, during an anti–Civil Rights protest on the Plaza outside City Hall. There Joseph Rakes, a white teenager wielding an American flag like a spear, lunged at Theodore Landsmark, an African American attorney who happened to be passing by a demonstration protesting court-ordered school integration. A photograph in the *Boston Herald America*, by Stanley Forman, became nationally famous, shaming the city.[64]

But Boston, as we have seen, has become a gentler, more diverse and tolerant city. It has lost the dubious distinction of being called "proper Boston," where books were banned and outsiders need not apply for inclusion, and it has attracted a richness of colors, tones, tastes, and modes of expression. Boston's citizenry no longer gathers in a single-minded congregation. The city upon a hill has spread, diversified, and become, at long last, playful as well as purposeful.

On a walkway of the Boston Public Garden, arrayed over thirty-five feet, stands *Make Way for Ducklings*, a bronze representation of a mother duck leading her eight ducklings toward the pond. Installed in 1987 by the Friends of the Boston Public Garden, the exhibit, created by Nancy Schon, is a tribute to Robert McCloskey's children's book, a best-seller since it was published in 1941. His *Make Way for Ducklings* shows Mr. and Mrs. Mallard seeking a home in Boston, which seems at first a hostile environment, particularly its threatening traffic. However, with the help of a friendly (apparently Irish American) policeman, they are able to cross busy Beacon Street and locate a safe haven on an island in the Public Garden pond. Designed in 1850 by George F. Meacham to reflect the Serpentine in London's Hyde Park, the gracefully curving pond of some four acres was variously known as the Lagoon, the Pond, the Duck Pond, the Lake, even "the Mimic Sea"—a small body of water enclosed by a public park artfully composed of landfill taken from Boston's hills. This pond and its encircling garden replaced a mudflat when Bostonians reconceived and reshaped their urban landscape.[65] In McCloskey's parable of a redemptive Boston, "the ducklings liked the new island so much that they decided to live there. All day long they follow the swan boats and eat peanuts."[66] E. B. White offered another fable of Bostonian acceptance in *The Trumpet of the Swan* (1970), where he portrays Louis, a Trumpeter Swan who, though born without a voice, overcomes his disability by learning to play a trumpet. Louis gets a job leading the swan boats.

Everyone wanted to ride the Swan Boats behind a real live swan playing a trumpet. It was the biggest happening in Boston in a long time. People *like* strange events and queer happenings, and the Swan Boat, with Louis out front leading the way, suddenly became the most popular attraction in Boston.[67]

From the Hub of the Solar System to a haven for odd ducks and disabled swans, Boston continues to be an inspiration for its writers, its symbolic center now shifted from Beacon Hill to the Public Garden Lagoon, where ducks, real and imaginary, float freely around the swan boats. The story of Boston, inscribed by writers from John Winthrop to Robert Lowell, revised over nearly four centuries, remains an unfinished story.

SELECTIONS

Arthur C. Inman, from *The Inman Diary: A Public and Private Confession* (1985)

Arthur Crew Inman (1895–1963), a reclusive, eccentric Bostonian, kept his 17-million word diary from 1919 to 1963. In the words of Daniel Aaron, who edited the diary for publication, "Boston figures primarily as a backdrop for the Diary's 'plot.'" Inman's "plot" reveals his voyeuristic observation and disapproval of most Bostonians.

July 10, 1920: This minute in from an hour's ride to South Boston and City Point/ It is over 90 degrees. I had an idea that there would be more or less a crowd over there along the drive and in swimming, as it is always cool. A crowd? There was a mob. It was an interesting sight.

South Boston has a reputation for being a rough place. It is filled with Irish. In fact, nearly every face you see is either Irish, Italian or Jewish. It is strange how Jews do love to swim. Perhaps it is cheaper than taking a bath at home. It was on the whole a pretty hard-looking crowd, consisting for the most part of working girls dressed in their cheap-looking best and working men whose straw hats almost invariably were tilted to one side or the other. These paraded up and down the walk, sat on the benches or the sand, or found places on the grass on the other side of the drive. Here some were merely sitting, some sitting and talking, some lying full length asleep—all at their ease under the shade. Many mothers were robing or disrobing their children preparatory to swimming. Some parties were eating lunches. In one place three girls were sitting talking (one of them tipped backwards facing the drive, hugging her knees with both hands, so that her legs were visible to every passer-by). Here a large-breasted Italian woman was suckling her infant. Here a man in a swimming suit was propped against a tree with a girl in the scantiest of clothes leaning most suggestively over him. She grinned mockingly at us as we passed. Here were a man and a girl dismounted from a motorcycle, drinking some villainous-appearing red drink by turns out of a bottle, the girl in man's clothes and leggings, her hair bobbed. Here was a Jew, fat and perspiring, helping his wife, also fat, out of a small Ford. And here was a girl in a pink bathing suit tossing a ball to a very sunburned man who wore a very infatuated look upon his face.

February 27, 1938: Overcast. Sunday. Streets without traffic have appearance of being wide. Columbus Avenue. Houses that once were fine look more squalid with neglect than houses which never were fine. Negroes living in the houses that once were fine, sauntering the streets with the air of being in their own African village, idling before poolrooms and drugstores. The mansion with the carved lion recumbent before it is now a colored undertaking establishment. Before that it was a religious meeting place. Before that it was empty. The building still beautiful, though soiled. A nurse in black, a child with golden curls, a man wearing a top hat, a woman in silks should be coming down those red sandstone stairs which turn so gracefully, and an equipage with jingling harness should be waiting at the curb. But that is fancy. Down the steps comes a small black negro with oiled hair.

December 23, 1938: I have been reading 'The Rise of Silas Lapham' by William Dean Howells. Twenty years ago, this American classic would have bored me. Now to my surprise I find myself enjoying it immensely. It is a novel about life in Boston and the social adjustments between old blue-bloods and rich new-bloods. Lately I have reread the remainder of 'The Oregon Trail' and all of 'Two Years Before the Mast.' Those old Bostonians certainly thought well of themselves. They were, in their own minds at least, the salt of the earth. In large measure the secure fortunes of the nation were centered in Boston. The elite of the city felt themselves to be the social and cultural arbiters of America. Behind them were Emerson and Thoreau, Holmes and Longfellow, Dana and Parkman and Ticknor and Prescott. They were snobs and proud of it. Bryce called their debates in their Bullfinch State House the finest in the world. The Bostonians of the last century must have been charming among themselves and in the presence of foreigners (whom they considered their equals or their superiors) but insufferable to others outside their circle—insufferable, condescending and boorish.

Samuel Eliot Morison, from *One Boy's Boston* (1962)

Samuel Eliot Morison (1887–1976) is represented in a statue on the Commonwealth Avenue Mall as an "Admiral" because of his service in

World War II and his compilation of *The History of the United States Operations in World War II* (1947–1962) in fifteen volumes. He taught history at Harvard and wrote many other books, including *The Oxford History of the United States* (1927). In *One Boy's Boston* Morison portrays his idyllic Beacon Hill boyhood and defends his class against critics, those "gossip columnists and novelists masquerading as historians."

THOSE ALLEGED PREJUDICES

What of opinions and prejudices, political and social? There I have a bone to pick with gossip columnists and novelists masquerading as historians. According to them, Boston society was stuffy, provincial, purse-proud, prejudiced, and one hundred percent Republican. So far as my observations go, it was none of these. My grandfather and father were independents, then known as "mugwamps." The first mention I remember of politics was Grandfather talking with marketmen, bewailing the fact that McKinley instead of Thomas B. Reed won the Republican nomination for President in 1896. Grover Cleveland was regarded as the best President since Abraham Lincoln; and we all knew by heart this ditty, to help memorize the names of the presidents:

> WASHINGTON *first of all the Presidents stands,*
> *Next placid John Adams attention commands;*
> *Thomas Jefferson's third on the glorious score,*
> *And square Jimmy Madison comes number four,*
> *Fifth on the list is plain James Monroe,*
> *And John Quincy Adams is sixth—don't you know?*
> *After Jackson comes Martin Van Buren, true blood,*
> *Then Harrison, hero of Tippecanoe.*
> *Then Tyler, the first of the Vice's to rise;*
> *Then Polk, and then Taylor, the second who dies.*
> *Then Fillmore, a Vice, takes the president's place*
> *And small Franklin Pierce is fourteenth in the race.*
> *Fifteenth is Buchanan; and following him*
> *The great name of* LINCOLN *makes all others dim.*
> *After Johnson comes Grant, with the laurel and the bays,*
> *And following him is one Rutherford B. Hayes.*
> *Then Garfield, then Arthur, then Cleveland the fat;*

Then Harrison wearing his grand-daddy's hat.
Adroit little Ben, twenty-third in the train;
And following him, the bold CLEVELAND *again.*

My father, a member of the Civil Service Reform Association and the Tariff Reform League, and a contributor to Godkin's New York *Nation,* ran for the City Council in 1892 as a Democrat, and for representative in the General Court four years later, as in Independent. His candidacy, in the latter instance, was endorsed by such men as Major Henry L. Higginson, William Minot, and Dr. Maurice H. Richardson, the celebrated surgeon. The *Boston Evening Transcript* even promoted him in an editorial. In both contests he was defeated; in the latter by the regular Republican candidate, a Negro. This did not, however, create any race prejudice in the 44 Brimmer Street household.

My description of the social life may have created the impression that our family at 44 Brimmer Street lived only for calls and parties. That would not be correct. Grandfather worked many hours at his desk on the affairs of the Massachusetts General Hospital, the McLean Hospital, the Perkins Institute for the Blind and other major charities of which he was director or chairman of the board and he often visited them, sometimes with little me in tow. It was thus that I met the remarkable Helen Keller. The Boston Public School Association, which for many years did keep the schools out of politics, was organized in our library. My grandmother and mother were particularly interested in the Society for the Prevention of Cruelty to Children. My father and mother frequently attended hearings at the State House to support or oppose some pending bill. One which they vigorously advocated was a bill to prevent the taking out of life insurance on very young children. Workers of the S.P.C.C. found that insurance agents were working over the slums, persuading parents to take out policies on babes and sucklings for a few cents a day; the prize being that if the poor child died the insurance would pay for a swell funeral. In effect, children were being denied food so that they could be buried in style. I well remember my parents' indignation over this state of affairs, and their scornful imitation of a prominent Republican politician, a friend of theirs too, who defended the insurance company: "Nobody would be so croo-el as to deny food to a little che-ild!"

Nor was there, among Bostonians we knew, any of the snobbish eighteenth century despising of "trade," which persisted, though in an attenuat-

ed form, in other cities. Most of the families we knew were professional people or bankers, but many were not, and almost everyone, including the Eliots
and the Otises, had mercantile ancestors, whose advertisements you could
read in the old *Columbian Continental*. Aunt Leslie Morison, one of Boston's
great ladies, was the daughter of a wholesale grocer, and it was observed
with tolerant amusement that her son Mac, my pal, started a little "store" in
a room of their Commonwealth Avenue house, where he made a tidy profit
selling spools of thread and similar household requirements to his mother
and her friends, at a markup of one cent. Boston's most famous lady, Mrs.
Jack Gardner, derived the fortune that built Fenway Court from Stewart's
department store in New York. Here I may cite an exception that provoked
general mirth. At the Museum of Fine Arts may now be seen the portrait by
John Singleton Copley of Paul Revere at his workbench, making one of
those silver teapots for which he became famous before he took to dispatch
riding for the Sons of Liberty. The Revere family of Canton, who owned this
portrait, were ashamed of it "because it showed Mr. Revere in his shirt-
sleeves, like a common workman," kept it in the attic, and allowed it to be
exhibited but once in the last century.

Within the Boston society in which I grew up there were no distinctions
of wealth. We were vaguely conscious our families were "top drawer,"
although there was not yet any Social Register to tell us so. One you were
"in," more or less wealth made no difference. Captain John Bigelow USA,
and his beautiful wife, who was Mary Dallam of Baltimore, came to Boston
in 1894, he having been assigned by the Army to teach at M.I.T. They had
nothing but army pay to live on, and dwelt in a modest wooden house near
Coolidge Corner, but they went everywhere, although unable to "pay back"
with anything more than good conversation and charm; and their children,
who went to public school, were among my best friends. It was not until I
went to St. Paul's School, then favored by Pittsburgh and New York million-
aires, that I encountered the notion that one's social rating depended on
such externals as steam yachts, stables of race horses and Newport "cottages." It is true that Boston society was too simple to attract bloated "gate-
crashers"; nor did it breed multimillionaires. People such as they stormed
the social citadels of New York, Washington, Newport and London.

Social status, which, according to Vance Packard [in *The Status Seekers*,
1959], every American seeks to win (or, if he has it, to keep) did not trouble
us or our friends for a moment. New families were being accepted every year.

The way to get in was to buy a town house on Commonwealth Avenue or Beacon Street, and a place on the North Shore, and send your children to private schools in the Back Bay. A certain minimum of breeding and manners were required, and that minimum, I believe, was much higher than in New York; possibly lower than in Philadelphia or Baltimore. Ancestry did not count in the least. Many families of ancient lineage dropped out of society simply because they did not care to incur the expense and trouble incident on dining out constantly. I remember my mother saying of one mousy little lady, "Poor Mary, she wouldn't make an effort, so now nobody calls on her." And there was no social institution in Boston like the Philadelphia Assembly or the Baltimore Bachelors' Cotillion, to which one simply *had* to belong to be "in." The Boston Assembly, a take-it-or-leave-it affair, was given up after World War I.

Bostonians, according to the novelists, were supposed to be highly race-conscious, bigoted Protestants, nasty to the Irish. I never heard any of that. Both sides of my family were proud of their Irish blood; the Morisons had a transmitted story of the 1689 Siege of Londonderry, in which their first American ancestors spent hours watching a rathole in the hope of catching his dinner. George Duncan, ancestor of the Eliots, was one of the founders of the Charitable Irish Society. In close daily contact as we were with Irish maids and workmen, we could believe no ill of the Irish; and my grandmother, after visiting friends in Ireland, used to tell everyone, "The Irish gentleman is the world's finest gentleman." The family was, to be sure, down on corrupt Irish politicians, but it was down on corruption of any kind, by no matter whom. The one man whose name (as I remember) roused their anger and contempt was General Benjamin F. Butler, that "hero" of New Orleans and Bermuda Hundred. A hardy perennial bill offered in the General Court was to provide an equestrian statue of General Butler in the State House grounds. It was first promoted by William L. Reed, the Negro who defeated my father; and later by Martin Lomasney, boss of old Ward 8. Grandfather used to say that if ever a statue were erected to "that rascal Butler" in the State House grounds, he would sell 44 Brimmer Street and move out of the Commonwealth.

There are fashions in churches, as in everything else; and it was rumored that ambitious ladies from the outer periphery joined the "right" church in order to meet the "right" people. The Anglo-Catholic Church of the Advent, on the corner of Mt. Vernon and Brimmer Streets, north of our house, was not at all fashionable; but I should hate to think that my parents and grand-parents left it for that reason. Phillips Brooks (I can just remember seeing Bishop Brooks, as he then was, on a street, a majestic figure in frock coat, white tie and top hat) was probably responsible for their being drawn to Trinity Church; he was not only a personal friend, but the most eloquent and inspiring preacher Boston has ever heard. The Church of the Advent, in my childhood, had as rector the rather severe, ascetic Dr. Frisbie. Services at Trinity, in those days, were decidedly "low"; there was no altar, only a communion table, no vested choir of boys and men, but an adult quartet who occupied the gallery at the west end, behind the congregation. Since I was not interested in sermons, it was a treat for me occasionally to be taken by my mother to the Church of the Advent, where one had the beauty of the traditional ritual, and superlatively good music.

Friendships, however, were not sectarian; most of our friends were Uni-tarians, and attended King's Chapel or the Arlington Street Church or the First Church in Boston. All the Eliots except my grandparents were Unitar-ians. Kings Chapel was a peculiar compromise worked out by conscientious New Englanders who couldn't take the doctrine of the Trinity, yet yearned for beauty and tradition in worship. So they got up a special edition of the Book of Common Prayer, with references to the Trinity and the Divinity of Jesus deleted. A traveling Englishman who strayed into King's Chapel one Sunday shortly after met President Eliot, and complained that the service seemed "expurgated," to which "Prexy" retorted severely, "Not expurgated, *washed*."

The brick church designed by Asher Benjamin and built in 1807, at the corner of Charles and Mt. Vernon Streets, has passed through the hands of a number of sects. During my childhood it was African Methodist, serving the respectable colored community that lived on the northern slope of Bea-con Hill. After most of the West End Negroes moved to Roxbury—a change they must have regretted—the Charles Street meeting house became for a time a community church, and is now Universalist. When I asked Grandfa-ther to tell me the difference between Unitarians and Universalists, he replied, "The Universalists believe that God it too good to damn anyone, but the Unitarians believe that they are too good for God to damn!"

A branch of the Otis family were Roman Catholics, and we respected that ancient faith even though we did not embrace it. The only thing I every heard of the American Protective Association, the "A.P.A." which tried to revive the anti-Catholic Know-Nothingism of the 1850's, was a ditty we used to sing.

> *Where is the mick that threw the brick?*
> *He'll never throw another—*
> *For calling me an A.P.A.*
> *He now is under cover!*

As for anti-Semitism, I never even heard of it. My father died before the furor about Louis D. Brandeis's appointment to the Supreme Court; but I expect he would have approved, as he admired Brandeis professionally, and as our neighbor at 4 Otis Place, we often talked with him. I do not believe that our family was exceptionally liberal. If they had been regarded as mavericks, a small boy would certainly have heard thereof in a disagreeable way. It was simply that nineteenth century liberalism, an atmosphere of live and let live, was the climate of opinion in that time and place.

Another favorite cliché of latter-day gossip columnists is that Beacon society was fanatically pro-British, aped the English aristocracy, and all that. My recollections are all to the contrary; and one of my boyhood friends from New York, a girl who married a Bostonian, told me that the one thing that struck her on coming here was that Boston was still fighting the War of Independence. The traditions of the American Revolution were central to my upbringing; memorials and landmarks of it were all about. Popular extracurricular reading was Charles Carleton Coffin's *Boys of '76*—Philip Weld told me that I must read it, or fight him! I was proud of Faneuil Hall and the Adamses, highly approved the Cleveland-Olney diplomatic sock-in-the-jaw to Lord Salisbury, firmly believe America to be the best country and Boston the finest city on earth; and that the United States Navy, having "licked England twice," could do so again, if necessary. It was only after growing up that I began to entertain feelings of kindness and admiration toward our mother country.

Boston society certainly was provincial in some respects—what society of a non-metropolitan city is not? But it was worldly too. Almost every family we knew had connections abroad, and in other parts of the United States, My mother, as a girl of seventeen, was taken to Germany by the William F. Apthorps, who were well know there in musical circles; she heard the *Ring* at Bayreuth, met Frau Cosima Wagner and Franz Liszt. My grandparents were then staying at the Chateau de Rabodanges in Normandy, which belonged to a French gentleman who had married an Otis. They had just been entertained by the Playfairs and Sir Richard Temple in London, and might well have continued to Florence, where they had friends among the American artistic community described by Van Wyck Brooks in *The Dream of Arcadia*. It was the same in the United States. Hospitable houses were open to us in New York, Philadelphia, Baltimore and Washington; and when I visited the far west in 1904, I was passed on from one family friend or cousin to another in Arizona and California.

Someone explaining the decay of American cities since 1940 observed that we had no solid core of nobility and bourgeois, as in Amsterdam, Strasbourg, Bordeaux, Bristol, and Milan, who insisted on living in town, interested themselves in local politics and supported cultural activities. But Boston had just that sort of group in my childhood. Not nobility, of course, but families who endowed Harvard and other universities, founded the Museum of Fine Arts, the Symphony Orchestra and the Opera House, and took pride in supporting great charitable foundations such as the Perkins Institute for the Blind and the Massachusetts General Hospital. And Boston had something more than that. Despite all the sneers and jeers at "Proper Bostonians," "Boston Brahmins" and the like, there was a remarkable pattern of living here that existed nowhere else in the United States. When a family had accumulated a certain fortune, instead of trying to build it up to further to become a Rockefeller or Carnegie or Huntington and then perhaps discharge its debt to society by some great foundation, it would step out of business or finance and try and try to accomplish something in literature, education, medical research, the arts, or public service. Generally one or two members of the family continued in business, to look after the family securities and enable the creative brothers or cousins to carry on without the handicap of poverty. Of course there were families like that in other cities, but in Boston there were so many of them as to constitute a recognized way of life. One only has to think of the Prescott, Parkman Shattuck, Cabot, Holmes, Lowell, Forbes, Peabody, Eliot, Saltonstall and Sargent families and what they have accomplished for the beauty and betterment of life, to see what I mean.

For this atmosphere I am deeply grateful, for it was never suggested that "Sammy" should go into business, or make money, or do anything but what his tastes and talents impelled him to do, no matter how unremunerative. By way of contrast, my best friend at St. Paul's School was a New Yorker, who went to Yale. He had a nice talent for writing—made *Yale Lit.* in college—and also at painting; and he had far more wealth behind him than I. But, when we talked over life on summer cruises, and I outlined what I hoped to accomplish with my pen, he shook his head sadly over my urgings that he become a writer or an artist. It was expected of him, he said rather wistfully, that he go on the New York Stock Exchange in order to keep his family's financial standing at a high level. He did just that, and has had a pretty miserable time in so doing.

Robert Lowell, from "91 Revere Street" (1959) and "For the Union Dead" (1960)

Robert Lowell (1917–1977) was descendant of two lines of Boston's first families: the Lowells and the Winslows. He was related to poets James Russell Lowell and Amy Lowell. Beginning with *Lord Weary's Castle* (1946) and climaxing in *Life Studies* (1959), Lowell drew upon his family's past to reimagine Boston, as had Hawthorne before him.

FROM "91 REVERE STREET"

In 1924 people still lived in cities. Late that summer, we bought the 91 Revere Street house, looking out on an unbuttoned part of Beacon Hill bounded by the North End slums, though reassuringly only four blocks away from my Grandfather Winslow's brown pillared house at 18 Charles Street. In the decades preceding and following the First World War, old Yankee families had upset expectation by regaining this section of the Hill from the vanguards of the lace-curtain Irish. This was bracing news for my parents in that topsy-turvy era when the Republican Party and what were called "people of the right sort" were no longer dominant in city elections. Still, even in the palmy, laissez-faire '20s, Revere Street refused to be a straightforward, immutable residential fact. From one end to the other, houses kept being sanded down, repainted, or abandoned to the flaking of decay, Houses, changing hands, changed their language and nationality. A few door to our south the householders spoke "Beacon Hill British" or the flat *nay nay* of the Boston Brahmins. The parents of the children a few doors north spoke mostly in Italian.

My mother felt a horrified giddiness about the adventure of our address.

She once said, "We are hardly perched on the outer rim of the hub of decency." We were less than fifty yards from Louisburg Square, the cynosure of old historic Boston's plain-spoken, cold roast elite—the Hub of the Hub of the Universe. Fifty yards!

As a naval ensign, Father had done postgraduate work at Harvard. He had also done postgraduate work at M.I.T., preferred the purely scientific college, and condescended to both. In 1924, however, his tone began to change; he now began to speak warmly of Harvard as his second alma mater. We went to football games at the Harvard Stadium, and one had the feeling that our lives were now being lived in the brutal, fashionable expectancy of the stadium: we had so many downs, so many minutes, and so many yards to go for a winning touchdown. It was just such a winning financial and social advance that my parents promised themselves would follow Father's resignation from the Navy and his acceptance of a sensible job offered him at the Cambridge branch of Lever Brothers' Soap.

The advance was never to come. Father resigned from the service in 1927, but he never had a civilian *career*; he instead had merely twenty-two years of the civilian *life*. Almost immediately he bought a larger and more stylish house; he sold his ascetic, stove-black Hudson and bought a plump brown Buick; later the Buick was exchanged for a high-toned, as-good-as-new Packard with a custom-designed royal blue and mahogany body. Without drama, his earnings more or less decreased from year to year.

But so long as we were on Revere Street, Father tried to come to terms with it and must have often wondered whether he on the whole liked or disliked the neighborhood's lack of side. He was still at this time rather truculently democratic in what might be described as an upper middle-class, naval, and Masonic fashion. He was a mumbler. His opinions were almost morbidly hesitant, but he considered himself a matter-of-fact man of science and had an unspoiled faith in the superior efficiency of northern nations. He modeled his allegiances and humor on the cockney imperialism of Rudyard Kipling's swearing Tommies, who did their job. Autochthonous Boston snobs, such as the Winslows or members of Mother's reading club, were alarmed by the brassy callousness of our naval visitors, who labeled the Italians they met on Revere Street as "grade-A" and "grade-B wops." The Revere Street "grade-B's" were Sicilian Catholics and peddled crummy second-hand furniture on Cambridge Street, not far from the site of Great-

great-Grandfather Charles Lowell's disused West Church, praised in an old family folder as "a haven from the Sodom and Gomorrah of Trinitarian orthodoxy and the tyranny of the letter." Revere Street "grade-A's," good North Italians, sold fancy groceries and Colonial heirlooms in their shops near the Public Garden. Still other Italians were Father's familiars; they sold him bootleg Scotch and *vino rosso* in teacups.

The outside of our Revere Street house was a flat red brick surface unvaried by the slightest suggestion of purple panes, delicate bay, or triangular window-cornice—a sheer wall formed by the seamless conjunction of four inseparable facades, all of the same commercial and purgatorial design. Though placed in the heart of Old Boston, it was ageless and artless, an epitome of those "leveler" qualities Mother found most grueling about the naval service. 91 Revere Street was mass-produced, *regulation-issue,* and yet struck Boston society as stupidly out of the ordinary, like those white elephants—a mother-of-pearl scout knife or a tea-kettle barometer—which my father used to pick up on sale at an Army-Navy store.

The walls of Father's minute Revere Street den-parlor were bare and white. His bookshelves were bare and white. The den's one adornment was a ten-tube home-assembled battery radio set, whose loudspeaker had the shape and color of a Mexican sombrero. The radio's specialty was getting programs from Australia and New Zealand in the early morning hours.

My father's favorite piece of den furniture was his oak and "rhinoceros hide" armchair. It was ostentatiously a masculine or rather a bachelor's chair. It had a notched, adjustable back; it was black, cracked, hacked, scratched, splintered, gouged, initialed, gunpowder-charred and tumbler-ringed. It looked like pale tobacco leaves laid on dark tobacco leaves. I doubt if Father, a considerate man, was responsible for any of the marring. The chair dated from his plebe days at the Naval Academy, and had been bought from a shady, shadowy, roaring character, midshipman "Beauty" Burford. Father loved each disfigured inch. . . .

[While a Brimmer School student] one day when the saucer magnolias were in bloom [in the Public Garden], I bloodied Bulldog Binney's nose against the pedestal of George Washington's statue in full view of Commonweath Avenue; then I bloodied Dopey Dan Parker's nose; then I stood in the center of a sundial tulip bed and pelted a little enemy ring of third-graders with wet fertilizer. Officer Lever was telephoned. Officer Lever telephoned my mother. In the presence of my mother and some thirty nurses and children, I was expelled from the Public Garden. I was such a bad boy, I was told, "that *even* Officer Lever had been forced to put his foot down."

FOR THE UNION DEAD
"RELINQUUNT OMNIA SERVARE REM PUBLICAM."

The old South Boston Aquarium stands
in a Sahara of snow now. Its broken windows are boarded.
The bronze weathervane cod has lost half its scales.
The airy tanks are dry.

Once my nose crawled like a snail on the glass;
my hand tingled
to burst the bubbles
drifting from the noses of the cowed, compliant fish.

My hand draws back. I often sigh still
for the dark downward and vegetating kingdom
of the fish and reptile. One morning last March,
I pressed against the new barbed and galvanized

fence on the Boston Common. Behind their cage,
yellow dinosaur steamshovels were grunting
as they cropped up tons of mush and grass
to gouge their underworld garage.

Parking lots luxuriate like civic
sandpiles in the heart of Boston.
A girdle of orange, Puritan-pumpkin colored girders
braces the tingling Statehouse,

shaking over the excavations, as it faces Colonel Shaw
and his bell-cheeked Negro infantry
on St. Gaudens' shaking Civil War relief,
propped by a plank splint against the garage's earthquake.

Two months after marching through Boston,
half the regiment was dead;
at the dedication,
William James could almost hear the bronze Negroes breathe.

The monument sticks like a fishbone
in the city's throat.
Its colonel is as lean
as a compass-needle.

He has an angry wrenlike vigilance,
a greyhound's gentle tautness;
he seems to wince at pleasure,
and suffocate for privacy.

He is out of bounds now. He rejoices in man's lovely,
peculiar power to choose life and die—
when he leads his black soldiers to death,
he cannot bend his back.

On a thousand small town New England greens,
the old white churches hold their air
of sparse, sincere rebellion; frayed flags
quilt the graveyards of the Grand Army of the Republic.

The stone statues of the abstract Union Soldier
grow slimmer and younger each year—
wasp-waisted, they doze over muskets,
and muse through their sideburns . . .

Shaw's father wanted no monument
except the ditch,
where his son's body was thrown
and lost with his "niggers."

The ditch is nearer.
There are no statues for the last war here;
on Boylston Street, a commercial photograph
shows Hiroshima boiling

over a Mosler Safe, "the Rock of Ages"
that survived the blast. Space is nearer.
When I crouch to my television set,
the drained faces of Negro school-children rise like balloons.

Colonel Shaw
is riding on his bubble,
he waits
for the blessed break.

The Aquarium is gone. Everywhere,
giant finned cars nose forward like fish;
a savage servility
slides by on grease.

Dan Wakefield, from *Returning: A Spiritual Journey* (1985)

Dan Wakefield (1932–) has been a successful journalist, novelist, television writer, and screenwriter. In *Returning* he writes of his escape from a self-destructive life in Hollywood, his return to Boston, and his spiritual recovery at King's Chapel.

Watching the national weather forecast on "Good Morning, America," I pictured myself on the bottom left-hand corner of the map in the dot of Los Angeles and felt I had slid to the wrong hole on a giant pinball machine, wanting to tilt the whole thing so I could get back to the upper right-hand corner to Boston, where I felt pulled by internal gravity. My Southern California disorientation deepened because I no longer knew when anything happened in the course of a year since all the seasons looked the same to me; when I saw a videotape of Henry James's *The Europeans* the New England autumn leaves and sunlight falling on plain board floors brought tears to my eyes. . . .

[Boston] was succor, a feast of familiar tradition from the statues of heroes (Alexander Hamilton, William Lloyd Garrison. Samuel Eliot Morison among them) in the wide swath of Commonwealth Avenue to the long wharves on the waterfront reaching out toward Europe. Walking the brick streets of my old neighborhood on Beacon Hill, I felt in balance again with the universe, and a further pull to what seemed the center of it, the source of something I was searching for, something I couldn't name that went far beyond the satisfaction of scenery or local color. I headed like a homing pigeon to the pond in the Public Garden and, without having planned it, sat down on a bench, and at the same time that tears of gratitude came to my eyes the words of the psalm also came to mind: " . . . he leadeth me beside the still waters. He restoreth my soul."

I recited the psalm from the start and at the end said "Amen" as if it were a prayer, and it was, of thanks. It would not have occurred to me to go to any church or chapel, but the pond in the Public Garden seemed precisely the place to have offered this. . . ..

There was a calm reassurance in the stately language of litanies and chants in the Book of Common Prayer (King's Chapel is "Unitarian in theology, Anglican in worship, and Congregational in governance," a historic Boston amalgam that became three centuries old in 1986). I was grateful for the sense of shared reverence, of reaching beyond one's flimsy physical presence, while praying with a whole congregation.

The connection of church and [Beacon Hill] neighborhood reinforced one another, gave depth and dimension to the sense of "home" that I had felt so cut off from in Hollywood. Church was not just an abstraction or a separate enclave of my life but a part of the place where I lived, connected with people I knew and encountered in my daily (not just Sunday) life. I think the deep sense of pleasure and solace of *place* I derived from returning to the neighborhood was—along with my physical improvement—part of the process of calming and reassembling myself that nurtured the desire to go to church. . . .

Once I began going to church, the age-old religious rituals marking the turning of the year deepened and gave a fuller meaning to the cycle of the seasons and my own relation to them. The year was not only divided now into winter, spring, summer, and fall but was marked by the expectation of Advent, leading up to the fulfillment of Christmas, followed by Lent, the solemn prelude to the coming of the dark anguish of Good Friday that is transformed by the glory of Easter. Birth and death and resurrection, beginnings and endings and renewals, were observed and celebrated in ceremonies whose experience made me feel I belonged—not just to a neighborhood and a place, but to a larger order of things, a universal sequence of life and death and rebirth.

John Updike, "Personal Considerations" (1999)

John Updike (1932–2009)—novelist, poet, short story writer, art and literary critic—came to Greater Boston from Shillington, Pennsylvania, to study at Harvard (class of 1954). After working in Manhattan for *The New Yorker,* he settled with his family on the Massachusetts North Shore. As he notes in his most famous essay, "Hub Fans Bid Kid Adieu" (*The New Yorker,* 1960), and here in an essay that responds to the question "Why do I live in New England?" posed by the journal *The Improper Bostonian,* he was drawn to the Boston region in part by his admiration for Ted Williams, the superlative hitter who played left field for the Boston Red Sox (1939–1960).

Like many another auslander, I came here to college (Harvard) and, after testing the climate elsewhere, returned and stayed. I had married a Radcliffe girl, when there still *were* Radcliffe girls, and I thought she as well as I might prosper in the salt air and the cultural aftermath of Hawthorne and Whittier, Thoreau and Oliver Wendell Holmes. Foreign art movies were showing in Harvard Square back then, Ted Williams played left field for the Red Sox, and Cardinal Cushing ripped through the radio rosary like a buzz saw quartering a cedar of Lebanon. My objective was to see if, away from the energy-wasting, ego-eroding literary hustle of New York City, I could make my modest way as a free-lance writer, and it turned out, one year at a time, that I could. Also one year at a time, my children grew into New Englanders, and now have produced seven New England grandchildren, so that moving elsewhere, to fashionable venues like Florida or Montana, gets harder instead of easier.

When William Dean Howells left Boston for Manhattan in the 1890s, he took the last slant ray of the Emersonian heyday with him, but, in the century since, Boston has retained the aura of a place where civilization, if not dynamically generated, is affectionately regarded. Its brick raggle-taggle bespeaks of a horse-drawn past; its vast student population keeps even the mustiest neighborhoods young. Tucked in its northern suburbs, I have remained something of a Harvard boy, handing in term papers, but by mail to editors in New York. Boston's distance to New York seemed about right forty year ago and, though it has grown less, as a fifty-minute shuttle flight has replaced a five-hour train ride, still seems about right—within easy reach but beyond instant intimidation. New England is one of the oldest areas on the American map, yet, perhaps because so many have left it for flatter farmland and broader avenues, it still has space within it, where a man can breathe and a writer can write.

Eve LaPlante, Introduction, *American Jezebel* (2004)

Eve LaPlante (1959–), journalist and descendant of Boston's original settlers, has explored her family and regional past in two biographies of Greater Boston worthies: *American Jezebel: The Uncommon Life of Anne Hutchinson, the Woman Who Defied the Puritans* (2004) and *Salem Witch Judge: The Life and Repentance of Samuel Sewall* (2007). If contemporary Boston is, as she says, a palimpsest, a written-over manuscript version of seventeenth-century Boston, then her biographies offer revised readings of the exemplary lives of her ancestors and of Boston.

One warm Saturday morning in March, as I let my children out of our minivan alongside a small road in rural Rhode Island, a part of America we'd never visited before, a white pickup truck rolled to a stop beside us. Leaving my baby buckled in his car seat, I turned to the truck's driver, a middle-aged man with gray hair. "This is where Rhode Island was founded, you know," he said to me. "Right here. This is where Anne Hutchinson came.

"And you know what?" the friendly stranger added, warming to his subject. "A lady came here all the way from Utah last summer, and she was a descendant of Anne Hutchinson's."

For a moment I wondered how to reply. "See those girls there?" I said, pointing at my three daughters, who watched us from a grassy spot beside the dirt road. "They're Anne Hutchinson's descendants too."

In fact, I had driven my children from Boston to Portsmouth, Rhode Island, to explore the place that their eleventh great-grandmother, expelled from Massachusetts for heresy, had settled in 1638.

Anne Hutchinson is a local hero to the man in the pickup. But most Americans know little about her save her name and the skeleton of her story. To be sure, Hutchinson merits a mention in every textbook of American history. A major highway outside New York City, the Hutchinson River Parkway, bears her name. And a bronze statue of her stands in front of the Massachusetts State House near that of President John F. Kennedy. Yet Hutchinson herself has never been widely understood or her achievements appreciated and recognized.

In a world without religious freedom, civil rights, or free speech—the colonial world of the 1630s that was the seed of the modern United States—Anne Hutchinson was an American visionary, pioneer, and explorer who epitomized the religious freedom and tolerance that are essential to the nation's character. From the first half of the seventeenth century, when she sailed with her husband and their eleven children to Massachusetts Bay Colony, until at least the mid-nineteenth century, when Susan B. Anthony and others campaigned for female suffrage, no woman has left as strong an impression on politics in America as Anne Hutchinson. In a time when no woman could vote, teach outside the home, or hold public office, she had the intellect, courage, and will to challenge the judges and ministers who founded and ran Massachusetts. Threatened by her radical theology and her formidable political power, these men brought her to trial for heresy, banished her from the colony, and excommunicated her from the Puritan church. Undeterred, she cofounded a new American colony (her Rhode Island and Roger Williams's Providence Plantation later joined as the Colony of Rhode Island), becoming the only woman ever to do so. Unlike many prominent women in American politics, such as Abigail Adams and Eleanor Roosevelt, Hutchinson did not acquire power because of her husband. She was strong in her own right, not the wife of someone stronger, which may have been one reason she had to be expunged.

Anne Hutchinson is a compelling biographical subject because of her personal complexity, the many tensions in her life, and the wide-spread uncertainty about the details of her career. But there is more to her story. Because early New England was a microcosm of the modern Western world, the issues Anne Hutchinson raised—gender equality, civil rights, the nature and evidence of salvation, freedom of conscience, and the right to free speech—remain relevant to the American people four centuries later. Hutchinson's bold engagement in religious, political, and moral conflict early in our history helped to shape how American women see ourselves today—in marriages, in communities, and in the larger society.

Beside being a feminist icon, Hutchinson embodied a peculiarly American certainty about the distinction between right and wrong, good and evil—a certainty shared by the colonial leaders who sent her away. Cast out by men who themselves had been outcasts in their native England, Hutchinson is a classic rebel's rebel, revealing how quickly outsiders can become authoritarians. The members of the Massachusetts Court removed Anne because her moral certitude was too much like their own. Her views were a mirror for their rigidity. It is ironic, the historian Oscar Handlin noted, that the Puritans "had themselves been rebels in order to put into practice their ideas of a new society. But to do so they had to restrain the rebellion of others."

Until now, views of Anne Hutchinson in American history and letters have been polarized, tending either toward disdain or exaltation. The exaltation comes from women's clubs, genealogical associations and twentieth-century feminists who honor her as America's first feminist, career woman and equal marital partner. Yet the public praise is often muted by a wish to domesticate Hutchinson. The bronze statue in Boston, for instance, portrays her as a pious mother—a little girl at her side and her eyes raised in supplication to heaven—rather than as a powerful figure standing in the Massachusetts General Court, alone before men and God.

Her detractors, starting with her neighbor John Winthrop, first governor of Massachusetts, derided her as the "instrument of Satan," the new Eve, and the "enemy of the chosen people." In summing her up, Winthrop called her "this *American Jezebel*"—the emphasis is his—making an epithet of the name that any Puritan would recognize as belonging to the most evil and shameful woman in the Bible. Hutchinson haunted Nathaniel Hawthorne, who used her as a model for Hester Prynne, the adulterous heroine of *The Scarlet Letter*. Early in this 1850 novel, Hutchinson appears at the door of the Boston prison.

> This rose-bush, by a strange chance, has been kept alive in history; but whether it had merely survived out of the stern old wilderness, so long after the fall of the gigantic pines and oaks that overshadowed it,—or whether, as there is fair authority for believing, it had sprung up under the footsteps of the sainted Ann ["sic"] Hutchinson, as she entered the prison-door,—we shall not take upon us to determine. Finding it so directly on the threshold of our narrative, which is now about to issue from that

inauspicious portal, we could hardly do otherwise than pluck one of its flowers and present it to the reader.

Hutchinson never "entered the prison-door" in Boston, as Hawthorne imagines, but she is rightly "a rose at the threshold" of a narrative that is itself a sort of prison.

"Mrs. Hutchinson," Hawthorne's eponymous story in *Tales and Sketches*, depicts her as rebellious, arrogant, fanatical, and deeply anxiety provoking. "It is a place of humble aspect where the Elders of the people are met, sitting in judgment upon the disturber of Israel," as Hawthorne envisions her 1637 trial. "The floor of the low and narrow hall is laid with planks hewn by the axe,— the beams of the roof still wear the rugged bark with which they grew up in the forest, and the hearth is formed of one broad unhammered stone, heaped with logs that roll their blaze and smoke up a chimney of wood and clay."

Apparently unaware that the Cambridge, Massachusetts, meeting-house that served as Hutchinson's courtroom had no hearth, Hawthorne continues,

A sleety shower beats fitfully against the window, driven by the November blast, which comes howling onward from the northern desert, the boisterous and unwelcome herald of the New England winter. Rude benches are arranged across the apartment and along its sides, occupied by men whose piety and learning might have entitled them to seats in those high Councils of the ancient Church, whence opinions were set forth to confirm or supersede the Gospel in the belief of the whole world and of posterity— Here are collected all those blessed Fathers of the land . . .

"In the midst, and in the center of all eyes," Hawthorne imagines, "we see the Woman." His Anne Hutchinson "stands lofty before her judges with a determined brow. . . . They question her, and her answers are ready and acute; she reasons with them shrewdly, and brings scripture in support of every argument; the deepest controversialists of that scholastic day find here a woman, whom all their trained and sharpened intellects are inadequate to foil."

In *Prophetic Women*, a trenchant analysis of Hutchinson's role in America's self-image, Amy Schrager Lang observes, "As a heretic, Hutchinson opposed orthodoxy; as a woman, she was pictured as opposing the founding fathers, who, for later generations, stood as heroes in the long foreground of the American Revolution. In the most extreme version of her story, Hutchinson would thus come to be seen as opposing the very idea of America." A woman who wielded public power in a culture suspicious of such power, she exemplifies why there are so few women, even today, in American politics, and why no woman has attained the presidency.

Unlike most previous commentators, I aim neither to disdain nor to exalt my central character. I strive instead for a balanced portrait of Anne Hutchinson's life and thought, in all their complexity, based on painstaking research into all available documents, which are extensive considering she was a middle-class woman living in a wilderness four centuries ago. I've had the pleasure of visiting all the sites of her life—in Lincolnshire and London; in Boston, England, and Boston, Massachusetts; and in Rhode Island and New York. In rural England I climbed the steps to the pulpit where her father preached and sat on a bench in the sixteenth-century schoolroom where he taught village boys to read Latin, English and Greek. I walked on the broad timbers of the manor house that was being built as twenty-one-year-old Anne and her new husband returned from adolescent years spent in London to the Lincolnshire town of Alford to start a family. I touched the plague stone that Alfordians covered with vinegar, their only disinfectant, during the 1620 epidemic that killed one in four of the town's residents. In the Lincolnshire Wolds I explored Rigsby Wood, where she took her children to see the bluebells bloom each May. Back in the States, I kayaked to an isolated beach on a Rhode Island cove where she lived in the colony she founded, and I rode on horseback through the North Bronx woods to the vast glacial stone marking the land on which she built her final farmstead.

I first heard of Anne Hutchinson when I was a child and my great-aunt Charlotte May Wilson of Cape Cod, an avid keeper of family trees, told me that Hutchinson was my grandmother, eleven generations back. Aunt Charlotte was a character in her own right, a crusty Victorian spinster with Unitarian and artistic leanings, a proud great-granddaughter of the Reverend Samuel Joseph May, a niece of the nineteenth-century painter Eastman Johnson, and a fist cousin to Louisa May Alcott. Longtime proprietor of the Red Inn, in Provincetown, Massachusetts, Aunt Charlotte served tea and muffins every morning to her guests, including me. Evenings, after the sun set over Race Point Beach, she would nurse a gin and tonic and read aloud from her impressive collection of browning, brittle-paged volumes of poetry. When she recited Vachel Lindsay's "The Congo"—"Mumbo-jumbo will hoo-doo you. . . . Boomlay, boomlay, boomlay, boom!"—her aging eyes closed and her ample torso swayed.

Even earlier, curled into an armchair in her little red house across Commercial Street from the inn, hardly a block from the Provincetown rocks where the Pilgrims first set foot on this continent in November 1620, I listened to Aunt Charlotte's tale of the exploits of our shared, known ancestors. My aunt seemed to favor the abolitionist and minister Samuel Joseph May and Samuel Sewall (1652–1730), the judge who so repented of his role in condemning nineteen "witches" to death in Salem Village in 1692 that for the rest of his days he wore beneath his outer garments a coarse, penitential sackcloth. "For his partaking in the doleful delusion of that monstrous tribunal," James Savage observed in 1860, Judge Sewall "suffered remorse for long years with the highest Christian magnanimous supplication for mercy." To me, though, Anne Hutchinson was most compelling on account of her vehemence, her familiarity, and her violent death.

Once I was old enough to pore over the minute glosses around the edges of my great-aunt's handwritten genealogies, I read wide-eyed of the dramatic contours of Anne Hutchinson's life. At fifty-one, after her husband died, she moved with her young children from Rhode Island to New York, to live among the Dutch. When her Dutch neighbors, who often skirmished with local Indians, advised her to remove her family during an anticipated Siwanoy raid, she stayed put. Always an iconoclast, she had long opposed English settlers' efforts to vanquish Indian tribes. Not for the first time, she risked her life for her beliefs.

As a sixteen-year-old in high school American history class, I listened, ashamed, as my teacher described the religious sect called Antinomianism and Hutchinson's two trials. The ferocity and moral fervor I associated with her were attributes I disliked in my relatives and feared in myself. Reading about her, I'd learned that one of her heresies was knowing that she was among God's elect and then presuming that she could detect who else was too. Since then, I've come to see that this view, which her opponents imputed to her, was not hers alone. An excessive concern with one's own and others' "spiritual estate" was also typical of her judges. Salvation—who had it, who didn't—was the major issue of her day, as it may be, in various forms, today.

In my high school classroom I raised my hand despite my adolescent shame. Called on by my teacher, I blushed and said that Hutchinson was my great-great-great . . . great-grandmother. The teacher's bushy white eyebrows rose in an expression that I interpreted as horror. Not long ago, thought, I ran into him and recalled the scene. I was wrong about my reaction, he said. It was more like awe.

Now, as an adult studying Hutchinson's story, I understand his response. Among a raft of fascinating ancestors, Anne is most alluring and enigmatic. As a wife, mother, and journalist living in modern Boston—a palimpsest of the settlement where Anne had her rise and fall—I am intrigued by her life and thought. How, in a virtual wilderness, did she (like countless other women) raise a huge family while also (unlike the rest) confronting the privileged men who formed the first colony and educational center in the United States? According to Harvard University, it is she rather than John Harvard who "should be credited with the founding of Harvard College." In November 1637, just a week after her first trial and banishment, colonial leaders founded Harvard to indoctrinate young male citizens so as to prevent a charismatic radical like Hutchinson from ever again holding sway in Massachusetts, observes the Reverend Peter J. Gomes, the Plummer Professor of Christian Morals at Harvard University.

Were she alive today, Anne Hutchinson might be a minister, a politician, or a writer. Four hundred years ago, when the vast majority of women could not even write their names, how did she emerge boldly to question the leading men of the day as to the nature of salvation and grace? What fueled her self-confidence and her sustained anger at colonial authorities? Where did she find the strength of character to stand for hours before scores of seated men, parrying their every Gospel quotation, replying again and again with wit? This book is a response to those and other bedeviling questions. Through it, I hope, Anne Hutchinson may claim her rightful place as America's founding mother.

Archibald MacLeish, "Night Watch in the City of Boston" (1975)

Archibald MacLeish (1892–1983), distinguished American poet, was Harvard's Boylston Professor of Rhetoric and Oratory (1949–1962). "Night Watch in the City of Boston" commemorates the American Bicentennial in Boston. The colleagues of the opening stanzas, invoked as guides to Boston's past, are Puritan historians and Harvard professors Perry Miller and Samuel Eliot Morison.

NIGHT WATCH IN THE CITY OF BOSTON

Old colleague,
Puritan New England's famous scholar
half intoxicated with those heady draughts of God,
come walk these cobble-stones John Cotton trod,

and you, our Yankee Admiral of the Ocean Sea,
come too, come walk with me.
You know, none better, how the Bay wind blows
fierce in the soul as in the streets its ocean snows.

Lead me between you in the night, old friends,
one living and one dead, and where the journey ends
show me the city built as on a hill
John Winthrop saw long since and you see still.

I almost saw it once, a law school boy
born west beyond the Lakes in Illinois.
Walking down Milk Street in a summer dawn,
the sidewalks empty and the truckers gone,

I thought the asphalt turned to country lane
and climbed toward something, glimpsed and lost again—
some distance not of measure but of mind,
of meaning. Oh, of man, I could not find.

What city is it where the heart comes home?

City of God they called it on the hills of Rome
when empire changed to church and kings were crowned
to rule in God's name all the world around.

City of God!
Was this the city, then, of man?—
this new found city where the hope began
that Eve who spins and Adam's son who delves
might make their peace with God and rule themselves?—

this shanty city on a granite shore,
the woods behind it and the sea before,

where human hope first challenged Heaven's will
and piled a blazing beacon on a little hill?—

city where man, poor naked actor on his narrow stage,
confronted in the wilderness the God of Ages?
Lead me between you to that holy ground
where man and God contended and the hope was found.

Moses upon the Sinai in the cloud
faced God for forty days and nights and bowed;
received the Law, obedient and mute;
brought back to Israel the Decalogue of Duty.

Not so New England's prophets. When their arguments were done
they answered thundering skies with their own thunder:
"We have the Lord," wrote Hooker with his wild goose quill,
"We have the Lord in bonds for the fulfilling."

City of Man! Before the elms came down
no village in American, no prairie town,
but planted avenues of elms against the sky
to praise, to keep the promise, to remember by—

remember that small city of great men
where man himself had walked the earth again:
Warren at Bunker Hill who stood and died
not for a flag—there was none—but for human pride;

Emerson who prayed and quit the church,
choosing not Heaven's answer but the human search;
Thoreau who followed footprints in the snow
to find his own—the human journey he had still to go;

Holmes dissenting in a sordid age,
the Court against him and rich man's rage—
Holmes who taught the herd how human liberty is won:
by man alone, minority of one.

City of Man, Oh, city of the famous dead
where Otis spoke and Adams' heart was bred:
Mother of the great Republic—mother town

before the elm trees sickened and came down . . .

The darkness deepens. Shrieking voices cry
below these fantasies of glass that crowd our sky
and hatred like a whirling paper in a street
tears at itself where shame and hatred meet.

Show me, old friends, where in the darkness still
stands the great Republic on its hill!

Patricia Powell, from "A Literary Landscape: From Jamaica to Boston" (2004)

Patricia Powell (1966–) was born in Jamaica, grew up in England, and reluctantly came to Boston in 1982, a journey she recounts in "A Literary Landscape." She is the author of three novels: Me Dying Trial (1993), A Small Gathering of Bones (1994), and The Pagoda (1998).

I used to think that I became a writer by accident, that a career in economics was where I was headed until I began failing advanced economics and had to switch to English literature. But I have since come to believe that there are no accidents. That all along I was meant to be a writer. And that early childhood experience—of separation from my mother, of being raised by my great-aunt, who was perpetually on the brink of death, of the mystery surrounding my birth father, and of being united with my mother years later in a foreign country—were not accidents of birth, but were experiences meant to mark me so profoundly that they would become the grist that I would spend the next twenty years of my life milling. And I would feel too that it was no accident that the place where all of this would happen was Boston—the city where I have met, one by one, all of the people who would propel me in the direction of a literary life, the city where I would develop all the tools necessary to live out the writer's life.

We arrived at Logan [Airport] in the heart of winter, my brother and sister and I. My mother, who had fled years earlier to Boston from Jamaica to escape her marriage, and had settled here, met us at the airport. In batches of twos and threes, she had sent for her children, and my siblings and I were the last batch. She bundled us up immediately into thick warm coats, for against the fierce New England cold our flimsy clothes were like pieces of tissue paper, and hurried us out to the car waiting at the curb that would take us to the section of Boston called Dorchester. I was sixteen, and I had never before been outside Jamaica. I had never seen real snow, and from the back of the slow-moving car, it did not have the clean white powdery look I often saw on the postcards my uncle sent from Canada with money. The snow had been piled up on the sides of the road for days, and was blackened with dirt and the exhaust from many cars and trucks that hurtled by; pieces of garbage clung to the snow, and dogs, it seemed, had found neat little places to defecate.

From the front of the car, my mother bombarded us with a steady stream of questions about all the relatives and friends she had left in Jamaica. Just a few years behind me in age, Dermot and Jacqueline were happy to see her again, and they filled her in on all the details. But I didn't have answers for any of my mother's questions and even if I did, my answers were short and blunt. I was not happy to see my mother, for my mother and I were not friends. I did not understand why, of all her children, I was the one she had sent away at three months and had never reclaimed until now. And I wanted to know the details of the mystery surrounding my birth father. I didn't know these people. I had never been very friendly with any of my immediate family members, except for my older brother, and yet here I was thrust suddenly into this newly assembled, makeshift family, after sixteen years of estrangement, and in this cold, strange place. I was furious and I was desperately missing my great-aunt Nora, the woman who raise me and who was really my mother. And I was terrified. But this wintry city was to be my home and the place where another phase of my life was beginning, and I felt that my only choice was to settle down into the new existence, in this unknown city that was said by everyone to be a place full of opportunities. . . .

Our part of Dorchester near Grove Hall, on the border of Roxbury, was a predominantly working-class and black neighborhood. The Jews and Irish who once lived in this section of town had long since escaped to the suburbs, and before them, the wealthy Bostonians who had made this area their safe quiet getaway when Dorchester was still a country landscape, a retreat from the city proper. . . .

The first winter living in Boston, there never seemed to be enough light. Night came promptly at four-thirty and I was rarely ever truly warm, no matter what I wore. I thought constantly of Jamaica's long, hot, dusty days, of the everlasting heat and those rainstorms that could bear down heavily on us for five steady minutes, but in the end, roads would disappear, houses would flood, and animals would be washed away. . . . But that world was gone, and here in front of me like a rude awakening was Boston, my new home. . . .

In 2003 I was offered a job in California. I was ready to go, my books were packed up in boxes, I was already dreaming of the heat and the sun; the realtor had begun showing my place here in Boston. And then, at the last minute, I decide to stay. Just like that. I had no job lined up here. I had no love waiting. But I decided to stay, to make Boston my home. It was a leap and it required faith. But I accepted the challenge. I wanted to see if indeed I could grow wings. The year after making that decision felt like my very first year in Boston. I felt as if I was living here in this city with brand-new eyes. I moved fifteen minutes away into what feels like the country though it is only a metropolitan suburb, but there are trees around me now, and I have learned their names and the names of birds. I lived through a bitter winter, and it was as if I was seeing snow for the first time. The spring was long and wet and chilly, and summer didn't come until mid-July. Every day I watched blue jays and robins and squirrels from my kitchen windows, busy at the feeder, and one by one, I saw the birch and cherry trees clothe themselves in leaves, and I heard the boy next door striking the piano, and the neighbor's fat brown cat watched me steadily.

My mother, who now lives in Florida, recently came to visit. We took the train into downtown Boston and walked all over this famously walkable city. She wanted to see Haymarket again, the old Italian market near City Hall, where she and I used to go early on Saturday mornings to buy produce and fresh fish and goat meat and live crab for curried stew. At Faneuil Hall we stopped to have lunch, and then we wandered through the Public Gardens. We sat on a bench and admired the tall trees, the towering buildings, the thickets of flowers, and the kids on skateboards.

It is the first time that my mother has visited me since I left her yellow house in Dorchester at eighteen. It has taken us almost twenty years to get close. Patricia, she says to me, you alone here, you alone here in this cold place. You're not lonely? She pulls her sweater tighter around her, it's late June and we are still bundled up. It's my home, I say, smiling, a little alarmed at myself, for I've never said that before, that a place is my home, that Boston is my home. Not just this place where I live and work or go to school, but a place that I have chosen, a commitment that I have made to be fully present here, to be fully conscious. And in that moment I knew that for the first time, I was willing to let Jamaica recede into the background and allow Boston to emerge fully into the foreground. That I was really now to face the city and its peculiarities. I was ready finally to be here, now.

I. BOSTON, FROM WINTHROP TO HAWTHORNE

1. Nathaniel Hawthorne, *The Scarlet Letter, The Scarlet Letter: An Authoritative Text, Backgrounds and Sources, Criticism*, 2nd ed., Sculley Bradley, Richard Croom Beatty, E. Hudson Long, and Seymour Gross, eds. (1850; New York: W. W. Norton, 1961), 110.

2. Samuel Eliot Morison, *Builder of the Bay Colony* (Boston: Northeastern University Press, 1980), 135.

3. Hawthorne, *The Scarlet Letter*, 42.

4. Darrett B. Rutman, *Winthrop's Boston: A Portrait of a Puritan Town, 1630–1649* (New York: W. W. Norton, 1972), 4.

5. Ibid., 10.

6. Joseph A. Conforti, *Imagining New England: Explorations of Regional Identity from the Pilgrims to the Mid-Twentieth Century* (Chapel Hill: University of North Carolina Press, 2001), 31.

7. Cited in ibid., 37.

8. *Johnson's Wonder-working Providence, 1622–1651*, J. Franklin Jameson, ed. (New York: Barnes & Noble, 1937), 70, 76.

9. Cotton Mather, *Magnalia Christi Americana, The Norton Anthology of American Literature*, 7th ed., vol. A, Nina Baym, General Editor (New York: W. W. Norton, 2007), 320–23.

10. Cited in Conforti, *Imagining New England*, 57.

11. Rutman, *Winthrop's Boston*, 22.

12. John Winthrop, *The Journal of John Winthrop, The Norton Anthology of American Literature*, 7th ed., vol. A, 159.

13. Hawthorne, *The Scarlet Letter*, 39.

14. Hawthorne, "The Custom-House," *The Scarlet Letter*, 11.

15. Conforti, *Imagining New England*, 40.

16. Garry Wills, *Head and Heart: A History of Christianity in America* (New York: Penguin Books, 2007), 34.

17. Samuel Danforth, *A Brief Recognition of New England's Errand into the Wilderness, Writing New England: An Anthology from the Puritans to the Present*, Andrew Delbanco, ed. (Cambridge: Belknap Press of Harvard University Press, 2001), 12–17.

18. Anne Bradstreet, "To My Dear Children," *The Works of Anne Bradstreet*, Jeannine Hensley, ed. (Cambridge: Belknap Press of Harvard University Press, 1967), 241.

19. Alan Heimert and Andrew Delbanco, "Anne Bradstreet, Poems and Prose," *The Puritans in America: A Narrative Anthology*, Alan Heimert and Andrew Delbanco, eds. (Cambridge: Harvard University Press, 1985), 130.

20. Anne Bradstreet, "Contemplations," *Works*, 210–11.

21. Anne Bradstreet, "Meditations Divine and Moral," *Works*, 283.

22. Charlotte Gordon, *Mistress Bradstreet: The Untold Life of America's First Poet* (Boston: Little, Brown, 2005), 258–59.

23. Benjamin Franklin, "Dogood Papers, No. 4," *Writing New England*, 207–10.

24. John H. Lienrad, "Benjamin Franklin and Cotton Mather," *Engines of Our Ingenuity*, No. 1611, www.uh.edu/engines/epi1611.htm.

25. Phillis Wheatley to John Thornton, 30 October 1774, *The Collected Works of Phillis Wheatley*, John C. Shields, ed. (New York: Oxford University Press, 1989), 184.

26. Thomas H. O'Connor, "John Adams," *Eminent Bostonians* (Cambridge: Harvard University Press, 2002), 6–8.

27. John Adams to Abigail Adams, 29 October 1775, *The Norton Anthology of American Literature*, 7th ed., vol. A, 620–21.

28. *Adams Family Papers: An Electronic Archive*, Massachusetts Historical Society, www.masshist.org/digitaladams/.

29. O'Connor, "Abigail Adams," *Eminent Bostonians*, 1–3.

30. Nathaniel Hawthorne, *The American Notebooks, Centenary Edition of the Works of Nathaniel Hawthorne*, Claude M. Simpson, ed. (Columbus: Ohio State University Press, 1972), 7–8.

31. Nathaniel Hawthorne, "My Kinsman, Major Molineux," *The Snow-Image, and Other Twice-Told Tales* (1832; New York: New American Library, 1962); "The New Adam and Eve," *Mosses from an Old Manse* (1854; Boston: Houghton Mifflin, 1882); "Sights from a Steeple," *Twice-Told Tales* (1851; Boston: Houghton Mifflin, 1879).

32. Hawthorne, "The Custom-House," *The Scarlet Letter*, 28–29.

33. Hawthorne, *The Scarlet Letter*, 39–40.

34. "Mrs. Anne Hutchinson—Trial at the Court at Newton. 1637," www.piney-2.com/ColAnnHutchTrial.html.

35. Hawthorne, *The Scarlet Letter*, 185.

36. Rutman, *Winthrop's Boston*, 114–34.

37. Michael J. Colacurcio, "Footsteps of Anne Hutchinson: The Context of *The Scarlet Letter*," *The Scarlet Letter: An Authoritative Text, Backgrounds and Sources, Criticism*, 2nd ed., 227–46.

38. Cited in James R. Mellow, *Nathaniel Hawthorne in His Time* (Boston: Houghton Mifflin, 1980), 316.

39. Cited in J. Stanley Mattson, "Oliver Wendell Holmes and 'The Deacon's Masterpiece': A Logical Story?," *New England Quarterly* 41, no. 1 (March 1968), 104–14. Mattson disagrees with Wendell's reading.

40. William C. Dowling, *Oliver Wendell Holmes in Paris: Medicine, Theology, and The Autocrat of the Breakfast Table* (Durham: University of New Hampshire Press, 2006), 110–35.

II. BOSTON AND THE AMERICAN RENAISSANCE

1. Van Wyck Brooks, *The Flowering of New England* (1936; New York: E. P. Dutton, 1952), 494.

2. Paul M. Wright, "The Old Corner Bookstore: A Boston Focal Point for Publishers and Authors," *Nineteenth Century* 3, no. 2 (Summer 1977), 94.

3. Cited in John Harris, *Historic Walks in Old Boston* (Chester, Conn.: The Globe Pequot Press, 1982), 113.

4. Herman Melville, "Hawthorne and His Mosses," *The Shock of Recognition: The Development of Literature in the United States Recorded by the Men Who Made It*, Edmund Wilson, ed. (New York: Farrar, Straus and Cudahy, 1955), 187–204.

5. James R. Mellow, *Nathaniel Hawthorne in His Times* (Boston: Houghton Mifflin, 1980), 313.

6. Cited in Sharon O'Brien, *Willa Cather: The Emerging Voice* (Cambridge: Harvard University Press, 1987), 315.

7. Brooks, *The Flowering of New England*, 494–96.

8. Edmund Wilson, *Patriotic Gore: Studies in the Literature of the American Civil War* (New York: Oxford University Press, 1962), 743–44.

9. William C. Dowling, *Oliver Wendell Holmes in Paris: Medicine, Theology, and The Autocrat of the Breakfast Table* (Durham: University of New Hampshire Press, 2006), 116–24.

10. Cited in Harris, *Historic Walks in Old Boston*, 114.

11. Oliver Wendell Holmes, Sr., to John Lothrop Motley, 16 February 1861, quoted in Louis Menand, *The Metaphysical Club: A Story of Ideas in America* (New York: Farrar, Straus and Giroux, 2001), 67.

12. Oliver Wendell Holmes, *Elsie Venner: A Romance of Destiny* (New York: Signet Classics, 1961), 15–19.

13. Cited in Thomas H. O'Connor, "Oliver Wendell Holmes," *Eminent Bostonians* (Cambridge: Harvard University Press, 2002), 137–39.

14. Oliver Wendell Holmes, "At the Saturday Club," *The Complete Poetical Works of Oliver Wendell Holmes*, Horace Scudder, ed. (Boston: Houghton Mifflin, 1895), 3–4.

15. Cited in Harris, *Historic Walks in Old Boston*, 119.

16. Ellery Sedgwick, *A History of the Atlantic Monthly, 1857–1909* (Amherst: University of Massachusetts Press, 1994), 4.

17. Brooks, *The Flowering of New England*, 494–95.

18. F. O. Matthiessen, *The American Renaissance* (London: Oxford University Press, 1941), vi.

19. Thomas H. O'Connor, *The Boston Irish: A Political History* (Boston: Northeastern University Press, 1995), 63.

20. Cited in ibid., 73.

21. Cited in ibid., 76.

22. Cited in ibid., 60.

23. Cited in Thomas H. O'Connor, *Civil War Boston: Home Front & Battlefield* (Boston: Northeastern University Press, 1997), 29.

24. Cited in ibid., 44.

25. Castle Freeman, Jr., "Vita: Wendell Phillips," *Harvard Magazine*, May–June 2007, 38.

26. Cited in Brenda Wineapple, *White Heat: The Friendship of Emily Dickinson and Thomas Wentworth Higginson* (New York: Alfred A. Knopf, 2008), 31.

27. Ibid., 6–7.

28. Cited in O'Connor, *Civil War Boston*, 29.

29. Cited in Sedgwick, *History*, 35.

30. Ralph Waldo Emerson, "The American Scholar," *Ralph Waldo Emerson: Essays & Lectures* (New York: Library of America, 1983), 70–71.

31. Sedgwick, *History*, 21–43.

32. Ticknor & Fields (1854–1868), Fields, Osgood & Co. (1868–1870), J. R. Osgood & Co. (1871–1878), Houghton, Osgood & Co. (1878–1880), Houghton, Mifflin & Co. (1880–1908), Houghton Mifflin Company (1908–).

33. Sedgwick, *History*, 284.
34. Ibid., 217.
35. William Cranston Lawton, *The New England Poets: Emerson, Hawthorne, Longfellow, Whittier, Lowell, Holmes* (London: Macmillan, 1898), 2.
36. Robert Frost, "The Gift Outright," John F. Kennedy Presidential Library and Museum, www.jfklibrary.org/Historical+Resources/Archives/Reference+Desk/The+Gift+Outright.htm.
37. See Matthiessen, *The American Renaissance*.
38. Susan Cheever, "Concord, Massachusetts," *American Bloomsbury* (New York: Simon and Schuster, 2006), 3–6.
39. Cited in John Matteson, *Eden's Outcasts: The Story of Louisa May Alcott and Her Father* (New York: W. W. Norton, 2007), 87.
40. Ralph Waldo Emerson, "Nature," *Ralph Waldo Emerson: Selected Essays*, Lazer Ziff, ed. (New York: Penguin Books, 1982), 5–6.
41. Ken Gewertz, "Emerson impression remains clear at Harvard," *Harvard University Gazette*, 1 April 2003.
42. Henry David Thoreau, *Walden, or, Life in the Woods* (New York: Library of America, 1985), 471.
43. Cheever, "Emerson Pays for Everything," *American Bloomsbury*, 35–38.
44. Cited in Gay Wilson Allen, *Waldo Emerson: A Biography* (New York: Viking Press, 1981), 344.
45. Ralph Waldo Emerson, "Concord Hymn," *Selected Writings of Emerson*, Donald McQuade, ed. (New York: Modern Library, 1981), 891.
46. Cited in Charles R. Anderson, "Introduction," Henry James, *The Bostonians* (New York: Penguin Books, 1986), 14.
47. Ralph Waldo Emerson, "Boston Hymn," *Selected Writings*, 895.
48. Ralph Waldo Emerson, "Boston," *Historic Poems and Ballads*, Rupert S. Holland, ed. (Philadelphia: George W. Jacobs, 1912).
49. Ralph Waldo Emerson, cited in Alfred Habegger, introduction to Henry James, *The Bostonians* (Indianapolis: Bobbs-Merrill, 1976), xii.
50. *Emerson in His Journals*, Joel Porte, ed. (Cambridge: Belknap Press of Harvard University Press, 1982), 420.
51. Ibid., 306.
52. Matteson, *Eden's Outcasts*, 55–85.
53. Cheever, *American Bloomsbury*, 14–15.
54. Ibid., 114–15.
55. Matteson, *Eden's Outcasts*, 377.
56. Thoreau, *Walden*, 446.
57. Ibid., 461.
58. Meg McGavran Murray, *Margaret Fuller: Wandering Pilgrim* (Athens: University of Georgia Press, 2008), 124.
59. Elizabeth Hardwick, "The Genius of Margaret Fuller," *New York Review of Books* 33, no. 6 (10 April 1986).
60. Elizabeth Hardwick, "Boston: The Lost Ideal," *The Penguin Book of Contemporary American Essays*, Maureen Howard, ed. (New York: Penguin Books, 1984).
61. Hardwick, "The Genius of Margaret Fuller," 18.
62. Brooks, *The Flowering of New England*, 494–95.

63. O'Brien, *Willa Cather: The Emerging Voice*, 315.

64. Harris, *Historic Walks in Old Boston*, 268–69.

65. *The Complete Notebooks of Henry James*, Leon Edel and Lyall H. Powers, eds. (New York: Oxford University Press, 1987), 20.

66. Cited in Jean Strouse, *Alice James: A Biography* (Boston: Houghton Mifflin, 1980), 200.

67. *The Notebooks of Henry James*, F. O. Matthiessen and Kenneth R. Murdock, eds. (New York: Oxford University Press, 1947), 47.

68. Willa Cather, "148 Charles Street," *Not Under Forty* (1936; New York: Library of America, 1992), 838.

69. O'Brien, *Willa Cather: The Emerging Voice*, 317.

70. Cited in ibid., 321, 337, 345.

71. Van Wyck Brooks, *New England: Indian Summer* (1940; New York: E. P. Dutton, 1965), 23.

III. POST–CIVIL WAR BOSTON

1. Henry Adams, *The Education of Henry Adams: An Autobiography* (Boston: Houghton Mifflin, 1918), 3–5.

2. Ibid., 7–9.

3. Henry James, *Hawthorne, Henry James Literary Criticism: Essays on Literature, American Writers, English Writers* (1879; New York: Library of America, 1984), 389.

4. Adams, *Education*, 41–42.

5. Henry Adams, 1875 letter, cited in Van Wyck Brooks, *New England: Indian Summer* (1940; New York: E. P. Dutton, 1965), 8.

6. *Mark Twain–Howells Letters*, Henry Nash Smith and William M. Gibson, eds. (Cambridge: Belknap Press of Harvard University Press, 1960), 530. See James B. Stronks, "Mark Twain's Boston Stage Debut as Seen by Hamlin Garland," *New England Quarterly* 36, no. 1 (March 1963), 85–86.

7. Mark Twain, 1869 letter, cited in Brooks, *New England: Indian Summer*, 8.

8. Mark Twain, "A First Visit to Boston," San Francisco *Alta California*, 25 July 1869. www.twainquotes.com/18690725.html.

9. Howells's letter to Twain cited in Henry Nash Smith, *Mark Twain: The Development of a Writer* (Cambridge: Belknap Press of Harvard University Press, 1962), 93.

10. Mark Twain, "New England Weather," *Mark Twain: Collected Tales, Sketches, & Essays, 1852–1890* (New York: Library of America, 1992), 674.

11. Cited in Susan Goodman and Carl Dawson, *William Dean Howells: A Writer's Life* (Berkeley: University of California Press, 2005), 191.

12. Cited in Smith, *Mark Twain*, 97.

13. William Dean Howells, *Literary Friends and Acquaintances: A Personal Retrospect of American Authorship* (Bloomington: Indiana University Press, 1968), 49, 51.

14. Cited in Goodman and Dawson, *William Dean Howells: A Writer's Life*, 120.

15. Cited in ibid., 54.

16. Cited in ibid., 168.

17. Leon Edel, *Henry James: The Master* (Philadelphia: J. B. Lippincott, 1972), 38.

18. Howells, *Literary Friends and Acquaintance*, 64.

19. Mark Twain, *Huckleberry Finn, Mark Twain: Mississippi Writings*, (New York: Library of America, 1982), 807; Chapter XXVIII title in various editions.

20. William Dean Howells, *The Rise of Silas Lapham* (1885; New York: Penguin Books, 1985), 3.

21. Alfred Kazin, *On Native Grounds: An Interpretation of Modern American Prose Literature* (Garden City, N.Y.: Doubleday, 1956.), 1.

22. Cited in Leon Edel, *Henry James: The Untried Years* (London: Rupert Hart-Davis, 1953), 274.

23. Henry James, "William Dean Howells," *The Shock of Recognition*, Edmund Wilson, ed. (New York: Farrar, Straus and Cudahy, 1955), 507–8.

24. Henry James, *Hawthorne* (1879; New York: St. Martin's Press, 1967), 76–77, 109.

25. *The Complete Notebooks of Henry James*, Leon Edel and Lyall H. Powers, eds. (New York: Oxford University Press, 1983), 214.

26. Henry James, *The Europeans, The American Novels and Stories of Henry James*, F. O. Matthiessen, ed. (New York: Alfred A. Knopf, 1947), 37–38.

27. Henry James to Thomas Sergeant Perry, in Alfred Habegger, appendix to Henry James, *The Bostonians* (Indianapolis: Bobbs-Merrill, 1976), 430.

28. David Mamet wrote a play titled *Boston Marriage* and directed it at Cambridge's American Repertory Theater in 1999. In 2004 Massachusetts became the first state to legalize same-sex marriages.

29. James, *Notebooks*, 19.

30. Henry James, *The Bostonians* (1886; Harmondsworth: Penguin Books, 1983), 17, 31.

31. *Henry James Letters*, Leon Edel, ed. (Cambridge: Belknap Press of Harvard University Press, 1974), 3: 106.

32. James, *The Bostonians*, 384–85.

33. Henry James, *The American Scene* (1907; Bloomington: Indiana University Press, 1968), 228, 231–32.

34. Douglass Shand-Tucci, *The Art of the Scandal: The Life and Times of Isabella Stewart Gardner* (New York: HarperCollins, 1997), 114–15.

IV. "VIEWED IN BOSTON LIGHT": TURN-OF-THE-CENTURY BOSTON

1. Thomas H. O'Connor, *Civil War Boston: Home Front and Battlefield* (Boston: Northeastern University Press, 1997), 60.

2. Cited in ibid., 54–55.

3. Oscar Handlin, *Boston's Immigrants: A Study in Acculturation*, rev. and enlarged ed. (1941; New York: Atheneum, 1976), 94, 62.

4. Thomas H. O'Connor, *Boston Catholics: A History of the Church and Its People* (Boston: Northeastern University Press, 1998), 93–95.

5. Cited in Thomas H. O'Connor, *Fitzpatrick's Boston, 1846–1866: John Bernard Fitzpatrick, Third Bishop of Boston* (Boston: Northeastern University Press, 1984), 188.

6. O'Connor, *Civil War Boston*, 236–37.

7. Ibid., 132.

8. Thomas H. O'Connor, *Eminent Bostonians* (Cambridge: Harvard University Press, 2002), 236–38.

9. Richard Powers, "The Robert Gould Shaw and 54th Regiment Monument," *A New*

Literary History of America, Greil Marcus and Werner Sollors, eds. (Cambridge: Belknap Press of Harvard University Press, 2009), 434.

10. Louis Menand, *The Metaphysical Club: A Story of Ideas in America* (New York: Farrar, Straus and Giroux, 2002), 148.

11. Oliver Wendell Holmes to his parents, 10 May 1864, cited in ibid., 56.

12. Ibid., 69.

13. Cited in Edmund Wilson, *Patriotic Gore: Studies in the Literature of the American Civil War* (New York: Oxford University Press, 1962), 759.

14. Cited in G. Edward White, *Oliver Wendell Holmes, Jr.* (Oxford: Oxford University Press, 2006), 23–24.

15. Wilson, *Patriotic Gore*, 786.

16. Van Wyck Brooks, *New England: Indian Summer* (1940; New York: E. P. Dutton, 1965), 338.

17. Menand, *The Metaphysical Club*, 432–33.

18. See Brenda Wineapple, *White Heat: The Friendship of Emily Dickinson and Thomas Wentworth Higginson* (New York: Alfred A. Knopf, 2008).

19. Ellery Sedgwick, *A History of the Atlantic Monthly, 1857–1909* (Amherst: University of Massachusetts Press, 1994), 78–79.

20. Colm Toibin, *The Master* (New York: Scribner, 2004), 177.

21. Cited in Wilson, *Patriotic Gore*, 664.

22. William James, "Robert Gould Shaw" (1897), *Essays on Religion and Morality, The Works of William James*, 72–73; cited in Menand, *The Metaphysical Club*, 147–48.

23. Thomas J. Brown, "Civic Monuments of the Civil War," *Hope & Glory: Essays on the Legacy of the Massachusetts 54th Regiment*, Martin H. Blatt, Thomas J. Brown, and Donald Yacovone, eds. (Amherst and Boston: University of Massachusetts Press in association with Massachusetts Historical Society, 2001), 154–55.

24. Cited in Robert D. Richardson, *William James: In the Maelstrom of American Modernism* (Boston: Houghton Mifflin, 2007), 369.

25. Henry Adams, "Treason (1860–1861)," *The Education of Henry Adams* (Boston: Houghton Mifflin, 1918), 99.

26. Wilson, *Patriotic Gore*, 654.

27. Douglass Shand-Tucci, *The Art of Scandal: The Life and Times of Isabella Stewart Gardner* (New York: HarperCollins, 1997), 11–13.

28. Hermione Lee, *Edith Wharton* (New York: Alfred A. Knopf, 2007), 69.

29. Brooks, *New England: Indian Summer*, 339.

30. Cited in Thomas H. O'Connor, *Bibles, Brahmins, and Bosses: A Short History of Boston* (Boston: Trustees of the Boston Public Library, 1976), 82.

31. Martin Green, *The Problem of Boston: Some Readings in Cultural History* (New York: W. W. Norton, 1966), 22, 24.

32. Henry Adams, *The Life of George Cabot Lodge, The Shock of Recognition*, Edmund Wilson, ed. (New York: Farrar, Straus and Cudahy, 1955), 750, 755.

33. Cited in Lyndall Gordon, *Eliot's Early Years* (New York: Noonday Press, 1977), 17.

34. George Santayana, *Persons and Places: Fragments of Autobiography*, critical ed., William G. Holzberger and Herman J. Saatkamp, Jr., eds. (Cambridge: MIT Press, 1986), 49.

35. Cited in Brooks, *New England: Indian Summer*, 452.

36. Santayana, *Persons and Places*, 158.

37. Ibid., 180.

38. George Santayana, *The Last Puritan: A Memoir in the Form of a Novel* (New York: Scribner, 1937), 16.

39. Ibid., 32.

40. Ibid., 6.

41. Ibid., 581–82.

42. Cited in Millicent Bell, *Marquand: An American Life* (Boston: Little, Brown, 1979), 254.

43. Katherine Wolff, *Culture Club: The Curious History of the Boston Athenaeum* (Amherst: University of Massachusetts Press, 2009), 7.

44. Cited in ibid., 252.

45. Mark A. De Wolfe Howe, "The Literary Centre," *The Atlantic*, September 1903, www.theatlantic.com/doc/190309/literary-centre.

46. Helen Howe, *The Gentle Americans, 1864–1960: Biography of a Breed* (New York: Harper and Row, 1965), 84.

47. M. A. De Wolfe Howe, *Memoirs of a Hostess: A Chronicle of Eminent Friendships Drawn Chiefly from the Diaries of Mrs. James T. Fields* (Boston: Atlantic Monthly Press, 1922), 284, 305.

48. John P. Marquand, *The Late George Apley* (1937; New York: Pocket Books, 1971), 3, 5.

49. Ibid., 236.

50. Ibid., 69, 71–74.

51. Ibid., 83.

52. Ibid., 148–49.

53. See Peter Davison, *The Fading Smile: Poets in Boston from Robert Frost to Sylvia Plath* (New York: W. W. Norton, 1994), 24–31.

54. Bell, *Marquand: An American Life*, 251.

55. T. S. Eliot, "Henry James," *The Shock of Recognition*, Edmund Wilson, ed. 859.

56. Ibid., 861.

57. Cited in Paul Mariani, *Lost Puritan: A Life of Robert Lowell* (New York: W. W. Norton, 1994), 151.

58. T. S. Eliot, "Cousin Nancy," *Collected Poems, 1909–1935* (New York: Harcourt Brace, 1952), 17–18.

59. Eliot, "The Love Song of J. Alfred Prufrock," *Collected Poems*, 3–7.

60. Brooks, *New England: Indian Summer*, 442.

61. Sam Bass Warner, *Streetcar Suburbs: The Process of Growth in Boston, 1870–1900*, 2nd ed. (Cambridge: Harvard University Press, 1962, 1978), 1.

62. Ibid., 3.

63. John Winthrop, "A Model of Christian Charity," *The American Puritans: Their Prose and Poetry*, Perry Miller, ed. (Garden City, N.Y.: Anchor Books, 1956), 79–80.

64. Cleveland Amory, *The Proper Bostonians* (New York: E. P. Dutton, 1947), 14.

V. THE "OTHER" BOSTONIANS: NEW VOICES AND VISIONS

1. William Dean Howells, *The Rise of Silas Lapham* (1885; New York: Penguin Books, 1986), 145.

2. Kermit Vanderbilt, "Appendix, *Silas Lapham* and Anti-Semitism," in ibid., 366–68.

3. John P. Marquand, *The Late George Apley: A Novel in the Form of a Memoir* (Boston: Little, Brown, 1937), 25–26.

4. George Santayana, *The Last Puritan: A Memoir in the Form of a Novel* (New York: Scribner, 1937), 32.

5. Cited in Marilyn Richardson with Edward Clark, *Black Bostonians: Two Hundred Years of Community and Culture: An Exhibition of Books, Paintings, and Sculpture by and about Blacks in Boston; Drawn Chiefly from the Collections of the Boston Athenaeum* (Boston: Athenaeum, 1988), 5.

6. Thomas H. O'Connor, *The Hub: Boston Past and Present* (Boston: Northeastern University Press, 2001), 138.

7. Museum of African History, Boston. www.afroammuseum.org/index.htm.

8. Phillis Wheatley, "On Being Brought from Africa to America," *The Collected Works of Phillis Wheatley*, John C. Shields, ed. (New York: Oxford University Press, 1988), 18.

9. Cited in Eve LaPlante, *Salem Witch Judge: The Life and Repentance of Samuel Sewall* (New York: HarperCollins, 2007), 228.

10. Cited in Sidney Kaplan and Emma Nogrady Kaplan, *The Black Presence in the Era of the American Revolution* (Amherst: University of Massachusetts Press, 1989), 8.

11. Abigail Adams, cited in ibid., 13, 15.

12. John Daniels, *In Freedom's Birthplace: A Study of the Boston Negroes* (New York: Negro University Press, 1968), 2.

13. Alan Lupo, *Liberty's Chosen Home: The Politics of Violence in Boston* (1977; Boston: Beacon Press, 1988); J. Anthony Lukas, *Common Ground: A Turbulent Decade in the Lives of Three American Families* (New York: Alfred A. Knopf, 1985).

14. William D. Pierson, *Black Yankees: The Development of an Afro-American Subculture in Eighteenth-century New England* (Amherst: University of Massachusetts Press, 1988), x, 26.

15. Frederick Douglass, *Narrative of the Life of Frederick Douglass, an American Slave, Written by Himself*, Benjamin Quarles, ed. (Cambridge: Belknap Press, 1960), 153.

16. Charlotte Forten Grimke, "Journals," June 2, 1854, *Norton Anthology of African American Literature*, Henry Louis Gates Jr. and Nellie Y. McKay, eds. (New York: W. W. Norton, 1997), 478.

17. W. E. B. Du Bois, "A Negro Student at Harvard," in *Black and White in American Culture: An Anthology from the Massachusetts Review*, Jules Chametzky and Sidney Kaplan, eds. (Amherst: University of Massachusetts Press, 1969) 185, 123.

18. Ibid., 130.

19. W. E. B. Du Bois, "William Monroe Trotter," "Articles from *The Crisis*," (May 1934), *W. E. B. Du Bois: Writings*, Nathan Huggins, ed. (New York: Library of America, 1986), 1250–51.

20. Pauline E. Hopkins, cited in *Black Bostonians*, 23.

21. Pauline E. Hopkins, *Contending Forces: A Romance Illustrative of Negro Life North and South* (New York: Oxford University Press, 1988), epigraph.

22. Dorothy West, in Mary Helen Washington, *Invented Lives: Narratives of Black Women, 1860–1960* (Garden City, N.Y.: Anchor Press, 1987), 344.

23. Malcolm X, with the assistance of Alex Haley, *The Autobiography of Malcolm X* (1965; New York: Grove Press, 1966), 34.

24. Ibid., 34–35.

25. Ibid., 40.

26. Ibid., 73.

27. David Bradley on *The Autobiography of Malcolm X*, *A New Literary History of America*, Greil Marcus and Werner Sollors, eds. (Cambridge: Belknap Press of Harvard University Press, 2009), 934.

28. Douglass Shand-Tucci, "Saint Phillips Brooks," BackBay Historical—The Global Boston," June 1, 2009, www.backbayhistorical.org/blog/.

29. Richardson, "Community and Culture: A Dual Tradition," in Richardson and Clark, *Black Bostonians*, 1.

30. William Stanley Braithwaite, *The William Stanley Braithwaite Reader*, Philip Butcher, ed. (Ann Arbor: University of Michigan Press, 1972), 167.

31. Ibid., 184.

32. T. S. Eliot, "The Boston Evening Transcript," *The Complete Poems and Plays, 1909–1950* (New York: Harcourt, Brace, 1958), 16.

33. Cited in *The William Stanley Braithwaite Reader*, 1.

34. Ibid., 53–54.

35. Ibid., 187.

36. William Stanley Braithwaite, "In the Public Garden," *The House of Falling Leaves and Other Poems* (Boston: John W. Luce, 1908), 54.

37. Pierson, *Black Yankees*, 160.

38. "The History Place," www.historyplace.com/worldhistory/famine/america.htm.

39. Lawrence J. McCaffrey, "Irish American Politics: Power with or without Purpose?" *The Irish in America*, P. J. Drury, ed. (Cambridge: Cambridge University Press, 1985). See too Lawrence J. McCaffrey, *Texture of Irish America* (Syracuse: Syracuse University Press, 1992); Thomas H. O'Connor, *The Boston Irish: A Political History* (Boston: Northeastern University Press, 1985); Kevin Kenny, *The American Irish: A History* (London: Longman, 2000), 228.

40. Nathan Glazer and Daniel Patrick Moynihan, *Beyond the Melting Pot* (Cambridge: MIT Press, 1963), 287.

41. Thomas N. Brown, "Holding Boston Together," *Boston Globe*, 19 June 1989.

42. Cited in Doris Kearns Goodwin, *The Fitzgeralds and the Kennedys: An American Saga* (New York: Simon and Schuster, 1987), 63.

43. Ralph Waldo Emerson, cited in Thomas O'Connor, *Selections from Ralph Waldo Emerson*, Stephen E. Wicher, ed. (Boston: Houghton Mifflin, 1957), 280.

44. Henry David Thoreau, *Walden, Henry David Thoreau* (New York: Library of America, 1985), 487–89.

45. Henry Cabot Lodge, cited in Dennis P. Ryan, *Beyond the Ballot Box: A Social History of the Boston Irish, 1845–1917* (Amherst: University of Massachusetts Press, 1983), 75.

46. Martin Green, *The Problem of Boston: Some Readings in Cultural History* (New York: W. W. Norton, 1966), 103.

47. Oscar Handlin, *Boston's Immigrants, 1790–1880* (1941; Cambridge: Harvard University Press, 1969), 142.

48. Cited in William V. Shannon, *The American Irish: A Political and Social Portrait* (New York: Collier Books, 1966), 135.

49. Cited in George Potter, *To the Golden Door: The Study of the Irish in Ireland and America* (Boston: Little, Brown, 1960), 603.

50. Ryan, *Beyond the Ballot Box,* 103.

51. John Boyle O'Reilly, "The Exile of the Gael," in *Life of John Boyle O'Reilly, Together with His Complete Poems and Speeches,* James Jeffrey Roche and Mrs. John Boyle O'Reilly, eds. (New York: Cassell, 1891), 414–18.

52. John Boyle O'Reilly, "The Fame of the City," *Harper's,* January 1881, 177–78.

53. Patrick A. Collins, in John T. Galvin, "Boston's Eminent Patrick from Ireland," *Boston Globe,* 17 March 1988.

54. Cited in Jack Beatty, *The Rascal King: The Life and Times of James Michael Curley (1874–1958)* (Reading, Mass.: Addison-Wesley, 1992), 89.

55. James Michael Curley, *I'd Do It Again: A Record of All My Uproarious Years* (Englewood Cliffs, N.J.: Prentice-Hall, 1957); see too Shannon, *The American Irish,* 231.

56. Tip O'Neill, with William Novak, *Man of the House: The Life and Memoirs of Speaker Tip O'Neill* (New York: Random House, 1987), 334.

57. Beatty, *The Rascal King.*

58. Joseph F. Dineen, *The Purple Shamrock: The Hon. James Michael Curley of Boston* (New York: W. W. Norton, 1949), 322.

59. Joseph F. Dineen, *Ward Eight* (1936; New York: Arno Press, 1976), v.

60. Robert Taylor, "A Labor of Love and Laughter," *Boston Globe,* 21 June 1989; *Fred Allen: His Life and Wit* (Boston: Little, Brown, 1989).

61. Charles F. Duffy, *A Family of His Own: A Life of Edwin O'Connor* (Washington, D.C.: Catholic University Press, 2003), 173.

62. Edmund Wilson, "'Baldini': A Memoir and a Collaboration," *The Best and Last of Edwin O'Connor,* Arthur Schlesinger, Jr., ed. (Boston: Atlantic Monthly Press,, 1970), 344.

63. Cited in Beatty, *The Rascal King,* 514–15.

64. Edwin O'Connor, *The Last Hurrah* (1956; New York: Bantam Books, 1967), 340.

65. Ibid., 66.

66. James Carroll, *Mortal Friends* (Boston: Little, Brown, 1978), 244.

67. Taylor, *Fred Allen,* 254.

68. Cited in George V. Higgins, *A City on a Hill* (1975; New York: Carroll & Graf, 1985), 2.

69. William M. Bulger, *While the Music Lasts: My Life in Politics* (Boston: Houghton Mifflin, 1996), 1.

70. George V. Higgins, *The Friends of Eddie Coyle* (New York: Alfred A. Knopf, 1972), 175.

71. Lukas, *Common Ground,* 246–47.

72. Michael Patrick MacDonald, *All Souls: A Family Story from Southie* (New York: Ballantine Books, 1999), 59.

73. Ibid., 201.

74. Michael Patrick MacDonald, *Easter Rising: An Irish American Coming Up from Under* (Boston: Houghton Mifflin, 2006).

75. Lawrence J. McCaffrey, *The Irish Diaspora in America* (Washington, D.C.: Catholic University Press, 1976), 10.

76. Jonathan D. Sarna, "The Jews of Boston in Historical Perspective," *The Jews of Boston,* Jonathan D. Sarna, Ellen Smith, and Scott-Martin Kosofsky, eds. (1995; New Haven: Yale University Press, 2005), 4.

77. O'Connor, *The Hub,* 171–72.

78. Cited in Sarna, "The Jews of Boston in Historical Perspective," 8.

79. Ibid., 3–12.

80. Thomas H. O'Connor, "The Jewish-Christian Experience," *The Jews of Boston,* 340.

81. Cited in Ken Gewertz, "Revisiting 'The Promised Land,'" *Harvard University Gazette,* 6 March 1997.

82. "Mary Antin," *The Norton Anthology of Jewish American Literature,* Jules Chametzky, John Felstiner, Hilene Flanzbaum, and Kathryn Hellerstein, eds. (New York: W. W. Norton, 2001), 190–91.

83. Mary Antin, *The Promised Land* (Boston: Houghton Mifflin, 1912), 195.

84. Isaac Goldberg, "A Boston Boyhood," *The American Mercury* 17, no. 67 (June 1929), in *The Many Voices of Boston: A Historical Anthology, 1630–1975,* Howard Mumford Jones and Bessie Zaban Jones, eds. (Boston: Little, Brown, 1975), 354–55.

85. Charles Angoff, *When I Was a Boy in Boston* (Boston: Ruttle, Shaw and Wetherill, 1947), 95–96.

86. Theodore H. White, *In Search of History* (New York: Warner Books, 1981), 78.

87. Nat Hentoff, *Boston Boy* (New York: Alfred A. Knopf, 1986), 4.

88. Sarna, "The Jews of Boston in Historical Perspective," 13.

89. Hentoff, *Boston Boy,* 12.

90. Ibid., 122.

91. Ibid., 134.

92. Sarna, "The Jews of Boston in Historical Perspective," 14.

93. Douglass Shand-Tucci, "Boston's Need for a New History: Redefining the Boston Brahmin," 1 November 2009, www.backbayhistorical.org/blog/.

94. Sarna, "The Jews of Boston in Historical Perspective," 15.

95. MTA press release (18 September 2002), "Leonard P. Zakim Bunker Hill Bridge Dedication Events Set for October 3–6" (retrieved 28 April 2008): "He worked tirelessly to build personal bridges between our city's diverse people and neighborhoods": Joyce Zakim, wife of Lenny Zakim.

96. O'Connor, "The Jewish-Christian Experience," 341.

97. U.S. Census Bureau, www.census.gov/main/www/cen2000.html; en.wikipedia. org/wiki/Boston.

98. John Hanson Mitchell, *The Paradise of All These Parts: A Natural History of Boston* (Boston: Beacon Press, 2008), 47.

99. Stephen Puleo, *The Boston Italians: A Story of Pride, Perseverance, and Paesani, from the Years of the Great Immigration to the Present Day* (Boston: Beacon Press, 2007), 3–25.

100. Roland Merullo, *In Revere, in Those Days* (New York: Vintage Books, 2002).

101. James Carroll, "Charting Boston's Course," *Boston Sunday Globe Magazine,* 10 October 1999.

VI. "THERE IT WAS": BOSTON, CITY OF SELF AND SPIRIT

1. Samuel Eliot Morison, *Builders of the Bay Colony* (1930; Boston: Northeastern University Press, 1981), 3.

2. Thomas H. O'Connor, "Samuel Sewall," *Eminent Bostonians* (Cambridge: Harvard University Press), 234.

3. Henry David Thoreau, *The Heart of Thoreau's Journals*, Odell Shepard, ed. (New York: Dover, 1961), 2.

4. Perry Miller, "A Journal of No Very Wide Circulation," *Consciousness in Concord: The Text of Thoreau's Hitherto 'Lost Journal' (1840–1841) Together with Notes and Commentary* (Boston: Houghton Mifflin, 1958), 3–7.

5. Henry David Thoreau, *Walden, or Life in the Woods*, from *Henry David Thoreau: A Week on the Concord and Merrimack Rivers, Walden; or, Life in the Woods, The Maine Woods, Cape Cod* (New York: Library of America, 1985), 325.

6. Kenneth B. Murdock, review of *Samuel Sewall's Diary*, Mark Van Doren, ed., *The New England Quarterly* 1, no. 2 (April 1928), 258.

7. Cited in O'Connor, "Samuel Sewall," 234.

8. Eve LaPlante, *Salem Witch Judge* (New York: HarperCollins, 2007), 68.

9. Samuel Sewall, *Phaenomena quaedam Apocalyptica*, in *The Puritans in America: A Narrative Anthology*, Alan Heimart and Andrew Delbanco, eds. (Cambridge: Harvard University Press, 1985), 293.

10. *The Puritans*, Perry Miller and Thomas H. Johnson, eds. (New York: Harper and Row, 1963), vol. 2: 461.

11. Edward Johnson, *Wonder-Working Providence of Sions Savior*, in *The Puritans*, 2: 145.

12. Eve LaPlante, *American Jezebel: The Uncommon Life of Anne Hutchinson, the Woman Who Defied the Puritans* (New York: HarperCollins, 2004), vi–xvii.

13. Andrew Delbanco, *The Puritan Ordeal* (Cambridge: Harvard University Press, 1989), 137.

14. Keith W. F. Stavely, *Puritan Legacies: Paradise Lost and the New England Tradition, 1630–1890* (Ithaca, N.Y.: Cornell University Press, 1987).

15. Delbanco, *The Puritan Ordeal*, 236.

16. Ralph Waldo Emerson, "Nature," *Ralph Waldo Emerson: Essays and Lectures* (New York: Library of America, 1983), 7.

17. Sacvan Berkovitch, *The American Jeremiad* (Madison: University of Wisconsin Press, 1978), 9. See too Berkovitch, *The Puritan Origins of the American Self* (New Haven: Yale University Press, 1975).

18. Alexis de Tocqueville, cited in Berkovitch, *The American Jeremiad*, 19.

19. Daniel Aaron, "Introducing Arthur Inman," *The Inman Diary: A Public and Private Confession*, Daniel Aaron, ed. (Cambridge: Harvard University Press, 1985), 1: 5, 11.

20. Cited in John Patrick Diggins review of *The Inman Diary*, *New England Quarterly* 59, no. 2 (June 1986), 284.

21. Cited in ibid., 282.

22. Nat Hentoff, *Boston Boy* (New York: Alfred A. Knopf, 1986), 93.

23. Samuel Eliot Morison, *One Boy's Boston, 1887–1901* (1962; Boston: Northeastern University Press, 1983), 62–68.

24. Robert Lowell, "Antebellum Boston," *Robert Lowell: Collected Prose*, Robert Giroux, ed. (New York: Farrar, Straus, Giroux, 1987), 291.

25. Peter Davison, *The Fading Smile: Poets in Boston from Robert Frost to Robert Lowell to Sylvia Plath* (New York: W. W. Norton, 1994), 252.

26. Seamus Heaney, "Robert Lowell," *Robert Lowell: Interviews and Memoirs*, Jeffrey Meyers, ed. (Ann Arbor: University of Michigan Press, 1988), 245.

27. Lowell, "Antebellum Boston," 291.

28. Robert Lowell, "91 Revere Street," *Robert Lowell: Collected Prose*, 313.

29. Ibid., 329–30.

30. Cited in Steven Gould Axelrod, *Robert Lowell: Life and Art* (Princeton: Princeton University Press, 1978), 158.

31. Ibid., 165–66.

32. Robert Lowell, "For the Union Dead," *For the Union Dead* (New York: Farrar, Straus and Giroux, 1964), 70–72.

33. Helen Vendler, "Art, Heroism, and Poetry," from *Hope & Glory: Essays on the Legacy of the 54th Massachusetts Regiment*, Martin H. Blatt, Thomas J. Brown, and Donald Yacovone, eds. (Amherst and Boston: University of Massachusetts Press in association with Massachusetts Historical Society, 2009), 207, 209.

34. Elizabeth Hardwick, "Boston, The Lost Ideal," in *The Penguin Book of Contemporary American Essays*, Maureen Howard, ed. (New York: Penguin Books, 1984), 249.

35. Davison, *The Fading Smile*, 14.

36. Jean Stafford, *Boston Adventure* (Garden City, N.Y.: Sun Dial Press, 1944), 128.

37. Lowell, "New England and Further," *Robert Lowell: Collected Prose*, 190.

38. Dan Wakefield, *Starting Over* (New York: Delacorte Press, 1973); *Home Free* (New York: Delacorte Press, 1977); *Selling Out* (Boston: Little, Brown, 1985).

39. Dan Wakefield, *Returning: A Spiritual Journey* (New York: Doubleday, 1988), 195–96.

40. Ibid., 5–6.

41. Ibid., ix.

42. Ibid., 224.

43. John Updike, *Self-Consciousness* (New York: Alfred A. Knopf, 1989), 254.

44. John Updike, "A response to the question of why do I live in New England, posed in this case by a fledgling journal called The Improper Bostonian," *Due Considerations: Essays and Criticism* (New York: Alfred A. Knopf, 2007), 668.

45. Updike, *Self-Consciousness*, 232.

46. John Updike, *Roger's Version* (New York: Alfred A. Knopf, 1986), 323.

47. John Updike, "Hawthorne's Creed," *Hugging the Shore: Essays and Criticism* (New York: Alfred A. Knopf, 1983), 76, 80.

48. John Updike, "The Boston Red Sox, as of 1986," *Odd Jobs: Essays and Criticism* (New York: Alfred A. Knopf, 1991), 92.

49. Ibid, 93.

50. John Updike, "HUB FANS BID KID ADIEU," *Assorted Prose* (New York: Alfred A. Knopf, 1965), 127.

51. Ibid., 137.

52. Ibid., 142.

53. Ibid., 146.

54. ESPN Baseball, 27 December 2002, espn.go.com/mlb/news/2002/1226/1482493.html.

55. Updike, "The Boston Red Sox, as of 1986," 95.

56. Dan Shaughnessy, *Curse of the Bambino* (New York: Penguin, 2004).

57. Dan Shaughnessy, *Reversing the Curse* (Boston: Houghton Mifflin, 2006).

58. Cited in David Mehegan, "Toil & trouble: A local author digs up common ground with her ancestor, witch trial judge Samuel Sewall," *Boston Globe*, 29 October 2007, www.boston.com/ae/books/articles/2007/10/29/toil__trouble/.

59. Paul S. Grogan "Introduction: The Comeback City," *The Good City: Writers Explore 21st-Century Boston*, Emily Hestand and Ande Zellman, eds. (Boston: Beacon Press, 2004), 2.

60. John Hanson Mitchell, *The Paradise of All These Parts* (Boston: Beacon Press, 2008), 15.

61. Joseph A. Conforti, *Imagining New England: Explorations of Regional Identity from the Pilgrims to the Mid-Twentieth Century* (Chapel Hill: University of North Carolina Press, 2001). 5.

62. Patricia Powell, "A Literary Landscape: From Jamaica to Boston," *The Good City*, 43.

63. Ibid., 44.

64. Louis Mazur, *The Soiling of Old Glory: The Story of a Photograph That Shocked America* (London: Bloomsbury US, 2008).

65. *The Public Garden Boston* (Boston, Mass.: Friends of the Public Garden, Inc., 2000), 25.

66. Robert McCloskey, *Make Way for Ducklings* (New York: Viking Press, 1941), unpaged.

67. E. B. White, *The Trumpet of the Swan* (New York: Harper & Row, 1970), 121.

SOURCES

I. BOSTON, FROM WINTHROP TO HAWTHORNE

John Winthrop, from "A Model of Christian Charity" (1630), a sermon, long circulated in manuscript but not published until 1838 by the Massachusetts Historical Society. *The American Puritans: Their Prose and Poetry*, ed. Perry Miller (Garden City, N.Y.: Anchor Books, 1956), 79–80, 82–83.

Anne Bradstreet, "Before the Birth of One of Her Children" (1678); "Meditations Divine and Moral" #53 (published 1867). *The Works of Anne Bradstreet*, ed. Jeannine Hensley, (Cambridge: Belknap Press of Harvard University Press, 1967), 224, 283.

Benjamin Franklin, from *The Autobiography of Benjamin Franklin* (1771). *Benjamin Franklin: Writings Boston and London, 1722–1726; Philadelphia, 1726–1757; London, 1757–1775; Paris, 1776–1785; Philadelphia, 1785–1790; Poor Richard's Almanack, 1733–1757; The Autobiography* (New York: Library of America, 1987), 1323–26, 1329–30.

Phillis Wheatley, from *Poems on Various Subjects, Religious and Moral* (1773): "On Being Brought from Africa to America" and "To The University of Cambridge, in New-England." *The Norton Anthology of American Literature: Volume A: Beginnings to 1800*, 7th ed., Nina Baym, general ed. (New York: W. W. Norton, 2007), 752–53, 755–56.

Letters from Abigail Adams to John Adams, 1775–1776. *The American Revolution: Writings from the War of Independence* (New York: Library of America, 2001), 61–65, 116–18.

Nathaniel Hawthorne, "The Prison Door," from The Scarlet Letter (1850). *Nathaniel Hawthorne: Collected Novels* (New York: Library of America, 1983), 158–59.

Oliver Wendell Holmes, "The Deacon's Masterpiece; or The Wonderful 'One-Hoss Shay'" (1858). *American Poetry: The Nineteenth Century*, vol. 1, *Philip Freneau to Walt Whitman* (New York: Library of America, 1984), 560–63.

II. BOSTON AND THE AMERICAN RENAISSANCE

Henry Wadsworth Longfellow, "Paul Revere's Ride" (1863). *Henry Wadsworth Longfellow: Poems and Other Writings* (New York: Library of America, 2000), 362–65.

Oliver Wendell Holmes, "Old Ironsides" (1831) and "The Last Leaf" (1831). *The Complete Poetical Works of Oliver Wendell Holmes*, ed. Horace Scudder, (Boston: Houghton Mifflin, 1908), 3–4.

Thomas Wentworth Higginson, "Letter to a Young Contributor" (1862). *Atlantic Monthly*, 9 (April 1862), 26–36, 401–11.

Ralph Waldo Emerson, "Concord Hymn" (1837) and "Boston Hymn" (1863). *Ralph Waldo Emerson: Collected Poems and Translations* (New York: Library of America, 1994), 125, 163.

Louisa May Alcott, from "How I Went Out to Service" (1874). *Alternative Alcott*, ed. Elaine Showalter (New Brunswick, N.J.: Rutgers University Press, 1997), 350–52, 354–58, 361–63.

James T. Fields, from "Hawthorne" (1872), from *Yesterdays with Authors* (Boston: Houghton, Mifflin, 1893), 48–55.

Annie Fields, from "Oliver Wendell Holmes: Personal Recollections and Unpublished Letters," from *Authors and Friends* (1896; New York: AMS Press, 1969), 117–55.

Willa Cather, from "148 Charles Street," from *Not Under Forty* (1936). *Willa Cather: Stories, Poems, and Other Writings* (New York: Library of America, 1992), 838–40, 842–48.

III. POST–CIVIL WAR BOSTON

Henry Adams, from *The Education of Henry Adams* (1906, 1918). *Henry Adams: Novels, Mont Saint Michel, The Education* (New York: Library of America, 1983), 723–24, 726–29, 739–40, 756–58.

Mark Twain, "The Whittier Birthday Dinner Speech" (1877). *Mark Twain: Collected Tales, Sketches, Speeches, and Essays, 1852–1890* (New York: Library of America, 1992), 695–99.

William Dean Howells, from *Literary Friends and Acquaintance: A Personal Retrospect of American Authorship* (New York: Harper & Brothers, 1900), 113–19.

William Dean Howells, from *The Rise of Silas Lapham* (1885). *William Dean*

Howells: Novels, 1875–1886 (New York: Library of America, 1982), 861–63.

Henry James, from *The Bostonians* (1885). *Henry James: Novels, 1881–1886: Washington Square*, (New York: Library of America, 1985), 814–23.

IV. "VIEWED IN BOSTON LIGHT": TURN-OF-THE-CENTURY BOSTON

Oliver Wendell Holmes, Jr., from *Dead, Yet Living: An Address Delivered at Keene, N.H. Memorial Day, May 30, 1884* (Boston: Ginn, Heath, 1884), 3–8, 10–12.

Edith Wharton, from "The Lamp of Psyche" (1895). *Edith Wharton: Collected Stories, 1891–1910* (New York: Library of America, 2001), 36–42.

George Santayana, from *Persons and Places: Fragments of Autobiography* (1944; New York: Charles Scribner's Sons, 1963), 112–13.

John P. Marquand, from *The Late George Apley: A Novel in the Form of a Memoir* (1937; Boston: Little, Brown, 1965), 84–92.

T. S. Eliot, "The Boston Evening Transcript" and "Cousin Nancy." T. S. Eliot, *The Complete Poems and Plays, 1909–1950* (New York, Harcourt, Brace, 1958), 16–18.

Edward Bellamy, from *Looking Backward* (1888; New York: Penguin Books, 1982), 37–39, 41–44.

Cleveland Amory, "The Hub," from *The Proper Bostonians* (New York: E. P. Dutton, 1947), 11–14, 30.

V. THE "OTHER" BOSTONIANS: NEW VOICES AND VISIONS

Charlotte Forten Grimke, from her Journal, 1854. *The Norton Anthology of African American Literature*, ed. Henry Louis Gates and Nellie Y. McKay, (New York: W. W. Norton, 1997), 478–79.

W. E. B. Du Bois, from "A Negro Student at Harvard" (1960). *Black and White in American Culture*, ed. Jules Chametzky and Sidney Kaplan, (Amherst: University of Massachusetts Press, 1969), 119–24, 126.

Dorothy West, from *The Living Is Easy* (1948; New York: Feminist Press, 1982), 37–49. Malcolm X, with the assistance of Alex Haley, from *The Autobiography of Malcolm X* (New York: Grove Press, 1965), 38–43, 49–50.

William Stanley Braithwaite, from "I Saw Frederick Douglass" (1948). *The William Stanley Braithwaite Reader,* ed. Philip Butcher (Ann Arbor: University of Michigan Press, 1972), 187–92.

William Stanley Braithwaite, "Quiet Has a Hidden Sound," 1948. *The Norton Anthology of African American Literature,* ed. Henry Louis Gates and Nellie Y. McKay, (New York: 1997), 923.

John Boyle O'Reilly, "The Exile of the Gael" (1887) and "The Fame of the City" (1881). *Life, Poems and Speeches of John Boyle O'Reilly, by James Jeffrey Roche,* ed. James Jeffrey Roche and Mrs. John Boyle O'Reilly, (New York: Cassell, 1891), 416, 443.

J. Anthony Lukas, from *Common Ground: A Turbulent Decade in the Lives of Three American Families* (New York: Alfred A. Knopf, 1985), 380–81, 384–85, 390–91.

Edwin O'Connor, *The Last Hurrah* (Boston: Little, Brown, 1956), 172–79, 183–84, 216.

Fred Allen, Letters (1935), from Robert Taylor, *Fred Allen: His Life and Wit* (Boston: Little, Brown, 1989), 253–54.

George V. Higgins, from *The Friends of Eddie Coyle* (New York: Alfred A. Knopf, 1972), 174–79.

Michael Patrick MacDonald, from *All Souls: A Family Story from Southie* (Boston: Beacon Press, 1999), 1–3.

Mary Antin, from *The Promised Land* (Boston: Houghton Mifflin, 1912), 286–300.

Nat Hentoff, from *Boston Boy* (New York: Alfred A. Knopf, Inc., 1986), 34–35, 37.

Roland Merullo, from *In Revere, in Those Days* (New York: Vintage Books, 2002), 5–9.

VI. "THERE IT WAS": BOSTON, CITY OF SELF AND SPIRIT

Arthur C. Inman, from *The Inman Diary: A Public and Private Confession,* ed. Daniel Aaron, (Cambridge: Harvard University Press, 1985), vol. 1, 178–79; vol. 2, 828–29, 891–92.

Samuel Eliot Morison, from *One Boy's Boston* (1962; Boston: Northeastern University Press, 1983), 59–69.

Robert Lowell, from "91 Revere Street" (1959), and "For the Union Dead" (*Atlantic Monthly*, November 1960). *Life Studies and For the Union Dead* (New York: Farrar, S0traus and Giroux, 1964), 14–17, 31; 70–72.

Dan Wakefield, from *Returning: A Spiritual Jo* (New York: Doubleday, 1985), 5–6, 15, 17.

John Updike, from "Personal Considerations: Why Do I Live in New England?" (1999), *Due Considerations: Essays and Criticism* (New York: Alfred A. Knopf, 2007), 668–69.

Eve LaPlante, "Introduction," *American Jezebel: The Uncommon Life of Anne Hutchinson* (New York: HarperCollins, 2004), xv–xxi.

Archibald MacLeish, "Night Watch in the City of Boston" (1975). *Collected Poems, 1917–1982* (Boston: Houghton Mifflin, 1985), 3–6.

Patricia Powell, "A Literary Landscape: From Jamaica to Boston," from *The Good City: Writers Explore 21st-Century Boston*, ed. Emily Hiestand and Ande Zellman, (Boston: Beacon Press, 2004), 43–44, 56–57.